D1188027

Nationalism and the Crowd in Liberal Hungary,
1848–1914

Suffrage demonstration in 1912 in front of the Millennium monument on Heroes Square at the entrance to the City Park in Budapest. Photograph by János Müllner (BTM Kiscelli Museum, Budapest)

Nationalism and the Crowd in Liberal Hungary, 1848–1914

ALICE FREIFELD

THE WOODROW WILSON CENTER PRESS
Washington, D.C.

THE JOHNS HOPKINS UNIVERSITY PRESS
Baltimore and London

EDITORIAL OFFICES

The Woodrow Wilson Center Press
One Woodrow Wilson Plaza
1300 Pennsylvania Avenue, N.W.
Washington, D.C. 20004-3027
Telephone 202-691-4010
http://wwics.si.edu

ORDER FROM

The Johns Hopkins University Press
P.O. Box 50370
Baltimore, Maryland 21211
Telephone 1-800-537-5487
www.press.jhu.edu

© 2000 Alice Freifeld
All rights reserved
Printed in the United States of America on acid-free paper ♾

2 4 6 8 9 7 5 3 1

Library of Congress Cataloging-in-Publication Data

Freifeld, Alice.
   Nationalism and the crowd in liberal Hungary, 1848–1914 / Alice Freifeld.
      p.   cm
   Includes bibliographical references (p.   ) and index.
   ISBN 0-8018-6462-3 (alk. paper)
      1. Nationalism—Hungary—History—19th century.   2. Nationalism—
   Hungary—History—20th century.   3. Liberalism—Hungary—History—
   19th century.   4. Liberalism—Hungary—History—20th century.   5. Crowds—
   Hungary   I. Title.
   DB933.F74 2000
   943.9′042—dc21   00-008814

THE WOODROW WILSON INTERNATIONAL CENTER FOR SCHOLARS
Lee H. Hamilton, Director

BOARD OF TRUSTEES

Joseph A. Cari, Jr., Chair; Steven Alan Bennett, Vice Chair. Public Members: Madeleine K. Albright, Secretary, U.S. Department of State; James H. Billington, Librarian of Congress; John W. Carlin, Archivist of the United States; William R. Ferris, Chair, National Endowment for the Humanities; Lawrence M. Small, Secretary, Smithsonian Institution; Richard W. Riley, Secretary, U.S. Department of Education; Donna E. Shalala, Secretary, U.S. Department of Health and Human Services. Private Citizen Members: Carol Cartwright, Daniel L. Doctoroff, Jean L. Hennessey, Daniel L. Lamaute, Paul Hae Park, Thomas R. Reedy, S. Dillon Ripley, Nancy M. Zirkin. Designated Appointee of the President from within the Federal Government: Samuel R. Berger, Assistant to the President for National Security Affairs.

WILSON COUNCIL

Albert Abramson, Cyrus A. Ansary, J. Burchenal Ault, Charles F. Barber, Theodore C. Barreaux, Lawrence E. Bathgate II, Joseph C. Bell, John L. Bryant, Jr., Conrad Cafritz, Nicola L. Caiola, Raoul L. Carroll, Scott Carter, Albert V. Casey, Peter B. Clark, William T. Coleman, Jr., Michael D. DiGiacomo, Frank P. Doyle, Donald G. Drapkin, F. Samuel Eberts III, I. Steven Edelson, John H. Foster, Barbara Hackman Franklin, Chris G. Gardiner, Bruce Gelb, Jerry P. Genova, Alma Gildenhorn, Joseph B. Gildenhorn, David F. Girard-diCarlo, Michael B. Goldberg, William E. Grayson, Raymond A. Guenter, Robert R. Harlin, Verna R. Harrah, Eric Hotung, Frances Humphrey Howard, John L. Howard, Darrell E. Issa, Jerry Jasinowski, Brenda LaGrange Johnson, Dennis D. Jorgensen, Shelley Kamins, Anastasia D. Kelly, Christopher Kennan, Steven Kotler, William H. Kremer, Kathleen D. Lacey, Donald S. Lamm, Harold Levy, David Link, David S. Mandel, John P. Manning, Edwin S. Marks, John J. Mason, Robert McCarthy, C. Peter McColough, Stephen G. McConahey, James D. McDonald, Philip Merrill, Jeremiah L. Murphy, Martha T. Muse, Gerald L. Parsky, Donald Robert Quartel, Jr., Edward V. Regan, J. Steven Rhodes, Edwin Robbins, Philip E. Rollhaus, Jr., Otto Ruesch, George P. Shultz, Raja W. Sidawi, Ron Silver, William A. Slaughter, Timothy E. Stapleford, Christine Warnke, Pete Wilson, Deborah Wince-Smith, Herbert S. Winokur, Jr., Joseph Zappala.

ABOUT THE CENTER

The Center is the living memorial of the United States of America to the nation's twenty-eighth president, Woodrow Wilson. Congress established the Woodrow Wilson Center in 1968 as an international institute for advanced study, "symbolizing and strengthening, the fruitful relationship between the world of learning and the world of public affairs." The Center opened in 1970 under its own board of trustees.

In all its activities the Woodrow Wilson Center is a nonprofit, nonpartisan organization, supported financially by annual appropriations from the Congress, and by the contributions of foundations, corporations, and individuals. Conclusions or opinions expressed in Center publications and programs are those of the authors and speakers and do not necessarily reflect the views of the Center staff, fellows, trustees, advisory groups, or any individuals or organizations that provide financial support to the Center.

To Peter

Contents

Acknowledgments

This study has been informed by two locales, Berkeley and Budapest, where crowd politics has been more romanticized than demonized, lingering in popular memory, yet provocative to outsiders.

I owe a special debt to the late William Slottman, my mentor at the University of California, whose moral imperatives, astounding wit and intelligence guided this project in its initial stages. Reginald Zelnik generously steadied the course over the long haul. Richard Gringeri made valuable suggestions in his close reading of the later text as did Martin Malia in his reading of an earlier portion. Loránt Czigány, Andrew János, George Orban, and Laura Schiff helped guide my initiation into Hungarian culture.

Ferenc Glatz and the late György Ránki of the History Institute of the Hungarian Academy of Sciences were most gracious in facilitating my research, as were Péter Hanák, Károly Vörös, and especially, Atilla Pók. I am particularly grateful to Iván Berend, Csaba Gombár, and Daniel Szabó for their stimulating readings of the text. Éva Havasi, Gabrielle Kocsis, and Agnes Szokolszky provided invaluable transatlantic help in preparing the manuscript.

As I have moved on to new locales, various professional and university colleagues provided encouragement and guidance, including Geoffrey Giles, Sheryl Kroen, John Lampe, and Maria Todorova. The East European Studies program at the Woodrow Wilson International Center for Scholars provided the opportunity to revise the manuscript in a most stimulating environment. I owe a special debt to the program for its repeated support and to Joseph Brinley and Carol Walker of the Woodrow Wilson Center Press for their unfaltering involvement through the publication of this manuscript. László Deme's East European studies conferences in Sarasota, Florida, provided a forum to present and refine my ideas. Peter Pasztor's careful reading helped focus the revision process. My students have provided a valuable link between research and one's audience, stimulating this project in all sorts of directions.

This project was generously supported by the University of Florida's Division of Sponsored Research and the Department of History. At earlier stages this project also benefited from support in part by grants from the Joint Committee on Eastern Europe of the American Council of Learned Societies and Social Science Research Council, the Carnegie Mellon Foundation, the Slavic Center at the University of California, Berkeley, and the International Research Exchanges Board, with funds provided by the National Endowment for the Humanities and the United States Department of State. None of these organizations or those individuals previously acknowledged are responsible for the views expressed.

From my parents, Transylvanian Holocaust survivors, I learned of the hopes and travails of assimilation in new nations such as Hungary, Romania, and America. Most of all, thanks to Ben, Max, and Sophie who made festivity and riot, building and disassembling an everyday occurrence. I dedicate this book to Peter Bergmann, who has always remained for the hangover and the long agony that this book has represented in our lives, spiced admittedly with the moments of celebration.

Nationalism and the Crowd in Liberal Hungary, 1848–1914

The return in 1906 of the remains of Ferenc Rákóczi II (1676–1735), the leader of an anti-Habsburg rebellion, 1703–11. Photograph by György Klösz (BTM Kiscelli Museum, Budapest)

1

The Chastened Crowd

This is a study of the aftermath and legacy of the central crowd experience in Hungarian history, the revolution of 1848. Revolutionary defeat was not simply an ordeal in itself, experienced for a generation and forgotten. It was mythologized, casting a long shadow over public life. But why study the hangover rather than the party? Because the strictures of the day after often lead to long-range resolutions, and bittersweet memories can conjure powerful myths. Fear of defiance resurfacing remained an obsession of the counter-revolution; some defiance did survive, but most importantly, people survived defiance with an underground nationwide discourse that linked the would-be nation in a way hardly known before 1848. The code of words and symbols sustained a sense of a common solidarity that was palpable and recognizable. Elsewhere, as in Germany, the revolution was quickly relegated to the status of the "crazy year," but in Hungary the myth of revolution was saddled with no embarrassing aftereffect. No Hungarian Bismarck could dare counterpoise the oratory of 1848 to the new realities of "blood and iron." Rather, 1848 became a defining element in national consciousness. The top-hatted crowd of March 15, 1848, lingered in Hungarian historical imagination.

Perhaps the memory of 1848 proved strongest in Hungary because it was the only country to have a total revolution in 1848 and, consequently, the only one to experience total defeat. In the last 150 years a revolutionary Budapest crowd burst into European history four times: 1848, 1918, 1956, and 1989. Hungary was the only country to go full cycle, from bourgeois to communist to counter-revolution at the end of World War I, and it was the only nation to take up arms against the Soviets in Eastern Europe. Each of the first three revolutions failed: 1848 and 1956 were both suppressed by the Russian army, the revolutions of 1918 and 1919 crumbled under French and Romanian pressure and peasant resistance. While Hungarians concede that 1918 was shipwrecked by internal contradictions in Hungary (as in Germany), the Hungarians are reluctant to make this same indictment of either 1848 or 1956. Instead, the failed gamble was always going it alone: taking on the Turks alone, fighting on in 1849 alone, and then again in 1956. The crowd had coalesced, erupted, organized, taken decisive action, tackled the giant from without, and then and only then did it fall subdued: David had yielded to Goliath. The emphasis was on the dignity of failure, on having fought the impossible fight rather than simply acquiescing. And if impossible odds had not deterred the revolution in the first instance, what was to prevent a reoccurrence? Perhaps no country has so successfully exploited revolutionary failure for political gain. The tactic of turning failed revolutions to the national advantage as a means to achieve political concessions became the backbone of Hungarian political praxis, the fulcrum around which compromise and semi-independence were fashioned in the dualist period, 1867–1918, and in the era of détente, from the 1970s to the fall of communism.

Since revolutionary defeat was cast in heroic terms, the potential for the crowd's reappearance remained, if only in a chastened form. This study follows the history of the 1848 crowd from defeat and forced quiescence to revival and institutionalization. This chastened crowd had the experience of previous defiance, which was savored, milked, and ritualized. Neither those defied nor those who had defied would ever view collectivities in the same manner again. Not that this concern remained active for more than the life of these individuals or, perhaps, their children, but for a generation it did mold a debate over public life. Rather than a spontaneous entity, the crowd recalled all too well, and it is the crowd's capacity for memory and replay that provides a key to the understanding of the emergence and development of the chastened crowd. Crowds, Elias Canetti argued, sought to discharge "stings," the many absorbed wounds and resentments built up over time. Crowd memory gives weight to the latent crowd, and it is the injunction of memory that moves crowds to throw over the burden of inflicted commands.[1] If one takes into account the importance of defeat in the tenor and vocabulary of crowd politics, then another crowd, that of nationalism, becomes visible. A central achievement of the chastened crowd was to transform the pain of revolutionary defeat into a positive vehicle of national identity. Crowds would play a critical role in the legitimation of liberal rule in Austria-Hungary, for it was not enough to identify oneself as a Magyar; affirmation of being a Magyar could be found in the crowd. It is through the chastened crowd of revolutionary defeat that the Hungarians constructed and reconstructed their sense of nationality and polity in the second half of the nineteenth century.

Between 1848 and 1914 the chastened crowd was a continually self-defining entity: born in revolution, chastened by defeat, revived in compromise politics, unchastened by long decades of success and hegemony, and ending in an ironic celebration of its undoing in August 1914. Hungary is, thus, an ideal place to study the later history of nineteenth-century crowds. The specter of the revolutionary crowd was never fully dispelled. Even after the Hungarians were vanquished in 1849 the Kossuth legend grew, and during the state of siege (1849–1854) a patriotic martyrology developed consecrating the absent crowd. The weight of the mass was felt at funerals— large, politically significant displays of mourning. The penalty of revolution stamped all contemporaries. The community, though forced into silence, was nevertheless linked—or thought itself linked—by the knowledge that those around them harbored the same feelings. Memory was remolded into myth, complicating the struggle for legitimacy between a conquering regime and the public. Myth transformed the gentry into the suffering class, promoting the pre-1848 masters into the natural leaders of the patriotic crowd when, or if, the Magyar nation was allowed to organize again. Repression of public politics stifled the crowd of the present, but not necessarily of the future, nor had it extinguished the memory of its past heroics.

The regime countered with its own symbols of political legitimacy. Official ceremonies first emphasized the illegitimacy of the nationalist sentiment but ultimately offered an avenue for compromise with Magyar legalisms. Manipulation of crowds by autocratic regimes saps them of spontaneity, but the manipulated crowd is not simply a polar opposite of the crowd beyond or above rules. With the royal tours of the 1850s, neo-absolutism acknowledged that it could not dispense with the crowd, and the groundwork was laid for a new celebrity monarchism that would do much to sustain the Habsburg Monarchy for six decades. Hungarian crowd politics made its return in 1859 in a chastened form. For this chastened crowd, memory had both a motivating and a delimiting function: reminding it of the cherished and unfulfilled goal, of the intoxication of revolution, but also of the dangers of extreme action. The chastened crowd had been chastised (reprimanded) but had not become chaste (purified); it had become cautious rather than repentant. While the chastened crowd is activated by memory, memory also enclosed action within limits. Because the crowd has memory, it will avoid acting exactly in the same way again. The chastened crowd was post-revolutionary, but it was neither passive nor restive. It represented a domestication, not a repudiation of the revolutionary impulse.

In the 1860s the chastened crowd demanded that the uncrowned king legitimate himself through a coronation, which was finally produced as a public spectacle in Buda and Pest. The ceremonial of dualism would harmonize the formerly revolutionary, now chastened, crowd with the imperial order: a new tradition was made. How the revolutionary crowd was woven into the politics of liberal Hungary is the tangled tale of compromise. Out of defeat, first their own, and then that of their master, the Hungarians under Ferenc Deák had won the war for compromise. In 1867 the chastened crowd capitalized on the faltering of the Habsburg regime. This was encapsulated in the words attributed to Deák, the architect of dualism, when he was told of the outcome of the critical battle of 1866: "We lost the war! . . . We are now victorious."[2]

The construction of a new state in 1867, indeed a new concept of a state, gained public manifestation in festivity. In the dualist period, the state encouraged an elaborate practice of public festivity, mobilizing public support for itself and drawing upon the arcane rituals of Habsburg tradition and nineteenth-century crowd politics. Liberal nationalist crowd politics took advantage of prosaic gatherings, formal settings, theater openings, and statue unveilings, as well as moments of exigency, to dramatize the shifts in political structures. This work studies the dance between iconoclastic crowd politics and the ritual forms of state ceremonials. The subsuming of multiple loyalties into the new definition of identity as a Magyar and a Habsburg subject was new. It provided an avenue of entrance for Jews and other immigrants into its rapidly expanding cities, and at the same time generated a dynamic of public ritual, official and counter-festivity, that was decidedly Hungarian.

The chastened crowd of liberal Hungary was necessarily both a "civilized" and an "uncivilized" entity, both dutiful and moblike, both orchestrated and spontaneous.[3] Although it had experienced the high and low of revolution and revolutionary defeat, the mainspring of this chastened crowd was buoyed by the mixture of its defeat and triumph in Austria-Hungary. The fashioning of an almost prosperous and semi-autonomous identity required the assimilation of both poles into the discourse of public life. The chastened crowd simultaneously engaged the memory of revolution and national tradition. Herein lay its novelty: national identity would never permit a total eclipse of revolutionary values, but radicalism had also not big government on behalf of the disadvantaged. To the continental left, liberalism or, " 'wild' or 'savage' liberalism," as it is sometimes called in France, "has also come to mean, essentially, American civilization, in all its McDonald's . . . aspects. Therefore, to be anti-liberal in France is not to be against big government; it is to be for it."[18]

The root of the word *liberal* is *liber*, the free man; similarly, *city* or *citizen* is the ancient word for the free man in the polis. In the middle ages the two words were closely tied, at least in Central Europe; if you made it to the city, you were free. Thus the German proverb, "City air makes free." During the sixteenth and seventeenth centuries, in the period of religious wars and enthusiasms, investigation of conscience led to a concern with the errors of freedom. The word *liberal* came to have the connotation of being licentious, of uncontrolled liberality. But this pejorative meaning of liberal as libertine was again reversed in the eighteenth century, when the liberal was praised as someone freed from tradition, from prejudice; in fact, there was a certain delight in the conscious rule breaker. In Adam Smith's *The Wealth of Nations* (1776), the local, the factory, met the universal, the world market. The real antagonist was the state. What could stymie the entrepreneur was a rapacious state functioning from an aristocratic capital. Nineteenth-century Hungarian liberal politics operated through a gentry-controlled party system out of a booming metropolis/capital vying with the aristocratic capital in Vienna. Hungarian political self-interest was different from what Adam Smith had envisioned; yet virtually every political party preferred to call themselves liberal during the dualist period, at least until the fin-de-siècle.

Liberalism, nationalism, and the crowd are concepts that arose at the same moment of time—the late eighteenth century—and both were given a thrust by the revolutionism of 1789. The understanding of the crowd in the nineteenth century remained largely a liberal discourse. The crowd had no role in universal history before 1789. Crowd outbreaks were important as object lessons of the past, but they were sporadic and could be viewed as occasional nuisances. For instance, Edward Gibbon's account of the Nika riots of 532 reflects his patrician horror at the Gordon riots of 1780, but he does not present the crowd as playing a role in the decline and fall of the Roman Empire. Burke may have spoken of the swinish multitude, but it was with the taking of the Bastille that the urban crowd stormed into history.[19]

Historicism elevated the role of the crowd into the new major actor in history. In Thomas Carlyle's *The History of the French Revolution*, the sansculottic mob became "the crowning Phenomenon of our Modern Time."[20] This new engine of history, according to Carlyle, was both stupid and preternatural. But Carlyle, a hero worshipper, admired Napoleon, the hero worshipped by the crowd. Although he was unrelentingly critical of the Jacobin crowd in the name of individualism, his assessment of the nationalistic impulse was sober. He accepted that the crowd was no longer a disparate mass; it had become a conscious force of history. The nation as the giant crowd was an idea implicit in romantic historiography. From Carlyle it was just a short step to Jules Michelet's claim that it was the whole people, not just the crowd, who stormed the Bastille in 1789. Michelet's identification of the crowd with the nation raised it to a major player in universal history.[21]

The revolutionism of the unanimous people fueled the imagination of the national revivals of Eastern Europe in the 1830s and 1840s. The budding Hungarian journalist Dániel Irányi quoted Heinrich Heine in 1846, "Liberty is the new religion of our age. . . . The chosen people of this new religion are the French. They have written the first gospels of this new religion. Paris is the new Jerusalem and the Rhine is the River Jordan."[22] The Hungarian poet Sándor Petőfi decorated his room with engravings of the heroes of the 1789 revolution. The novelist Mór Jókai recalled, "We were all Frenchmen. We read only Lamartine, Michelet, Louis Blanc, Sue, Victor Hugo, and Béranger."[23] History infused the nation and the crowd with purpose.

The crowd and the nation never seemed more in union than in 1848. But as the revolution unraveled, the romantic vision of the crowd darkened, replaced by a polarized historiography of the crowd. Liberals, who had often idealized the crowd, came typically to demonize it. The free-trade Scottish liberal Charles Mackay, for example, had been among the very first in March 1848 to call for the creation of a United States of Europe, only to be distressed by the divisive nationalism of the revolutionary crowds.[24] In his *Extraordinary Popular Delusions and the Madness of Crowds* (1852), Mackay was out "to show how easily the masses have been led astray, and how imitative and gregarious men are, even in their infatuations and crimes."[25] He focused on those "seasons of excitement and recklessness" when "whole communities suddenly fix their minds upon one object, and go mad in its pursuit." Yet crowds as such hardly appear in his work. Instead, his pages are loaded with burst bubbles such as John Law's Mississippi scheme, the South Sea bubble, and the tulipomania. It was the nature of the folly, not the goal itself, which interested Mackay. A crowd, that is the tendency to madly flock together, whether in a consumer mania or a revolutionary flurry, was a mere metaphor for popular delusions. The phrase "the madness of crowds" was added to the title after 1849, when Mackay had despaired that men "think in herds; it will be seen that they go mad in herds, while they recover their senses slowly, and one by one."[26]

Marx, for his part, argued that the French bourgeoisie's willingness to crush the proletariat in the June Days marked the onset of a fearful new stage of crowd politics. The Marxists would turn to "scientific socialism" with only the Anarchists under Bakunin continuing to believe in spontaneous insurrections and revolutions. Marx drew a sharp distinction between the demonstrating and the festive crowd. He was critical of any utopian dream of festivity in a world of social harmony, because it led to a "fantastic standing apart from the contest."[27] To Marx, it seemed that the revolution had dissipated itself in festivity. Marx's critique of the utopian socialists reappeared in the 1860s in Lassalle's *Kulturkampf* against liberals as the fools of festivity who believed that patriotic assembly could be the catalyst of change.[28]

The festive crowd, as the forum for the unique individual, was a key theme in Jacob Burckhardt's *The Civilization of the Renaissance in Italy* (1860). In the brutal splendor of Renaissance festivity, Burckhardt found "the festival [was] a higher phase in the life of the people, in which its religious, moral, and poetical ideas took visible shape. The Italian festivals in their best form mark the point of transition from real life into the world of art."[29] Burckhardt aestheticized the problem of the crowd, inspiring Wagner's Bayreuth festival that became a celebration of the Bismarckian German nation-state. Burckhardt's art-historical vision would also be echoed in Hans Markart's grand historical pageant on the boulevards of Vienna in 1879. Such street pageantry became a staple of Hungarian liberalism.

Burckhardt, however, in idealizing the city-state civilization as the bearers of true festivity, increasingly despaired of the possibility of true festivity in the modern world, divided as it was by parties and classes, and organized into bloated nation-states rather than city-states. For Burckhardt, the city-state thrived in the tension between patrician hegemony and mob rule. Without the city-state, he assumed the festive crowd would be sucked into the void between peasant and aristocratic milieus. Burckhardt was a member of the Basel patriciate, nursing the wounds of a lost canton civil war in his childhood. In 1844 Burckhardt filed four reports with the *Basler Zeitung*, the leading conservative journal in Switzerland, on the Swiss Sharpshooters' Festival meeting in Basel. Burckhardt watched with some suspicion the huge assembling crowds of gun-toting sharpshooters, yet at the same time he was taken by the decorations—scores of different flags, festoons, wreaths and garlands everywhere—that gave "an aura of glorious splendor."[30] An "inestimable crowd" gathered at the festival meadow to greet the arriving processions of sharpshooters; volleys of cannon fire sounded from each side of the river. This festivity celebrated the Swiss peasantry's right to bear arms, and foreshadowed the renewed civil war in Switzerland. Burckhardt was appalled to hear "the most beautiful phrases of Swiss unity and fraternity misused for the most unpleasant party purposes." He thought that the radicals were fomenting discord among the crowd by flattering the sharpshooters, "by calling them the true parliament."[31]

The Paris Commune of 1871 further embedded a dread of the crowd into European culture. As the crowd became associated with socialism and liberalism with elitism, nationalism became the property of the right. The distinction between liberalism, nationalism, and the crowd was never complete, for multiple allegiances existed for most—a class solidarity, religious affiliations, and a new political sense of nation. But as socialism and the crowd seemed ever more closely linked, liberalism found itself on the defensive in most of Europe. The Paris Commune remained a bloody scarecrow on the European landscape. It prompted Hippolyte Taine's malicious commentary on the violence and viciousness of the crowd in *Origins of Contemporary France* (1876–1894): "Take women that are hungry and men who have been drinking; place a thousand of these together, and let them excite each other with their exclamations, their anxieties, and the contagious reaction of their ever-increasing emotions; it will not be long before you find them a crowd of dangerous maniacs."[32] As liberalism grew skeptical of the crowd, historians followed suit. History refocused on great moments, great men, and instructive moral lessons for the nation. While social inferiors were often portrayed as amorphous aggregates, liberal historians increasingly tended to think of their protagonists and themselves as unique and aloof individuals.

Nietzsche helped inaugurate modernism's ambiguous distaste for the crowd by launching the polemic against the audience, but the myth of the superman he cultivated also needed a following.[33] Modernists echoed Nietzsche's denunciations of the "all-too-many," but found themselves drawn to the most deviant aspects of gatherings—their spontaneity, emotionality and irrationality, mental disturbance and lower-class participation. Modernists, in short, were both fascinated and frightened by crowds. Guy de Maupassant expressed horror at feeling "one of a crowd": "I struggle with the spirit of the mob, which strives to take possession of me."[34] Modernism was elitist to the present but democratic to the future. The avant-garde kept themselves ahead of the crowd, but not that much ahead; in any event, they assumed that the crowd was headed in the same direction. The avant-garde's assumption was, however, that they, rather than the crowd, were the engines of history. Attention shifted from the mob to the hero.

Modernism's repudiation of history ensured that from the 1880s through the 1930s theorists of the crowd took over from the historians. Social psychologists, anthropologists, and sociologists focused interest on how crowd excesses occurred, and how they could or should be prevented or repressed. Rather than the sansculottic mob as a force of progressive history, outbursts of crowd violence were isolated, undergoing psychological analysis and condemned as pathological. Scipio Sighele's criminal crowd (1891), Le Bon's demagogic crowd (1895), and Gabriel de Tarde's public opinion (1901) all accorded a sinister centrality to the crowd by exploring crowd spontaneity, emotionality, and irrationality.[35] These leading theorists of the crowd were linked to the professions of law and order. Sighele's father was a judge and Sighele became a lawyer. Le Bon was an army doctor. Taine's father was a lawyer, and Taine became the founder of a school of political science concerned with stabilizing the Third Republic.

In *The Crowd* (1895) Le Bon reflected on the threatening promise and ultimate fiasco of the Boulanger agitation. During 1888 Boulangist crowds had surged through the Parisian streets, the Third Republic had trembled, but the leader of the new politics of the street wavered, delayed, and then fled. Like the South Sea Bubble, the seemingly unstoppable nationalist agitation surrounding General Boulanger on his black horse evaporated into thin air, leaving many puzzled as to the meaning of the whole affair. Le Bon, the father of crowd theory, characterized the crowd as irrational, spontaneous, feminine, susceptible to manipulation by the "leader."[36] Most disturbing was the deindividuation taking place in crowds. The pathological crowd was perceived as an intrinsic aspect of the metropolis, the new urban world that was enveloping late-nineteenth-century European culture. Le Bon's work appeared just as the Dreyfus affair was unfolding, lending the work an aura of prescience as pitched street battles developed between Dreyfusards and anti-Dreyfusards. While crowd theorists criminalized the crowd, they also wrote off liberalism as a generator of the crowd. They assumed crowd politics would be socialist. Marxists concurred, declaring the working-class crowd as their new force in politics. From the turn of the century, May Day became a major urban holiday, and huge, surging crowds demanding suffrage reform and the eight-hour day filled Europe's great public squares.

The crowd was no longer understood as a disparate mass, György Lukács later observed, but was perceived as a "Conscious Subject"; the masses no longer "have the appearance of a natural occurrence."[37] The potential and violence of crowds was embraced by syndicalists such as Georges Sorel, who imagined the crowd a hero of a coming General Strike.[38] Sorel's revolutionary myth advertised a new purpose to the working-class crowds who were demonstrating in the heart of the city. The crowd was not only seen as a thing-in-itself, but as an actor apart from its would-be leaders. He postulated that a great, overwhelming show of crowd force could by itself topple those in power and bring about revolution. Ervin Szabó, the leading Marxist intellectual in turn-of-the-century Budapest, promoted this syndicalist vision.[39] Szabó bristled at the notion of the crowd subservient to bombastic leaders and aggressively took up Marx's critique of Lajos Kossuth, the leader of 1848, as a means of discrediting the Kossuth cult, then at its height. He wanted to shift attention from the leader to the mass and presented Kossuth as the "past master of the secret of mass appeal, [i.e.] to call only on such sentiments that are already shared by his public and to propagate only such ideas that are already popular. He could adapt to the mood of his audience so that they believed their leader was speaking to them, although in fact they heard only their own mouthpiece talking."[40] Szabó also balked at the enthusiasm for memorializing that had dominated liberal politics since the massive funeral for Kossuth in 1894. It became his aim to debunk the liberal crowds as a thing of the past; socialist crowds would supplant them.

With the Hungarian left mesmerized by the potentiality of the liberating crowds of the General Strike, the Hungarian school of sociology incorporated the crowd into its political analysis. It was the conjunction of working-class agitation with massive demonstrations for suffrage reform, rather than simply working-class radicalism, as Szabó claimed, that gave the General Strike its impetus. Hungarian sociologists and criminologists studied strikes and suffrage agitation, as well as the centripetal pull of ethnic disaffection. There was reason to worry that the basis for compromise between elites and the Magyar crowd was breaking down over the imperative of suffrage reform and ethnic compromise. Viktor Jászi distinguished between Le Bon's riotous mobs and the disciplined crowds of the May Day parades. He conceded that spontaneous, unorganized crowds were endemic in liberal society and that these crowds showed the signs of de-individuation noted by Le Bon. But, Jászi argued, participants in planned and self-disciplined crowds did not lose their individuality.[41] Pál Angyal, a legal scholar, similarly wrestled with legal definitions of crowd criminality and individual criminal responsibility within a crowd. Writing during the crisis of 1905, he sought to introduce the word *tömeg* (crowd/mass) into the Hungarian legal code, which like the German term *Masse*, did not distinguish between the two concepts. Hitherto, the legal code had used *csoport* (group, military detachment, team, work shift) or *csoportosulás* (grouping, gathering). In Angyal's rendering a *csoport* was a lesser crowd, not a "criminal association," but rather one that was "at best capable of disturbing the peace." These more neutral terms lacked the inflammatory undertone of *tömeg*. He anguished over questions such as: "To what degree is the individual's responsibility mitigated by the dynamic of the crowd? Who is most responsible for damages, the leader or his followers? How can one most effectively fight crowd criminality?" Angyal's crowd was combustible, liable to transform even the most sober participant. But they were but short-lived conflagrations, whose actors were likely later to feel bitter remorse for complicity once the crowd "fever" had passed. "In the crowd, no one can know in advance what its members will do, least of all themselves." Yet, although Angyal found the "riotous crowd" to be "one of the most frightening expressions of human society," he struggled to balance questions of individual responsibility with collective crowd purpose.[42]

Angyal stepped back from the pessimism of Le Bon and the crowd psychologists, and drew on the Victorian concern with the fashioning of the civilized urban crowd. Since the 1850s the popular press had obsessively monitored the problem of street criminality. Social commentators delved into statistics, while setting forth elaborate rules for appropriate deportment on the street. This British tradition developed a picture of society as a structured crowd.[43] Hungarian liberalism emulated the Victorian injunction to urbane behavior, while seeking to remain open to the potentiality of the crowd, even as it remained fearful of the crowd in the present. In John Stuart Mill the crowd had become a shadowy entity, a blanket of smothering conformity. Yet even in Mill there were echoes of the Chartist crowds of the 1830s and 1840s threatening to overturn the social order. Angyal warned Hungarians that anticrowd legislation could inhibit the very crowds that sustained and nurtured liberal society, for example, at mass funerals, strikes, and patriotic/ loyal festive gatherings. Victorianism and late-nineteenth-century Hungarian liberalism enjoyed a moment of social equilibrium during which the nobility could adapt to the imperatives of a burgeoning metropolis. Victorian society made people feel more or less at home in the world. In its hierarchical arrangement, gentry Victorians made the politic adoption of the ethical and aesthetic standards of a middle class whose interests it contrived to make their own.

From Noble Horde to Chastened Crowd

The Hungarians are distinct among the European peoples in pinpointing their arrival on the European scene to around 896, and in their understanding of their arrival as an act of homesteading on the Pannonian plain. Descendants cultivated this memory in chronicle upon chronicle. The participants in the conquering army—it was emphasized by their descendants and historians—preserved the right of nobility or freedom. The crowd so-to-speak had arrived ennobled. And while the myth of the conquest (*honfoglalás*; literally, occupation of the homeland) legitimated a common entitlement, King Stephen's embrace of Christianity in the year 1000 transformed the horde of heathens into a Christian flock. The Hungarian chastened crowd integrated elements from the French revolutionary tradition, German romantic nationalist rallies, and the urbane crowd of Victorian England. But while Hungarian crowds drew from these three crowd experiences and corresponding literatures, they did so with a twist that reflected their own history and environment.

The myth of the collective arrival did not imply homogeneity. The seven Magyar tribes, each with their own structure, included affiliated ethnicities. Already by the time of St. Stephen, the nobility had absorbed numerous foreigners into their ranks. The demographic collapse during Ottoman rule necessitated the absorption of yet other groups, new peoples, and new elites. Habsburg rule overlaid a powerful magnate stratum enjoying fabulous wealth and influence from their vast latifundia. Hungarian noble rank represented a much larger and diverse category than its western counterparts. A lesser nobility retained considerable authority in the counties, while the poorer among them were eager to fill the expanding bureaucracy. But in addition to this middle stratum, the Hungarian nobility encompassed an impoverished and land-poor nobility. With some 6 percent of the public holding voting rights, the Hungarian electoral system in 1867 was relatively democratic, comparing favorably even to England and France. Nobles bearing such quaint designations as the "nobility with seven plum trees" or "sandaled nobility" held tenaciously to the national myth of the historic nation and its original noble horde, for it was the only real distinction between themselves and the peasantry. Despite the jealously guarded respectability and all the attendant snobbery, Hungarian gentry could claim with some justification to be close to the people. Nobles, by definition, share among themselves a presumed equality of discourse. The vast social/economic range of the Hungarian nobility made a dialogue between elite and crowd somewhat more accessible than elsewhere. And this circled back to Magyar national identity, to which the land-poor stratum's status was particularly identified.

During the liberal era, archaic, and hypermodern themes were spun together in ritualized processions: the gentry paraded the myth of the arrival in their finery down the new boulevards of Budapest, while the masses of the metropolis cheered the elegantly robed bearers of the "golden fleece" and men in animal skins. Such visual exercises helped paper over nagging questions of suspect noble patriotism during the revolution of 1848 and the general contradictions produced by dual loyalty to Habsburg sovereignty and Hungarian nationalism. Parading before a spectator crowd may have confirmed noble participants in their claims to be spokespeople of the nation, but the chastened crowd could also feel its presence was instrumental. Even as the chastened crowd became an instrument to advance the elite's agenda by rallying support within the nation, it was never a slave to the leaders on the podium or simply manipulated by them, for it, too, demanded deference from its pageant masters. The assumption that nationalist ideas move from elites to the people ignores the competing pluralities within the elites themselves as well as the role of the chastened crowd in defining the conversation over national goals.

Crowds fortified the sense of a national entity. Crowds might serve the interests of a ruling, or would-be ruling elite. This did not, however, erase the liberal oligarchy's fear of the crowd as a potential threat. Leaders operate within the parameters of a dialogue with their public. Elites necessarily trim claims to suit crowds, for crowds wield power not only by their numbers but also by their hubris. Crowds can respond in contrary or unrehearsed ways; they may step over boundaries and inflict damage. A dialogue was established between, across, and through the crowds. The chastened crowd could be dutiful and/or iconoclastic, but it was above all a conversant crowd helping to shape Hungarian liberalism. Far from destabilizing, the chastened crowd functioned as a crucial and valued interlocutor in dialogue with a changing group of elite leaders, reminding them of the failed yet heroic revolutionary past, while acknowledging the need for a new equilibrium. Indeed, it became involved in nothing less than a narration of a new nation—the Hungarian nation and its new metropolis. Budapest, the home and arena of the chastened crowd, welcomed the elite and reinforced its dominions, but its character was not gentry driven, and the elites remained dependent upon the chastened crowd to validate the existence of the nation. Crowds could be the goad, and, therefore, in part theorists of Hungarian liberalism when they paraded, shouted their slogans, or otherwise made manifest their agenda. Hungarians were still narrating the nation to themselves. English theorists, such as John Stuart Mill, did not have to narrate a nation, they had one. Mill was operating within the security of the most powerful nation-state with tendrils of influence reaching around the globe. Hungarian liberalism was, therefore, not simply a derivative of western liberalism.

During the 1850s Habsburg neo-absolutism succeeded only in driving the nationalist crowd underground, and when authoritarian controls crumbled in 1859 Viennese administrators scrambled to deal with those Hungarians who could claim be the stewards of a chastened crowd. Maintaining this arrangement required a continuous three-way dialogue between Vienna, the chastened Hungarian elite, and its crowd. As advertisers of a liberal capitalist future, Hungarian pageant masters simultaneously sought—differently in every decade, to be sure—to reconcile the claims of national identity and imperial loyalty, to assert the national market while ensuring international credit. Hungarian liberals forged a compromise, but they operated without the security of national autonomy, international power, or economic well being.

This was a different problematic than that faced by the Austrian half of the monarchy. Carl E. Schorske's *Fin-de-Siècle Vienna* argued that Austrian liberals failed to enliven their *Ringstrasse* with supportive crowds.[44] The great architectural edifices of the all-too-short liberal era became trophies to a facade—magnificent but lifeless in their enormity. Schorske utilized the architectural, art historical, literary, and intellectual facets of Vienna to illustrate the growing isolation of Austrian liberalism and its largely Jewish avant-garde, but he was too quick to cede the crowd to the new demagogic leaders. Like Sigmund Freud himself, around whom Schorske fashioned his portrait of fin-de-siècle Vienna, the dominating crowd image is derived from Le Bon's charismatic leader-driven crowd. Freud resisted Wilfred Trotter's wartime assessment of the "herd instinct" for having left "no room at all for the leader; he is merely thrown in along with the herd, almost by chance; it follows, too, that no path leads from this instinct to the need for a God; the herd is without a herdsmen."[45] Freud remained convinced of the power of the father. His analysis is pre-fascist, even liberal, while Schorske's is postfascist.

While Schorske greatly enlivened interest in turn-of-the-century Budapest, the focus alternated between the disadvantaged and the bourgeoisie. But recent portraits of turn-of-the-century Budapest, its cityscape and architecture, have tended to absent the crowd from the squares.[46] Outside of Hungary, the overpowering reflex has been the Vienna gate notion that modernism flows from Vienna. More generally, Hungarian liberalism has played the supporting role of the overshadowed younger brother imitating the anguish of the older. Consequently, the degree of bifurcation in liberalism in Austria-Hungary has been obscured by the persistent tendency to conflate Viennese and Austrian liberalism, to parallel German and Austrian liberalism, while ignoring the tandem of Hungarian and Austrian liberalism.[47] The focus on the making and unmaking of Austrian identity has further obscured taking seriously the web of allegiance in the Habsburg Monarchy. In 1848 both Austrian and Hungarian liberalism had been defeated. However, after the second defeat in 1866, Austrian liberalism enjoyed a reprieve, while Hungarian liberalism felt at a new beginning. By the 1880s, Vienna politics shifted into an antiliberal sharper key, but in Budapest the chastened crowd continued to enjoy a longer and more vigorous life. The Viennese liberals, twice defeated, and soon to be overwhelmed again, were viewed with suspicion and generally lacked a popular base. By contrast, liberalism in Hungary had an emotional resonance throughout the population, with virtually every political party calling itself liberal. Under dualism, Hungarian liberalism was in power for a generation and therefore provided a more substantial target for the dissonant voices of the turn-of-the-century than did the paper tiger of Austrian liberalism. Hungarian liberalism needs to be distinguished not only from its Austrian variant, but even more from the Eley and Blackbourn interpretation of a suffocating German liberal "notable politics."[48] By viewing 1848 as an aberration and the notable politics that followed as the norm, they denuded liberalism of its social activism and conflated it with a conservative politics fearful of crowds. Unlike the inexpressive politics of German liberalism, the Hungarian public was accustomed to gathering in protest, for it was unified and galvanized by a shared anti-dynasticism after 1848.

In the push-pull of Austria-Hungary, Hungarians seemed destined for the role of spoiler. The agreement of 1867 may have only secured Hungary semi-independent status, but the territory over which Hungary ruled was 282,000 square miles compared to 93,000 square miles today; its population was eighteen million rather than the present eight million.[49] The power Hungary wielded in the monarchy between 1867 and 1918 would prove formidable, and its leaders were major players in great power politics. Hungary's "nation-space" was at its full reach, while its cultural authority was still, to borrow from Homi Bhabha, "ambivalent . . . in the act of 'composing' its powerful image."[50] After the demise of Austria-Hungary, revanche mobilized the Hungarian masses in a politically charged festivity drenched with would-be monarchist-nationalist symbolism. While the Kingdom of St. Stephen remained the object of much nostalgia inside Hungary, the memory of an influential Hungary has dissipated abroad. More accessible than Magyar apologias has been a historiography derived from German-language sources, which has tended to contrast the pig-headed program of turn-of-the-century Magyar gentry nationalists to an enlightened Austro-Marxist vision of the future. Hungary has been caricatured as the obstacle that had prevented the needed reform of the monarchy in the liberationist-revisionist historiography of the former ethnic minorities. Pointing to the arrogance of greater Hungary has become a convenient explanation for what went wrong in Central Europe.

The historiography of Hungarian liberalism has further suffered from the confluence of two arguments, one dating from the immediate aftermath of the liberal epoch itself and the other from the modernization theories of the cold war era. The former arose from the disaster of World War I, a catastrophe that made everything before it seem irrelevant. Hungarian liberalism was discredited as a foreign, largely Jewish intrusion into indigenous, i.e. gentry, politics, and by definition as a German and/or Jewish-led or dominated movement liberalism necessarily lacked a genuine crowd base. Liberalism, in short, became the scapegoat of historic Hungary's downfall. On the other hand, modernization theory discounted Hungarian liberal politics as too backward, too low on the ladder of development to warrant respect. On the scale of liberal perfectionism, Hungarian liberalism has been found wanting, for liberalism failed to resolve the ethnic tensions tearing at the fabric of the Kingdom of St. Stephen. Of course, this indictment could also be made against British liberalism for failing to resolve the Irish issue or American liberalism for sustaining slavery as long as it did. Even in terms of modernization theory, the Hungarian liberal era proved more dynamic than the periods that followed. But whatever its economic or social achievements nineteenth-century Hungarian liberals did little to temper the impatience with the dualist/liberal epoch as a tedious excursion through the minutiae of stale oratory, parliamentary disputes, and a fraudulent electoral system. The liberal era was thus prey to overarching structural analyses that presumed the sterility of the liberal tradition in Hungary.

World War I had brought the crowd and nationalism together as never before so that a final closure seemed to have been brought on liberalism. The model became no longer the marches down broad boulevards but the milling crowds of the trans-European war enthusiasm of August 1914, i.e., the nation in love with itself demonstrating the power of the patriotic crowd. War crowds shattered the nineteenth-century notions of civility, compromise, and defeat, and prompted disillusioned polemics against the "instincts of the herd."[51] Man, the gregarious animal, had shown his suicidal side. Mussolini would demonstrate conclusively that the crowd could be the tool of a new right. The success of fascism was aided by its willingness to defend defiantly and make a cult of war enthusiasm, while at the same time copying the proletarian processions and party rallies of the pre-1914 period. In the grim setting of the interwar years, public festivity turned inward, unleashing a mood of civil war. Street marches devolved into contests or assertion of wills. A resentful Horthyite regime clothed itself in hypernationalist festivity during the interwar years. In defeat and constriction, celebrations of myths of Hungarian greatness stoked the fires of revanchism. Such festivity also established a comfort zone in a much diminished Hungary.[52]

Twentieth-century Hungarian historiography has yet to recover from Gyula Szekfű's anti-liberal polemic of 1920, *Három nemzedék* (Three generations). He presented a seductive portrait of three generations infected with a liberal worldview that was extraneous and hostile to the "Magyar soul." The first generation (1825–49) was checked for a time by reform conservatism, but "revolutionary liberalism" plunged Hungary into the catastrophe of 1849. Defeat brought forth a temperate liberalism that succeeded in arranging a workable compromise with Vienna but did not prevent the second generation (1850–90) from furthering a liberalism "shallowed into materialism." In the third generation (1890–1918) the rotten fruit of liberalism became visible in the social and political chaos that brought the downfall of the Kingdom of St. Stephen. By the 1930s an alarmed Szekfű had begun warning his own fourth generation from his earlier celebration of "Christian German civilization." But unlike other disenchanted rightists he saw little potential salvation emanating from the liberal west, making his peace with communism rather than liberalism after 1945, becoming ambassador to Moscow. Szekfű's book remained a not-so-underground classic during the communist era, for while he viewed liberal revolution as inimical to Hungarianness, communists repudiated the chastened crowd as a half-way house, not revolutionary enough, and thereby an obstacle to true revolution.[53]

Szekfű's nostalgia for the bucolic world of a lost Hungary has to be seen in light of the imbalance between Budapest, a metropolis, and the dwarf state it dominated after World War I. By default Szekfű's critique reflected the degree to which Budapest itself had lost its dynamism and direction after 1914, lending credence to his saga of an anemic liberalism undone by success. The emphasis was placed not on the making of the compromise, grounding a capitalist economy, and presiding over the rise of interest group politics, but rather on a spent liberalism that had exhausted its historic role by the turn of the century. Liberal limitations had become barriers: they were unable to represent the interests of workers and peasants. By clinging to the fiction that liberalism represented a modern Hungary that was expansive but not clerical or subversive, liberal notables maneuvered Hungary into a blind alley, according to Szekfű.

Szekfű's repudiation of liberalism was essentially a critique of urbanism, of the winnowing away of power from the Magyar gentry to the urban middle classes, in which newly assimilated Jews and Germans were quite visible. That Budapest Jewry had a stake in the ascendancy of liberalism does not deny the essence of liberalism: the fashioning of a Magyar nation. Where were the Jews in the conversation between crowd and nation? They were prominent in the press, in the urban commercial culture. But it was not just a Jewish conversation, and certainly the Jews were not leading the conversation.

In the 1970s and 1980s a more complex, if still largely critical, view of liberalism developed. Nationalist and Stalinist historiography had converged in postulating nineteenth-century Hungary as a colony. For the former it was an outpost of French enlightenment thought; for the latter an economic colony of Austria. The colonial model was questioned in the sixties and seventies, particularly by Péter Hanák, who initiated a reassessment of the advantages offered by the Compromise. However, he and his students focused their attention on the fin-de-siècle, still leaving the core years of Hungarian liberalism relatively unexamined. The periphery theory advanced by economic historians suggested Hungary's relative economic status in Europe could, at least in part, be explained by the nexus of location and natural resources. This allowed for consideration of Hungary's economic dilemmas in a less judgmental framework and expanded the options for fruitful intellectual analysis and economic diplomacy.[54] Western impatience with János Kádár's half-measures toward democracy and political or economic freedoms coincided with Andrew Janos's critique of Hungarian liberalism as neo-corporatism: "a bureaucratic polity, a pseudo-market, and a neo-corporatist society" run and organized for its own benefit.[55] This structuralist analysis simultaneously telescoped nineteenth-century liberalism into the twentieth century and focused so tightly on the workings of bureaucratic and parliamentary structures that the nonvoting public was all but extraneous.

We should guard against the tendency of allowing liberal Hungary to be swallowed up in a historiography of disappointment. László Tarr, writing in 1976 with a mixture of disapproval and wry affection, sought the ambiguity of the era in an 1891 eulogy to Count Gyula Andrássy, the political architect of liberal Hungary, which declared Hungarians were pursuing a "mirage." A decade later András Gerő similarly depicted Hungarian parliamentarianism chasing a false image, resulting in a "mirage of power." By dissecting the mirages of the liberal era, they were preparing readers to understand the mirages of the communist era. While the one mirage did eventually lead to the other, both, nevertheless, deserve also to be viewed on their own terms, mirages, and all. To paraphrase the poet Randall Jarrell's statement, "we never understand the normal better than when it has been allowed to reach its full growth and become abnormal," we never understood liberalism better than when it had been allowed to reach its full growth and become illiberal. Nevertheless, without the benefit of hindsight, liberalism had appeared normal to the chastened crowd.[56]

On the eve of the collapse of communism liberalism garnered renewed interest.[57] In his introduction to a new edition of Szekfű's writings published in 1989, Ferenc Glatz began with the striking sight of the crowd of cars and people massing at the newly opened Hungarian border checkpoint to Vienna in 1988. Contrary to Szekfű, Glatz argued that 1867–1918 was the high point in modern Hungarian history, the period in which Hungary came closest to the western European standard of culture and development. He embraced a liberal future as "the only possibility for a modern Hungary."[58] Liberalism seemed to be the antidote to seventy-five years of isolation and provincialism. If one surprise of the post-1989 period was the vehemence of nationalism in the volatile and sometimes dysfunctional politics of the region, the other surprise to many has been the strength of liberalism. While the importation or welcoming of capitalism was not a surprise, the ideological embrace of a liberal ideology was. Even astute analyses of the transference of power in 1989 do not include discussion of liberalism as a relevant political ideology. Ironically, many of the same social scientists who have critiqued the notable politics of the past celebrated Hungary's "negotiated revolution" of back-room politics and deals, the very doings of notable politics. But as this study will seek to demonstrate the back room and the filled plaza are complementary sites. Dripping with irony, Kálmán Mikszáth, the noted liberal novelist, journalist, and politician of the nineteenth century, wrote, "Liberalism is a gala dress like the robes that the French judges wear in the courtroom but discard at the doorstep. Liberalism exists only in official meetings and outside of those, no one ever takes it seriously."[59] If we can also see the chastened crowd at those official meetings and scores of unofficial ones as well, we are in a position to begin.

A'német játékszin belsöjének tekintete.
Inere Ansicht des teutschen Theaters.

The German theater of Pest, 1812–47. Engraving (Capitol's Ervin Szabó Library, Budapest Collection)

2

The Crowd as Threshold of the Nation

In his 1792 tour of Hungary and Transylvania, the Hungarian playwright Sándor Kisfaludy found to his horror more Slovaks, Saxons, Romanians, and Germans than Hungarians. The Hungarians are lost, he feared, unless they succeeded in buttressing and expanding the Hungarian language. Preserving their threatened language meant marginalizing what Hungarian literary reformers termed alien languages. The small nationalities of Eastern Europe are haunted by the fear of national extinction. Hungarian is a language that is disconnected from its neighbors, an odd ball within a continent of some twenty-seven different languages; this can make Hungary a more isolated, defensive, or paranoid place. Nineteenth-century liberals, Eric Hobsbawm notes, assumed there was a threshold small peoples had to cross before they could be taken seriously as a nation.[1] Hungary labored under the threat that it had not reached, or might someday slip below the crucial threshold. A litany developed around the examples of foreign hostility, indifference, or callousness. One of the oft-repeated sayings dates back to the Counter Reformation when the Jesuits are said to have convinced Leopold I that it was necessary to render Hungary miserable, then Catholic, finally German. And then there was the aside by Herder wondering whether Hungarian was an obsolescent language destined to disappear. This fear of national extinction is even the central concern of the Hungarian "Himnusz" (national anthem). Its refrain, from an 1823 poem by the romantic poet Ferenc Kölcsey, was also the hymn of the Hungarian revolution of 1848.[2] The recurring nightmare of "national death" (*nemzethalál*) reached poetic height in Mihály Vörösmarty's "Szózat" (Appeal) (1836), which offered up a whole nation swallowed in a gigantic communal grave, while Europe stood by and watched.[3] The pathos of endangerment and the reverberations of political defeat were defining features of Hungarian nationalism.

The Magyar aspiration to move a multilingual to a monolingual state corresponded to a European pattern. In 1789 only 15 to 20 percent of France's twenty-five million people could understand French.[4] This suggests that the modern French state was also formed as much by the exclusion of dialects and weaker languages by a dominant one as it was by the domination of one class by another. Competition between an "advanced" German and an "authentic" Hungarian during the nineteenth century produced a linguistic shift in Hungary. And in turn, a similar inferior relation was inferred toward Hungary's own minorities. The caustic proverb, "The Slovak is not human" (Tót nem ember) expressed Magyar disdain for nationalities still seemingly submerged in linguistic limbo.[5] This Hungarian arrogance and paranoia was different only in degree from the fear of language death propelling much of the German *Sturm und Drang*. By the 1760s, Germans feared their language might rot into obsolescence if it did not exert itself vis-à-vis the French. During the Napoleonic occupation, the playwright Heinrich von Kleist could even wonder if Germans would still be speaking German in 1910. The German idea of theater as a medium of cultural revival developed out of this pathology. There is an element of irony in the Hungarians adopting the German idea of theater as a powerful tactic in their contest with the Germans, all the more so, since the Magyar conquest of the Budapest stage would, in the eyes of Magyar nationalists, ultimately demarcate the formal de-Germanization of Budapest culture.

The Theater Crowd

The narrative of nationalist history embeds the story of the creation of the National Theater in the drama of liberation and cultural revival. In this essentially political analysis, the National Theater was a central venue of patriotic activity.[6] It is history on an epic or heroic scale: one of maturation, a coming of age. The emphasis is on the struggle for dignity, respect, and equality. From the beginning of the dream of a national theater in the last decade of the eighteenth century to its realization in 1837, the theater offered one of the clearest reflections of the Hungarian march to progress. Hungarian nationalists were not content simply to resuscitate the language; survival was not sufficient, or rather, survival required expansion. The vision of a national theater became the antidote to the specter of national death. The theater crowd could become the vehicle of the national language.

In northern and eastern Europe from the second half of the eighteenth century to the beginning of the twentieth century, country after country made the creation of a national theater a highest priority.[7] These national theaters were political institutions, serving both high and low culture. Two processes were going on simultaneously: the public assertion and refinement of the national language, and less publicly, the extension of the cosmopolitanism of the literati to the audience. This involved familiarizing educated Magyar speakers who were not educated in Hungarian with the possibilities of the language, as well as introducing slightly educated Magyars to higher levels of the spoken language. Popular culture was being satisfied or being created; drama, opera, light opera, and ballet were all integral to this process. Parallel to this was a growth in newspaper culture, which would make celebrities of actors even among non-theatergoers. For Hungarian activists translation of Shakespeare was a priority, because they were determined to lift Hungarian from a "coarse" to an "eloquent" tongue. But the theater could stage a rendition of Shakespeare one night followed by a farce or animal act the next. The theater was not directed at a small elite stratum; understanding the language was often more of a strain for aristocrats than commoners. The fact that the words were spoken in Hungarian made the theater accessible to those unschooled in foreign languages. So whether it was Shakespeare or a fluffy French comedy, the Hungarian theater appealed to the commoners as directly as it did the elites. Pantomimes and tableaux were also popular. With the appearance of its own Magyar playwrights and composers, a rich and complex theater culture could evolve, spurring forward the refinement of the Magyar language.

The early Hungarian literary lions such as Kisfaludy and Ferenc Kazinczy turned to the stage as the first proving ground.[8] While this was clearly an example of elites "inventing tradition," the primacy of the theater rather than print media in this process deserves closer scrutiny. Metternichean censorship allowed the press little opportunity to pursue a nationalist agenda. On the other hand, a vision of Hungarian as the operating language of the region and the language of the school could be advanced in the theater. Theater could circumvent political restrictions on the right of assembly, while those in attendance could experience the gathering as a crowd daring the margins of political legality. The theater was the obvious forum for the enactment of the drama of the liberation of the nation, and in the theater the revival of culture was received as a collective experience. Although newspapers would become important instruments in the process of establishing a Magyar national identity, the crowd was the starting point even of the top-down phenomenon. Nationalism was not simply foisted upon the crowd by the elite; the elite was itself formed by the crowd experience of the national theater. Forced to demonstrate to themselves and to Europe that Magyars had sufficient mass, the creation of a crowd arena was a central preoccupation for Hungarians. The upper classes were bolstered in their subjective certainty to call themselves the people by their own crowd experience; their ambition was to grow this crowd. Albeit more sheltered than open air occasions, auditoriums or rotundas can also be the locale for crowd experiences. For the tentatively Magyar-speaking aristocrat, the Magyarizing urbanite, and others, the theater could serve as a national seminar. The theater crowd experience could present and facilitate the rational debate, but theatrics could also let loose the gregarious sentiment and tie people together who were not otherwise associated.

While a national theater was critical in the Hungarian program for cultural revival, the initial impetus for the construction of a Hungarian national theater was reformist rather than linguistic. In 1779, three years after Joseph II elevated the Viennese Burgtheater from "Court Theater" to "National Theater," a German-language pamphlet appeared in Pozsony (Bratislava, Pressburg) subtitled "In a speech to the homeland," calling for the establishment of a "Hungarian national theater," operating and performing, it was taken for granted, in the German language.[9] A permanent German-speaking theater, called the Rondelle, had been in existence in Pest since 1774. By 1783 Buda also had a regular theater season, and both German theaters caught the attention of Joseph II, for whom the twin cities in the middle of Hungary were a potential emanating point in his new centralizing and Germanizing policies. Joseph II involved himself in moving the German theater of his Hungarian kingdom to Buda, where in 1786 he oversaw the creation of the Buda Fortress Theater (1787). The new theater reflected Joseph II's keen awareness of the importance of a German theater in fostering his cultural and administrative goals. He was planning a much larger theater in Pest that could seat 1,200, but his death in 1790 brought this effort to an end. Although historians tend to distinguish Joseph II's administrative centralization efforts from ethnic or linguistic Germanization, the German theaters he built or imagined building were to be vehicles for imparting the imperial culture, with Buda and Pest as German cultural centers. Joseph II's 1784 decision to substitute German for Latin as the administrative and official language aroused furious opposition among Hungarians, who interpreted centralization as Germanization, and consequently, viewed the emergence of a German theater in Pest and Buda with a jaundiced eye.

Joseph II's patronage of German culture mobilized a Hungarian language revival. The theater concept began to percolate. Emotional pleas for a Hungarian national theater in the Hungarian capital of Pozsony were again made at the meeting of the Diet in 1790, but this time the primary language was to be Hungarian. One Magyar troupe run by László Kelemen sought to establish itself permanently in Buda and Pest in the 1790s. The Kelemen troupe attempted to perform international plays in Hungarian as an alternative to the German theater. The German theater countered by performing plays with Hungarian themes before they could be translated into Hungarian. The first Magyar language opera was also produced in 1793. But there would be nothing again for forty years.[10]

Instead, in 1812 the largest German-speaking theater in the world opened in Pest, a city of around 33,000.[11] The theater contained between 3,000 and 3,600 seats—there is some dispute as to actual number. But even 3,000 is double the capacity of the Vienna Burgtheater today, a thousand more than the Vienna Staatsoper and only a few hundred less than the New York Metropolitan Opera in Lincoln Center. Palatine (Viceroy) Joseph, liked because of his city boosterism, was the galvanizing force behind this huge Pest theater, under construction from 1806 and 1812. The Pest city fathers were skeptical about the new theater, fearing it might divert funds from education, poor relief, and hospitals, but the palatine was persuaded of the imperial advantage of a Pest German theater that could help draw Hungary into Imperial culture. Both Palatine Joseph and Pest city authorities concurred in their financial rationale for retaining an exclusively German-speaking schedule for the new theater. A Hungarian troupe did inherit the old Rondelle theater when the German actors moved out in 1812, but they failed after only three years. The Hungarian theater had yet to prove its profitability (or ability to draw a crowd).

The flowering of the German theater between the 1810s and the 1830s coincided with a fleeting German-Hungarian literary movement whose most emblematic figure was the poet Nicholaus von Lenau, but it would not survive the language rivalries of the coming decades.[12] Hungarian German-speakers fell into three camps. Along the Austrian-Hungarian borderland a classic bilingual push and pull of two rivals resulted in language shifts.[13] In Transylvania, the Military Frontier, and southern Hungary, pockets of German-speakers fought a rear-guard action against Magyarization in the defense of a status quo of multilingualism.[14] Pest, Buda, and other German-speaking towns in the Hungarian heartland assumed a more ambiguous stance. German-speaking Pestiek were as eager as their Magyar neighbors to see Budapest the capital and center of a new autonomous Hungary, and were much more willing to accept a subordinate linguistic role in the governance of the country. They had the most to gain from linguistic collaboration; the most to lose from intransigence.

The Pest German theater succeeded in attracting some European attention, such as when Emperor Franz, Czar Alexander, and King Frederick William III attended a gala performance in 1814. Unfortunately, the acoustics in the cavernous hall of the German theater were so poor that directors all but abandoned serious drama in favor of spectacles of all kinds. Supposedly, one woman is said to have watched a drama from the balcony, only to compliment the actors on their fine pantomime. The large stage was conducive to ballet; it presented stage set designers with a tremendous backdrop. Similarly, operas could be put on as lavish spectacle that did not require close attention to the dialogue.

From 1815 to 1837 the Hungarian theater project retreated into the provinces. One magnanimous magnate, Count George Festetics, gathered the literary lions of the land and feted them with unparalleled largesse twice a year at his agricultural institute, the Georgikon.[15] These Keszthely Helicon holidays began with a theater performance. They ended with Festetics's death after five years, but they had trumped the Rousseauian presumption that theater was culturally corrupting. The Hungarian intelligentsia had become convinced that until it created a theater crowd of its own it would lack any popular base. The first self-proclaimed national theater was in Kolozsvár (Cluj), Transylvania. It took to heart Count Stephen Széchenyi's slogan "in the language lives the nation." In Kolozsvár the attitude toward the national theater movement was different from deep in the mother country and garnered more patronage from the well-to-do aristocracy. It would be Kölcsey, in an 1827 speech to the Szatmár (Satu-Mare) county assembly in Transylvania, who galvanized the nationwide drive for a national theater. Kölcsey rooted the future security of the national language and culture in the theater. He posited the theater as a safe haven, a "home" for the Magyar language at the end of its long "exile."[16]

The opening of the National Theater in Pest in 1837 galvanized the oppositional cultural politics of the Metternichean period.[17] Whereas most cities like Vienna had only one serious opera company and dramatic theater, Pest now had two. This prompted a most unusual competition between the German and Hungarian theaters between 1837 and 1847. Yet even as this theatrical duel ratcheted up cultural life of the twin cities, it soon became apparent that it was an unequal contest—in favor of the Magyar. The

Hungarian theater was subsidized, the German was not, and after three years in operation, the Hungarian theater received official designation as the National Theater. The first patriotic voices in favor of a Magyar theater were not building from an indigenous foundation, the mid-nineteenth-century critic Pál Gyulai later argued, but rather attempting to transplant something new and foreign. It was a "contrived tool" in the reassertion of the national culture. Theater was but an "abstraction," and as such "the stage became Magyar, but the spirit remained foreign. However, the weak imitation of German theater could not satisfy the Germanized cultured public," while the common people were not attracted. The actors also did not know what to do. "One can not have national theater without national theater literature."[18]

However, the Hungarian theater had a clear focus, to develop the clarity and power of a popular idiom. In other countries "patriotism just raises and ennobles respect for the arts, but here it almost single-handedly bore and nourished it," Gyulai reflected.[19] Some more ambitious directors sought with varying success to reserve the smaller, more intimate Buda German theater for serious dramatic works, taking cues from the repertoire of the Burgtheater in Vienna. The primary function of the German theater, however, had devolved into that of a conduit to European theatrical and operatic life. At the German theater guest performances became pervasive, with the Viennese stars prominent in Pest summer theater. This emphasis on imported talent left the Pest ensemble weak and no match for the Hungarian national theater. As the German theater had never been experimental or even classical, the Hungarian theater quickly seized the dramatic high road, and then, in Ferenc Erkel found a composer, conductor, and manager who quickly established the primacy of the Hungarian opera company, as well. Erkel's *László Hunyadi* became the first Hungarian-language box office success. Debuted on January 27, 1844, it has been performed regularly ever since. As the bilingual opera divas moved over to the Hungarian theater, foreign guest performances became standard at the German theater. The Pest German ensemble consequently remained weak and soon was no match for the Hungarian national theater.

The Pest German theater was committed to a broad cosmopolitan offering rather than a specifically German dramatic tradition; the theater fell more under the influence of Rossini than Schiller. The Pest theater, on the other hand, courted Magyar patriotism to fill the hall, performing Theodor Körner's *Zrínyi* and tableaux on patriotic topics. In 1815 they were able to pack the house with Kotzebue's *Béla's Flight*, which enacted a favorite motif, that of the alienated Hungarian nobleman who saves the king. When Kisfaludy's *The Tatars in Hungary* proved a smash hit in the Hungarian theater in Székesfehérvár, the German theater brought the performance to Pest where it was performed in Hungarian (thirty nights in 1818, nineteen times in 1819), a sign that Magyar drama had arrived.[20]

Passage of the protection of the national language act by the 1830 Diet spawned a number of projects; notable among them was a commission for the "Protection of the Spread of the Native Tongue," with Gábor Földváry, the subprefect of Pest (the top administrator in Pest County), as its most enthusiastic member, and two corporations for the building of a Magyar Playhouse, one led by Földváry and the other by Stephen Széchenyi. No longer was the actor a glorified barker, begging for audience and scraping together the fillers for a meager living. Indeed, actors dared to claim themselves "apostles of the national language."[21] The changing role of the actor was symptomatic of the rise of the theatrical crowd. Richard Sennett observed that the "public man" who had emerged in the eighteenth century, defined himself largely in terms of the theater. The actor had originally held a servant-like status, but in the early nineteenth century he was beginning to represent a quasi-independent worldview of his own, and by the 1830s he was the model for the oppositional politician.[22]

Széchenyi had founded several key institutions, such as the racetrack, National Academy, and the National Casino, that is, the clubs of the like-minded modeled on the English club, which combined gambling and factional politics with socializing. He now pamphleteered for a "Magyar stage," in large part to block the financial interests of the speculators in the Földváry theater land deal. The call for a Hungarian National Theater became a major political issue, pitting the liberal Pest County authorities against the conservative magnates in the Diet. Széchenyi's patriotism was born out of a profound pessimism about backward Hungary. He recommended a small subdued theater near the Danube and made all the prudent arguments, such as the lack of actors and financial resources, in his call for lowered expectations. Földváry dismissed Széchenyi's recommendations as an overestimation of Hungary's economic and cultural limitations, and organized the lesser county nobility around the building of a grander structure. The difference of opinion became quite acrimonious. Széchenyi actually had Pest municipal contributions to the Földváry project sequestered, but through guild donations by Pest burghers sufficient funds were raised; the county nobility won this battle of wills and built the Pest Magyar Theater just outside the Hatvan gate.[23] Placed on a busy but still dusty thoroughfare leading from the plain to the town of Pest, the County and municipal authorities were assuming development along Pest's highways, and displayed an ambitious vision of future population growth swelling beyond the inner city, beyond the locus of the river.

The Pest Hungarian theater building itself manifested the difference in the cultural mission of the German and Hungarian theater. Ostentatious elements were absent; seating capacity was modest (200–500 seats). People sat and mingled in a rather plain audience space, although the boxes were decorated by the subscribers as elaborately or distinctively as they wished. This was the place to be noticed for one's serious attention to the drama of cultural/linguistic renewal. The theater opened with the prologue of Vörösmarty's *Árpád ébredése* (Árpád's awakening). Vörösmarty not only empowered the Hungarian theater with his own plays but added to its repertoire by translating Shakespeare's *Julius Caesar* and *King Lear*. Petőfi translated *Coriolanus*, while János Arany translated *Hamlet*, *A Midsummer Night's Dream*, and *King John*. In the rush to create a classical theatrical canon, the Hungarian dramatists and actors often sacrificed natural Hungarian intonation, producing stilted oration and iambic pentameter that tripped over its unnatural Magyar rhythms. Some true gems were produced, but to fill an entire season's repertoire there was recourse to endless repetition and quick, clumsy translations of often weak German works. All too often attending the theater amounted to two hours of boredom in the name of patriotism.

As linguists demanded back Hungarian intonation, contemporary French plays were introduced alongside Shakespearean plays or Hungarian dramatic verse. This adopted French realism evolved into a Hungarian theatrical form by Ede Szigligeti (1814–1878) called a *népszínmű*. These tableaux with music were of uneven quality but produced a set of stock caricatures of village life, ranging from the fatuous notary to the peasant bumpkin, which were popular with theatergoers and were able to draw the migrating peasants into the theater as well. In the 1840s political comedies by József Eötvös, Ignác Nagy, and Imre Vahot became another staple. The Hungarian theater was able to complement its serious repertoire with comedies and even light operettas. While a dramatic theater was no direct threat to the German Pest theater, the introduction of music was.

When the German theater burnt to the ground on February 2, 1847, there were rumors that the management, exhausted and defeated in the theatrical duel, had torched the structure. Clearly, the contest was over. The German theater's future became a source of controversy. Pamphlets appeared on both sides. The two principal arguments in favor of its reconstruction, that the German theater had brought European culture to Pest and was a school for Hungarian theater, seemed old-fashioned. The detour through the German language no longer seemed necessary. The Hungarian theater was, in any case, by now less involved in outshining the German theater than in galvanizing the nation behind revolutionary changes. A Pest German theater would linger for another forty-two years, but with its glory years behind it. It would subsist increasingly on the margin, despite sporadic efforts from Vienna to revive it.

Kossuth and the Crowd: From the Theater to the Streets

The theater was the first venue of Magyar as a mass political language. The theater, as seminar, prepared the public for a political conversation over national identity. But for a co-narration of Hungarian nationality to occur the conversation had to move beyond the theater. While the rise of the Hungarian National Theater was a product of the older generation of magnates, by mid-century it would be Lajos Kossuth's mastery of the new public language that established him as the preeminent leader. When Kossuth gave

Electoral crowd for Kossuth in Pest (detail), 1847. Colored lithograph by Franz Weiß (Budapest Museum of History)

political agency to the Magyar language, he turned it from a seminar to a forthright political mobilization. Széchenyi, as so many of the magnates of the older generation, spoke Magyar in a halting way; he could not stir crowds with rousing speeches. In contrast, theatricality was a central feature of Kossuth's oratorical talents. Kossuth's direct, popular, and effective speech landed him in prison in 1837; his journalism and public speeches represented a new and dangerous challenge to bureaucratic authority. He emerged from prison three years later with an even more highly charged oratorical style, having spent his time learning English by memorizing Shakespeare. For young writers, such as Petőfi and Jókai, the theater was the center of their lives. Mór Jókai, the most prolific Hungarian writer of the nineteenth century, married the leading actress of the day, and while Petőfi proved a terribly awkward actor, the soaring theatricality of his poetry would be the script of the greatest theatrical event of his generation, March 15, 1848.

The Hungarian case seems to confirm Richard Sennett's thesis that "The political personality is now by 1848 defined by crowds and judged by the purity of his impulses and what a politician believes is less and less important in judging him." The spectator became "a voyeur," Sennett argues, because the political actor assumed the role of the virtuoso in the public realm. Such virtuosity was a means of gaining mastery over that "unworthy mob" whose praise the politician craved, even though he artfully disguised that desire.[24] Once a spectator audience was in place, the crowd hero could emerge and move his crowd from the theater onto the street. In the process, the applause or indifference of the audience could dash the hopes of some while buoying the efforts of others.

The political crowd became a definite factor in Central and Eastern European politics in the early 1830s. The Parisian July Revolution of 1830 linked revolution in Western Europe with a nationalist rising in Eastern Europe. Metternich had supposed that even if future revolutions reoccurred, they would not be long lasting, likening them to an old coquette, arousing resonance among amateurs perhaps, but true romance only among youths and crazies. Yet when the Poles rose up in November 1830, Metternich immediately ordered the palatine to dissolve the Hungarian Diet. But more infectious than revolutionism was the cholera that spread after the suppression of the Polish revolt from Galícia (Galicia) to Kassa (Košice, Kaschau) and Eperjes (Prešov) in northern Hungary, leading to hair raising excesses. Cholera provoked panic all over Europe with tumults in Berlin and Paris. Pest was quarantined in July 1831. When university students heard the news, they confronted the city's head doctor demanding permission to return home. The frightened and angry crowd filled the streets from city hall to the bridge. While the besieged physician scurried away across the river to Buda, troops on horseback squeezed the students back into University Square and ordered them to disperse. Some students responded by hurling stones at the soldiers. Others yelled, "Long live the Poles! Long live freedom!" Seeing that this was no longer a simple question of public medicine, the county administrators and assistant sheriff took the most expedient way out. They quickly distributed internal passports to the students and sent them packing. But gangs of local youths (nonstudents) continued to roam the city, vandalizing a few coffeehouses and knocking down a customs gazebo at the bridge. By evening order was restored.[25]

Nowhere was the unrest more terrible than the mass hysteria in northern Hungary in 1831. As cholera decimated the countryside, peasant paranoia turned on landlords, Jews, officials, and doctors, whom they believed were trying to poison them.[26] Officials who came to distribute medicine were bombarded with stones and some were endangered. In the three northern counties, military troops were sent in, and there were trials and mass floggings. The cholera panic would be treated as a great cautionary episode after 1848, becoming one of the favorite metaphors for a feverish social order. The provincial world was the potential arena of a crazed peasantry and morbid gentry. Yet in Zsigmond Kemény's novel of this episode, *A rajongók* (The fanatics),[27] he attacks the demagogues, extremists, zealots— people who misled the crowd. As terrible as had been the crowd of murderous peasants, the chaotic power of the crowd was no longer denied. From this region, and out of these years, Kossuth began his extraordinary career as the great orator of the mid-century crowd. Kossuth demonstrated his political acumen by successfully calming things down in his home region during the cholera scare. From it he gained confidence that he could speak for and to the crowd, be it in Pest, Pozsony, Vienna, or on the *puszta*.

Kossuth would ride the wave of crowd excitement that swept Central Europe between 1832 and 1848. These were not the ominous crowds of peasant Jacquerie and pogroms, or at least that was not the fantasy of the European liberals who planned them. It was imagined that festival would follow upon festival, leading, a few hoped, to the greatest festival of all— a revolution. The German Hambach festival was especially a portent. From May 26 to May 28, 1832, some 25,000 to 30,000 people assembled at Hambach, the site of an old castle ruin in the Bavarian Palatinate. It was the largest mass meeting in Germany since the Peasants War of 1525.[28] As the population of Frankfurt am Main, then one of the largest cities in Germany, was only 45,000 and considering that most of the people at the Hambach festival were men between the ages of twenty and fifty, the assembly raised the specter of revolution in the courts of Central Europe. An amassing of people of this size created a set of expectations that challenged the bureaucratic politics of the Metternichean era, for massing of more than twenty was forbidden, except for specially designated holidays. Anniversaries and monuments would become the pretext of politics. "One said Gutenberg and meant press freedom."[29]

Such politicized festivity flourished in the Swiss Confederacy. The freest area in the region, the Swiss were poised on the edge of the Swiss civil war. Jacob Burckhardt described this charged festivity in four reports he filed in 1844 with the *Basler Zeitung*, the leading conservative journal in Switzerland, about the Swiss Sharpshooters' Festival convoked in Basel.[30] The festival began "under beautiful and happy auspices," he began, "already yesterday the whole town was in movement, foreigners and Swiss filled the street in colorful confusion, a marvelous moonshine drew everyone into the open."[31] Burckhardt, a member of the Basel patriciate, wrote with equanimity while he faced the huge assembling crowds of gun-toting sharpshooters. Indeed he wrote with pleasure and with nationalist pride. The decorations—scores of different flags, festoons, wreaths, and garlands everywhere—gave "an aura of glorious splendor," he wrote.[32] The Swiss peasantry had won the right to bear arms in medieval times.

An "inestimable crowd" watched as a procession of city worthies marched to the festival meadow to greet the columns of approaching sharpshooters. They signaled their presence to the approaching procession by volleys of cannon fire from each side of the river.[33] Patriotic festivals of the Swiss Confederacy had evolved to celebrate the first successful democratic revolution and to keep alive that revolutionary tradition. But Burckhardt's reportage changed as he heard "the most beautiful phrases of Swiss unity and fraternity misused for the most unpleasant party purposes." He thought that the Radicals were fomenting discord among the sharpshooters by flattering them, "by calling them the true parliament." And he hoped that soon the sharpshooters "will no longer want to build a people within a people but will be happy to represent voluntarily its modest part in the national splendor."[34] Burckhardt would increasingly despair of the possibility of true festivity in the modern world divided by parties and classes.

Kossuth was the very type of crowd radical that the conservative Burckhardt had come to hate. Kossuth's trial of 1837 aroused vocal crowds; a subscription campaign on behalf of his widowed mother and sister fanned the flames during his three-year imprisonment, and joyous crowds greeted him upon release. The object of crowd attention, Kossuth turned his charismatic personality toward the organizing of four Pest Industrial Fairs between 1842 and 1846. These fairs, meager examples of the arts and crafts movement, were formidable as springboards of polemic.[35] Kossuth, a journalist of genius, sensed the publicistic import of the industrial fairs and the unceasing flow of copy these fairs would generate even in a censored press.[36] The first European industrial fairs, those by the French in the Napoleonic period, were intended to promote the promise of a liberal, technological society in the making. The purpose of Kossuth's fairs had not been to demonstrate economic promise, but rather to highlight the inhibitions and obstacles toward economic advance. For all the froth of praise extended to the individual exhibitor and the potentialities of the manufacturing sector in Hungary, it was apparent in these fairs of the forties that Hungarian manufacturing was an infant without fine motor control. How could it be otherwise, when manufacturing goods only represented some 5.3 percent of total Hungarian goods, or when Hungarian manufacturing represented a mere 16 percent of Austrian manufacturing output in the 1840s? The competitive fiction fostered in the summer displays had helped give shape and public character to the unfortunate fact of Hungarian lag and implanted the notion of Austrian exploitation of Hungarian backwardness. The positive impact of the initial fairs lay in their negative message. In the Napoleonic period the fair became the place to display new technology; Kossuth used the fair as a political arena to make his point that Hungary was backward. The exhibition made visible those who were behind and galvanized those involved in overcoming the problem of backwardness; only then could the race to catch up commence. Count Lajos Batthyány and Baron József Eötvös took up the call for the establishment of an industrial association to promote modernization. The young Batthyány became the titular head of the Industrial Union that sponsored these events; he would become the prime minister and principal martyr of the revolution of 1848. In the provinces young aristocrats like Dénes Pázmándy junior wrote flaming manifestoes and threw fund-raisers in his hometown.[37] The fairs served as an advertisement for Hungarian nationalism and Hungarian goods, and as a critique of Austrian benevolence. Foreign participation also had the practical purpose of spreading technology; instead of spying or traveling to England to copy the latest technology, one displayed it and at the same time tried to win a public for it.

The industrial fairs were held coincidentally with the great fair week in Pest at the end of August. Business and pleasure mixed in this tumultuous fair season. While the thousands of carts trundled into Pest, St. Stephen's Day festivities on August 20 created a truly holiday mood. St. Stephen's Day was decreed a national holiday by King Franz in 1818, and it steadily gained in importance, eventually to become the national holiday. There were fireworks and festivity in the park, after the solemnity of the national-religious rite. The fairs were cultural high points in the city's year. Books benefited from the freedom of the fair setting; books were generally released at this moment, because the censor was most lenient at these times. Art also received a boost with wealthier merchants taking the opportunity to commission portraits and paintings. Artisan production became an ever more important part of the fair activity. Tariffs and custom duties were also traditionally reduced during fair season. Kossuth wanted to revive the Socratic practice of the agora, or marketplace, as the arena of intellectual and market exchange. In the middle of the nineteenth century the definition of a metropolis was that it had several, and Pest had at least five, large marketplaces.[38]

In June 1845 Pest added a new urban holiday to its calendar, holding its first folk festival. The 1845 placards advertised the coming event as "one day of the year for everyone where everyone is part of the people." In 1845 the "folk" was understood as primarily "middle class" in tone and manner. It was to be the one day in the year when citizens blended into a crowd of equals, all reveling in the sense of mutual strength and power. The impulse of 1845 was to enter, for a day, the earnest good crowd of middle-class people. The newspapers promoted the holiday. "To celebrate a genuine folk festival is not easy, one can't bring one's elegance. And the folk, or what is called the folk, the creative middle class, is concerned with good manners,"[39] the newspaper editorialist enthused. The model for the town's folk festival was the parish fairs of Buda, Óbuda, and the Pest districts. The adjoining square of the local church was filled on its saint's day with merrymakers moving through the stalls and temporary structures. What had begun as an appendage to a religious pilgrimage in Buda, was destined to become something quite different. By the 1860s the notion would expand, or deteriorate to that of entertainment for the masses. It had become a kind of revelry for the general public, providing an opportunity for letting off steam in the urban setting.[40] Between 12,000 and 15,000 people attended the folk festival of 1845, highlighting the need for a holiday that served the new urban environment.

Kossuth utilized his industrial fairs to advance a political polemic for tariff barriers, for protection from the "rapacious" Austrian market. The some 14,000 men and women who attended the first Industrial Fair in Hungary in 1842 were potential recruits in a new campaign for economic nationalism. The Pest fairs helped mobilize sentiment behind a boycott of Austrian goods. The slogan became "Buy only Hungarian goods!" At the fourth annual Pest fair in 1846 the number of exhibitors had climbed from 213 to 516 and the number who attended rose to over 22,000.[41] The Palatine visited and allowed himself to be ushered around by Kossuth. Students celebrated the fair by gathering for a "gyűlde," a torchlight parade under hundreds of torches.[42] Visitors to the fair were impressed by the array of silk, velvet, glassware, or white beet sugar, and improving porcelain and wool manufactures.[43] These initial exhibitions generated public concern about economic change. They made visible and graspable both facts and causes of backwardness. They became the vehicles of a higher salesmanship, first to convince the elite itself to invest in the manufacturing sector, and then to persuade the nation, and finally the whole region that liberal industrialism could harness safe and comfortable passage through the wrenching process of modernization. The Kossuth fairs presented a counter option to Széchenyi's fatalistic, agrarian conception of the Hungarians as an "Eastern people," and helped to free Kossuth and his allies from Széchenyi's schizophrenic hesitations, and his underlying ambivalence and skepticism about the possibilities of Hungary's emergence as a liberal industrial society.[44] The attendance of some 22,000 people was modest, but it indicated that nationalism and liberalism were beginning to mobilize a crowd.

In October 1847 a convergence of political festivity—monarchic and radical—brought Pest and Buda to new levels of excitement. Kossuth revolutionized the politics of the notable Diet by staging a modern electoral campaign, the likes of which had never been seen before in Hungary. Precisely at the moment when Kossuth's electoral campaign in Pest County reached its climax, the seventeen-year-old Franz Joseph won the "nation's love," according to Kossuth, when he arrived unexpectedly in Buda for his first official visit.[45] In the week preceding the election, people streamed into Pest from the villages and provinces. Gentry electors had been arriving by trains, by ships, and in a procession of carriages from every direction. Even conservative magnates patriotically appeared in Hungarian folk costume.[46]

The election campaign happened to coincide with the installation of a new palatine. Palatine Joseph, who had died in January, had been particularly beloved in Pest for his efforts to enhance and beautify the city, and his son Stephen was expected to continue the tradition. Since the beginning of the century, this branch of the Habsburg family had taken on the responsibility of mediating between Hungarian interests and Austrian concerns. The palatine had developed a real sympathy for and among Hungarians, raising his children within Hungarian culture. A public subscription campaign was organized immediately upon Palatine Joseph's death for a statue in his honor in the City Park. Had revolution not interceded, this would have been the first public monument erected to a Habsburg in Hungary in three-hundred-and-fifty years of rule.[47] The campaign for a statue to Palatine Joseph was revived during the first wave of statue building in the city in 1860. The installation of the new palatine was orchestrated in the fashion of a mini-coronation, preceded by an official tour of Hungary. The tour had the makings of a triumphal event. But at its conclusion, a bridge at Komárom (Komorn, Komárno) collapsed after the archduke's carriage and a hundred-man banderium, a mounted procession of nobles in traditional garb, passed over it. Fifty spectators were plunged into the river and only twenty-three could be rescued.[48]

The appearance of the Archduke Franz Joseph helped shift the focus away from the tragedy. Buda crowds strained to see the nephew of the sovereign. At the installation on October 17 the sight of the young Habsburg Archduke Franz Joseph in a Hussar officer's uniform, speaking fluent Hungarian surprised and delighted the audience. He upstaged the new palatine as the darling of the event. Ferdinand V had produced similar excitement when he had addressed the Hungarians with a few words of Magyar—the first Hungarian king in three hundred years to do so.[49] But now the young Franz Joseph appeared before them able to speak their language. "The heart throbbed, joy came to people's eyes, and thousands of voices said that the nation finally had someone to love," Ferenc Toldy would enthuse decades later.[50] Toldy reported to the Academy of Sciences that Franz Joseph could say "I came, I saw, and I conquered."[51] Franz Joseph confided in a letter to his mother that he had felt ill at ease during the volcanic eruption and found it uncomfortable to be the object of such adoration.[52] Széchenyi was alone in his unenthusiastic response to Franz Joseph's cool demeanor.

On the very evening of the installation, Kossuth supporters were rallying across the river in Pest. One youthful admirer, Baron Frigyes Podmaniczky told the crowd he knew of four special days since the creation of the world: the first when light was created out of chaos; the second when

Christ was born; the third when the French revolution broke out, and the fourth would be tomorrow when it would be decided if Kossuth is elected or not.[53] Gypsy bands accompanied the Kossuth supporters in their march through town; demonstrators carried pictures of Kossuth and waved the tricolor. A group of conscripts were so taken by the demonstration as it passed the barracks, that *en masse* they joined the several-thousand strong march. The appearance of the soldiers in the already noisy crowd emboldened the whole.[54]

Although the city remained orderly, conservatives felt beleaguered, for those who did not raise their hats to Kossuth's portrait were insulted as "Schwabs." They complained of the "ear-splitting mob" that stopped at every bar "to drink and shout."[55] All reports concur on the tumultuous street activity and the packed taverns on the eve of the election. On election morning thousands marched in the electoral procession through the center of downtown. The crowd was massive enough to span the one mile distance from Calvin Square around Museum Ring Boulevard to Ferenc Deák Street, and then snaked back through Szervita Square to the County Courthouse. Electors carried tricolor national flags, posters for Kossuth, or slogans such as "For the good of the nation" (*haza*). In glittering gold lettering signs proclaimed the names of the different delegates' regions. At the head of the procession was a Gypsy band, followed by village notaries and electors. They were followed by wagons filled with wine barrels. Over four thousand electors filled the courthouse. Eötvös spoke to the delegates of a wider significance of this election, which was inspiring a new era in Hungarian politics. The candidates each addressed the crowd, although much of what they said was drowned out by all the cheering and yelling.[56] When Kossuth won with over a two-to-one margin, Pest celebrated. By late evening the increasingly raucous, liquored up electors filled the downtown streets taunting the conservative opposition who bitterly resented the "Magyar mob" and "*betyár* (robber) terrorism" that seemed to accompany the new politics.[57] Social license was being inserted into the nascent urban setting of Pest. Moralists complained of "scandalous scenes in doorways involving some of the offspring of Pest's leading families!"[58]

Just five months before the outbreak of revolution, a curious mix of monarchic festivity and radical crowds appeared in the twin cities. Deputy Kossuth drew crowds in Pozsony whenever he appeared in public. His star was rising. Inside the Diet chamber, crowds grew so boisterous that conservative politicians found it difficult to make themselves heard. In a speech on March 3, 1848, twelve days before the outbreak of revolution, an expansive Kossuth included the young Archduke Franz Joseph as another who had gained Hungary's affection. The crowd as expression and monitor of that affection had become a player in Hungarian politics.[59]

Kossuth had first expanded the public forum modestly from the theater to the fair grounds, from Magyar words to Magyar goods; but eventually his political agitation moved out onto the streets. At the theater only those who were willing to pay admission entered. It was a "closed crowd" and the elite were predominant.[60] On the streets the crowd became open ended, no longer confined by the walls of the theater or the gates of the fair. The indifferent, cynical, or hostile were still present. The conversation broadened to include the semiliterate, the illiterate, and non-Magyars. The language renewal had aestheticized a political problem; Kossuth repoliticized the quest. His oratory was a bridge between the elite and crowd experience. He brought the focus back to the Diet chamber, but the crowd would not be shut out. What the country would do, and how it was to be done remained an open question, to which the politicians in their Diet, the peasants awaiting emancipation, and the entrepreneurs and students in the cities would offer answers.

1848 revolutionary rally at the steps of the National Museum, Budapest. Engraving (Hungarian National Museum, Historical Picture Gallery)

3

Crowds Shaking Nations

1848 is the year of crowds shaking nations. As Hungary had no urban tradition of "bargaining by riot," the revolutionary crowd exploded with unusual force upon the Hungarian scene. On March 15, 1848, Sándor Petőfi
(1823–July 31, 1849), the poet of Young Hungary, rallied Pest by reciting
his just-completed poem, "Nemzeti dal" (The national song), with its call:
"On your feet Hungarians!" (Talpra magyar!) To his own half-suppressed
amazement, he kindled a revolutionary crowd. How they acted and how the
crowd responded on March 15, 1848, is among the most embroidered events
of Hungarian historical memory.[1] Those who were frightened or shrank
from participating have seldom been heard from. March 15 became almost
from the initial moment a heroic victory celebration. But Pest was also con-
forming to the revolutionary dynamic sweeping Central Europe: huge gatherings, triggered by a tiny circle that had prepared for such a moment—
usually in a tavern or café. A series of political demands were read. Although barely comprehensible to the majority in the crowd, they were affirmed by acclamation in the knowledge that by doing so long-held constraints and inhibitions suddenly would lose their force.[2]

The urban revolutions of 1848 would spread as a pebble dropped in a
still pond sends out ring upon ring. Since the news that Parisian crowds
had toppled the Orléans Monarchy in late February, the anticipation of a
revolutionary tidal wave had reached a thunderous pitch in cities throughout the continent. On March 14, the British foreign secretary was instruct-
ing his diplomats in Vienna to counter alarmist reports of Chartist rioting
in Glasgow, not himself cognizant that crowds were already convulsing the
Habsburg capital.[3] When word reached Pozsony, the seat of the Hungarian
Diet, on March 14 that crowds had taken to the streets of Vienna, Kossuth

was buttonholed by a student who urged that "if you will make a speech, in two hours you can incite a public meeting to proclaim a republic."[4] Kossuth angrily rejected such adventurism. Still people took to the streets of the official Hungarian capital to celebrate the imminence of revolution. Students and uniformed Civic Guards conducted a torchlight procession complete with a musical band that wound its way through the streets to the residences of the palatine and Kossuth. The red-white-green tricolor was proudly displayed, forbidden marches were played and sung, and sabers were brandished, but after a few words from Kossuth on his balcony the crowd quietly dispersed. On the morning of March 15 Kossuth departed with key political leaders for Vienna, where he intoxicated the huge, swelling crowd with his rhetoric that same afternoon. A successful revolution in Vienna, he reasoned, would assure liberal reforms in Hungary. It could be said that Kossuth was projecting a liberal-revolutionary version of dualism between the two halves of the monarchy; in any case, neither he nor the politicians of Pozsony were to be part of the soon-to-be legendary events of the Hungarian March 15.[5]

The outbreak of the revolution in Pest contained all the pathos of light opera. Petőfi and perhaps a dozen others who left the Café Pilvax in the early morning hours armed with a poem and a twelve-point program were certain (or wished to be certain) that everything had prepared them for this moment.[6] "The history of the French Revolution is my daily bread," Petőfi wrote.[7] Young Hungary, subversive young intellectuals that had come together in the coffeehouses of the new city, caricatured the romantic vision of revolution that day, confidently believing that they had the script of revolution in their hands. The Parisian barricades of the July Revolution of 1830 inaugurated a new tactic for nineteenth-century urban revolution. But Hungarian radicals worried that the twin cities of Pest and Buda, their one significant urban complex, still in its infancy, might be an insufficient staging ground for mass popular action. And even in Buda-Pest the majority of the population was German-speaking. Buda, with 35,000 inhabitants, was the seat of the Vice-Regal Council, and protected by high bluffs and the fortress the Habsburg palace looked down upon the Danube and the city of Pest beyond. But what had made Buda an ideal location for the Habsburg bureaucracy and German-language culture in Hungary also restricted its population growth. Pest and Buda were two separate towns about to be linked by a permanent chain bridge then under construction, with Pest the more dynamic of the two. Pest melded into Hungary's agricultural heartland, and thus would be the natural hub of transport and food processing industries, which in the coming decades would propel Hungarian economic development. Much hope was placed in Pest; it was the home of Hungary's only university, the Academy of Sciences, National Museum and Library, National Theater, Hungary's largest printing presses, and important newspapers and journals. Not only German-speaking burghers, but also significant Serb, Greek, and other ethnic communities prospered in Pest. Pest was growing rapidly; it was the natural migrating point for Magyar peasants. But still in 1848 its population was 110,000. Pest County as a whole had a population of some 600,000, but it seemed only during the fair seasons that it could swell to a size that would make the crowd a formidable political actor. It so happened that on March 15, peasants were beginning to stream into Pest for the Joseph Day fair, one of the principal fairs of the year. The March Youth, as they would come to be called, had been talking about holding a mass meeting on the nineteenth at the Rákos fair grounds to take advantage of the mass influx.[8] They had been working on a petition since the ninth, while liberals had been maneuvering to frustrate their plans for a mass gathering.[9] But when the news arrived on the evening of the fourteenth that the revolution had carried the day in Vienna and that Metternich had fallen, the dynamic changed. Petőfi and his friends were impatient to act; the only question remaining was when. Petőfi urged immediate action: "The day after tomorrow may be too late."[10]

After a night of feverish debate the young radicals of the Café Pilvax agreed to reassemble at eight in the morning to attempt the act of defiance that could spark a popular uprising. The distress that only six of the conspirators dared to appear punctually at the appointed morning hour was overcome by the sense that there was no turning back, especially with Petőfi declaiming, "Now is the time, now or never!"[11] Petőfi had arrived dressed for the part: crossing his narrow chest was a blood-red, wide silk sash from which dangled a broad sword that hit his side as he moved. An ostrich feather rose from his felt cap that was tilted at a rakish angle over his right ear. Silver buttons adorned his black silk attila, the native jacket worn by the gentry. Tightly tailored pants and tufted evening shoes rounded out his ensemble.[12] Petőfi penned some of the most lyrical romantic poetry in Hungarian, which coupled with his forceful political poetry, has made him incontestably the most important Hungarian poet of the nineteenth century. Petőfi recited his poem first in the café; the writer Mór Jókai declaimed the Twelve Points, and the little band of conspirators melodramatically stepped onto the early morning sleet-drenched streets. They attracted a curious throng of perhaps sixty or seventy, half-following, half-removed, accompanying them, and occasionally cheering slogans as they made their way to the medical school.[13]

Pál Vasvári (1826–July 1849) ran through the building heralding their arrival. His loose pleated cape draped over his right shoulder fluttered behind him. He wore a cockade on his chest and a little Magyar hat decorated with a streaming feather. Vasvári was a historian and teacher at a progressive school for girls in Pest, but now he brought classes to a halt. Some professors dismissed their classes with patriotic gestures, others made disdainful utterances,[14] but in the courtyard cheers of approval accompanied the reading of the Twelve Points by Jókai. When Petőfi stood on a chair and recited his poem, the refrain: "We swear that we won't be slaves any longer!" triggered a tremendous response.

The scene was repeated at the law school where the cadre fused with the ever-widening crowd of one thousand.[15] From the third-floor window of the liberal arts building one student described it as a large assembly of black top hats; words could not be discerned, just the buzzing and cheering and the sense that below was a crowd of the elegant and privileged.[16] In the courtyard, the crowd chanted "We swear that we won't be slaves any longer" six times. This assembled group, cheering and chanting as one, heeded the call for action. They determined to defy censorship by publishing the poem and points immediately. What the crowd of 2,000 had so ecstatically embraced would now be made concrete and spread. Like a buzzing swarm the crowd approached Pest's major print shop. They were awaited at the entrance, where a brief charade of demand and surrender took place. Inside the pressroom the journalist József Irinyi (1817–1895) put his hands on the large printing press and said, "We seize this press in the name of the people." His sharp voice carried throughout the shop.[17] During the negotiations in German and the printing of leaflets in Hungarian, the crowd, now some five thousand, listened to Petőfi declaim again. Police had forewarned Lajos Landerer, the proprietor, of Young Hungary's plans already the night before, but he had turned down the offer of armed protection "saying that if the crowd were small there would be no need for them and if the crowd were large they would only make matters worse."[18] Landerer had made sure there was sufficient paper stock and staff on hand for the task.

The crowd had become dense and insatiable. Even though all could not hear or even understand the Magyar being spoken, each newcomer to the crowd wanted to see the poet repeat his performance. As they awaited the leaflets, others took to the soapbox, with Vasvári, the most gifted orator among the radicals, intensifying the excitement with his sonorous flowing speech, alive with images and peppered with historical analogies from antiquity. The initial distribution of the leaflets resembled a sacramental act to those lined up directly outside the print shop.[19] Soon a missionary fervor took over and the leaflet was rushed through the streets, handed out, and stuck on buildings. Despite the rain, more and more people streamed in from the outlying districts. With the leaflet in their hands, peripheral crowds reenacted the central drama for newcomers. Hearing the poem and points read aloud integrated them into the crowd experience.[20]

At noon the revolution declared an intermission. But even the normal noon-day church bells rang more incessantly that day to mark an ancient triumph over the Turks, adding to the now intoxicating holiday mood that not even the rain could dampen. After lunch an even larger and more polyglot crowd of 10,000 regrouped in the marketplace before the steps of the National Museum. Artisans and burghers were there, but so were nobles, overseers, and peasants. Many now took to the podium.[21] The dream of reaching a mass public was at this moment a reality for Pest's young literati.[22] A few of the patriotic speeches were delivered in German, and some moderate politicians joined the principals, hoping to steer the infectious mood in a more moderate direction. Having already successfully violated the letter of the law by voiding censorship regulations, the crowd moved on to the Pest City Hall to face the politicians and magistrates directly. The 100-man Pest city council was addressed by an eight-member delegation of the March Youth, who demanded the actions of the crowd be ratified and affirmed.[23] The inclusion of two liberals in the delegation made the city council more receptive, but with some 15,000 to 16,000 people milling around in the square below them, it was the breakdown of order that most concerned them. The liberal Assistant Mayor Lipót Rottenbiller legitimated the sense of breakthrough when he declared that "We should not let history later blame us for having kept Pest behind the other European movements." He praised the crowd's representatives, for having "brought us the hope of full liberty," and pleaded with them that "under your aegis our city will avoid disruptions of public order."[24] Amidst the speeches and cheers for freedom and equality, there were cheers and words of deference to the king and the palatine as well. The Vice-Regal Council had dispatched Móricz Almássy, the king's commissioner, down to Pest to reason with the popular crowd or masses (*néptömeg*).[25] Despite a polite reception, nothing was going to keep the Pest crowd from replaying Bastille Day: a living trophy of their action was to be rescued.

    With the city seal affixed to the Twelve Points and waved to the waiting
crowd below, the crowd was now spurred on by cries of "To Buda!" "Let's
open Táncsics's cell!" Mihály Táncsics was the principal political prisoner
in Buda, jailed for seditious writings. The crowd of some 20,000 swept
down fashionable Váci Street where merchants had hurriedly shut their elegant shops. The mass march that crossed the pontoon bridge to Buda was
both tame and passionate: an interminable line of umbrellas, thousands and
thousands, occasionally spurred by flamboyant individuals. The passionate
desire to include all, women very much included, was characteristic of this
crowd. Given the theatricality of the event, it is fitting that the one woman
that we know stood out in the crowd was Mrs. Lujza Farkas Szathmáry, an
actress of the National Theater, who seized the tricolor and gave direction
to the milling crowd. The act gained her such notoriety that she was obliged
to spend seven years in hiding after the revolution.[26]

    Watching "a procession longer than the eye could see" marching up
to Buda, the alarmed Vice-Regal Council hurriedly reconvened.[27] As the
crowd filled the grounds, the seven thousand largely Italian defenders of
the Buda Castle paid the immense crowd the due it desired with cries of
"Evivia l'Ungheria!" Within five minutes the council had granted the three
principal demands: the end of censorship, the creation of a National Guard,
and the release of Táncsics, and the revolutionary delegates announced
their success to the "cheering crowd" from a palace window. To liberate
Táncsics the crowd proceeded to the Buda prison. When the warden went
to Táncsics's cell to tell him that the crowd had come to free him, he
begged Táncsics for protection.[28] Unlike Bastille Day, all agreed that in this
enactment one could dispense with gratuitous violence. Táncsics' wife,
Teréz, who headed the group of young liberators, hugged him and said:
"There is no more censorship!"[29] The abolition of censorship, the first of
the Twelve Points, had been the central focus and crowning achievement of
the entire day. In the hour-and-a-half it took the crowd to overcome the authorities in Pest and Buda not a single individual had been hurt. The crowd
of 20,000 to 25,000 had "behaved calmly," committing not even the small-
est infraction to disrupt the peace.[30] A move to raid the arsenal was fore-
stalled by Rottenbiller and Jókai's assurance that a National Guard would
be quickly formed and weapons distributed.[31] Instead, the mass exaltation
of having taken justice into one's own hands by freeing an innocent culminated the crowd action of that day. The newspaper headline recounting the
day's events would read: "revolution without blood."[32]

    With Táncsics amongst them, the jubilant crowd turned back to Pest,
guiding Táncsics's carriage in a festive procession through streets aglow in

candles. The evening of March 15 in Buda-Pest the candles flickered in the windows, "awake the city was dreaming," János Arany would recall a few months later.[33] The procession ended in front of the theater. "The theater was an altar today," Jókai reported.[34] Arrangements were already made in the afternoon to put on a special gala performance that night of József Katona's *Bán Bánk* (1820), considered the best of Hungarian nineteenth-century historical dramas. Bánk was a thirteenth-century bán (palatine), loyal to his monarch, but who nevertheless kills the queen—and is not gravely punished for his deed. No admission was charged; people filled the theater in holiday dress, a cockade on every chest. The excited audience had little patience for Katona's drama of conflicting loyalties; instead, the audience turned the spotlight on itself, fêted Táncsics, and cheered their heroes in the audience. They chanted Petőfi verses, and turned the "National Song" into a song, lustily singing a hurriedly composed musical arrangement of the poem.[35]

Placards the next day announced the new freedoms, and many newspapers stamped "free press" across their front page.[36] In Pest on the sixteenth women passed out cockades, bandannas, and flowers. Radicals affected "'immense red feathers' in their hats."[37] Male and female attire announced the triumph with sashes of red white or green around wrists, shoulders, or waists. A crowd of "uncountable number" stopped in front of the publishing house while a speaker told the assembled, "This is a saintly place. Here began the free Magyar press." Twenty national flags with the slogan "Magyar Press Freedom" adorned the building, and its employees sported Magyar emblems and tricolors on their work clothes.[38] On the streets the popular crowd (*néptömeg*) milled around boisterously cheering: "Long live Hungarian freedom!"[39] The palatine's residence and the Mátyás Church were bathed in celebratory light on the evening of March 16, shedding a reassuring glow on the revolutionary project under way in Pest. With nothing and no one threatening, the crowd turned celebratory in the days to come. An exciting flow of conversations and street debate became melodic by the interjection of revolutionary songs.[40]

What happened in Pest on March 15 was retold, imitated, and reinterpreted by young radicals in provincial cities throughout Hungary. In Győr "the whole city" and the rural folk flooded in "like waves in the street," and "hundreds and hundreds of cheering voices" could be heard from the central square. From Transylvania the telegram to Vienna began: "Events have moved forward with horrible speed and descended upon us with an unpredictable velocity."[41] March 15 was a kind of epic drama that would be visualized and transformed into a mythic event almost immediately.

The soapbox orators that appeared all over Győr would be remembered decades later as emotional catalysts, who appealed not only to the "excitable youth" but moved "the souls of the old people" as well. These March Youth of Győr began traveling about the countryside to deliver their message.[42] On the morning of March 16, 1,500 young men signed up for the national guard in the Szeged city hall market plaza.[43] One man recalled the lovely "girls with gentle hands" passing out tricolor ribbons: "Some fellows sent me over" to the girls, who pinned the required ribbon on the twenty-six-year-old bachelor, thus designating him a national guardsman.

With prohibitions and inhibitions loosened, citizens sported swords on the street. "Students took them to school and actors took them to rehearsals."[44] Júlia Szendrey, Petőfi's wife, cut her hair and donned pants, in the manner of George Sand. Radical women asserted a new style and public presence, insisting on an active role for women in public affairs. These honeymoon days had a rhythm of their own, documented every evening at the National Theater in Pest, and propelled forward with the arrival of the evening steamship carrying the daily news from Vienna, Pozsony, and abroad. Citizens rushed to the museum grounds to hear the latest. The steps of the museum—the launching pad of revolution—became the forum of innumerable official and unofficial gatherings. The grass and flowers were trampled, and the museum grounds turned into mounds of dirt; but from the steps information was transmitted, solidarity established, and actions were organized. People were emboldened by the new flow of information. Although rumors still abounded, the newly freed press imbued news with an exhilarating authenticity and immediacy. News itself could take on a vivid and important character. From here the news was received that King Ferdinand V of Hungary (Emperor Ferdinand II of Habsburg) had acquiesced, and a decree had been issued providing for a separate Hungarian administration. On March 17 in Vienna the sovereign received the ministerial deputation of the newly constituted Magyar government with Count Lajos Batthyány at its head. From the museum grounds Pest could follow the reverberations of their actions. The opportunity to report these events was in itself newsworthy. "The author of these lines feels himself fortunate that in a public manner he can inform the sons of his homeland," began a news account of "Vienna celebrates the Magyars."[45] The mass of anonymous celebrants were uplifted when they thought themselves enacting a drama that linked them with the urban masses all over Europe.

Kossuth returned from Pozsony with the message that absolutism had collapsed at its very center in Vienna. He moved to mobilize immediate legislative action in Pozsony, to seize the moment—but also to contain the danger of the crowd unleashed. Parliamentary radicals (about ten percent of the voting deputies) pushed through legislation to end serfdom. Compromises "went through both Houses in the first fright," wrote the palatine.[46] What might Young Hungary do with a captive audience of tens of thousands of peasants? It was not Petőfi as the magician and lyricist of the urban crowd, but as the magician and agitator of the peasants on market day that filled the imagination of the magnate and gentry politicians. The still-recent memory of Galician peasants massacring over a thousand Polish nobles two years before gave fearful credence to a rumor that reached Pozsony on March 16 or March 17 that Petőfi was mobilizing an excited crowd of serfs, as many as 30,000 to 40,000.[47] This false rumor of an imminent Jacquerie and Petőfi's "really mad poem" produced a "certain kind of panic" that propelled the Diet into the process of dismantling the feudal order.[48] Seventy-four percent of Hungary's serfs were emancipated; the land formerly worked by statute labor passed into the ownership of the peasantry. Nobles became taxpayers, but nobles were also to be compensated for the land relinquished to the peasants—at least in theory—for the legislature feared precise stipulation of these provisions might unleash the mob. Thus, a great peasant Jacquerie did not materialize. By discharging the peasant anger before it escalated the revolution, the Pozsony legislators avoided the chaos and violence of the "Great Fear" of August 1789. The economic advantages to the peasant were still unclear; many remained landless or consigned to very meager plots. Over half of the arable land stayed in the hands of the large estate owners.[49] In April further legislation would extend the new freedoms, but compensation to the nobles was also written into the law.

While the Diet moved out of fear of the peasants, Petőfi reveled in his provocateur image. Moderates were in charge of the government, while radicals divided into two camps: the parliamentary radicals and the revolutionary intellectuals in the capital (Petőfi, Vasvári, and their friends). Kossuth was adamant on March 19 that Buda-Pest was not to play the role of Paris leading a second revolution; the twin cities were to be "the heart of the country" but not its "master."[50] Simultaneously, the Diet sought to quench the call to move the seat of government to a unified "Budapest"; seeking to keep the crowd at bay, they were not about to move into the hornet's nest. But the energy and imagination of this revolution inevitably pulled government and politics to its center. "Budapest spoke in its own name but was convinced that the whole country would follow its example," wrote Petőfi. "The party that can create general movements . . . can surely count on the sympathy of the countryside."[51]

The first news of Pest's "umbrella revolution" temporarily calmed the worried Széchenyi in Pozsony, although he hardly shared the enthusiasm of a friend who wrote him from Pest: "Let's take our hats off to Petőfi, who is one of the most capable men in the country. As he exercised the magic of his poems and speeches to create mass excitement before, so now he promotes quiet and order . . . a religious belief has awakened in me that a noble, sublime common spirit arising from here would become the greatest guarantee of the nation's inner vitality, and that the gods did not raise this spirit as a symptom of future agony."[52]

The old reformer Miklós Wesselényi wanted to wish it away. From Transylvania he wrote Kossuth that the demonstrations in Pest and the copy-cat events elsewhere in Hungary were no more real than the Potemkin villages fabricated by Catherine the Great.[53] But Pozsony continued to be disturbed by rumors of wild actions by Pest crowds, including the supposed storming of the Buda Citadel by the crowd and the National Guard. Pozsony wanted to slow things down. After Pest crowds tore down and destroyed the imperial colors and insignia from public buildings, those in Pozsony were surreptitiously removed on March 23.[54] Worried that the press was inflaming crowd violence, on March 20 the Diet passed a new publishing law that levied a steep registration fee, thus drawing a distinction between the abolition of censorship and actually setting the press free.[55] This retreat from March 15's article of faith brought Pest revolutionaries out onto the street. They burned the edict at a public rally in City Hall Square.[56] This significant step backward in press freedom brought renewed calls to move the legislature to Pest, away from Pozsony, with its "vapors of the overthrown regime."[57] Eötvös, leading moderate intellectual, received a threat that if a suitable ministry were not instituted post haste a band would storm the royal arsenal at Buda. On the twenty-fifth the Pozsony Diet retreated somewhat on the publishing law, reducing the deposit by half.

The revolutionary crowd became reactive in the last days of March. Rancor between the sovereign and the Hungarian Diet turned into a thunderous rebuttal in the Diet. With the emperor/king seeming to abandon his conciliatory pledge toward the revolution by withdrawing the royal decree of March 17 and Kossuth yelling vituperative remarks, Batthyány threatened his resignation, and the Diet rejected the latest Royal Rescript. Kossuth took the risky step of appealing to the streets, István Deák argues, in order to help out the Diet.[58] In any case, angry crowds would have appeared in Pest and Pozsony. A large crowd gathered on the fashionable promenade at Theater Square in Pozsony to watch while the decree announcing the royal change of heart was burned.[59] Later that evening a crowd of youths broke into a residence of a baroness seeking the bearer of the decree. Ferenc Deák, a moderate liberal, chided the crowd: "The greatness of the French Revolution did not consist in breaking into private homes, persecuting individuals, or threatening personal safety."[60] The anxious Széchenyi warned his fellow legislators that the French Revolution could well come to look "like an innocent comedy, an insignificant joke, compared to what is about to unfold here."[61] Leading politicians hurried to Vienna to plead their case.

The Buda-Pest Committee of Public Safety had been trying to move the revolution in a more radical direction. At a mass meeting on March 27, they called for the immediate convocation of a national convention, the repudiation of the Batthyány ministry, and the proclamation of a republic. With difficulty, moderates calmed the crowd then, but when word arrived of Emperor/King Ferdinand's reversal, the city was gripped in an insurrectionary mood.[62] A massive crowd marched on City Hall demanding weapons, waving red flags, and wanting to fly a red flag over the building.[63] Only the announcement of a massive demonstration the next day calmed the unruly throng. The demonstration of March 30 was so thunderous that some have suggested that it surpassed that of March 15.[64] Pest was in such a state that Kossuth could have easily raised the call of revolt and a march on Vienna. "It is certain," writes István Deák, "that Kossuth had encouraged these manifestations with his passionate speeches, and by stressing to the delegate of the Pest radicals that the 'March Youth' ought to 'risk everything for fatherland.'"[65] Many arrived at the Pest County executive committee meeting wearing red buttons as symbols of their anger. Outside orators made sporadic calls for a "republic" and severing of the personal union with Austria. Some wanted the Palatine Archduke Stephen named King of Hungary. At least "20,000 people assembled in front of the National Museum to hear Petőfi proclaim the coming of world revolution," an event that seemed not all that improbable at that moment.[66] Virtually all the great cities of Europe were being shaken by huge street crowds. Even in England, where the revolution was avoided, Chartists had mobilized crowds in Manchester and Glasgow, and a quarter-of-a-million would gather in London in the following week-and-a-half.

Barricades suddenly appeared in the streets of Pest, against whom or for what purpose was not clear. Certainly the mood had become more violent.

The thrill of the fifteenth had been the release, the breaking of taboo, the exploration of the unknown. Two weeks later the desire for confrontation was ascendant. The memory of the Magyar Jacobins was called forth. A resolution was introduced in parliament that the remains of Ignác Martinovics and his compatriots, "martyrs for national freedom of 1795," be reburied in a manner that expressed the nation's appreciation. Their graves should be "covered with national decorations" so that such persecution never happens again.[67]

Vienna backed down, and Hungary's Batthyány government gained Habsburg recognition and wrenched a whole agenda of reforms from the king. The April Laws legitimated Hungary as a semi-autonomous territory, tied to the Habsburgs only as a constitutional hereditary monarchy with its own elected annual parliament. Monarchic decrees would henceforth require a counter-signature, and Habsburg governance was further impeded by a set of parallel competing bureaucracies for finance and military affairs, and Hungarian internal administration was ceded to local administration, the domain of the Magyar gentry.

The new suffrage laws were extremely progressive by the standards of the era. Extended to about one-quarter of the adult male population, it compared favorably to the other great franchise reforms of western Europe and Great Britain in the 1830s and was even more generous than the one proclaimed by the Prussian revolutionary assembly. About half the peasants, and all the notables and educated received the franchise. No nobles lost their franchise whatever their wealth or education. This was a masterstroke, for it preserved noble political privilege uninterruptedly, permitting noble lawmakers to continue to govern. The national "popular assembly" through 1848 and 1849 was almost exclusively composed of nobility. These politicians at the reform Diet had passed legislation at an exhilarating rate in the first weeks of the revolution, but henceforth the national assembly would play a role of moderation, and little dramatic reform legislation could be expected.

This aristocratic dominance of Hungarian politics for the remainder of the revolution insured a preference for legalistic solutions. The critical issue of the next phase of the revolution was relations between the states within the state: Hungarians vis-à-vis the Habsburgs; Hungarians vis-à-vis the Kingdom of Croatia, vis-à-vis the other minorities. The Hungarian politicians desperately wished to approach these issues in a traditional manner, as issues of political negotiation between diplomats and political leaders. The result was a distancing of the political from the crowd; the process would be a fiasco of arrogant misjudgments, or hopeless attempts to stem the inevitable. Whichever, when the revolution was lost, the nobility would be chided, but remain strong. The franchise proved to be a coup that secured the hold of the nobility on Hungarian politics. "The provincial nobility actually increased its influence and power," [68] and this facilitated the continuance of aristocratic dominance of Hungarian politics from the 1860s revival of Magyar politics to the end of the monarchy. So while the street demonstrations may have been the winning card in the struggle between the Diet and the Habsburg Court, it would be Kossuth rather than the Pest radicals who would profit from the victory. The Pest crowd now set bonfires to acclaim "Citizen Kossuth," while the substantive radical demand for a new government, a republic, was sidestepped. Despite the revolutionary rising, the nobles remained at the helm. On March 30 Petőfi penned "The Sea has Risen":

Föltámadott a tenger,	The Sea has risen,
A népek tengere;	the sea of the peoples
Ijesztve eget földet,	terrifying heaven and earth,
Szilaj hullámokat vet	its dread might casts up wild waves.
Rémítő ereje.	
Látjátok ezt a táncot?	Do you see this dance?
Halljátok e zenét?	Do you hear the music?
A kik még nem tudtátok,	Those who still don't know,
Most megtanulhatjátok,	now can learn,
Hogyan mulat a nép.	how the people celebrate.
Reng és üvölt e tenger,	The ocean shrieks and howls,
Hánykódnak a hajók,	The ships are tossed about,
Süllyednek a pokolra	sinking to hell,
Az árbóc és vitorla	their masts and sails
Megtörve, tépve lóg.	broken, hang ripped.
Tombold ki, te özönvíz,	Let the torrent surge,
Tombold ki magadat,	Let it surge
Mutasd mélységes medred,	Display your wild foam
S dobáld a fellegekre	Heave your angry crest to the clouds.
Bőszült tajtékodat.	
Jegyezd vele az égre	Let it mark the heavens
örök tanulságul:	as an eternal lesson:
Habár fölül a gálya,	Even if the galley is above,
S alul a víznek árja,	and the water's current is above,
Azért a víz az úr!	still the water is the master! [69]

Petőfi's image of the crowd was as an overwhelming surge of power, un-navigable, crashing over authority. The crowd was tumultuous and threatening, washing away all that impeded it. But the poem was like a warning foghorn near the harbor; while the threat to the ruling elite seemed strident, Petőfi and a few around him sensed that the role of the Buda-Pest crowd had been trumped and that Kossuth had usurped the energy of the revolution.[70]

The crowd had unleashed the revolution and then it had rallied to its defense. With tension lifting, the period of victory celebrations continued. In the preceding weeks the public spaces remained alive. By mid-April, after a month of illuminations and processions celebrating the origin of revolution rather than its direction, radicals like Petőfi sighed: "How many holidays in one month! Take care that dark days do not follow the bright nights."[71] He worried, "We are a terribly ceremonial people! We must always have holidays, and if we ever lack something to celebrate, we go to the moon with a torchlight procession and light up the world. The reason we are impoverished, perhaps, is that we always want to shine. . . . But I believe and want to believe . . . that we will cast off this showy character, along with the monarchy, as a flower falls to make place for a fruit."[72]

"The Sea of Peoples"

Although Petőfi extolled "the sea of peoples," he turned a blind eye to the specter of peoples facing Hungary from within. The "peoples" (*népek*— plural) invoked in the first stanza referred to those nations already in revolt, whose risings magnified the potency of the activity in Hungary. In stanza two the "people" in revelry is singular (*nép*), i.e. the Magyar people. In the ethnic heartland around Budapest, Magyars possessed the confidence to proclaim an inclusive revolutionary mission that projected a cultural unity coinciding with the wider territory of the Kingdom of St. Stephen. However, Petőfi, Kossuth, and many other prominent Magyar activists came from the periphery regions. Petőfi was of Slovak parentage; his father, a baker's apprentice had a Slavic name and a hint of Slovak in his speech, while his mother labored under a thick accent. Kossuth was of the Hungarian minority gentry in Slovakia. Their Magyar pride was self-conscious and all the more ardent for being chosen or endangered. Petőfi's blindness was typical of Magyar nationalists raised within the multiethnic regions of the kingdom.

In the borderlands a high proportion of Hungarians lived in separate enclaves in close proximity to other groups. None of the non-Magyar minorities were in a position to threaten seriously the Magyars by themselves. The Magyars comprised less than 40 percent of the population of fourteen and a half million. But, none of the other ethnic groups came close to that number. The Romanians in Hungary and Transylvania together comprised 17 percent, while the Slovaks numbered 13 percent, the Germans and Jews about 10 percent and 2 percent respectively, the Croats 9 percent, and the Serbs were around 7 percent, and a range of others, including Roma, Armenians, and other Slavic peoples living in the kingdom.[73] The Hungarians may have occasionally fantasized about the grand future of their revived Magyar culture displacing German in the area, but the Magyars had no similar hold in the region, at best they had but a head start on the other regional vernaculars. With the exception of the Jews, who craved inclusion and acceptance, the other nationalities had not embraced Hungarian. The incompatibility of the French model is evident. French was a language and culture that so dominated beyond its borders that the Germans had recoiled with a counter nationalistic cultural revival of their own. The Hungarians occasionally evoked a specter of Pan-Slavism, but none of the nationalities came to this juncture in order to embrace German, Russian, or a pan-Slav interlingua.

The mixture of preeminence and vulnerability was reflected in Hungarian political vocabulary. The more evocative expressions of the patriot (*hazafi*), e.g. *nemzet* (nationality) (homeland, as in the French *patri*), or alternatively the more literary *hon* (homeland), were much more frequent in the speeches and popular journalism of 1848 than the cooler, neutral term *ország* (state, country). *Ország* was a central, familiar, legal and geographical expression, as in *Magyarország* (Hungary, or the state of the Magyars), *országgyűlés* (parliament—national assembly), or *országszerte* (countrywide), but *nemzet*, *haza*, and *hon* were essential vocabulary in the cultural nationalist revival and the revolution it spawned. *Ország* was assumed to coincide with the notion of *nemzet*. For example, Ferenc Deák, the master of legalistic language and conciliatory state politics, wrote in one worried letter: "The state of the *ország* (country) is unsettling; . . . while in Pest every hour there is some sort of hot-tempered, not-carefully-thought-out outbreak that endangers the *haza* (homeland) with insurrection. . . . *Hazánk* (Our homeland) was perhaps never in greater danger."[74] Although Deák was appalled by revolutionary excess, he also used the terms for state and nation interchangeably. This practice reflected inner contradictions in the revolution. The initial goal of the *nemzet,* to which politicians such as Deák subscribed, was only a semi-realization of *ország* status, e.g. remaining within the Habsburg Monarchy. Still, the fulfilled Magyar *nemzet* within a Habsburg state would incorporate several ethnic minorities not granted nation status. Intertwining the terminology of state and nation led to fatal assumptions and political misjudgments.

When the revolutionaries were confronted by the ethnic crowd that claimed a different sense of solidarity—one based on common language, common origin, and common ancestry—there was a conundrum that pointed to a breakdown of the concepts of both revolution and nation. That the other nationalities would rise up against the Hungarian revolution was not at all clear at the outset. In the initial days or weeks minority politicians championed the Pest crowd, much as the Magyar crowd had applauded the fall of Metternich in Vienna. The demonstration effect moved the minority populations to rally crowds of their own. Đorde Stratimirović, one of the leaders of the Serbian national movement, told a Újvidék (Novi Sad) rally on March 21 that as a result of the Hungarian revolution "liberty . . . has erected its altars in our country as well." On March 22 at a rally in Pancsova in the Banat, the so-called Military Frontier, crowds singing the Hungarian national anthem drove the loyalist municipal leaders out of town. On March 24 in Zimony a crowd similarly turned out the city authorities.

But once the initial concessions were wrested from the Viennese authorities and the revolution could declare itself victorious, the issues of Hungary as a pluralistic state containing not only various minorities but three ethnic homelands needed to be faced, but was not. In addition to the three ethnic homelands of Croatia, Slovakia, and Hungary, the territory included two minorities, the Serbs and Romanians, whose core homelands lay directly across the Hungarian borders. Also the Transylvanian Saxons had in the course of their nine-hundred-year history come to view their ethnic enclave as a historic homeland as did the Székely who were more Magyar than the Magyar. Finally the "diaspora minorities"—Jews, Roma, and "Swabians" or Germans—were a wild card, vulnerable and scattered.

Antisemitic violence accompanied the Viennese revolution from the outset. Such attacks against Jews, as well as machine-breaking, caused loss of property, death, and the declaration of martial law from March 16 to 22.[75] This rioting rapidly spread to nearby Pozsony and spilled over to the German Catholic towns of western Hungary, and ultimately to Pest. The first Hungarian pogrom of the revolution was on March 20 in Pozsony, coinciding with the Diet's consideration of a law that would have extended local suffrage rights to financially secure Jews. The pogrom caused considerable property damage, but no loss of life.[76] Stephen Széchenyi con-

Youth had lionized the young Serbs of Pest who had joined the National Guard on March 18, they became angry when they learned of the March 16 petition. They attacked the local Serbs for "wanting to present themselves as a nation" because in Hungary "there existed only one nation, the Magyar."[86] When a similar petition from a March 27 assembly in Újvidék demanding to be recognized as an independent nation within Hungary was brought to Kossuth, he declared: "I shall never ever recognize any other nation and nationality under the Holy Hungarian Crown than the Hungarian. I know there are peoples and races who speak other languages, but there is only one nation here." Stratimirović responded that if their demands were not met in Pozsony, the Serbs would "turn elsewhere." This prompted Kossuth's reply: "In that case the sword shall decide."[87]

Growing ethnic tension in southern Hungary and in various Hungarian cities exploded during Easter Week, 1848. In the market square of Nagy-kikinda in the Banat, Serb peasants engaged in wild ethnic violence with some deaths.[88] The rhetoric of ethnic cleansing aimed at the Magyars was now first heard. On April 19 a pogrom erupted in the Pest inner-city. Crowds ran riot through the streets ransacking businesses. Several individuals were wounded in the process of expelling Jews from the city. Albert Pálffy, editor of the newspaper *Márczius Tizenötödike* (March Fifteenth), wrote that such riots "defile this decent and outstanding city," and were it possible, he would erase that day from the city's history.[89] On April 24 in Pozsony the most violent of the pogroms occurred; ten Jews were killed and about forty wounded. The government took the expedient alternative of ordering the Jews out of Pozsony. But once authorities had capitulated to the crowd, it became clear that non-Jewish property was also being looted, and strong action was directed at the rioters as well. Regular army troops were able to control the crowds, but as soon as the troops were withdrawn the pillaging and violence resumed. However, persistent police pressure on the rioters and the Jews did bring quiet. The government sought prosecution of those involved in the "violation of security of the person and property of peaceful citizens," and acted to curb freedom of assembly.[90] Not even radicals objected when mass gatherings could now only take place if authorities were notified in advance of their purpose.[91] Radicals spoke out against the pogroms. When Jewish enlistees in the national guard were booted out by their Magyar brethren, Vasvári, Petőfi, and Táncsics organized Jewish national guard units. However, on April 25 Batthyány, at Kossuth's urging, "excused" Jews from service in the militia. They acted to protect the fledgling government from turmoil and to protect Jewish recruits from bodily harm, but in so doing they temporarily removed a critical avenue for earning civil rights.[92] Episodes of antisemitic violence continued in April and May in Kassa (Kaschau, Košice), Eperjes (Prešov), Újhely (Neustadt), Szeged, and other towns.[93] Anti-Jewish disturbances and peasant unrest in the northern counties became an excuse to recall the Hungarian army. The government lacked the power to maintain peace.[94] These April riots were more violent than the ones a month before, had hit the heart of the country, were not an expansion of plundering from Vienna, and could no longer be dismissed as aberrations.

The Hungarian Interior Ministry responded to the growing ethnic challenge by the Serbs by issuing a decree of martial law that, unlike previous ones, essentially made any illegal act punishable by execution—in theory, this could include any criticism of the existing order. On April 9 the call for a first national assembly of the Serbs in Hungary had gone out, and at an April 14 meeting the demand for a separate Serb Vajdaság (Voivodate) governed independently from Hungary was raised. But distribution of the intimidating martial law statute throughout Serb areas prompted the Serbs to schedule the general assembly not in Újvidék but in Szerémségi Karlóca, which was not only the seat of the Orthodox Church but also propitiously located in the Military Frontier, thus outside Hungarian jurisdiction. On April 20 two thousand Serbs from Újvidék marched to Szerémségi Karlóca where the Metropolitan Josif Rajačić formally announced that the Serb national assembly would be held there on May 13.

While the Serbs met in Szerémségi Karlóca from May 13 to 15 and the Romanians in Balázsfalva from May 15 to 17, Vienna experienced a second wave of revolution, prompting the flight of the Habsburg family to refuge in Innsbruck. In the political chaos of the third week of May the historic peasant assemblies assumed special importance. Both the Serbs of southern Hungary and the Transylvanian Romanians utilized the one institution under their control, the church, to mobilize their peasants. These rallies were held in their spiritual centers and with a spiritual patina absent in the crowds of Pest and Zagreb. The Serbs also benefited from the old millet system of the Ottomans that made religion rather than ethnicity the identifying factor. The Serbs had inherited the control of Orthodoxy's institutions in Hungary and now attempted to use the church not only to advance their national aspirations but also to exercise dominance over the Orthodox Romanians in southern Hungary who outnumbered them two to one.

The shift of attention to growing fears of a Croatian military invasion helped deflate antisemitism.[95] Not the urban minorities but the borderland minorities were the concern. The weakest nationality and most easily squashed was that of the Slovaks. The Slovaks lacked the political structure of the Croats and the ecclesiastical organization of the Serbs. Their gentry had been significantly Magyarized, their burghers often Germanized, and both their Lutheran and Catholic hierarchies were dominated by Magyars. Theirs was the weakest of the national revivals and consequently the strongest on pathos. The Magyar-Slovak conflict brought out the clash between the French equation of the indivisible nation with the "people" and the German fashion of identifying the nation with the language. Slovak intellectuals followed Herder in viewing the state as an artificial phenomenon deserving at best formal loyalty while the nation as a product of nature had an inborn right to develop its own language and culture; to deprive the nation of this right was a crime against humanity. The Magyars followed the French model, having formally replaced Latin with Magyar in the 1844 Diet for its proceedings and that of the country's administration. Magyar was now known widely as "the national language" (*a nemzeti nyelv*). Since Slovak political acumen was weak, Slovak intellectuals had most fervently fostered a cultural Pan-Slavism and then the Czechoslovak idea before 1848. The Slovak leader Jozef Hurban told a crowd on April 28, "You have for several centuries been concerned only with forests, fields, manure and livestock" yet "the main thing is, nonetheless, nationality, in other words the right to be worth as much as any other nation in the country."[96] While the Slovak national movement was able to rally small groups of several thousand by late April, the largely Protestant leadership sensed its lack of support in the 80 percent Catholic Slovak population. On May 10 forty Slovak national leaders met to formulate a petition in Liptószentmiklós, but then declined to stage a rally presenting their petition the next day in the market square in front of the county hall, because they feared this event might only demonstrate the indifference of the locals. Slovak demands were most modest, but as the weakest they were also the ones the Magyars were least inclined to appease. Also, concessions to Slovak nationalism would undercut the Magyarized Slovak gentry, the very group where Magyarization had been most successful. Expulsion of the Slovak leaders eliminated the threat, and a subsequent invasion by a small Slovak legion was easily turned back.

While the threat in the north was manageable, by early May large parts of southern Hungary and Transylvania were panicked by the imminent peasant rallies of the Serbs and Romanians. In Transylvania, Baron Miklós Wesselényi wrote on May 9, Hungarian nobles, burghers, students, and peasants were arming themselves as best they could; lances were the easiest to obtain, then pitchforks or shovels. The Romanians were said to be similarly equipped though with fewer firearms.[97] In Pest it was the threat of a Croatian invasion led by Jellačić that aroused the nationalist crowd. On May 10 two thousand Pest demonstrators marched to the home of General Lederer, the commander of the Buda garrison, to protest his policy of withholding arms from the Batthyány government. A military detachment fired upon the demonstrators, wounding many and killing a Jewish medical student—thus producing the first Jewish martyr of the Magyar revolutionary cause. Two days later Petőfi held another large protest rally at Museum Square, where he excoriated the Batthyány regime for its passivity, shocking the country if not his listeners by declaring that he "would not trust his dog to this government, even less the fate of the motherland!"[98] While ethnic violence underscored the barbaric in the crowd, the radical heroes of the crowd appeared demagogic or paralyzed in this new round of Pest demonstrations. Petőfi's extremism seemed subversive and petulant, and he would never again regain the role of tribune of the revolution. The moderates were reluctant to turn on the radicals by curbing the crowd and limiting further its freedom of action. Batthyány's call for a declaration of martial law and a ban on "provocative speech and press" was tabled when Széchenyi responded: "Let us avoid dictatorship."[99] Martial law could have unintended consequences, he argued. During the crisis Kossuth had been nowhere to be seen, claiming illness when the crowd implored him to form a new government, only to reappear healthy when the storm had passed.[100] The episode had not been Kossuth's finest hour. When the eighty-year-old General Lederer beat a hasty retreat to Vienna, it was the Battyhány government, not Petőfi and the radicals, that could claim victory.

The Serb national assembly proclaimed archbishop Rajačić patriarch, demanded the independence of the Serbian districts from Hungarian administration, and claimed union with the kingdoms of Croatia, Slavonia, and Dalmatia—without actually repudiating the Hungarian crown. The few voices calling for conciliating gestures toward the Magyars were shouted down by a crowd of some six to eight thousand recruited primarily from the villages of the Military Frontier—i.e., outside Hungary proper. The drafted resolution proclaiming the Serbs a "politically free and independent nation" in a new Vajdaság made as little mention of the fact that the Serbs were as much a minority in their projected Voivodate as the Magyars were in the Kingdom of St. Stephen. An alarmed Batthyány called the Székely to arms on May 19 for use against the Serbs, and on June 10,

Whitsuntide, Szerémségi Karlóca was bombarded and taken from the "Illyrian rebels." The burning of the Serb Jerusalem aroused the Serbs. Mobilization brought 20,000 to three encampments. Largely recruited from the border guards regiments, they were soon joined by between 10,000 and 12,000 volunteers from the principality of Serbia. Although they outnumbered Hungarian troops in the region some five to one, they were uniting the Magyars, Germans, and Romanians of southern Hungary against them. Aware of this three-fold opposition Serb forces engaged in small-scale raids on Magyar and German towns rather than attacking in force in the coming months.

In Transylvania the issue of union with Hungary became the lightning rod of ethnic conflict. Instead, the Transylvanian Romanians had not initially opposed the union. Kolozsvár's Magyar burghers, students, and nobles had demonstrated on behalf of union in the third week of March, but by mid-May they had come to see union as a plot to permanently suppress the Romanian majority. "Poisoned is every morsel taken from the table of Hungarian liberty," Simion Bărnuțiu told the assembled leadership of the Romanian National Committee on the eve of the Balázsfalva rally. While holding up Switzerland as the land to emulate, he accused Hungary of seeking expansion, adding "without the union, the ties between the Magyars of Transylvania and the Magyars of Hungary will break and the Magyars of Transylvania will slowly undergo a process of natural extinction." Magyar nationalists, for their part, had been calling for the union since the 1790s; it had been among Petőfi's twelve points; and the slogan of the Kolozsvár demonstrations of May, "Union or Death," was symptomatic of the passionate polarization of these weeks. With Switzerland torn by its own civil war, the conciliatory notion of a multinational mountain state seemed out of step in 1848.

The May 15 national assembly at Balázsfalva, the religious and educational center of Transylvanian Romanian life, had sought to have one or two representatives from each village, but when up to 40,000 (five times the Serb rally) assembled on the "Field of Liberty," it was clear that a watershed had been reached. Bărnuțiu told the crowd "liberty could not exist without nationality"; that if the Romanians "lost their nationality," "they would lose everything." On the other hand if they achieved national equality, "the rest would follow as a matter of course."[101] Various peasant groups declared, "We want to be a nation: we want Romanian lords and our Romanian language." The meeting culminated with a petition that was taken to the Transylvanian Diet in Kolozsvár, which ignored them, voting for union of the "two brother homelands," Hungary and Transylvania, on May 30. A subsequent Romanian delegation to Innsbruck also returned home empty-handed. With the Austrian empire weak and seemingly on the verge of collapse, the Habsburgs were out to mollify the Magyars. When on June 2 Székely troops fired on Romanian peasants who received them with pitchforks and scythes in the village of Mihályfalva (Mihalț), killing at least a dozen, there was talk of a rising, which led to the banning of the Romanian National Committee. The Transylvanian Romanians were also on their own, since the Romanians in southern Hungary were more concerned with the Serbs, and the Romanian revolutionaries were anxious to win liberal Magyar support for the Wallachia and Moldavia revolution that broke out in June.

Meanwhile Hungarians held their breath as their initial inspiration, the crowds of Paris, faced the artillery pieces of General Cavaignac from behind flimsy barricades. The 1,500 killed in the June Days were a sobering lesson, as was the Prague fighting, which had the same result with fewer casualties. Of the four hundred barricades constructed in Prague, Field Marshal Prince Alfred Windisch-Graetz deemed only fifteen as representing a military obstacle; the rest had served as an outlet for the energies of a poorly armed popular crowd.[102] The revolutionary crowd might inaugurate revolution, but the lesson of June 1848 seemed to be that they could not sustain revolution on their own. Yet despite the triumph of the counterrevolution in Prague, the Magyars had the satisfaction of seeing the disarray and collapse of the Slav Congress, which dissolved when Windisch-Graetz struck. The Magyars succeeded in having the king dismiss Jellačić as ban. It seemed in June that the minorities had rallied, only to be stymied by Habsburg dependence on Hungary.

The Commandeered Crowd

Yet by mid-summer, Field Marshal Joseph Radetzky's victories in Italy were changing the balance of power, and it was becoming evident that revolutionary Hungary might well be standing alone as the final battleground of the revolution of 1848. If historical parallels came to the minds of those on the Pest streets that summer, it was no longer Bastille Day or the July Revolution. Robespierre's rallying the revolution to meet the foreign invader was more apt, although usually avoided. Széchenyi transformed his Pest quarters into a miniature armory in preparation for a Jacobin blood bath as he became unbalanced and then went mad in these months. On the streets and public squares crowds assembled to see off the troops. These were emotional scenes. For instance on July 2, a young volunteer recalled that when he left it felt like the whole city's population escorted the troops to the railroad station. "Citizens were overflowing the square; and all the bands of Budapest played without being asked." When the train pulled out, cries of "God be with you!" rang out, and he and his fellow Honvéds departed "with the expectations of the most glorious return, filled with visions from our fairy-tale scenarios on our journey to the sacred conflict."[103]

What was euphoric in the capital was something else in the borderlands. The besieged mentality, the fear of being overtaken by enemies from without and infiltrated by hostile ethnic minorities from within produced its own version of crowd theater: the public hanging of traitors. The first hanging in Temesvár (Timişoara) in southern Hungary drew a huge crowd, estimated at "50,000 people." "Never before in my life had I seen so many people collected in one group; one could see people of every kind of costume and language, Bulgarians from Vingár and Besenyő, Serbians from the nearby countryside, Romanians, Germans, etc." The soldiers placed themselves between the convicted traitors and the crowd, aligning themselves in a large circle to maximize the crowd's view of the hanging tree. The charges against the accused were read in Magyar, repeated in German, and then the first victim, a tall, muscular border guard of about forty, made his way to the gallows, so shaken he could barely walk. And "as if the devil had grabbed him by the feet, he died immediately." While the victim was still dangling above, the other accused, a businessman, started cursing the Magyars and the government, and shouted defiantly that he was not going to die, because thousands of supporters were on their way from nearby Versec and Pancsova to rescue him. They strung him up quickly, but even while he was being pulled up the gallows, he kept yelling: "There come my saviors!" From the crowd someone shouted, "The Serbs are coming!" The frightening, all-too-plausible words rippled through the crowd, repeated in German, and Romanian, until an incredible tumult ensued. Rumors had been circulating that the Serbs were organizing, and a Serbian rising would occur. The people panicked, running in all directions. About forty soldiers had been circling on horseback a fair distance from the scene of the execution. Seeing the riotous confusion, they assumed that the crowd had disputed the death sentence. The crowd was rushed by men on horseback brandishing their swords. The people panicked, convinced that these were the Serbian enemies. When it was all over, bracelets, necklaces, and earrings were strewn about where they had fallen as women ran for their lives. "Hundreds were lying on the ground," some had been trampled to death; in the river, women and children took refuge "half-dead." "The scene was like Judgment Day."[104]

Most likely there had been plenty of "enemies" in that crowd; those who sympathized with the victims must have been numerous. Belgrade, Serbia, was less than one hundred miles to the south, and within a week of this demonstration the emperor reinstated Jellačić as ban (governor) of Croatia and Slavonia. Jellačić had visions of saving the monarchy as commander of the Habsburg Imperial forces in Croatia by mobilizing the south Slav peoples against the Hungarians. Antagonism to both the existing order and the aspirations of the Magyars was palpable all around them. The reality of internal and external hostility made fear a potent force. The army feared the crowd; the crowd feared itself. Even without weapons passions could foment unrest. Such confused outbursts happened elsewhere, also as the execution of collaborationists became common as revolution turned to war. The army would perform these executions as displays of power meant to establish authority, instill fear, obtain obedience, and maintain order. However conservative their intent or stylized and frequent the executions would become, crowds would persist in spilling from their homes to witness them as theater. On one occasion in Veszprém, when a confused old woman and an official from a neighboring town were put to death as traitors, the crowd enjoyed the entertainment and murmured approval.[105] In Gyöngyös twelve hanging trees with two nooses each would be erected at the edge of town as a warning to all. About six weeks later at least one resident would complain about the oppressive environment. He looked forward to the true day of freedom when one could voice one's opinions without fear of reprisal, he wrote on October 8, the day the Vienna revolution fell.[106]

In these six weeks the crisis of foreign war and civil war fell onto the nation. In a last ditch effort to avert this ultimate confrontation, a Hungarian parliamentary deputation had an audience with the king on September 9 in Vienna. Anticipating a government crisis, the March Youth brought out the crowd. On September 10, the evening the delegation returned, a crowd—the thickest, most tumultuous since the March days—was waiting for them at the Danube bank and all along the parade path to the museum steps.[107] Traffic was stopped, particularly around a coffeehouse where young people had gathered en route. At the club of the Society for Equality incendiary speeches sought to trip the mood of imminent doom into one of radical anticipation. The Society for Equality itself was of recent vintage, a product of the sense of crisis and the pull toward a more radical revolution. It had one thousand members, more than thirty deputies, and kept its pulse on most Buda-Pest newspapers. Kossuth tried to keep a watchful eye over the radical agitators, but radicals were dreaming of mobilizing the Pest crowds for one last climactic demonstration that could drive the revolution finally to the left. Failure in Vienna might provoke that radical turn and unseat the entrenched nobility. The delegation did return with dismal news: the king had withdrawn his mandate for the Batthyány government. On the eleventh the heated speeches in parliament were in conversation with the tumult outside. In the public squares conscripts were switching from imperial to Honvéd units.

On September 12, Batthyány informed the parliament that Jellačić had invaded Hungary. He called for a people's rising in the southern region along Jellačić's path. But forced conscription took a violent turn. When Romanian villagers forcibly kept recruiters out of their northern Transylvanian village, a two-hundred-man force attacked, killing dozens. The death of these Romanian peasants at Aranyoslóna became a rallying symbol for popular resistance against the Magyar national political program. Adding to the resonance of this image was the myth of the good emperor endangered now by the Hungarian rebels. By the time the government put a stop to the forced conscription in Transylvania, it was too late, the ethnic tinderbox of Transylvania had cracked apart. While Romanian peasants were forcefully resisting conscription in Hungary, Romanian peasants in southern Hungary were volunteering for the frontier regiments that would be under Jellačić's command in the assault on the Hungarian revolutionary government. Two different Romanian agendas—that of the Romanian majority asserting its rights in Transylvania and that of the Romanian plurality in the Vajdaság (Voivodina) fending off both Magyar political and Serbian ecclesiastic domination—fed upon each other. Romanian peasants had not been mollified by an emancipation that was too reluctantly granted and was more restricted and more slowly instituted in Transylvania than in the rest of Hungary. The need to conciliate the minorities had been stonewalled in the legislature in Pest. A month earlier a majority of the parliament had rejected the education bill proposed by Cultural Minister Eötvös that would have permitted the mother tongue of the local inhabitants to be the language of elementary schools.

From September 16 to 28 Balázsfalva looked like an encampment as tens of thousands of Romanian peasants made their way to a mass assembly. There they clamored for representation—proportional representation—

in a Transylvanian government and Diet, and they rejected the political union with Hungary. Still offers of negotiation were made, only to be tabled by the Hungarian parliament, feeding the rage at Balázsfalva. The raw anger in Transylvania was now exposed, but unaddressed. The assembly at Balázsfalva moved toward action: alarm trees were organized and legions began drilling with scythes and spears. Hungarians met the turn in events with great trepidation. When the prime minister relayed bad news to his advisory council that Gen. Count Ádám Teleki refused to march against Jellačić, there was deep quiet and a sense of great danger in the room. But outside the hall, the beseeching of the crowd disturbed the advisory council. The crowd yelled for the general's head.[108] Throughout the crisis the radicals kept the popular agitation in Pest at a fever pitch.

An attempted coup-d'état by Palatine Archduke Stephen was averted, leaving many wrestling with the thorny question of loyalty. When Gen. Ferenc Lamberg, Archduke Stephen's choice, was appointed royal commissioner and commander-in-chief of all armed forces in Hungary, the parliament, the capital, and the press flew into a rage. Lamberg, himself a Hungarian, had participated in the upper house of the Reform Diet of 1847–8 as a conservative reformer and had the backing of the Conservative Hungarian magnates. But Kossuth spoke in angry condemnation of Lamberg's appointment, and the Hungarian parliament declared his appointment null and void.

When General Lamberg arrived in Buda-Pest in late September to assume command, the invading Croatian army was just miles outside the capital. According to the wild rumors swirling about, Lamberg was also arriving with 15,000 to 20,000 soldiers and cannons prepared to level Pest from Buda.[109] The press attacked Lamberg, and an excitable crowd hunting him discovered Lamberg on September 28 crossing the bridge connecting Buda and Pest. He was brutally murdered. This crowd was primarily composed of the urban lower class, with a sprinkling of peasant volunteers on their way to the front. The collective killing was to mark a point of no return and a heightened danger for the revolution. For moderates like Eötvös the killing indicated that the period of compromise and reform had come to an end. "The Hungarian situation has reached the point where discussion is impossible, and he who does not want to bow to the prophet's orders . . . has only two options, the hanging tree and exile." Eötvös fled the country. He was not, he explained to a friend, designed to be a revolutionary and felt himself to be "superfluous" in the new conditions.[110] Kossuth was quick to have the assembly condemn the murder.

József Irinyi, one of the core agitators of the March Youth whom Széchenyi had feared from the outset, opposed Kossuth's motion, regretting only that Lamberg was not tried and sentenced before being executed by the crowd. The ultraradicals determined to make the murder of Lamberg a watershed in the revolution. Petőfi wrote a poem lauding the murder as a sign that the "people" were taking the reins and warning Europe's sovereigns that the same fate awaited them. But what would be remembered as the epitome of violent crowd behavior proved to be the finale of the urban revolutionary crowd in the Hungarian revolution. Lamberg's killing became the icon of crowd violence, embellished over time. Half a century later a witness who had been caught and swept along by the "human wave" still railed against the "screaming" crowd that had pounced on its victim. The horror of that crowd, a "bloodthirsty" mob, was the relish with which "it took revenge on its prey."[111]

Kossuth had taken charge of the revolution when Jellačić invaded Hungary. The court's support of a Jellačić invasion was a dangerous signal that the monarchy had regained its stride and was shoring up its defenses by mobilizing the resentment of the other peoples against Hungary—its only serious remaining adversary. The militarization of the Hungarian crowd proceeded. Kossuth quickly crowded out all rivals on the streets of Pest, focusing the eyes of the nation on the threatened city of Veszprém, "where the whole Hungarian people shall assemble, as mankind will be assembled on the Judgment Day." The orator with "the flaming tongue" continued: "To arms! Every man to arms; and let the women dig a deep grave between Veszprém and Fehérvár, in which to bury either the name, fame, and nationality of Hungary, or our enemy. And either on this grave will rise a banner, on which shall be inscribed, in record of our shame, 'Thus God chastiseth cowardice'; or we shall plant thereon the tree of freedom everlastingly green, and from its foliage shall be heard the voice of the Most High, saying, as from the fiery bush to Moses, 'The spot on which thou standest is holy ground.' "[112] On the day following the murder of Lamberg, a crowd from Buda-Pest assumed its new passive role of spectator when thousands went out to observe the Hungarian forces turn back Jellačić's army near Pákozd on Lake Velence, about thirty miles from Buda-Pest. The new national army, smaller than its rival, had saved the capital and the revolution. The victory was one day too late to lead to reconciliation with the court. It was the military that now held the balance. Residents of the capital were introduced to the dreary reality of conducting a war. "Enthusiasm is not an army," wrote a friend to Kossuth's sister. "You can't put enthusiasm out on the battlefield in fighting formation. One needs the real thing, trained, skilled troops, tactics, financial resources, and military discipline."[113]

For months the peasantry, hitherto lethargic and outside the political world, had begun hearing of Kossuth the virtuoso orator and of the doings of the self-proclaimed capital, Budapest. Even though the actual military benefit was slight, the political and psychological effect of Kossuth's tour had been "inestimable."[114] Kossuth's success in recruiting the peasantry ensured their place in the subsequent patriotic martyrology alongside their hero and transformed Kossuth into a mythological figure. Kossuth's biographers have employed religious metaphors, for example, "Kossuth became a saint, the god to the peasants."[115] Certainly, the orator spoke to the peasantry in a language they had never heard before, but which they immediately grasped. Kossuth had mastered romantic oratory: lucid logic; clear purpose; the raised voice full of high pathos; allusions to high aspirations and patriotic ideals, all encircled with statements glorifying God. His eloquence made him appear both a man of the people and an extraordinary talent. It was, moreover, the first time that a direct appeal was made to the peasantry on their own ground. Kossuth's skill in repeatedly presenting an oratorical performance that seemed completely alive and unrehearsed, coupled with the undeniably grave crisis of the country, left a resonance in the countryside that no politician in succeeding generations has matched.

With Hungary's back to the wall, Kossuth was mobilizing the peasants in a way that the Pest radicals had been unable to do. Jókai, who accompanied Kossuth on this tour, had written despairingly in May, that it had been but a "self-deception to think that they had a people (*nép*)." They "will follow us to the grave with curses and snide remarks." The peasants credit their freedom to anyone "but not to his *haza*." The peasant would rather *do robot* or go hungry than "to rise up to protect the *hon* against the Cossack." The great mass of agricultural workers were and remain unfamiliar with the word *haza*, unmoved by the national colors, and hate and distrust the man in a frock coat, and "to him the law isn't law, until it has the emperor's stamp on it with the double-headed eagle."[116]

Kossuth had begun his recruiting tour by taking the train to Cegléd to rally the people to the cause. "In half an hour I'll have a flag in my hand and will begin," he wrote his wife. "I have said where I am starting, where I will go, I don't know, the people's mood and response will give me direction."[117] The whole town gathered in the market square, and three hundred enlisted that day. The scene would be later immortalized in countless

Kossuth statues showing him addressing the people of the Great Plain while the peasants, young and old, male and female, sat at his feet with arms upraised in gratitude. In Nagykőrös Kossuth was greeted with a similarly tumultuous crowd, with similar results. In Kecskemét there happened to be a fair, allowing him to speak to a crowd of over 10,000. He expected 5,000 recruits, but eventually as many as 8,000 signed up for military service in Kecskemét.[118] The popular energy of the preceding six months seemed to have flowed into the countryside. Kossuth wrote his wife, "I never saw such a demonstration. They were kissing my clothes and passing out the proclamation everywhere."[119]

The enthusiastic response of village and town crowds on the Great Plain to his stump speech made his own position as leader virtually unassailable.[120] While Kossuth had worked over the crowd, he seemed also to have succumbed to the power of the crowd as intoxicator. Kossuth believed that the enthusiasm of the faithful and the excitement of the crowd gathered before him were an accurate reflection of the attitudes of the public. He projected from the will of the crowd a political force greater than it was. Even where the crowd initially seemed cool, Kossuth soon had women in tears and men volunteering. "The so-called indifferent people fired up like a lightning bolt," Kossuth wrote home.[121] After three or four stops, he had collected more than 11,000 enlistees. Kossuth had the power of his charisma continually reconfirmed. He was so enamored of his elementary ability to move the people, that he ignored his advisers' urging that he return to address the military crisis in the Danube region. Instead, he set out to move the people in the sizable city of Szeged.[122] To observe Kossuth in operation in the provinces it appeared that the revolution had only now taken root, although in reality the revolution was now entering a rear guard action.

Hungarian regimental commanders were scornful of these untrained, poorly armed peasants in their units, insisting instead, that they be cordoned off in Mobile National Guard units or other new makeshift entities. But Kossuth continued his recruiting drive; a crowd of national guardsmen followed him to Komárom, and hundreds more joined him as he left. Soon the news of his coming preceded him. When Kossuth arrived in Esztergom on October 18, he was greeted with torchbearers and music at the boat landing, and a few hundred enlistees carried him on their shoulders into the city. "And if I went all the way through the Hungarian homeland a migration of people would follow me and the news of which in itself would be enough to stop the enemy," he wrote.[123] According to tradition, it began to rain, and an anonymous poet sang out a song beginning "Esik eső kari-kára" [The raindrops in ringlets]. The crowd sang the tune all the way into town, and later it became a popular song throughout the country.[124]

In March fear of a peasant Jacquerie had stampeded the Hungarian gentry to uncharacteristic concessions, in the autumn fears of ethnic massacres galvanized the Hungarian peasantry, making them responsive to the message of war, sacrifice, and patriotism. When General Jellačić marched into Hungary, he commanded an uneasy mix of professional soldiers, border guards seeking booty, and peasants with pitchforks defending their property. The Hungarian army commanders who faced Jellačić were not willing to fight their Habsburg army comrade. At first the Hungarian force retreated to avoid battle, then the commanders opted for maneuvers to stall and frustrate the intruder. The military commander changed three times before they found Field Marshal Lieutenant János Móga, who was willing to use arms against Jellačić. Móga's army was small and weak, still Jellačić's campaign failed. When the undisciplined Border Guards of Jellačić's forces moved through villages and towns they "loot and steal without shame," recorded one of their frustrated officers.[125] In response peasants heeded the call for a "people's rising." The Hungarian government made sure word spread rapidly about atrocities, looting, thieving. Border guards were traditionally unpaid and extracted their livelihood from their interception of smugglers and their wares. The thought of them moving on Hungarian villages, galvanized the Hungarian peasantry on the invasion route to a desperate resistance.[126] While officers agonized over questions of allegiance to their emperor or their nation, the peasants were protecting their turf with guerrilla warfare that targeted any Croatian soldier who strayed from the march route. Jellačić soon found himself cut off from reinforcements and foiled to no small degree by amassed peasants. By October Jellačić was in retreat, crossing the Austrian-Hungarian border on October 8—just two days after the court fled to Olmouc (Olmütz), Moravia, to escape the revived Viennese revolution.

The spread of ethnic violence and guerrilla tactics was antithetical to the regimental culture that had dominated European life since the fall of Napoleon. Regiments, typically one thousand strong, had become a characteristic nineteenth-century institution with garrison towns dotting the landscape. Their success in pacifying a Europe rent by a quarter century of warfare led to both a willingness to conduct policelike operations to maintain order and a conception of a "true war" as one fought out by professionals in elaborate campaigns.[127] The warfare in 1848–9 defied their expectations, and worse, brought civil war within the officer corps itself. The failure of the Habsburg bureaucracy to prevent the disaster encouraged the regiments to see themselves as the nemesis of the urban and rural crowd, as the civilizer of society's disruptive elements. Reforming colonels had long used regiments as laboratories of reform; regimental schools educated young officers and taught soldiers how to read and write; and all the while regiments provided a splendid spectacle before town crowds. No other common institution in the monarchy was so rent by the Hungarian revolution that pitted brother officers and regiments against each other. The uneasy relationship between the military and town authorities in Hungarian regimental towns since April abruptly ended in October. The lynching of the War Minister, Gen. Theodor Baillet von Latour, from a lamppost in the last days of the Viennese revolution became with the assassination of General Lamberg the touchstone of loyalist indignation. With the call for loyalists to turn on the revolution, the war crowd overwhelmed the revolutionary crowd. In German-speaking Temesvár the German-speaking garrison that had flown the Hungarian tricolor since April now demanded the disarming of the town's National Guard. When the pro-Magyar city council balked, the commandant had the drums sounded and within a few minutes the main squares were filled with four to five thousand soldiers. Cannons were brought into place to fire on the city hall and the county hall if need be. The five-hundred-man National Guard then surrendered, and the city hall was occupied. The October triumphs of the counter-revolution in Berlin and Vienna confirmed the summer's premonitions that the Hungarian revolution was on its own.

As the peasant masses were drawn into the conflict, as either volunteers or conscripts, some villages coalesced in a defensive posture against the nationalities of neighboring villages, while some villages were torn apart with suspicion of their neighbors and fear of the regiments barracked in their vicinity.[128] In Transylvania, panicked Hungarians placed their hopes in the fearsome Székely. In mid-October sixty thousand, virtually the whole Székely male population, gathered at Agyagfalva (Lutiţa) where they swore an oath to uphold the Hungarian constitutional monarchy and acclaimed Kossuth as its leader. They were to disperse and organize for war within their villages, but rumors of imminent attack propelled the assembled into immediate guard formations. In Marosvásárhely they marched through the town in a solemn ceremony, with lit candles, singing psalms, as if on a crusade. But when the Székely arrived in the small German-speaking town of Szászrégen (Reghin), they looted homes, set them on fire, and lost more lives pillaging than they would fighting on the battle-field. When they finally encountered imperial forces, this Székely band fled at the first cannon shot.

The Székely attacked Romanian communities and hung resistance lead-ers. Romanian peasants in turn took revenge. Romanian bands massacred hundreds of Hungarians in the town of Zalatna (Zlatna, Kleinschlatten) and village of Alsó-Fehér, and in Nagyszeben (Sibiu, Hermannstadt) more than a hundred noblemen and their families were killed when the large manor house in which they had taken refuge was burned. As the situation in Transylvania spiraled out of control, the Polish revolutionary strategist, General Bem, offered his services to the Hungarian revolution in early No-vember. The support of Polish volunteers was seized upon as a hopeful omen. On November 26 a huge Pest crowd came out to see Kossuth's sis-ter consecrate the flag of the Polish legion, for their presence meant that Hungary was still not utterly alone.[129] The brilliant Bem would register striking military victories in Transylvania. But the monarchy was recon-stituting itself. The mentally incompetent Emperor Ferdinand V resigned on December 2; his brother also stepped aside in favor of his eighteen-year-old son Franz Joseph. With a vigorous new emperor at the helm, who had not been a party to the April Laws, these could be repealed and prepa-rations were made to attack. The Habsburg army struck first from the northeast, from Galicia and Moldavia into Transylvania, Hungary's most vulnerable region. By December 13, 1848, Windisch-Graetz was ready to invade Hungary on the orders of the new emperor. It was Windisch-Graetz who had mopped up the Prague revolution in June and the Viennese revo-lution in October. Windisch-Graetz and the other prominent figures to emerge from the counter-revolution were regimental commanders on the eve of the revolution—notably Jellačić, Julius von Haynau, Johann von Kempen, and Heinrich Hentzi. It was up to the regimental commanders to chastise the crowd that had followed youthful orators in the revolution of 1848; these regimental commanders would emerge from the revolution as the essential force of the monarchy. The empire was ready to reassert its control over its insubordinate Hungarian subjects.

An increasingly desperate tone marked Kossuth's war propaganda. "They have attacked Hungary from nine sides!" he announced in the press.[130] The Hungarian Parliament shed the mantle of legal reformism, accepting its role as a revolutionary government. The six weeks it took Windisch-Graetz to clean up Vienna had allowed the Hungarians to reor-ganize their army, their government, and to prepare a popular rising and guerrilla warfare. "The people . . . are unbeatable. . . . What can ten or a hundred armies do against the people in the millions, against a people who do not allow the enemy peace day or night, against a people who hide all food stuffs from them, a people who finally if they rise up in the millions can beat apart their enemy with their batons? . . . You, the multitude of people, rise up," Kossuth proclaimed. "Justice is with us." "God is with us."[131] Petőfi issued his "Csatadal" (Battle song) in late December: "We will perish, not the homeland (*haza*)!"[132]

Windisch-Graetz took Győr, moving closer to the capital. But that same day, Bem also liberated Kolozsvár. While Bem offered clemency to the defeated Romanian resistance in Kolozsvár, Buda residents prepared for the inevitable. On New Year's Eve, they stowed themselves in their basements for safety awaiting occupation by General Windisch-Graetz. Pest "was silent as a city of the dead; no light broke the gloom . . . , no music disturbed the solemn stillness of the streets."[133] The National Guard had passed its weapons on to the Honvéd, defending the city only with lances. Buda had been disconnected from Pest; the new chain bridge had been disassembled and floated down river. Pest's fall was inevitable, to be delayed by just a few more days. On December 31 the peace party insisted that this was the hour to sue for peace, but Kossuth wished to fight on, to move the government to Debrecen. And in the nervous stillness of that New Year's Eve a demonstration below Kossuth's apartment windows shouting patriotic slogans and war chants swung the balance toward the hawks.[134] On January 6, the Austrians occupied a denuded Pest, with several thousand people gone, including many of the providers of everyday essential services, such as bakers and pharmacists.[135] The active Magyar revolutionaries were gone. But for the time being Deák stayed in Pest, for once occupied it was, perhaps, the safest place in these months. Imperial forces did not enter an entirely hostile environment; many in the German-speaking cities sincerely supported the Austrians, others were ambivalent.[136] "Buda is even quieter than it once was. The residents not only avoid confrontation with the soldiers, but also any gatherings. If perhaps you can make it in to the city, come, believe me that no where is it safer for a quiet, trustworthy citizen than here."[137] Still those who remained, whether Austrian sympathizers or hapless residents, would continue to endure hardships. Budapest and other cities had been shelled, their streets and open spaces were trampled, and homes were opened up for the forced quartering of troops.

In Debrecen, the city on the Great Plain to which the Hungarian government had fled, the parliament reconstituted itself. Kossuth, the liberal, was now Kossuth, the military dictator. While everything was radicalized as the sense of danger was heightened, in Debrecen the fulcrum of the parliament became more moderate, since many liberals and radicals had left to take up commands in the army. Radicals had lost their critical venue, the capital; they no longer had the force of the urban crowd behind them. The moderate club, led by Zsigmond Kemény, toppled the key street orator and "grandmaster of terrorism," László Madarász.[138] While faced with a concerted attack from Austria, Hungary was also in danger of disintegrating from within, of losing Transylvania, and of being reduced to the status of an amputee state. Nationalist war rhetoric found its voice. The words democracy, liberty, or equality vanished from the banners; and the revolution became a series of bloody ethnic expeditions. There was an insurmountable contradiction between the rigid and peremptory nature of the nation and the elastic nature of revolution and its initial rhetoric of tolerance. The ethnic minorities inhabiting the Kingdom of St. Stephen took advantage of the slightest whiff of freedom to tear themselves away. Freedom was understood as detachment. The response in turn by the Hungarian revolution was an intolerant insistence that the recalcitrant give way to the Hungarian revolutionary state. Hungary found itself inextricably mired in an authoritarian position that wrenched the land in war.

Fighting continued, and troops criss-crossed the countryside. But the intimidation pressed even on one's sympathizers, as when the Honvéd arrived in Veszprém, to the delight of the great majority. Whitewash was distributed, and the populace was informed that the slogan "Éljen Kossuth" was to be painted on every house within twenty-four hours or else swift punishment would follow. "Hurry and light a candle and put it in the window," a barber's wife called out nervously in the night, "because otherwise they will break our windows right away." As new candles were lit, the trashing of his neighbor's windows could be heard. Youths roamed the streets shouting:

"Long live Kossuth! Long live the Magyars!
Candles in the window!
Smash the windows without candles!"

The houses of well-known loyalists, illuminated or not, were vandalized as the crowd took revenge for the previous occupation on its supporters.[139]

The conquerors on both sides placed great importance on their ceremonial entrances, intent on projecting an image intimidating to the doubters of the then ascendant cause. Typically conquests were accompanied by balls, band music, and military reviews. Street windows were crowded with ladies, who waved their handkerchiefs and little Hungarian flags as troops passed by, whilst the air resounded with éljens! Attempts were made contritely to excuse away earlier festivity on behalf of the other conquerors as beyond their control and due more to fear than goodwill.[140] The home front learned to become the commandeered crowd and suffered the traumas of a war zone. For instance, in Eger on February 22, 1849, the public came out to receive Klapka's eight hundred troops as they passed through the city, and three days later the city held a torchlight parade in honor of the three Hungarian generals. But on March 1, two thousand Austrian troops with six cannons conquered Eger. Less than two weeks later fortunes were again reversed, and as the Hungarian forces returned the most recently appointed mayor committed suicide. On March 30 Kossuth arrived in Eger, addressed the crowd from his carriage, and was fêted the next evening. The torchbearing men assembled below Kossuth's window swore allegiance to the revolution, while Kossuth admonished them to a patriotism of action and sacrifice.[141]

On March 15, 1849, in Debrecen the bells of the Rákóczi church rang out in the morning to mark the anniversary of the revolution and the beginning of a holiday. By nine in the morning the central square was packed with civilians and soldiers in dress uniform. The newspaper headlines proclaimed General Bem's victory in Nagyszeben, defeat of the Transylvanian Saxons, and the Russians on the run. Much was made of these victories, but, in fact, military prospects were bleak. Kossuth's "March Fifteenth Prayer," which was distributed and read aloud, better captured the pathos and anxiety of the moment. In the celebrations that day, he and his family were enthusiastically greeted with cheers as their coach made its way to the religious services. A capacity crowd filled the Catholic Church to hear the ceremonial mass conducted by the bishop of Nagyvárad (Oradea, Großwardein), and then the entire gathering, including the bishop, proceeded to the Reformed Church where a "golden-tongued" pastor delivered a moving sermon.[142] The morning ended with a military review, complete with cannon fire, music, and parade; the fun began in the afternoon in the city forest. Bands played, the young danced, and quite a crowd toasted March 15 at the spigots of free wine. Oxen roasted on the spits, and a soapbox was set up for the people. The celebrants returned to a city in festive illumination. A transparency had been set up in front of the pharmacy; fireworks were exploded, and that evening candles were lit in even the windows of the poorest houses.[143] The military marked the holiday by issuing a double pay bonus and welcoming new recruits.

But in Buda-Pest the one-year anniversary of March 15 could not be celebrated. "But still," wrote an elderly Pest citizen, "we celebrated March 15. True, just secretly. We looked at one another, we clicked glasses, and everyone knew whom we were toasting. Our lips were silent, but our hearts were filled with patriotic thoughts."[144] Throughout the land there was an overwhelming sense of catastrophe, that the year had been one of suffering and sadness. There was the "greatest insecurity on March 15, 1849, about our Hungarian forces. We have not heard good or bad. We do not hear a single word."[145] In areas occupied by Habsburg forces, parish churches had been ordered to conduct a thanksgiving mass (Te Deum laudamus) to "our new emperor, Ferenc József, tyrant, child king." Authorities had not been cognizant of the date. This gesture was prudently postponed, so that the people wouldn't think that they were celebrating March 15![146] "Magyar prayer is not permitted and the German God just can't become popular."[147]

By the spring of 1849 when the counter-revolution had triumphed everywhere else, the Hungarians held the international imagination by sustaining their resistance. Recruiting continued in earnest in the Hungarian core region. Recruiters went door to door, even signing up seminary students. A diarist still described the recruits going off "happily," as if "to a Mayday picnic."[148] And certainly they were ushered off with great fanfare. When the barrack gates opened, at one such departure, the drums rattled from inside, cheers resounded, and the recruits joyfully shoved out into the "crackling crowd," moving toward the Crown Restaurant, where the popular Szilasi Gypsy band awaited them. Playing the "Rákóczi March" the band led the three-hundred-strong little army through the city. People lined their path all the way up Palace Street and as far as one could see on the highway. Flags were expected to fly over every house, and every man's hat had some sort of national ornament on it.

Hungarian military strategy was also preoccupied with the symbolic, perhaps, disastrously so. Recapturing the capital became such a goal that it clouded tactical thinking. Kossuth declared Hungary independent from Austria on April 14, 1849; the National Assembly ratified the resolution five days later. The Hungarians initiated the siege of Buda on May 4. When the cannon fire began, it seemed as if the whole population of Pest was drawn out to the banks of the Danube to watch. At each firing of the Hungarian artillery at the defenses on top of the hills, the spectators cheered.

The sight of a jubilant crowd enraged the Habsburg Buda commander General Hentzi, a Swiss-born and naturalized Austrian. He retaliated with an order to lob a warning shot at the Pest crowd from the terraces of the castle gardens in Buda. In response the Pest side began firing at the castle. The Hungarians returned fire from the Buda Citadel under their control; when two additional shells struck the Buda side of the bridge, Hentzi apparently believed these also came from Pest. He now no longer felt obliged to follow his instructions not to damage Pest.[149] To the satisfaction of the troops, Hentzi ordered a two-hour bombardment of Pest that began at 8 p.m. His goal was not massive destruction. Of the 316 projectiles fired, thirty-two were hollow shells and 130 bombs were only half-filled with explosive, so not a single house in Pest caught on fire. Damage was limited to roofs and windows. Still Hentzi had made his point. The Pest crowd sought safety and no longer involved itself directly in the struggle. Finally, after seventeen days, the Hungarians did storm the Buda fortress on May 21, and General Hentzi, saber raised, led a final, futile counter-attack, suffering mortal wounds on Saint George Square.

Hardly had the shooting ended before a crowd streamed over from Pest into the fortress. On May 22 the victors held a parade in Buda. Medals were awarded; money was given the Hungarian soldiers; many were promoted, all to the cheers of the crowd. There was also a solemn burial procession for dead Honvéds. The next night the body of Hentzi was quietly taken on a peasant cart and thrown into a trench.[150] Buda had fallen, and the revolution believed itself triumphant. In hindsight, the whole strategy of taking Buda has been seen as a blunder.[151] But at that moment all over Hungary there were thanksgiving services and festivity.

On June 5, 1849, Kossuth made his triumphal entry into the reclaimed capital. He was greeted with a huge noontime demonstration in front of the city hall.[152] Accompanied by his wife and sister, Kossuth's carriage moved through the streets at the head of a stream of carriages that passed thousands of waving hats. He wore a simple Honvéd uniform. The capital was a wounded giant, yet at nightfall most of Pest and Buda's windows were illuminated. While some felt this improvised, rather modest illumination was a mistake, only highlighting the damage from the recent bombardment, others described it as giving the effect of a full moon, and apparently some transparencies and portraits of Kossuth served as magnets to the crowd. As the evening wore on, this crowd moved toward Kossuth's hotel where a chorus began serenading at around 11 p.m. But by midnight the assemblage turned ragged and belligerent, pelting darkened windows of

presumed Habsburg loyalists.[153] A detachment of thirty national guardsmen was called to the scene, only to be stoned so hard that they dispersed.
Finally, after an hour of abandon a single government official appeared in
a carriage, and he beseeched the crowd to desist, so as "not to spoil the
greatest night of Kossuth's life."[154] It was not an incident the patriotic
press of Pest relayed. Instead, they reported that the patriotic festival went
off without a hitch. Gen. Lajos Aulich would issue a proclamation thank-
ing the people for the demonstrations but beseeching them to return to
their normal occupations.[155] Liberation from Austria and the release from
the "fearful scourge to which it had so long been subject" was marked by
a joyous holiday in the town wood.[156] Gaily decorated tents and marquees
replaced the temporary shelters inhabitants had built among the trees of the
town wood for refuge during the bombardment. Oxen were roasted and
wine flowed.

Still there was plenty of trepidation behind the rejoicing. The fortress
walls were torn down rather than repaired, for if Buda could not be defended, better no walls to scale the next time a siege was attempted—were
there to be a next time. As the end approached, Petőfi condemned the public and the generals for dancing before a false god. He denounced Kossuth
for "fanaticiz[ing] the people of Pest to a resolute, last-ditch battle around
the capital city," although Kossuth "did not have the faintest intention of
fighting around Pest, and even less of giving up his life, but that at the
slightest rustle of a bush he would hotfoot it into the wide world where
since the time of Árpád we have had no enemies, and where the skin of the
savior may be more secure."[157] In those areas still under Hungarian control, the Hungarian declaration of independence was intoned from the
churches on the first Sunday of July 1849. The high sheriff of Veszprém led
the entire district's staff of civil servants first to mass, then the Calvinist,
Lutheran, and evangelical churches, concluding with a sermon in Magyar
at the Jewish temple in the afternoon.[158] Petőfi was not alone in anticipating the coming defeat in all its largeness. A nationwide fast underscored the
solemnity and danger pressing upon the nation.

The fighting continued. A couple days later three hundred Hussars
marched into Veszprém. At the rumor of their approach, girls rushed to the
town gardens and surrounding fields to gather flowers. The town's population spilled out, forming a greeting party at the town limits—much as
they had done several times before in Veszprém and everywhere else during the war. When the soldiers were finally sighted the young women ran
forward, and it seemed to one observer as if "two opposing armies were

meeting on the battlefield" when the women rushed to the soldiers and thrust flowers in their hands. The elite greeted the soldiers at the city limits; a Gypsy band played. And while the little battalion, dirty, dusty and ragged from battle, moved along Palace Street into the city, wreaths and bouquets flew toward "those who were suffering so much for the homeland."[159] This time formal speeches in front of the city hall were brief, for the men were eager to disperse into the burgher houses to sleep.[160]

The next day the town celebrated with a public ball and banquet, an ad hoc, potluck affair. In the afternoon servant girls began carrying bundles to the bishop's garden, and by 5 p.m. the Hussars marched in formation to the garden. At the banquet alternating Gypsy bands played the *csárdás* without pause. This Magyar dance was so newly revived, that burghers were startled to see women join the dance. The dancing frenzy relaxed other traditional prohibitions and distinctions, as well. Dancers included servant girls and Jewish women.[161] As defeat approached, "here was equality," one man observed. "The poor, the gentry, even the Jew, all celebrated and twirled. Pride and arrogance lost their advantage on the dance floor. The muscular women held the advantage over the fragile, corseted ones."[162] The next morning the Hussars moved on to battle.

The twenty-five-year-old Petőfi had joined the forces at the front and would be among the scores of Honvéd lost in the final battles. As catastrophe beckoned, he had asked: "Where will the new Mohács be? Where once again the homeland's sun sets, and for three-hundred years, or perhaps forever, does not show its face!"[163]

Mihály Munkácsy, *In the Cell of the Condemned* (detail), 1869. Oil on Wood, 137 x 195 cm. (Hungarian National Gallery)

4

The Martyrology of Revolutionary Defeat

By July 11, 1849, the revolution had reached its end in Budapest. The sister cities were desolate. Around the noon hour some five hundred Austrian troops arrived on the outer streets of Buda. Revolutionary placards still clung to the walls along the empty streets that led into the inner city. But their promise of inevitable victory contrasted with the shell-pocked streets in Buda and even more sharply with the bomb rubble that still littered Pest from the costly siege of the Buda castle. Here and there at crucial locations in Pest, such as the National Museum or the hospital, the militia maintained order. At three p.m. a large Pest crowd formed on the Danube bank to gape across the river for sight of the conquering Austrian force in Buda. Since the bridge crossings had been dismantled, a standoff ensued between the prostrate crowd and its imminent conqueror.[1] The remaining Buda city authorities formally offered homage to the entering army the following day making the customary request for safety for the citizenry. The women of the loyalist *Gutgesinnt* (the well-meaning) greeted the officers with flower bouquets. The Pest authorities remained a bit more recalcitrant, stalling the inevitable, but a day later, after additional warnings, they performed the rite of defeat.

When the Pest deputation made good their surrender, Habsburg imperial forces still remained across the river. Instead, a four-hundred man detachment of Cossacks rode through the Pest streets to the blare of trumpets and drums, pitching their camp at the unusable bridgehead. Frustrated Habsburg forces remained on the other side. In the evening the curious Pest citizens came out in significant number to peer at the Cossacks, their tents, and their horses.[2] The national tricolor disappeared from the Pest city hall once the Russian troops had arrived. The capital as a legal entity was no more; Pest and Buda were again divided. By the morning of July

14, Habsburg forces crossed the river; the black-yellow, double-headed eagle was formally raised at City Hall, and the state of siege was officially proclaimed: a 9 p.m. curfew went into effect; all national insignia and colors were strictly forbidden; the ringing of church bells was prohibited, with the exception of funerals and the noonday chimes.

Separate triumphs were staged for the conquering Romanov and Habsburg generals. Austrian troops flooded into Pest, occupying every available quarter, even the front yard of the National Museum. On this symbolic space, the launching pad of the revolution, they pitched their tents and set up shop for their blacksmith and butcher. Soldiers and their carts took possession of the inside courtyard and the ground-level hallway. Within a few days the grounds of the National Museum were ankle deep in litter and dung covered the walkways. Before the large steps of the museum, the Austrians prepared to stage their public executions. The first victim was a former imperial soldier who had deserted to the Hungarian side. Dressed in civilian clothes, he was executed as a spy. Behind the barrier set up around the museum yard a large crowd watched, and many came later to see the guarded corpse while it lay there overnight. In hangings, Michel Foucault noted, "the main character was the people, whose real and immediate presence was required for the performance."[3] A regimen of executions followed before the submissive crowd of revolutionary defeat. A miner from Szatmár could be tried at 10 a.m. for wounding an imperial soldier and shot by noon against the north wall of the museum steps. The finality of defeat had a breathless quality: harsh and swift.[4] Individuals were hung, but the culpability was hardly thought to be theirs alone. Such public executions accentuated the deadly adversarial relation between the forces in control and the entire society.

Although Buda-Pest was vanquished, fighting still continued in Hungary. The Austrian commander, General Baron Julius Haynau (1786–1853), could smell victory. He had a dispirited Hungarian army on the run, and the peasantry wanted desperately for the war to end. Haynau's ambition was to make Russian participation superfluous by ending the war as quickly as possible. He was furious that the Russians had allowed Hungarian General Arthur Görgey's Hungarian army to escape into eastern Hungary. Haynau had mocked the Russian commander's "retrograde" maneuvering, only to have to apologize, explaining he was "a soldier with a character that was an open book and as such I am used to expressing my feelings without diplomatic tact to state how things really are."[5] Haynau and later historians have questioned the military wisdom of inviting Russian intervention once defeat of the Italians had freed up at least 150,000

Habsburg troops. But the flurry of Hungarian victories in April and May had prompted Prime Minister Prince Felix zu Schwarzenberg to request Russian military aid. A cholera epidemic coincided with the Russian invasion. As the battle visited and revisited areas, cholera spread from the troops to civilians and back again, rendering darker a darkening threat. Between 20,000 and 30,000 Russian soldiers died in the epidemic, which slowed down the Russian offensive and demoralized the public.

By the late summer, Görgey's army was showing the classic symptoms of an army verging on dissolution. On his march eastward he executed a captain in the main square of Keszthely for failing his duty; Görgey also felt obliged to put some thirty young officers under arrest. But on August 3 Hungarian General György Klapka launched a successful sally from Komárom, the island fortress in the Danube. The besieging Austrian troops were routed and sent into flight westward as far as Pozsony. This fanned a flicker of hope. But just as expectations were again raised of some miraculous deliverance, Görgey unexpectedly surrendered to the Russians at Világos on August 13. A common metaphor of this capitulation was that of "a funeral attended by a crowd of 100,000."[6] In Pest the conquering forces announced the surrender at Világos by ordering a holiday illumination of the city streets; it marked the end of all hope. "On August 13 began Hungary's days of mourning."[7] When imperial soldiers captured his regiment and marched into their camp at noon playing the Habsburg hymn "Gott, erhalte," recalled one Honvéd, the sounds of the anthem made palpable the finality of defeat, and there was loud and uncontrollable sobbing.[8] Komárom, the last holdout, gave up on October 2, and an Austrian military dictatorship reigned over the whole country. Hungarian General László Újházy would recall the scene for an American audience: "Then came the saddest, most dreadful of my life's days, when the Austrians marched in, and were permitted to plant on the walls of the fortress their black and yellow flag— colors of envy and death."[9] Pathos mixed with anger as soldiers cracked the barrelheads of their weapons. They cursed the occupying "scoundrels," the "selfish" officers, and the "traitorous" commander Görgey.[10] Memoirs recount the small acts of defiance and opportunities for escape.[11] The comfortable camaraderie of soldiers within their battalions changed to the lonely crowd of defeat.

Haynau, the Villain

The experience of revolutionary defeat would be associated in the Hungarian mind with Haynau and his ten-month occupation. The blond, blue-eyed general with a white mustache assumed his role as conquering general in Hungary with an already fearful reputation, because of the vindictiveness he had displayed in Italy, where he had unleashed terror in Ferrara and earned the epithet "hyena of Brescia" for reprisals he took when a crowd massacred wounded Austrian soldiers. Empowered with dictatorial power over a subjugated Hungary, he made it painfully clear that the real power in the land was his.[12] Haynau took a much harder line than General Windisch-Graetz had at the beginning of the year.[13] Haynau's personal approach was also quite different from the impersonal, almost mechanical, Prussian repression imposed simultaneously in Baden. Haynau even seemed to relish his role as a lightning rod for public anger. It was Haynau's real but also cartoonlike malevolence that would make him a catalyst for a national martyrology.

To prevent children from wearing the Honvéd caps on the street, punishment of ten strokes was exacted on the father of an offender, and if there were no father, the punishment was to be applied to the mother. Though few in number, such incidents became widely known, as did the imprisonment of Kossuth's mother and sister. By having women arrested and flogged, Haynau offended the notions of propriety and incurred notoriety throughout Europe. Rather than dampen this negative reputation, he enhanced it by assuming the blame for onerous edicts that he enforced, but in reality, had not created. He knew that "the journalists will all come down on me with the dear English," but he countered by emphasizing that "over 100,000 lost their lives through murder, battle, and disease. Millions are impoverished, in whole counties the villages have been burnt down (as by the Serbs)."[14]

The Hungarian preference for surrender to the Russians irritated Haynau; the Russians' magnanimous treatment of the defeated Hungarians enraged Haynau. The Russians, he was convinced, were out to cheat him of an exclusive triumph. An apoplectic Haynau poured out his anger in his letters to Franz Joseph, complaining that the Russians were fueling illusionary hope among the revolutionaries that would only bring new dangers to the Austrian state. He found it incomprehensible that the Russians could treat the "rebel chiefs" with respect, allowing them to retain their weapons, revolutionary medals, and usurped titles when it was clear that the majority were no more than deserters and oath-breaking former officers of the Habsburg army. He objected to the word capitulation for he wanted the rebels to accept unconditional surrender (*unbedingt unterwerfen*). But most galling for him was one Russian general's comment that the rebel cause was not such a bad one and that poor policy of the Austrian government was responsible for much of the problem. "In short," he wrote the emperor on August 18, "it appears that they see in these individuals not rebels, not the murderers of General Count Ferenc Lamberg, not the leaders of the party who marched on the capital of the empire to support its rebellion, but rather—almost in the same sense as the English radical assemblies held on behalf of Hungary—the vanguard of a nation who is fighting against unjust repression and whose defeated, in their unhappiness, should be treated with respect."[15]

Russian leniency provoked the choleric Haynau to make the opposite demonstration. When the Russians suggested he issue a general amnesty, he made it clear his policy would be to hang all rebel chiefs and shoot all imperial officers who had fought for the revolutionaries. "I will pull the weed out by the roots and give all of Europe an example of how one should treat rebels so as to have order, quiet, and peace for a century. The Hungarians have been rebels for three hundred years, and there have been revolutions under almost all the Habsburg kings. I am the man who will bring order. I will shoot hundreds with a clear conscience, because I am convinced that this is the only means to create a warning example that will prevent all future rebellions."[16] Haynau declared he owed the army and the world the "terrible example" that he was going to inflict on those who had turned on the imperial army. The accused was simply asked if he had been in Habsburg service and then served with a weapon in the rebel army. "Without the help of our officers, they could not have carried out the war. All orders were given in German, because hardly anyone of these spoke Hungarian, even fewer could write it. . . . In the coming century no revolution will break out in Hungary, for that I mortgage my head if necessary . . ."[17]

While Haynau was unflinching in his exacting of retribution, he complained of insomnia and wrecked nerves. His victorious fate was not to be envied as the circumstances had made "me almost crazy."[18] Haynau's sense of professionalism scorned the chaotic, unregulated fighting of Serbs and Magyars in 1848, and he saw himself bringing regulated warfare to the end stage of the conflict. Haynau, a Hungarian himself, had been commandant of the Temesvár garrison from 1845 and prided himself on his dedication to the regimental officer's value of duty, which he raised to the status of a political creed that absolved him from deeper political reflection. Even before the revolution Haynau commanded through fear. As Temesvár commandant, he was insultingly stingy in bestowing praise. He was quick to incriminate, had a propensity to torment his subordinates, and often showered them with torrents of verbal abuse. "Because of his moral character everyone would be pleased if he were transferred, because no one likes to come into contact with him in the course of duty," General Pitt wrote in his 1847 review. Despite his admitted competence in military science, Pitt suggested that "perhaps the best thing would be to place him in retirement." Haynau was "sixty-one years old, but looks seventy, sickly."[19]

Instead, Haynau's rise in the ranks was swift. When he assumed command of the Hungarian campaign in the early summer of 1849, he scored a series of quick military successes over a collapsing Honvéd army. His patron and friend Radetzky, the hero of Austria's Italian campaigns, called Haynau a razor blade. Haynau's strategy was a combination of intimidation and the command "forward!" As the son of the Elector of Hesse, he also fully endorsed that House's paranoid legitimism, combative antiliberalism, and taste for counterrevolution. Haynau was so eager to play the role of chastiser, that he became identified with policies crafted in Vienna.

At the end of 1848 when it appeared that Windisch-Graetz was closing in on the Hungarian rebels, a memorandum established the principle that it was not enough that the rebels capitulate, they needed to be brought to "reason" or else one would not be able to rule in Hungary for more than a few years. No negotiations were to be entered into with the rebels, nor was there to be any talk of amnesty. The actual promoters of the rebellion were not many, it was reasoned in this document, and thus, these rebels were to be treated according to the laws of war and hung without fanfare. The less guilty were to be intimidated by placing them before courts-martial, proclaiming death sentences on them, announcing the scheduled date for execution, and only then letting them go.[20]

Stringent measures were taken toward wayward clergy and religious communities. Haynau lashed out at the Jewish population for its support of the revolution, slapping a heavy fine first on the Buda-Pest communities and then extending it to all Jews in the Hungarian lands.[21] The Bulgarian patriarch of the Balaton was shot. His crime was reading the independence declaration in church. Executions seemed directed as much at moderates as radical revolutionaries. In any case, Kossuth and many of his followers had fled. The Austrians were out to pacify the middle. Haynau became the final arbiter of life and death. His practice of executing centrists fueled a feeling of injustice, and made martyrs out of his targets. The most significant examples were the execution in Pest on October 6, 1849, of the former Prime Minister Count Lajos Batthyány and that of thirteen generals in Arad, memorialized as the Arad martyrs.[22] Haynau chose the anniversary of General Baillet von Latour's assassination for this retribution.

Batthyány was imprisoned in the New Building in Pest in an upstairs cell. The other prisoners could only hear footsteps from his cell on the floor above.[23] Such isolation was unusual, for most incarceration was communal—even death sentences were announced to groups of men at once. Trial, verdict, and punishment were pronounced upon the individual, but the crime was in the name of the community. The commiserating public outside, and the camaraderie of the defeated inside the prison altered the tenor. Chivalric language and Biedermeier gestures, romantic sensibilities and a firm sense of self-righteousness vis-à-vis one's captor camouflaged the individual, existential experience faced by each convicted person. Men generally gained strength from each other; however, women prisoners, few in number, were more likely to suffer prison as solitary confinement.[24]

Batthyány and others resigned themselves to their fate. Resistance or escape was rejected not necessarily actively, but fatalistically, as impossible. Batthyány refused his wife's promising escape plan, determined to fulfill the role of the martyr prescribed for him. But in order to prevent the shame of being hanged, Batthyány attempted to slit his throat with a dull knife smuggled to him by Countess Mihály Károlyi, his mistress and sister-in-law.[25] Although the wound was not fatal, it did prevent his hanging. Gen. Johann Kempen von Fichterstamm, the officer in charge, even allowed him to give the order to his firing squad: "Allez Jäger, éljen a haza!"[26] His last words, a composite of three languages, reflected the cultural fluidity of Hungarian nationalism at the time of the revolution. But Kempen would have to defend his action to Haynau. He explained that hanging the wounded man "might have excited the participation of the public."[27]

That day in Arad four more were shot, nine were hung, and no crowd disturbance took place. Seven of the thirteen were interred at the spot. Two were buried elsewhere, secretly. The rest were taken to family crypts. The public was barred from the executions, but a crowd gathered outside the fortress walls. Priests were implored to address and soothe the crowd. Reluctant at first, one priest made a short statement, which the public appreciated and the military command could not understand. Only later did they learn that the Hungarian statement had been critical.[28] The festivity of the gallows had once been a ghoulish day of community where citizens witnessed the powers of their state; the crowd took heed but was also drawn into the public polity. The executions of 1849, however, were symbols of final defeat and alienation, meant to dispel the public instead. Batthyány had been executed in Pest that same day, but it is the thirteen Arad martyrs who became the icon of persecution. Hungarian martyrology has shunned the discrete examples of victims, focusing, instead, on the image of a group of martyrs acceding to their death.

Fear, despair, and humiliation—a reversal of all political assumptions and actions—were essential to martial law. This fear and apprehension existed on both sides. The inchoate, despondent public may have become docile, but the possibility remained that the people were still excitable. If revolution gained its impetus and energy from a crowd experience, defeat gained its sustenance from fear and exhaustion of the individual. The forced dispersal and expulsion of the crowd, acts of supplication by the devalued leadership, were immediate, expected aspects of defeat. Defeat meant the end of a political crowd, a seeming devaluation of fraternity. The absence of all crowd activities and the suspension of the right of assembly are aspects of the standard picture of military repression. "Everyone woke up in fear, and went outside to hear the awful news or to read the latest placards, announcing the most recent restrictions or decrees."[29]

"The streets are empty. Only occasionally a rental-carriage rumbles through the empty streets. The clink of the gendarme's swords rudely disturbs the silence. . . . Pedestrians walk with heads down, saddened, hurriedly to the safety of their homes, they don't look right or left, just riveted to the ground. If one said anything, it was only to someone very trustworthy."[30] "One person hardly dared sit next to another in public places like casinos or coffeehouses, because if one started to talk to someone, they could hardly speak about anything else than the past battles. And if one started on that, one couldn't avoid criticizing one of the many enemies. One had to feel out the person to whom one was talking very closely. Among the locals there were many secret police who sat and drank among us, and if someone dared say something about the existing regime, that person got arrested."[31]

Since there was no real crowd for Haynau or the ruling Habsburg house, the theater became the crucial forum of official demonstration and the symbolic battleground of the military occupation. The conquering army insisted upon a special Pest performance of the play *Hans Sachs* to mark the emperor's birthday of August 18 and highlighted the evening with the illumination of the theater building.[32] The Hungarian National Theater's gala performances generally played to a packed house, but relatively few were paying patrons; thus, these galas were a financial hardship. Haynau's Pest arrivals and departures became formal spectacles. The illuminations, trumpet and drum roll entries, the enacted events that marked the state of siege were addressing a real, if invisible, crowd. The month ended with

General Haynau being fêted on his return to Pest. The new Austrian-appointed mayor received him at the railway station, and torch-carrying city Hussars escorted him to his residence; the city was illuminated, and Hungarian actors of the National Theater were obliged to present a special command performance in German in his honor.[33] Among Haynau's first acts was to force the National Theater to share its stage with the German theater that had burnt down a few months before the outbreak of the revolution. The National troupe felt threatened by this forced sharing of its stage and the various "command" performances. They worried that Haynau might go the next step and Germanize the National Theater. The theater as linguistic and cultural battlefield was already a fixed motif in Magyar nationalism.[34]

Not only was the Hungarian National Theater a theater of no nation, but Pest was reduced from a capital to the headquarters of one of the five military districts.[35] All traces of municipal self-rule remained with the military and police authorities until 1860. But dismantling of the capital took place simultaneously with the reconstruction and completion of the Széchenyi Chain Bridge connecting Pest and Buda. Ironically, a true unification was possible for the first time, because hitherto the bridge was only in place after the spring thaw and before the winter freezing of the Danube. One could cross in the dead of winter, but there were periods when access between the two cities had been impossible. It fell to Haynau to celebrate this ultimate symbol of the connection and future possibilities of a grand capital. At the dedication of the Chain Bridge on November 20, 1849, the Danube banks were filled with soldiers and civilians. Haynau made a splendid entrance, there were many official greetings, and then Haynau and the whole officer corps dismounted and walked across the Chain Bridge to Buda. But while Haynau was greeted with "boisterous ovations" on the Buda side, on the Pest side there had been utter silence and no one had "reached for their hat." But once the stiff ceremony was done with, the public came alive, delighting in the opportunity to cross the bridge without paying a toll. Army bands played as the public strolled.[36] This celebration typified a fundamental contradiction in the Habsburgs' stance toward the capital. While wishing to defuse the crowds of the capital and force the Hungarians into obeisance, the neo-absolutist regime oversaw the beginning of the urban, technological advance of Budapest and the solidification of the city's central role in the Hungarian economy.[37]

At the height of Haynau's power, Alexander Bach, the influential interior minister, was putting into place the features of what would eventually be called the Bach system. While this is often identified solely with the bureaucratic control exercised by the Interior Ministry, of equal, perhaps greater, importance was the creation of the gendarmerie. Napoleon I revived the French gendarmerie to protect the highways and to curtail robbery, recruiting its members from the local areas. The Austrians copied the practice, introducing gendarmerie regiments into South Tyrol and Lombardy in 1805. They capitalized on the Hungarian revolution's effort to create the first modern statewide police force in Hungary. The revolution had abolished the old police system of the pandurs; the counter-revolution now forged a new police-state around the gendarmerie.[38] The revolution of 1848 also eased the process of Habsburg police expansion into Hungary and the rest of the monarchy by dissolving the legal prerogatives of the landowners. Vienna was quick to see the possibilities of a monarchy-wide gendarmerie. Bach formally presented the proposal to the emperor on June 8, 1848, well before control was reestablished in Hungary. In July 1849 Kempen was entrusted with the task of creating a gendarmerie. By November Kempen had assembled 12,000 for regiments on foot and 2,000 on horse, and by June 1850 there were sixteen regiments with three in Hungary, headquartered in Kassa, Budapest, and Nagyvárad. Three additional regiments were stationed in Transylvania, the Vojvodina, and Croatia-Slovenia. The gendarmerie secured Habsburg domination, but it also was critical in moving beyond the state of martial law imposed by Haynau in the summer of 1849. A bitter Haynau complained on June 1, 1852, shortly before his death that "in Hungary there is no government, none at all; over there only the gendarmerie rules."[39] Haynau's traditionalist, heavy-handed oppression was replaced by an ideological, modernizing regime that was dependent upon three connected, but often competing hierarchies: the army, police, and bureaucracy.

The more alienated Haynau felt from Bach, the closer his conceptions seemed to those of Hungary's Old Conservatives, composed primarily of Hungary's high nobility, who complained that in the name of legitimacy, legitimacy itself was being undermined by a neo-absolutist *tabula rasa*.[40] Pál Somssich, their leading spokesperson, accused Bach of being willing to stoop to anything in "flattering the crowd."[41] Somssich argued the bureaucratic system was cynically manipulating the democratic principle to make itself popular among the lower orders. It was fatal for a hereditary empire to rest its legitimacy on the right of the stronger, he concluded.[42] Somssich also countered Bach's condemnation of Hungarians as revolutionaries by employing Metternich's imagery of the revolution as infection. Eighteen forty-eight did not happen out of antidynastic sentiments (which with only a few exceptions never existed), but rather was part of a chain reaction that swept through Naples, Paris, Brussels, etc. By this line of reasoning Hungarians simply caught the revolutionary pathogen in the air; without the March days in Vienna, there would have been no March days in Pozsony or Pest.[43] "The fatherland rent apart, the nationality repressed, the throne robbed of its thousand-year pillars: what more can come to torment the breast of the patriot?"[44]

The Old Conservatives' attempts to lobby against the Interior Ministry's policies toward Hungary were blocked. Silenced in Hungary and not permitted to appeal directly to the sovereign, the Old Conservatives began to make their case in the Viennese press and in brochures, often published in Germany. To their chagrin, the Old Conservatives had been pegged as a potentially subversive movement, but this rendered them more palatable to the Hungarian public.[45] Haynau also hoped to spruce up his image by courting the Old Conservatives, offering an alliance against the bureaucratic-police state that was emerging in the spring of 1850. In early 1850 Haynau startled Hungarians by issuing a magnanimous amnesty. In the taverns and wine cellars of Pest, it was speculated that Haynau was now out to play the role of a "second Radetsky," that is, to reshape his persona into that of a popular military hero.

Haynau found working with Bach's man in Pest, Baron Karl Geringer, increasingly burdensome. Their differences were visible to all during the memorial service for Gen. Heinrich Hentzi in May 1850 when Geringer avoided standing next to Haynau by engaging Baroness Haynau in animated conversation.[46] Choleric as ever, Haynau quarreled with the war minister and got himself summarily dismissed in July 1850. The Old Conservatives were startled and disappointed. The signal was clear: his hard-line measures were no longer appropriate, and his newly found mildness was even less so. Haynau was superfluous. The state of siege gave way to Bach's bureaucratic system and Kempen's police state. The institutionalization of the new regime was commencing.

There may have been no love lost between Haynau and the Hungarians, but Haynau would ultimately feel more at home among the great magnates in Hungary than he did among the bureaucrats in Pest or Vienna. He invested his "dismissal money" in an estate in Szatmár County. However, the estate was flooded by the river Tisza, and he caught swamp fever. After undergoing quack water cures, he ignored friendly advice and traveled to Western Europe and England. Police had to rescue him from a crowd in

Brussels. In London, while visiting a brewery, Haynau was recognized, cornered, and beaten by a group of draymen. In Austria the "terrible incident" was interpreted as an attempted assassination and "created outraged feeling." It became an international incident when Lord Palmerston rejected Austria's demand for action against the perpetrators.[47] Bits of the London brooms with which Haynau was beaten were set in handsome gold settings and worn as pins by Hungarian gentry women as a form of nationalistic defiance and also as a sign that the crowd was still alive, if not in Hungary, then at least in lands where liberalism still reigned.[48]

Myth Making

Neo-absolutism, rather than exploiting the bitter factionalism that had surfaced during the revolution, provided a unifying target. "The future was bleak, and the ruling power dealt with everyone as an enemy," lumping all together. "The differences of 1848 divided the nation into two parties, but the disaster of 1849 once again united them," reflected a contemporary.[49] There was a natural solidarity that came from a collectively suffered defeat and occupation. The depoliticized, troubled setting actually encouraged the healing of previous internal political wounds still evident in the revolution. Occupation forced Hungarians into a chastened, but nevertheless genuine, sense of internal unity. One example was the common resistance to a new tobacco tax in 1851. Peasants were arrested for burning their tobacco seeds in the town square of one small town.[50] The gentry may have showed greater business acumen by surreptitious cultivation and selling of tobacco, but both strata were caught up in a common rhetoric of resistance.[51] The end of serfdom had lifted the fear of a jacquerie that had gripped so many nobles in 1848; replacing this was now a legend of noble-peasant cooperation against the Austrian occupier. With defeat the aristocracy, the gentry, urban middle class, peasantry, Jews, and other minorities could all cohere around a common grievance against the Austrians and their Bohemian civil servants. Brushed aside was the former expectation of peasant compensation for land, but over 50 percent of the land remained in large gentry estates, while a considerable number of peasants were still without land or had acquired holdings of insignificant size.

In the unquiet wait of the fifties, Hungary possessed an internal unity only aspired to in the revolution. Defeat fostered the Magyarization of the elite. The higher nobility had typically learned to speak German and French better than Hungarian, and their patriotic utterances were often halting and flawed. But in the new "apoliticized" social whirl even the most apolitical or pro-imperial nobles found Vienna inhospitable. This was a dramatic shift, for since the reign of Maria Theresa the Hungarian magnates had been among the richest and most brilliant components of Viennese society, including such illustrious families as Andrássy, Apponyi, Károlyi, Batthyány, Pálffy, and, above all, Esterházy. The great change was that after 1850 the Hungarian nobles were rarely to be seen in Vienna. In the demonology of the period, the Habsburg capital was the lair of the arch-villainess, the Archduchess Sophia, architect of the anti-Hungarian policy of her son, the emperor.

The Hungarian liberal Ferenc Deák declined his liberal Austrian counterpart Anton Schmerling's invitation to attend a legal conference in Vienna in April 1850. Although his letter was polite and benign in itself, the refusal was reported in the newspapers and thereby publicized throughout the country. This tactic of dignified passivity had a resonance in the beleaguered land, especially among its rural gentry, already prone to a narrowminded insularity. Although in the long run encouraging isolationist proclivities proved a problem, the tactic of passive resistance was appropriate to a state of siege.

The gentry's identification with the suffering of the homeland was an extension of their own sense of decline. Withdrawal was a natural impulse. "I longed to return to the solitude of the country, where one was still less cognizant of the pathetic condition than in the capital."[52] Denied the outlet of local politics, largely confined to their lonely estates, gentry energy necessarily turned inward. What had once seemed so unthinkable, defeat, now had become overwhelming and crushing. Defeat conscripted those who had not been actors in the revolution itself, for they had to deal with a thick, dense fog of gloom that spread over daily life. Peace had come to mean defeat, and fathoming God's purpose prompted many to search for historical analogies; it was in this moment that many Hungarians identified themselves with the Hebrews as a "lost people." A German anagram developed: "Pannonia, vergiss deine Todten nie! als Kläger leben sie." (Pannonia, forget not your dead! as accusers they live on!)[53] Writers presented the national idea in a set of allegories. They were bound together by a shared secret code: the Jews lost in the desert, the destroyed people of Caledonia, the suffering of galley slaves, the destruction of Jerusalem, the chained lion. These were all understood by the public as references to the homeland's condition.[54] This collusion, the shared fight and its aftermath, was an important step in creating a nation out of Hungary.

Women of the rural elite played a critical role in the emotional crisis by striking the right notes of sentimentality, dignity, piety, and patriotism.[55] After the shock of defeat came the debilitating period of mourning in which "men's work" was interrupted and women became visible in developing the new politics of pain. Focus of the mourners was on the home, the gathering place where the healing process could begin, and where the new martyrology could be fostered. Women would be especially visible in developing the new politics of pain. A similar pattern has been observed in the American South after the fall of the Confederacy and the occupation of "rebel" territory. The level of casualties in the South was many times greater than in Hungary, and the one year of Hungarian resistance paled in comparison to the psychic drain of four years of unrelenting civil war. Hungarian women could still view defeat as righteous and temporary, while for southern women the Confederacy was clearly the Lost Cause.[56]

In the 1850s the crinoline matron in the countryside came into her own with her quasi-secret cult of the disappointed revolution. Women were freer than their male counterparts in defeat. They could display defiance with less risk. Passive resistance also diminished the distinction between the female and male role in politics. While it was "manly" to bear wounds stoically and politic to lay low, women could still exhibit the nation's wounds publicly, albeit in a restrained or indirect fashion. The counter-revolution scornfully labeled women partisans as "Kossuth Sisters."[57] The smoking, pant-wearing female bohemian had made an appearance at the outbreak of the Pest revolution, but during the war, the feminine had been cast into the role of applauding witness. The counter-revolution unwittingly elevated women into the key purveyors of a new martyrology. Shared suffering bound the isolated gentry women to the national cause. The periodic attempts of the authorities to make examples of high-placed women, as when one countess was imprisoned in 1851 for writing her sister in exile, only confirmed their new prominence. Gentry women copied forbidden documents; the last prayer of the Arad martyrs was a favorite, as were letters from exiles. They read them behind closed doors in family circles and private get-togethers.[58] In one district peasant women stitched the border pattern of the illegal Kossuth bank notes into their traditional costumes.[59] Legal reprisals followed, as an ever stricter dress code was enforced. Still, organizing the magnate/gentry women was difficult. When one magnate woman sought pledges of monthly donations toward prisoner aid, there were few comers.[60]

Incidents of confrontational gatherings of men were rare, but on March 15, 1850, at one secret meeting in Eger, a lawyer sang the refrain, "We don't need a tyrant king." The assembled cheered a speech that concluded with "Long live freedom. Long live the nation. Curses on every tyrant." The next day the police arrested the group and sent them before the military tribunal.[61] For a decade neo-absolutism would define remembrance and memorial as a surreptitious activity. What is remembered in the reverent essays fifty years later is the "silent clicking of glasses" when old comrades gathered at tables in coffeehouses.[62]

The state of emergency was marked by dead public space. The trumpet-and-drum-roll entries did not enliven the public squares, but they did send notice to all within earshot. After Haynau's departure, the state of siege lost its ad hoc quality. Regulations and limitations were more clearly set down, and previous gaps, such as in censorship practices, were tightened. Efficiency and order revealed itself in all sorts of petty ways. "If the walkway in front of one's house was unkempt, the police brought a clean up order. Everyone was working in front of their houses to keep their yards in good shape." A painting spree, officially ordered, transformed "rebellious" gates and fences into loyal ones of yellow or black.[63] The taverns and coffeehouses closed on time. "There wasn't such a swarm of prostitutes as today. There weren't work-shy loiterers hanging around at the market square, everyone found something to do."[64]

The occupiers set out to discipline and grow their crowd. Theater performances were ordered to open with the royal hymn "Gott, erhalte" on dynastic holidays, but this only ensured that the theater would be an emotional battleground. On Franz Joseph's birthday on August 18, 1850, the balcony could not restrain itself. Screeching, whistling, and banging by students and apprentices in the balcony forced the orchestra to interrupt playing of the anthem three times. The police arrested seventeen and gave them a thrashing; three sustained injuries.[65] The balcony was closed for weeks, causing a substantial loss in box office receipts. Thereafter, the audience was beseeched to swallow the "Gott, erhalte" quietly in the interest of the theater.[66] Being fashionably late became ever more fashionable. After an audience hysterically cheered a bit player, because he was dressed in a Hussar uniform, the theaters were forced to substitute Mecklenburg for Hungarian uniforms for the next decade. Musical performances with radical motifs were prohibited.[67] In 1850 the events in the Pest theater were followed by incidents in Besztercebánya and Vác, where Kossuth was hailed instead of Franz Joseph.[68] The nameday for Lajos was only six days after the emperor's birthday, making August 18 and 24 lightning rods for dissident voices. In Selmecbánya in 1851 the planned celebration for the ruler's birthday was pathetically attended, only to have the residents come out in force to celebrate Lajos day.[69] Organizers were similarly embarrassed the following year, as well.[70]

Occupation forces had to contend with the haunting presence of the revolution, whether in the depressive tones of the poetry in the one permitted literary journal, or the pregnant silence on the streets and in the cafes, and most of all, in the anger and fear consuming individuals behind their closed doors—all potentially combustible. During the state of siege literary life went into dormancy. Sándor Petőfi and many others had died; the remaining literary community dispersed. Prominent writers such as Mihály Vörösmarty, János Arany, and Mór Jókai were forced into hiding; Vörösmarty found his livelihood as a writer wrecked by the "winter" of the Bach period, as he called it in "Prelude" (1850).[71] He suffered dearly in hiding, becoming bitter and prematurely aged. Both his spirit and his health declined.[72] Arany's poem, "Cold Wind" (Hűvös Szél), similarly touched the emotional pathos of the period immediately following the revolution. Arany's image of a beggar going from door to door was recited throughout the country even though it could not be published. Under censorship and in a semiliterate society, the poet sustained the age-old role of the political troubadour. Publishing houses took refuge in the almanac, which bridged the gap between peasant society and literati most effectively. Publication of calendars doubled, their pages filled with essays and poems.[73]

In February 1850 Sándor Szilágyi, launched *Magyar emléklapok* (Hungarian Souvenir Pages), the first literary magazine of the post-revolutionary era. This palliative to the "general and dumbfounded quiet" lasted for six issues before it caved to the censors.[74] This was time enough to produce a font of images from which the literary martyrology would be fashioned. Pál Gyulai, a literary authority of the coming decade, included a ballad, "Debreczin Girl," evoking the apotheosis of the revolution: the maiden who had lost her homeland and her love; her only remaining prize was a madness that allowed her dead lover to remain alive in her mind.[75] Ferenc Mentovich's "The Grave of the Mad" also built on the same image.[76] With madness a metaphor of these years, Count Stephen Széchenyi's slide into insanity during the revolution actually seemed to enhance his mythic presence rather than diminish it. Until his death in 1860, "the greatest Magyar" remained the man who had cared most about the homeland.

In the deadened public space, the graveyard was the potent symbol of rebirth. Wives and mothers with their wreaths could not be banished from the graveyards. On April 21, 1850, Baron Miklós Wesselényi, the Transylvanian reformer, died in Pest. He had asked his wife and friends to bury him without fanfare, but his interment in the crypt at the Calvin Square Reformed Church became an opportunity for a national demonstration. Without prior public announcement, a large patriotic crowd solemnly, and in "the deepest quiet," followed his coffin.[77] Wesselényi's request to be buried in the family burial plot in Zsibó would be honored that winter. Dwelling on the catastrophe of 1849 may have been, Kemény would later argue, a form of madness in his time; still attention remained riveted on the funereal. Popular ballads retold the fate of "the ever-crying patriot" lamenting the demise of his "lovely homeland buried in a deep grave from which there was no resurrection." Even loyalists bemoaned the sad mood, and "the past's funereal history."[78]

Neither censorship nor surveillance was overarching in this state of siege. The intelligentsia still gathered. For instance, the contributors to *Magyar emléklapok* had a secret Pest meeting place they called the Golden Bull. Here, according to Szilágyi, discussion flowed freely and could be critical and biting for no spies were present.[79] Although "every rank of society was permeated with spies, there were countless places where one felt completely safe."[80] Subversive poems were passed from hand to hand. Journalists "found ways" to smuggle allusions into print. Some were imprisoned for their writings, but reemerged to write again.[81] And when words went public, such as in Szilágyi's journal, leading writers in hiding used pseudonyms that were quickly deciphered by insiders.[82] Jókai's histrionic style, for instance, was identifiable to all "except those in the New Building," that is, the Pest administrative center of the occupation. Even a previously unpublished poem by Petőfi appeared.[83] The censorship of the immediate post-revolutionary year was actually less stringent than it would become, for firm statutes and regulations did not yet exist. Theoretically anything was possible, or nothing was possible. Rules simply required that material be submitted after it had been printed, delaying distribution three to eight days pending review. This allowed for leakage in small amounts of subsequently banned material but led to self-censorship by publishers who needed to avoid potentially large losses. German language newspapers, such as the *Pester Zeitung* and *Pressburger Zeitung* were transformed into quasi-official organs aimed at the *Gutgesinnt.*[84]

A police spy who toured the markets and main squares of Pest that year reported no trace of "politicizing." He credited this to the inclement weather and the constant patrols of the gendarmes who seemed to pass by every three minutes.[85] With guns strapped across their shoulders, the gendarmes manned the gates of every city and small town. They checked travelers' passports and aimed to keep suspicious people out of urban areas.[86] In 1850 the gendarmerie made 48,000 arrests. This included: 19,180 suspicious persons, 4,228 recruits absent without leave, 1,484 persons for illegal weapon possessions, 206 agitators, 144 escapees, and 19 spies, as well as 320 highwaymen and 6,455 robbers.[87]

Every year yet another conspiracy seemed to be uncovered, such as the Makk conspiracy discovered in Transylvania in 1851, and others broken up in 1852 and 1853. The revolution of 1848 may have begun in Pest, but in the fifties the urban world was the domain of the *Gutgesinnt* and had to be written off by revolutionaries. Exiled revolutionaries could wax poetic about a specter of 180,000 lower class men who had taken up arms in 1848, and conjecture, that they would do so again "at the bidding of the educated class."[88] But Kossuth's insurrectionary plans now presumed guerrilla fighting in the countryside, rather than an urban revolution. His followers created conspiratorial organizations, but they were caught in the dilemma that once they went beyond the confines of secrecy, it inevitably led to mass arrests.

Gendarmerie regiments blanketed rural regions. Village outposts were manned by a corporal and between five and eight men, who reported to supervisory units staffed by three or four gendarmes and a non-commissioned officer. And these, in turn, were part of a larger net of two more posts. The system required constant correspondence, and at least six inspection tours a year. The gendarme was at first well paid and well disciplined; the posts were staffed by veteran non-commissioned officers whom Kempen had picked from the ranks. On their daily patrols the gendarmerie had made a favorable impression on the countryside where the peasantry was tired of marauding ex-soldiers and growing lawlessness. They were ordered to watch the eight hundred taverns, forty coffeehouses, and other public places, but were not to enter private homes without the written authorization from political authorities. In spiked helmets, double-breasted green coats trimmed with gold lace, and light gray pants with a red stripe down the side, the gendarmes investigated murders and robberies, and dealt with fires, floods, and other emergencies.

They patrolled the rural highways, stopped suspicious persons, and ferreted out conspiracies. Once the initial crisis of lawlessness had been checked the Hungarian peasantry relapsed into suspicion. The gendarmes could never overcome their image as the "brutal myrmidons," "selected from the army," or abroad.[89] Just the sight of an approaching gendarme could throw a village household into turmoil and fear.[90] When police cornered one former Honvéd, a crowd of neighbors watched in horror as the fugitive leapt to his death. The crowd's distressed scream was followed by threatening gestures that prompted authorities to call in the army.[91] Among the largely illiterate peasantry hope and defiance were identified with the highwayman, outlaw, and rural criminal caught in a cat and mouse game with the increasingly scorned gendarmerie. The gendarmerie came to view the problem of rural criminality as a special threat to their authority.

Their campaign against rural gangs was followed with avid interest but received little assistance from the public. "During the Bach period, rather than worry about our developing national feeling, the Germanizers worried about breaking Hungarian Robin Hoodism."[92] Perhaps, the *betyár* (bandit) label had been used too often as an epithet against Magyars generally. In any case, public sympathy was increasingly with the *betyárs*. Without aid from the people on the plain, the police did not do well in the hunt for the *betyárs*. The gendarmes were forced to play hide-and-go-seek with the highwaymen and found themselves being mocked and watched as they pursued the outlaw gangs. Ironically, the disarming of the populace had the effect of maximizing the power of the *betyár*. One resident living on the edge of the plain complained about the lack of law and order despite the frequent patrols, adding the *betyárs* were in effect "extracting a tax" and creating their own form of "relief institutions."[93] A cult of the brigand can be found in other distressed rural areas of Europe in the 1850s.[94] However, unlike southern Italy, the Hungarian phenomenon remained identified with the revolution. In the vast and desolate Hungarian plain, outlaw bands, occasionally as large as two hundred men, operated with an impunity and freedom that excited popular imagination. As long as these rebel bands roamed the plain, the prospect of a rising seemed to remain alive. The image of *betyárs* ready to rise was the last holdout of the rebellious crowd.

When a *betyár* was hung in Félegyház in 1852, he became the subject of a popular song among the young women of the town.[95] Just as ex-Confederate guerrilla fighters like Jesse James entered American lore as famous leaders of outlaw gangs, so Sándor Rózsa (1813–78) became the most famous of all Hungarian *betyárs*.[96] Rózsa's escapes from the gendarmerie were followed closely by the invisible crowd, and every time he cheated the hangman his legend grew. The Bach system had to contend with highwaymen, ex-Honvéd drifters, and the wealth of legends, folk ballads, and folk tales that developed around Sándor Rózsa. He captured the imagination of the populace, and "Sándor Rózsa" remains a favorite nickname for wild young sons. In ballad he became the Robin Hood of the *puszta* (prairie): "He took from the rich and gave to the vagabonds." [97]

Rózsa was usually portrayed as having never killed anyone in an act of thievery; his crimes, it was said, were fabricated by the Austrians, who wanted revenge for his exceptional success in revolutionary battle. The bandit had, in fact, joined Kossuth's divisions. At the end of the 1850s, when he was finally caught, the prosecutor warned that the connection of his name with revolutionary actions had won him "in the eyes of the people a kind of popularity and political meaning in which the revulsion at his misdeeds is outweighed by his political impact."[98] Rózsa was glamorized as Honvéd turned guerrilla, celebrated for his valor, and raised to mythic proportions. In this fantasy, he was invincible, no bullet ever struck him although he always led the charge; he was drinking buddy of Petőfi, intimate of Kossuth, and benefactor of the cause.[99] People took comfort and pleasure in these stories, in the imagined chase between the gendarmerie and Sándor Rózsa on the wild, barren puszta.

Unable to adjust to civilian life, many former soldiers had become half-guerrillas, half-criminals—blurring the line between suffering patriots and riffraff.

> I don't have a homeland; Görgey sold us out;
> I don't have law, the tyrant trampled it,
> What law governs me?
> Without my homeland, what can I love?
>
> I fought the battle,
> With sad heart now roam the puszta,
> This puszta, although no towering rock pile,
> I think of as freedom's temple.
>
> For freedom, I endure and wait,
> Where are those gendarmes
> Who dare not come into the puszta?
> If they came, they would arrest me sooner.
>
> I am a *betyár*, that's what I'm called.
> I swear to God, I am not ashamed of my calling.
> I will be that, perhaps not much longer,
> For soon they will need Honvéds and Hussars.[100]

These legends had their basis in fact. Former Honvéds were forced into hiding, sometimes living out in the puszta in desperate circumstances. Rural poverty persisted in these years. The newly freed peasants longed for land, but continuing bad harvests and increased taxes left them frustrated and discontented. The Magyar "Robin Hood" legends drew sustenance from the ubiquitous reports or rumors of Honvéd-*betyár*s stopping travelers and politely asking for money. Supposedly, if refused, they did not resort to violence, but rather, rebuked the traveler with a civics lesson on patriotism. At the telling, listeners would lament the "poor Honvéds!"[101] The notion that defeated soldiers had to steal for food pulled at the heartstrings of the population. By projecting the vision of a just society onto the brigand, the existing legal system was condemned as banditry.

The identification of Hungary with the condemned peasant criminal would be memorialized in Mihály Munkácsy's painting, *In the Cell of the Condemned* (1869).[102] In it a peasant criminal awaits his execution. As was customary in Hungary, visitors have come to say farewell. It is in fact a genre painting of peasants from the puszta, but with a difference, for the scenery is the unrelenting darkness of a prison cell. Despite the group of figures watching him, the convict remains quite alone in his misery; his young wife grieves alone, and the urchins stand alone. Yet the crime and the punishment have brought a shared grief to all. The painting provokes an unequivocal empathy and pathos possible only because the peasant-criminal on death row could be transposed to stand for Hungary's executed Honvéds. The convicted man possessed virtú, a strength unbroken by his fate. When first exhibited in Paris in 1870, it won acclaim from the leading French critics as a daring portrayal of a largely unknown people.[103] When Munkácsy repainted the scene in 1872, he removed the group of figures.[104] The uninterested guard remains in the background, but the *betyár* receives the viewer's full attention. The *betyár* had become the symbol of Hungary, of a people whose history was purely suffering and restriction, and still they remained strong.[105]

Kossuth's Foreign Crowd

A bust of Kossuth hung from a chain above one prison commander's desk. Every martyrology has a list of villains. The counter-revolution nailed their list to the gibbet, while the defeated particularly vented their wrath at the dictator Haynau, the traitor Görgey, and the villainess Archduchess Sophia. "Sophia, the mother of the present usurper of Hungary," was to be "cursed through all posterity," proclaimed Kossuth during his tour of America, for she was "the source of all misfortune which now weighs so heavily upon my bleeding fatherland." This "ambitious mother of the young Nero, Franz Joseph" was the "evil genius" oppressing the down-trodden fatherland. "History has, to be sure, recorded the downfall of mighty empires, of nations, to whom compared, the Magyars can scarcely claim a name. But the fall of those nations was precisely the revelation of the eternal justice of God. They fell by their own crimes. Nations die, but by suicide. That is not our case. Hungary is not the sacrifice of its own crimes. An ambitious woman has in the palace of Vienna the sacrilegious dream to raise a child to the seat of power upon the ruins of liberty."[106]

The counterpoint to a martyrology focusing on unjust defeat and persecution was a demonology, i.e. a negative dialogue with the repressors. Nationalist rhetoric blended demonology and martyrology. Its demonology was as extroverted as its martyrology was introverted. A martyr is a witness for his cause; the demon is a figure to be driven from one's environment. As a tool for mobilization, Kossuth excoriated individuals so as to indict the system that had gotten the upper hand. Archduchess Sophia was, however, simply a code word; for a demonology, unlike a martyrology, is usually not addressing individuals but damning a system. While martyrology is central to Christianity, symbolized by Jesus on the cross, Jesus had instructed his followers not to demonize their enemies. Christian martyrology focuses on the strength of one's own faith and accepts one's own defeat. Martyrs were to die and there was no need, therefore, to focus hatred on the blinded persecutors. Instead, hope lies in the exemplary purity of the act. A demonology insists on targeting opponents, because the hope is that once the repressor is identified and exposed reversal is possible. Demonology turns the martyr's aggression against the system. By externalizing the problem, demonology calls forth the hope of external liberation. Demonology extended the moral demand to outsiders. The foreign crowd would be needed to mobilize for that future deliverance. Meanwhile, the possessed wait, rethinking and reformulating their relation to the system in a way that the masochism of martyrology does not encourage.

Probably every army has a stab-in-the-back legend in reserve in case of defeat. In the Vidin Letter of September 1849, Kossuth fingered General Görgey as the "accursed man." Kossuth thus displaced the responsibility of defeat from his shoulders to that of Görgey and tried to turn the anger of the defeated from the Austrians to the Russians. The Hungarian army was quite probably on the verge of defeat when the Russians intervened, but the perception that the Russian invasion had been decisive served Kossuth's diplomatic purposes by appealing to a Russophobic public opinion in England and France.[107] Also the sorrowful theme of falling victim to a greedy traitor did much for Kossuth's reputation, and it blended well into the funereal mood of lamentation that was being spread through popular songs. The somber lyrics evoked the "darkening of the Hungarian sky" or "ancestral graves being stomped on by the *muzhik.*"[108] Mihály Vörösmarty's 1850 poem, "Átok" (Curse), gave the myth of the traitor high cultural resonance. The legend of Görgey's betrayal fostered a nagging "what if" in popular discourse.

With the Hungarian population cut off from the world, their passports confiscated, press controlled, and letters under surveillance, they became prone to rumors about external forces. As the populace was gradually losing its sense of what was still probable, military and administrative officials complained that the lack of newspapers opened the gate wide to all kinds of whispered propaganda and rumors. The most absurd tales—English-Turkish-Magyar armies amassing at the border, pressure from the Americans and English, the falling out of the Austrians and the Russians—were widely believed. The population proved susceptible to rumors of imminent war and revolution, especially with Kossuth and his émigré cadre mobilizing abroad.

During the revolution the identification with the Hungarian rebel fighters of the past, the *kuruc,* in their struggle with the *labanc,* the Hungarian imperial soldiers, underscored the historic reach of the present conflict. By 1849 an almost mystical connection was being drawn between Ferenc Rákóczi II (1676–1735) and Kossuth.[109] In Rákóczi's rebellion against the Habsburgs, Rákóczi had assumed the title of "governing prince," eschewing that of king. But by 1707 the rebellion had escalated into a struggle to dethrone the Habsburgs in Hungary. The charismatic leadership of Rákóczi, like Kossuth, was able to sustain the struggle even as Habsburg power had strengthened and the cost of resistance had grown. Rákóczi was finally betrayed by his supporters, who sued for peace while he was abroad seeking foreign assistance. After Világos, the surrender at Nagymajtény seemed all too relevant, and new historicizing legends cast 1848–9 into the mold of the failed revolt of 1703–11. The lessons of Rákóczi's failed anti-Habsburg war also fed the fantasy of a second chance. Rákóczi had mustered his anti-Habsburg forces and fashioned an international alliance in France during the War of the Spanish Succession. Perhaps, an opportunity would come for Kossuth to build a similar foreign alliance. The legends of an idealistic Rákóczi betrayed by a selfish Sándor Károlyi, Rákóczi's flight into Turkish exile and his imminent return were transposed unto Kossuth. The cult of Rákóczi was strongest in Protestant northeastern Hungary; *kuruc* legends had less resonance in Catholic Transdanubia. The oral tradition evoked the fallen hero's tragic situation, expressed nationalistic pride, and sustained hope in the leader's eventual return. The lament of Jeremiah was the model for these popular legends.[110]

In the poignant love ballads of separated lovers, popular at the time, the young Honvéd had gone off forever to fight for Kossuth in the noble cause. Hungarian boys continued to imagine themselves armed and prepared to march in Kossuth's army at that hour when victory was still possible, when they, too, could have been proud heroes of a living cause. "The Kossuth Song," with its six-hundred variants, was initially sung as a recruiting ditty during the general mobilization of December 1848. It evoked the experience of 1848 more strongly than anything else, and therefore, the public singing of "The Kossuth Song" would be the favored act of defiance in the next decade-and-a-half.[111] Cheers for Kossuth or wearing the national tricolor were grounds for arrest in the fifties. In Szeged, on one market day in 1851 when the town was filled with peasants, a file of prisoners crossed the spot where Kossuth had delivered a recruiting speech two years before. The first prisoner in line suddenly stopped, took off his hat, and shouted repeatedly "Éljen Kossuth!" The whole square suddenly joined the refrain, and Austrian forces were called out to prevent any serious incident.[112] The very cry "Éljen!" became suspect among the authorities, who feared any cheer would turn into a yell of "Éljen Kossuth!" Occasionally, prescriptions for disobedience, supposedly from Kossuth, appeared on wall placards, or in proclamations and manifestos that were passed around.[113] "Éljen Kossuth" graffiti was commonplace. One Miskolc placard sent the dynasty and Franz Joseph to hell. Even at the local casino someone penciled in "scoundrel" (*gazember*) under the picture of the emperor. The steady stream of reports from the elaborate governmental spy network only served to reinforce official apprehension.[114]

Eliminating the Kossuthite threat was frustrated by foreign interference. When the Habsburgs seized a former Honvéd from an American ship in Turkish waters, it created a major international incident, prompting the United States to issue the first international ultimatum in its history.[115] The Americans would subsequently welcome Hungary's fallen leader Kossuth with great excitement. In 1851 Kossuth attracted some of the largest political crowds the western world had ever seen in his impassioned rendition of Hungarian martyrdom and the tragedy of his exile. "My country was martyred! Her rulers are hangmen!" was the principal message he brought his audiences.[116] He succeeded in making of the Hungarians what the Poles had been to the previous generation of Englishmen and Americans— martyrs in the march to progress.[117] No revolutionary before or during the nineteenth-century had such an international impact or created such a stir as Kossuth.[118] In London his arrival seemed like a coronation day. Trafalgar Square was "black with people" and Nelson's Monument peopled "up to the fluted shaft."[119] Throngs crying "Long live Kossuth! Down with Austria!" filled the main arteries and the procession took hours to make its way through the main streets. Kossuth knew how to flatter his audiences. England was "the most glorious spot on earth," and he was vociferous in his toasts: "May England ever be great, glorious, and free!"[120] He told the English that "We are now where you were after 1665. Only time went on. It will not last so long. Look to history. Restored dynasties have no future."[121] With the English he stressed the legality of his actions and the promise of constitutionalism; in America he evoked republicanism.

A captivated throng of a hundred thousand awaited him in New York. It was the largest crowd that had ever gathered for a procession in America. The city rocked with tumultuous shouting. Kossuth's charisma must have been extraordinary for he presented his orations before over five hundred crowds in America, and everywhere he was heard by large excited audiences. Men cheered; women swooned. The telegraph made it possible for the literate of a vast region to follow Kossuth's tour, escalating the popular excitement.[122] His tour and the Crimean War were the two hot topics of the new mass press in the first half of the 1850s. As such, Kossuth's tour deserves to be acknowledged as a fantastic achievement, a world-wide press sensation. The attempt of the German revolutionary poet Gottfried Kinkel to emulate Kossuth by undertaking a similar tour of the United States met with little success. Kossuth had single-handedly upstaged the much larger German exile community. Within the popular mind in the English-speaking world, the problem of the defeated of 1848 came to revolve around Hungary. Heinrich Heine's poem, "In October 1849," paid homage to Petőfi and the Hungarians who went down fighting like heroes, unlike his fellow Germans for whom the end was theatrical and false. Friedrich Engels expressed similar sentiments.[123]

Not only had Kossuth been received with enthusiasm, but politicians and notables offered gestures of support at every juncture—a fact that did not go unnoticed in the home country. Kossuth, it was presumed, had created moral capital to use in barter later with the Austrians. This successful dramatization of the Hungarian cause in the English-speaking world came at a moment when gaining American support seemed important in Europe. Alexis de Tocqueville's prophecy of America's future had just been popularized. But more importantly, in 1848 America had become the symbol of a republican future. In his last Hungarian speech before fleeing into exile, Kossuth had declared, "My principles were those of Washington."[124] America, in turn, had become involved in European affairs during the revolutions, with many American politicians, such as Abraham Lincoln, joining the Hungary Committees of 1848.

The celebratory, affirming crowds abroad were assumed to be a portent of a future in which Hungarian crowds would grace a Hungarian Republic. But reversing defeat required action. "The most important lessons you give to Europe," he told a delegation from Newburgh, New York, the site of George Washington's headquarters, "is in the organization of the militia of the United States. You have the best organized army in the world, and yet you have scarcely a standing army at all. That is a necessary thing for Europe to learn from America—that great standing armies must cease."[125] Kossuth expressed the hope that Americans would become "the La Fayettes of Hungary."[126] And he asserted that "Either the Continent of Europe has no future at all, or this future is American Republicanism."[127]

Kossuth presented himself to his American hosts as "the wandering son of a bleeding nation," a homeless exile representing "my down-trodden land," with his authority resting on the fact that "my people took, and take me still, for the incarnated personification of their wishes, their sentiments, their affections, and their hopes. Is it not then quite natural that the woes of my people also should be embodied in myself? I have the concentrated woes of millions of Magyars in my breast."[128] He also occasionally likened himself to the defeated Hannibal in exile. In Philadelphia, he became so affected after declaiming "the dying bid you farewell! and in bidding you this farewell, I will bless you with the warmest wishes of my heart, and to pray to God that the Sun of Freedom may never decline from the horizon of your happy land," that he was overcome with tears. The audience was deeply moved, rising as a whole to their feet, and joining in hearty cheers.[129] At the banquet held by Congress in Kossuth's honor on January 7, 1852, he likened the American Congress to the Roman Senate, and then declaimed that the United States did the Romans one better, for while Rome scorned "unfortunate exiles," and "misfortune was only introduced with fettered hands to kneel at the triumphant conqueror's heels," in the New World "the persecuted chief of a down-trodden nation is welcomed as your great Republic's guest, precisely because he is persecuted, helpless and poor."[130] Kossuth was profuse in his gratitude to America for having freed him from an "Asiatic jail."[131] He contrasted his fate to that of his American audiences with their "happy home. Freedom and Home, what heavenly music in those two words! Alas, I have no home."[132]

The combination of Shakespearean rhetoric and a secularized martyrology gave Hungarian anger a resonating voice. Nationalist martyrology patterned itself on Christian martyrology. Of all religions, Christianity most vividly retains memory of its historical achievements through the cult of believers and martyrs. In the ecclesiastical histories of the lives and sufferings of martyrs, the profession of faith and the drama of persecution were at the center of religiosity. In the oldest surviving Christian martyrology, *The Martyrdom of Polycarp* (A.D. 155), the themes were set, including betrayal and courageous endurance of suffering. The Christians of Smyrna rushed to claim Polycarp's remains, "more precious to us than jewels, and finer than pure gold—and we laid them to rest in a spot suitable for the purpose . . . and with the Lord's permission we shall celebrate the birthday of his martyrdom. It will serve both as commemoration of all who have triumphed before, and as training and a preparation for any whose crown may be still to come."[133] Christianity historicized its own advance in these martyrologies and in annual ritual commemorations of the relics. Through the pilgrimage the medieval church wove this culture into peasant religious life, with localities everywhere seeking to sacralize their own saints and martyrs. Hungarian nationalist martyrology appealed to Catholic and Protestant sensibilities. The initial impulse of the Reformation was to severely restrict the cult of martyrs, but when Protestantism came under attack Protestants developed their own martyrology. The printing press publicized the persecution of co-religionists across Europe. The new vernacular reading publics also enjoyed the martyrologies as stories of personal heroism. Women, a growing element in the reading public, were also appreciative of the pedagogic value of martyrologies as companion volumes to the Bible in the home.

While Hungarian women nurtured martyrologies of defeat at home, Kossuth did not expect American audiences to spend their sympathy on a corpse. He could change the flow of sentiment and suddenly declare that Hungary had suffered a mere "temporary failure," proclaiming "the trumpet of the resurrection of the enslaved millions shall sound."[134] His Hun-

garian martyrology played on parallels with the Israelites or the New England Puritans, who had visualized themselves as holdouts of the true
covenant, suffering the martyrdom of the bereaved "colony" of faith. In
America, Franz Joseph was cast in the role of George III, and Kossuth per-
sonified a global struggle for republican principles. Kossuth's ideals made
sense to Americans, and they assumed that the right ideals would eventually prevail. Therefore, Kossuth was celebrated as a winner rather than a
loser. This was seen as a historical struggle over fundamental values in
which Hungarians, for the moment, were the people on the front lines. This
response toward Kossuth oxygenated Hungarian hope.

Kossuth's tour of America played on the Hungarian imagination. There
were fanciful folk drawings and tales told, such as a popular novel in
which Kossuth encountered Indians and fought wolves in the Wild West.
Hungarian popular culture reaffirmed its sense of alienation by turning
Kossuth into an icon of hope, the affirmation of the dignity of the fallen.
The laments of the period were associated with his name. His fame was
spread by folk ballad, and into his person were assimilated many older
myths and songs such as of the savior from outside, come to liberate the
people from harsh conditions and tyranny. "I was your king, Lajos Kossuth," answered the stranger to the squire; in another legend, "Kossuth
Wanders Through the Countryside," he is enforcing justice for the peasants
vis-à-vis the gentry.[135]

Kossuth's foreign adventures were, however, too unique to his person
and conditions abroad, making them impossible to emulate within the
country. Kossuth's demonology was, ultimately, too apocalyptic. The discrepancy between Kossuth's oratory abroad and the silence bred by enforced quietism at home highlighted the exile community's growing di-
vergence from the reality in the homeland and its impoverished political
speech.[136] In Hungary the experience of defeat required a recognition that
the system of ideas which had sustained action during the revolution had
collapsed and that action was unequivocally restricted. Hungarians continually combed over their memories in order to make sense of their situation.
Memory at home became a hybrid between that which had happened and
solutions for life in the present. Émigré memory was more static. Thus
Kossuth's actual political sway waned, even while he was being mythologized in a cult of hero worship.[137] Never again would Hungarian national
identity be so celebrated by foreigners but feel so vulnerable within the
country as in the reactionary early fifties. Kossuth's message from America to his people was, "Be patient; hope, and wait thy time!"[138] "Be faith-

ful as hitherto, keep to the holy sentences of the Bible, pray for thy liberation, and then chant thy national hymns when the mountains reecho the thunder of the cannons of thy liberators!"[139] This was the prescription for an unquiet wait: sustaining the invisible crowd through hymns, prayer, and memory. The 1848 revolution was pivotal, but the martyrology of defeat after 1849 only brought Hungary the sudden fame of an Andy Warhol variety: Each suffering small nation can be famous for fifteen minutes.

Lajos Kossuth greeted by a massive crowd in New York, December 6, 1851. Watercolor (Hungarian National Museum, Historical Picture Gallery)

5

The Unquiet Wait

Economic and social expansion in the post-revolutionary decade engendered a dynamism that dispersed but never dissipated the deep pools of nationalist sentiment. Neo-absolutism was never a still pond. Fear of the crowd remained a motivating factor in policy decisions, but to emphasize repression, the absence of activity, is to miss an essential quality of this period in which the newspapers took off and urbanization hit its stride. Mass communication and mass transportation meant public popular expression and public massing was inevitable. The counter-revolutionary system stepped into this era not to extinguish crowd politics, but to seize, refashion, and use it. To achieve stability and order the Habsburg regime needed to cajole and ultimately to convince the public of the efficacy of the new regime. Its new bureaucracy aimed to manage this crowd, while Hungarian nationalism settled into an unquiet wait until the system would be buffeted sufficiently for the crowd to return.

The difficulties of working with a population that was cowed, but hostile, quickly moved the Habsburg regime toward new tactics. The "Bach system" would attempt to master and stage the pageantry of urban life. The Habsburgs would reanimate the public space with festive programs that trumpeted their modern bureaucratic state. In the 1850s monarchism went on display. Napoleon III, Tsar Nicholas I, and Franz Joseph each subjected themselves to grand public tours of their domains. But in the interstices of official festivity, they also inadvertently permitted the scattered, occasional reappearance of the repressed liberal crowd. These were not just depoliticized, desultory, and disconnected moments. Hungarian nationalist sentiment was waiting backstage, convinced that counter-revolution would be unable to hold the audience's attention.

The Priesthood of Order

In pursuit of order, the regime harkened back to three basic pillars: support for dynasty, revival of religion, and creation of a modern, efficient bureaucracy. The figure of Alexander Bach (1813–1893) became the glue, symbol, and lightning rod of the 1850s. Often credited as the founder of the modernizing, if often Kafkaesque bureaucracy of Central Europe, Bach was "affable," "polite," perhaps even charismatic.[1] The minister of the interior was ideological in the manner of a renegade; he claimed to know what he opposed. The "barricade minister" of March 1848 had survived by reversing direction and moving ever further right. All historical experience since the revolution of 1830, particularly the convulsions of the preceding years, had shown, he argued, that the radicals were hardly going to be intimidated by their heavy defeat, but would rather find in the blows brought on them merely a stimulus to take up their international struggle with renewed vigor.[2] The administrative system he organized was counter-revolutionary rather than conservative, for its practitioners had learned from the revolution and in many ways attempted to outdo the revolutionaries in their tactics. While Metternich had sought to inoculate society against the "contagion" of revolution, Bach dreamed of so transforming society through bureaucratic initiatives that the revolutionary would find himself out of place in the new society. "Neo-absolutism" was "neo" in its insistence on public persuasion, and Bach would use the name "Neuösterreich" in all official terminology. Metternich had seen himself in a rearguard, lifelong battle against the temptations of revolution, an enlightenment man turning back the fantasies of romanticism; Bach emphasized his disregard for historical tradition. He prided himself on his realism.[3]

As Felix zu Schwarzenberg's indispensable man, his man Friday, Bach was in the position to develop a new propaganda apparatus. Not for nothing had he been called Caliban by fellow members of the Shakespeare Society of Vienna before the revolution. A friend of the poet Nicholas von Lenau, Bach was attuned to the power of the word. An amateur actor himself, Bach was convinced that the German theater was important as a social institution and practiced a fiscal largesse toward the German theaters in Pest, Buda, and the provinces. Simplicity, efficiency, and speed were the watchwords of his method; his practice was constantly to monitor public opinion through monthly mood reports from the counties, weekly reports dispatched from Pest on the Saturday night train, and use of the telegraph for breaking news. Bach was even willing to tolerate public opinion in the press and legal assemblies, although here he found himself often blocked by Generals Kempen and Karl Ludwig Grünne. Bach's propaganda aimed at forcing the Hungarian population to an awareness that the defeat of 1849 was final, that the power of the monarchy was invincible, and that foreign opinion had lost interest in the appeals of the exiles. Hungarians were to be convinced that they were not really in a position to maintain their statehood independently and only neo-absolutism ensured permanence and growth. It was in Hungarian self-interest to submit to Austrian leadership. In return, the Hungarian population was promised peace and prosperity, and to a surprising degree the Bach system would deliver on its promises. Nor would it be shy in advertising its achievements.

To his turn-of-the-century admirer Heinrich Friedjung, Bach was an enigma. He was "without any qualification the greatest administrative talent of Austria and Hungary in the nineteenth century."[4] Yet this "liberal" supported a clerical dismantling of the secular Josephinist tradition, becoming one of the architects of the Concordat with the Vatican in 1855. Bach was convinced that the Concordat would help solve not only the Italian and the Hungarian problems but would also overcome national prejudices.[5] Pope Pius IX, for his part, had abandoned Italian nationalism and now embraced Austria as his savior; together they could fight revolutionism.[6] Political opportunism played a role; Bach needed the protection of Archduchess Sophia, Bishop (later Cardinal) Josef Ottmar Rauscher, and Cardinal Schwarzenberg against the military who wished him gone. Bach's increasingly conspicuous piety would become a butt of mockery; many officers from the provinces made it a point to go to the church adjoining the ministries to see Bach in his daily devotions. There on his knees he seemed more pious than any of the other worshippers. His religious politics was not simply a ploy. Family background somewhat explains Bach's turn. Bach's uncle was a priest; his father had considered the vocation as well. When Bach was raised into the nobility he chose as his motto, *In cruce spes mea* (My hope is in the cross). Bach would conclude his government career as ambassador to the Vatican.

The religious component of neo-absolutism was not incidental but a motivating factor at its inception. Franz Joseph understood the Hungarian rebellion as a violation of the religious basis of monarchy that deserved whatever chastisement it received.[7] The "Bach system" would attempt to master the pageantry of urban life by invoking a spiritual mission predicated on remorse and redemption. But first the priesthood of order had to be purified. The Hungarian Catholic Church found itself compromised after the revolution. The revolutionary government had filled many vacancies in its effort to bind the church to the revolution; the counter-revolution responded by purging the hierarchy. At the war's end Cardinal János Hám, the prince primate, expressed his satisfaction that the nation was once again peaceful and the rebellion had been stopped. But Hám was forced to resign, for he was simply too compromised to head the religious reorganization of the monarchy that was planned by Bach and his allies. Hám was replaced by the loyalist Slovak, János Scitovszky, who had officiated thanksgiving services for the Habsburg victory on October 4, 1849, the day after the Komárom surrender and two days before the Arad executions as well as a funeral mass on November 8 for the fallen Habsburg soldiers. His pastoral letter on occasion of his induction in January 1850 declared: "We trespassed against God, against the church, the sovereign, the dear homeland," because "we listened to the advice of deceitful masters, we believed in false prophets." It was also rumored the primate even considered moving his official residence from Esztergom (the "Magyar Zion") to Pest because of the great coldness he had encountered in Esztergom.[8] Primate Scitovszky's repeated calls for a public act of penance for revolutionary sin became the source of bitter humor among those who wished to remain true to their political sin of having supported the revolution.[9] With an unsympathetic Slovak as the symbolic leader, a pall hung over the Magyar Catholic Church. Scitovszky would, however, insist on a measure of Hungarian church jurisdiction. He resisted the concordat in its centralization of church affairs. This would set into play a triangular relationship between Vienna, Esztergom, and Rome, which lessened the stigma of collaboration and would enable the Hungarian clergy to become a focus of opposition as the decade progressed.

While Bach's system ostensibly targeted the scattered "rebels," he downplayed their actual threat, opposing the state of siege already in December 1849, referring to it as a *testimonium paupertatis*. His true antagonists were the Old Conservatives, who rejected his policies even as they shared a number of Bach's assumptions, such as the desirability of monarchical rule in Hungary and the need for a continued long-term military presence. Bach's bureaucracy aimed at freeing Hungary from the control of a rigid caste. In Bach's view, Hungarians had lost the right to rule in the Kingdom of St. Stephen, in part, because of their historic weakness that had led to their subjugation by the Turks and because of their incompetence in dealing with other ethnic groups within the kingdom that had become manifest in the revolution. Hungarians were to be punished for their pride, their claim of separateness, which had upset the relations between the nationalities within the monarchy. Bach rejected the Old Conservative agenda of a reconstituted Hungarian aristocracy playing the role of loyal feudatories to their Habsburg sovereign as outdated and unrealistic. The counter-revolution's claim to realism rested on the assumption that the nationalist vision was backward looking, while the imperial bureaucracy was on an advanced track. New principles of public order would replace the old code. The aristocracy's monopoly over official posts and a backward decentralization needed to be replaced. A new theory of authority would counter the old assumptions and ideas about the nature and proper ordering of ethnic groups and their relationship to their Habsburg ruler. "We stick eternally to the observation: You have had no bureaucrats for a thousand years in your country. Why are the people poor, uneducated? Why is agriculture at such a primitive level? Why do you have no industry, no commerce? Why does one sink in your streets? Why is your elementary education with such a rich and powerful church so miserable? Why are your institutions of higher learning a satire of science/learning?"[10] Was it not time to turn one's back on the idol of the old county administration and the old patriarchal system and try to create a new *Kulturstaat*?

The unfolding Austro-Prussian war scare in the summer of 1850 revived nationalist sentiment and spread skepticism that multinational systems could expunge nationalism. The Austrian expatriate Anton Heinrich Springer wrote, that to ask the Italian, the Slav, the German, etc., to feel himself to be just an Austrian was to enforce a kind of celibacy on him.[11] Springer, living in Prussia, saw no future in Austria. The confident *kleindeutsch* view of Austria was that the multinational monarchy was finished. As Schwarzenberg's consummate bluffing drove the Prussians to a choice of war or diplomatic defeat, it seemed to one Viennese commentator that not since the Thirty Years War had Germany presented such a spectacle of turmoil, bitterness, resentment, and division.[12] In isolated Hungary the external crisis prompted rumors of imminent deliverance and fanned defiant public gestures. General Bem, it was said, was invading with a Turkish-Magyar force of forty thousand cavalry. As fantasies emboldened the oppositional spirit, Bach's reform plans became more central. Official mood reports continued to attest to a calm mood, but there was tension in the air. Authorities worried over what lurked below the surface. One report fretted over the fact that the educated classes "either completely hid their feelings or express them only to confidantes."[13] The Pest gendarmerie found itself breaking up dance hall fistfights between soldiers and civilians in September. The most serious confrontation was one with over fifty young artisans in the City Park sporting large black feathers in their caps and red bandannas around their throats, accompanied by young women, mainly cigar workers, wearing tricolors in their hats and hair.[14]

In the Austro-Prussian confrontation, Schwarzenberg succeeded in rallying legitimism against Prussia. Prussia's humiliating diplomatic retreat in November seemed to reverse the irreversible march of nationalism and validated the Bach system. Bach's revival of supranational imperial ideology appeared capable of challenging the prevailing sentiment of the age. From the Austro-Prussian war scare of 1850 to the outbreak of the Austro-Italian war of 1859, the strictures of neo-absolutism that had descended upon the Hungarian landscape assumed an air of normalcy. In face of what was being seen as the Schwarzenberg-Bach juggernaut, Old Conservatives and exiles converged in lamenting the loss of a way of life, "swept away" in the suppression of local "self-government . . . replaced by the most despotic centralization."[15] The exile Bartholomew Szemere remembered Hungary as among the least centralized polities in Europe, with one hundred-twenty local jurisdictions having oversight over "police, roads, sanitary regulations, hospitals, schools, charitable institutions, prisons."[16] Szemere considered these "municipal assemblies" as the "nursery of patriots . . . our training-schools for statesmen."[17] Now, however, the country, he lamented, was occupied by "two armies"—"one of *soldiers*, the other of foreign *placemen*."[18]

Until 1844 the bureaucracy in Hungary had been a noble monopoly. Expansion of the bureaucracy in the late 1840s, particularly 1848–49, had resulted in an increase of nonnoble Hungarian officials.[19] After the purge of 1849–50, many nonnobles remained but were viewed as mere adjuncts to the "swarm of foreigners" set to "prey" on Hungary.[20] This irritation with the newcomers intensified when the Bach bureaucrats began entertaining lavishly, performing their expected function as centers of local social life. In the immediate post-revolutionary years, the salaries of bureaucrats were ample enough to permit them to play out the representational role that Bach initially envisaged for them. This contrasted sharply with the debilitating, short-term economic distress many gentry were enduring as a result of the dislocations of the revolution and the worthlessness of the Kossuth bank notes.

The regime demonstrated its full faith in the new priesthood of order that replaced the unreliable bureaucrats of 1848 by returning the ceremonial swords that had been taken away from them in 1849. One of the first measures taken after the lifting of the state of emergency in the fall of 1851 was the dressing of officials in a fanciful pseudo-Magyar costume.[21] The elaborate uniform cost almost half the bureaucrat's annual salary. The fur cap and flowing cloak; thin, tight pants; high boots and spurs were uncomfortable and required a servant's assistance to put on. Moreover, the fur cap and cloak were stifling in the summer, and the thin trousers were equally impractical in the winter. In these ghostbuster suits the bureaucrats participated in the illuminations, trumpet and drum roll entries, addressing a real, but usually invisible, crowd. Bright and garish, they were like exclamation marks that underscored the new order. In his glittering, shiny helmet, the official announced his approach from afar. Széchenyi wrote that in the countryside they were likened to corncrakes, a bird of the grain fields, because the bird's screech invariably revealed its whereabouts to the hunter.[22] The new uniforms "will have a great impact on the Hungarians," wrote one journalist in Vienna, "because they are so concerned with externals."[23]

Wearing conspicuous uniforms was a traditional means of emphasizing the presence of law enforcement, but the neo-absolutist bureaucratic costume made Magyars fume. While the gentry could wear their native Hungarian outfits only during carnival, the bureaucrat came out in his red and green getup claiming to represent Hungarianness on official holidays. They projected imperial authority in the absence of public display. The majority who donned the new uniform were Germans, Czechs, and other Slavic officials who "chose" to transfer to Hungary. Many attained positions they might never have received elsewhere, but others were all but forced to accept appointment in this hostile social environment. Just as the American South would be regaled for decades with stories of carpetbaggers and scalawags taking charge, so Hungarians would create a treasure chest of similar lore about their travails under the newly arrived bureaucrats knowing no Hungarian and often only faulty German. The populace was united in scorning the foreigners. The Hungarians developed the art of the patriotic put-down, especially toward the Bohemian officials, particularly German-speaking Czechs, who were flooding into the region. In one apocryphal story a lady complimented an official who sang well: "So it is true that every Bohemian is either a thief or a musician." Nationalist anger transformed such crudities into examples of patriotic gesture.[24]

Carnival enjoyed a special luster during the Bach era, because it allowed for feasting and dancing and the channeling of the rebellious instinct of the urban population. In Catholic tradition carnival was the counterpart to Lent, the fling before the penitential rigors of the fast. Carnival balls became important charity fund-raising events for local Magyar organizations (who thereby enhanced their presence in the community). But carnival also played on the tradition of the charivari with its role reversal and excess. Given its "symbolic grammar," carnival had always presented a "dynamic, oppositional description of a society." It emphasized sins of the flesh, glorified feasting, drinking, and the release of sexual inhibitions, and it could indulge momentary snipes at authority. This was the moment when the daring remark might go unreported and unpunished, when those in power might permit some modicum of mockery of their authority. At carnival time laughter might break through the oppression of official ideology.[25]

Carnival in the Bach era became an occasion not only to let off steam but to make a point as well. It was both a tool for adaptation and a weapon against the new politics and the militaristic crowds. During the difficult "winter," carnival season became a Magyar fling. "Despite the terrible straits of our country, we went from one lively dance to another during the long carnival season" of 1851, jotted a diarist, "and one was livelier than the next."[26] The newspapers were full of advertisements for elegant and lively balls in Pest, Buda, and the provinces. This was an occasion when people were drawn in from the countryside, as in Szeged where the Gypsy band was brought from Nagykőrös, and gentlemen with their daughters came from all the neighboring areas.[27] People became so wrapped up in carnival that young and old seemed to have "not cared about the home-land's unhappy condition!" They were enjoying themselves "as though our mourning wasn't real." Yet, there was awareness of the imperial colors, "the yellow-black ribbons always fluttering over us," and complaints about the new taxes coming "one after the other. . . . We would have been much bet-ter off if things had remained as they were before the revolution."[28] Focus of regret was shifting from the defeat of the revolution to the loss of pre-revolutionary conditions. The long carnival season finally came to an end, and people attempted to accommodate the routine of an unquiet wait.

Authorities were naturally suspicious of carnival. Many dance halls were closed down as subversive gathering places. But in time, officials re-lented to community arguments that they were losing valuable sources of revenue. Aside from the politically evocative events, carnival season brought a spate of other complaints: officials registered friction between classes, between neighbors, between lovers.[29] During the decade, carnival became an ever more extravagant respite, in part because of the relaxation of the dress code enforced throughout the rest of the year. Extraordinary Magyar outfits were stitched for carnival. Women skirted the limits as they danced the *csárdás* in their lavish Magyar dresses at balls that lasted until five a.m., week after week through January and February and into March. Although the Kossuth revolutionary cap was still illegal, men could wear them, if they removed the wide band and buckle.[30] Carnival evolved into a Magyar holiday, an opportunity for the gentry to snub the Bach Hussars by not inviting them to their fancy masquerades. There were often toasts to prerevolutionary conditions, a better future, and the hellish torments that justice would bring the "foreign officials."[31]

The Tour of 1852

In October 1851, Archduke Albrecht, the emperor's older cousin, arrived in Hungary to assume the new dual position of general governor and commanding general in Hungary, combining the two key institutions of the counter-revolution: the army and the bureaucracy. Albrecht was the most powerful anti-liberal figure in the monarchy, representing an unsympathetic, strict Habsburg presence on Hungarian soil.[32] His reputation to that effect preceded him: he had ordered the firing on a Salzburg crowd on March 13, 1848; served with Radetzky in Italy, and during the war crisis of 1850, commanded the key fortress of Mainz. He identified himself with the policy of the iron fist. His new office would subsume the post of palatine. The unseasoned Palatine Stephen had found himself caught in the middle during the revolution. He had initially supported the demands of the "aristocratic revolution," then balked at the proposition that he proclaim himself king of Hungary or that he subvert what the Viennese court denounced as the illegitimate Batthyány regime. Once the fighting began, the institution of the palatine collapsed, brushed aside by a suspicious court.

Before Albrecht took up residence, the Buda castle, which had suffered extensive damage, was rebuilt with record speed.[33] In the Hungarian lithographic iconography of 1849, the castle in flames was a central image. Its rapid rebuilding erased that visual sign of the opponent's triumph and emphasized the cursory nature of Hungarian "insolence." The discrepancy between the restored castle and the remaining shell damage in Pest further underscored the Magyar defeat. Albrecht's mission was to rehabilitate the prestige of the Habsburgs, remove the vestiges of civil unrest, and establish a new sense of "normalcy," that is, he was to secure a stable society. A staunch advocate of the pluralism of the Habsburg army, he was committed also to diminishing the friction between the ethnic groups.

With the Bach Hussar in place, the royal residence restored, and Archduke Albrecht preparing the stage, Franz Joseph could undertake a tour of his Hungarian lands. In a public tour the emperor could project the power that he insisted was invested in his person, demonstrating this to the masses of his subjects supplicant before him. But the sudden death of Schwarzenberg on April 5, 1852, two months before the scheduled tour, unsettled everything. Schwarzenberg's death forced Franz Joseph to step out from the shadow cast by his mentor. The emperor's first choice to succeed Schwarzenberg was Bach, but older advisers and the military dissuaded Franz Joseph from having the counter-revolution so intimately identified with Bach, the "barricade minister." They convinced the Emperor to step into the limelight as the strong man himself. The twenty-one-year-old Franz Joseph assumed the role of undisputed "neo-absolutist sovereign." Since his accession in 1848, Franz Joseph had seemed a clone of his prime minister, simply acting out the military conception of statesmanship that Schwarzenberg had so successfully mastered in the crisis of 1848–50. Franz Joseph continued to cling stubbornly to the archaic notion instilled in him by Schwarzenberg that his subjects had ultimately nothing to do with government policy that was solely his affair and that of his selected ministers and officials. Schwarzenberg had invariably appeared before the public in uniform, and the young emperor adopted the same disdain for civilian attire. Martial law, the identification of the emperor with the army, and the fact that he always appeared in uniform soon earned Franz Joseph the epithet in Vienna of "Lieutenant Red Legs" (for the red stripe that ran down his white trousers). This predilection for military attire was a departure from the habit of the two preceding sovereigns and widened the gulf between him and the public in these years.[34]

The emperor had learned to live without privacy from childhood and had found his own remedies. He had none of the Viennese love of chat; he distrusted talkers, and he was too impatient to be a listener. After his marriage in 1854, he gave up dancing, his one spontaneous public activity. His demeanor at court festivities expressed his sense of obligation to represent the ruler almost impersonally.[35] Accustomed from boyhood to a stiff formalism of military manners, rigid obedience, and terseness in expression, he naturally took to this mode of interaction. His seemingly marble coldness in public froze the already stiff traditional Habsburg ceremonial. This constant preoccupation with form, as well as his penchant for written directives made him a distant sovereign. Since he had no real ties to anyone in Hungary, he could in these early years be abstract and cruel. Court etiquette became his moat, while his desk was his castle. Franz Joseph sought to simplify the issues that confronted him. Everything, he thought, should be simple, practical, and useful.

Where they could, the Viennese sought to embarrass Franz Joseph and the regime. The illumination of January 7, 1852, held to honor the city's Commandant Weiss von Starkenfels, was pitiful, despite the efforts of the bureaucracy to encourage a respectable response from the Viennese. Even in the inner city, the seat of the black-gold bourgeoisie, many houses remained dark, and in the suburbs there were candles in only a few windows.[36] Franz Joseph enjoyed little of the popularity commonly accompanying attractive young men who suddenly assume the role of head of state. Neither the peasantry nor the urban middle classes were drawn to the circumspect young monarch. No one in Hungary really knew much about him. He had been to Hungary only once in an official capacity, and his contacts with Hungarians were cursory. There was the occasional stopover as on a hunting trip through the small town of Csongrád, where preparations were made for weeks in anticipation of a fleeting visit by the emperor. A long festooned tent was constructed in the open area next to the tavern and painstakingly decorated by local women. The day before the sovereign's arrival numerous carriages drove in from nearby towns, and on the great day the restaurant and the square in front of the tavern were filled with curious people. Finally, around noon the bells rang announcing that Franz Joseph had entered the district, and the church bells continued to toll until the sovereign reached the festive tent, accompanied by a gala delegation and some one-hundred mounted landowners, who had joined the emperor's entourage at the district border. One childhood memory was of a jostling crowd straining to catch a glimpse of the emperor. Casually dressed in a hunting jacket, the sovereign entered the tent to roaring cheers. There he briefly addressed the notables and continued on his way.[37]

News of Schwarzenberg's sudden death had an electric effect on Hungarian public opinion. Loyalists experienced it as a hard blow, especially in the face of Magyar nationalist glee. Although the semiofficial publicity of the tour warned against excessive hopes, the *Österreichische Correspondenz* fed public expectations, announcing that the monarch would do all that was necessary to bring a resolution to existing problems. Hungarians wanted to believe this signaled the coming of some sort of return to civilian rule. There was endless speculation surrounding the symbols and symbolism of the tour. Would Franz Joseph appear in a Hussar uniform? Would the ship bringing him from Vienna fly the tricolor or only the imperial colors?[38]

Much was read into the conciliatory gestures that prepared the way for the tour, only to be confronted by the sobering realization that there was no intention of changing the principle of government. Instead of a hoped for general amnesty, death sentences were announced for prominent exiles in early May, just a month before the tour. One police official lamented having to squash such illusions, especially of the Magyarized elements, who seemed the most anxious that the tour bring some reconciliation. The gentry, whose stance toward the tour had been questionable but potentially supportive, became resistant to bureaucratic appeals for participation. Excuses were made, and local authorities scrambled to prevent anything that might be construed as a gentry boycott. They also worried that the tour not become the occasion to turn acclamations into demonstrations of Magyarism. The largely German-speaking Pest city council planned to have the mayor who spoke hardly a word of Hungarian present his welcoming speech in Hungarian. "Magyar-mania," officials complained, had hardly abated, and German-speaking businessmen in Pest were downplaying their German ethnicity so as not to lose their customers. Widespread was the hope that the Hungarian language would again become the official language in the judiciary. Continued economic crisis fanned rural discontent. In addition to the ever-increasing inflation, a wretchedly cold, dry spring had brought famine to northern Hungary. This reinforced the peasantry's "hostile attitude toward the close connection with Austria, hence the hatred of the Germans is still prevalent."[39]

The court viewed the tour with trepidation. An anxious Archduchess Sophia, accompanied by General Kempen, was at the Vienna dock to see the emperor depart down the Danube late on the night of June 4. The sovereign would spend most of June, all of July, and half of August in resentful, prostrate Hungary. When news came of a positive reception in Pest, there was general relief. The tour could now be officially scripted as a kind of victory procession in which a knightly emperor won glory without arms: "A never before experienced spectacle, Europe is amazed! From mouth to mouth this is how one gathers the wreaths of glory without weapons," enthused a semiofficial account.[40] After the emperor heard that a leader of the Old Conservatives, Baron Sámuel Jósika, had told several diplomats that the reports of a warm reception in Hungary were not true, the baron was warned that he should make himself scarce in Vienna.[41]

Nationalist historiography (particularly of the gentry variety) has played up the discontent left by the tour, and certainly this was important. Yet the very amassing of crowds, albeit with reluctant and cynical participants, played an important role in civilizing crowd activity in post-revolutionary Hungary. Telling is the comparison with Louis Napoleon's post-coup tour of France in these same months. Whereas massive crowds laid the groundwork for the proclamation of the Second Empire on December 2, 1852, the anniversary of Louis Napoleon's coup d'état, the Hungarian crowds were generally respectful but not enthusiastic. While Louis Napoleon was creating a party state that could exploit nationalism, Franz Joseph was attempting to conciliate an occupied kingdom that had to rely on monarchic identification. Louis Napoleon mobilized crowds to win plebiscites, but Franz Joseph could not. Nevertheless, certain similarities can be noted. Both the Bach Hussar and the Bonapartist prefect were pioneers of a bureaucratic politics in a post-revolutionary age. In the tours of the 1850s, crowds were brought out to demonstrate the neo-absolutist thesis that the masses of people were fundamentally loyal, that the revolutionaries misled the people, and that dynasticism had strong underpinnings and was growing stronger day by day. Royal tours are often dismissed as nothing more than a kind of show or folly, with little practical consequence, mere window-dressing to mask imperial realities.[42] But what was evident in 1852 was that the royal tour had become a test of the system, not a completely fair test, but a test that did have its own risks. Whatever their differences, Franz Joseph and Napoleon III succeeded in sending a common message that year, namely that the revolutionary tide was receding and a new order was in place.

There was no disguising the mixed messages of the tour. The subjugated Magyars were simultaneously courted and threatened. Commemorations of the imperial army alternated with gestures of reconciliation toward the insurrectionists, just as gestures toward the Hungarian national feeling alternated with expressions of gratitude toward the loyal minorities. On a few occasions, such as in the Kecskemét market square, Franz Joseph spontaneously left the march route to enter the crowd and was received with genuine enthusiasm. When he toasted the crowd in the Pest City Park, an excited throng responded by lunging forward and trampling the netting set up to keep them at a distance. For the most part, though, the tour remained a military spectacle, dominated by military parades featuring non-Hungarian units. Protocol was strictly prescribed.

Awaiting him at the Pest landing was the Catholic hierarchy (the primate and twenty-two bishops), together with the military, and bureaucratic leaders. The welcoming speech of the mayor of Pest was canceled, while his Buda counterpart made his.[43] That evening Franz Joseph was cheered for several minutes in Pest when he attended a German-language opera at the Hungarian theater. There followed a day of military inspections and visits to the hospital, National Museum, county administrative center, and German Buda theater, capped by a torchlight parade with military bands. As was intended, Franz Joseph gained respect for the manner in which he carried out these inspections: his graciousness and knowledge of their language and customs came across. The initial stay in Buda concluded with the celebration of Pentecost. Huge crowds of the pious assembled to observe Franz Joseph, three accompanying archdukes, high officials, and clergy. Franz Joseph's concern for detail, knowledge of institutions, and a certain sense of charity was already apparent.

The emperor departed by train the next morning in an easterly direction on a schedule that saw him visit a town a day. Along his route banderiums would greet him at the county borders; these would range from a hundred to several thousand horsemen. Along the highways through roadside villages, the people assembled in their Sunday clothes. When he entered villages, the church bell was rung, and he was greeted by officials, guilds, and schoolchildren gathered at a triumphal arch. Receptions included schoolgirls all in white, stereotypical speeches, and shouts of *Vivat*, *Zsivio*, or *Éljen*, depending on the locale's ethnicity. In the evening the locale would be illuminated. A large number of private carriages and the uncommonly large crowds in the streets until midnight gave provincial towns the flavor of a metropolis. The emperor rose early, typically departing around seven a.m. after inspecting the assembled military in the town square.

Yet what would distinguish this tour was the homage by the victors to their martyrs. The counter-revolution was determined to publicize its own history, consecrate its own martyrology, and mark the public landscape with memorials. In Temesvár the emperor dedicated the corner stone of a monument memorializing the loyalty of the inhabitants and troops during the 107-day siege and the culminating battle of August 9, 1849.[44] Such occasions were opportunities to display military emblems and white-red Austrian and black-yellow imperial flags. At the Arad fortress the emperor also issued four pardons and reduced the sentences of some 145.[45] The first of four excursions into the provinces ended after thirteen days with a short respite in Pest. After observing the emperor at the Pest folk festival, a visiting Otto von Bismarck commented: "The Hungarians are enthusiastic about his national pronunciation of their language and the elegance of his riding."[46]

Soon the monarch was off on a westerly tour, where he visited the grave of Count Jenő Zichy, who had been executed as a Habsburg spy. Franz Joseph commissioned a chapel for the site, and this was eventually dedicated by Archduke Albrecht in 1859.[47] At the fortress town of Komárom, he rebuked the mayor in Hungarian, warning that the city should live up to their loyal expressions better in the future than they did in the past, "otherwise I will have to bring the brunt of the law against you."[48] This stern pose was lightened somewhat by other scheduled events that highlighted the emperor's commitment to economic modernization, such as his visit to the exhibition of the industry and agriculture of Tolna county.

The liturgy of restoration would be performed on his return to Buda. On July 4 Franz Joseph prayed in the Buda chapel before the relic of the right hand of St. Stephen, and the feudal demonstrations of loyalty were made by aristocrats throughout the country.[49] Honors and rewards were presented to those who had demonstrated loyalty during the uprising of 1848–9. Often additional pensions and land grants, special privileges or exemptions from normal administrative procedures also accrued to Hungarian aristocrats, notables, and officials in attendance at these meetings.

The symbolic centerpiece of the tour was the dedication of the Buda statue to General Hentzi on St. George Square. The full import of the Hentzi statue needs to be underscored, for it was the first statue raised in a public square in Hungary in honor of the dynasty or its servants. Thus, the first political statue in Pest's public space would not be to the palatine remembered for beautifying Pest, but rather to Hentzi who had ordered the bombing of Pest. Patriotic fund-raisers had sputtered along for almost two decades in hopes of raising statues to the national heroes, but none had yet materialized on a public square. The one prerevolutionary Hungarian sculptor, István Ferenczy (1792–1856), carved a bust of Ferenc Kazinczy and a statue of St. Stephen for Esztergom. But when he attempted a monumental statue of King Matthias Corvinus, he was showered with aesthetic criticism rather than donations, for his conception lacked the heroic quality expected by the age. The embittered sculptor withdrew from the public eye.[50] A statuary association was formed to promote patriotic statues, but it too disbanded before the revolution.[51] During the revolution there was no time to raise durable statues. Instead, the leaders were hurriedly memorialized in portraits and plaster of paris. These were inexpensively reproduced, intended as part of the propaganda and paraphernalia of the revolution. The dream of a Kossuth statue would haunt Hungarian politics for the next half century.[52]

By the third anniversary of Hentzi's death, the counter-revolution had its monument. The statue was as histrionic as it was provocative. One was confronted first by a massive base, rising up a full story, on which were inscribed the names of Gen. Hentzi and Col. Alois Alnoch, along with those of 418 soldiers who had made the "supreme sacrifice for Emperor and Fatherland."[53] Atop this platform lay the figure of a dying soldier clutching his sword while an angel hovered over him bearing a crown of laurels. The

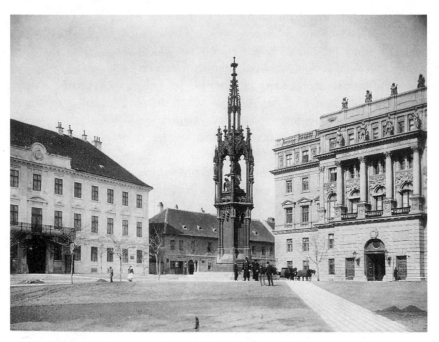

Hentzi Monument on St. George Square in the Buda castle area, ca. 1896. Photograph by Mór Erdélyi (BTM Kiscelli Múzeum, Budapest)

sculptor attempted to capture the poignancy of the martyrology by appealing to the romantic instincts of the time. The dying warrior was encapsulated within a richly decorated Gothic-style canopy, crowned with gables, and culminating in a miniature Gothic church steeple. From a distance, the spire rose above the surrounding single-story buildings on the square. It was as if the dying hero and his angel were safely housed within the House of Habsburg and the Catholic Church, which he had protected with his sword. Attached to the six pillars of the canopy were allegorical figures celebrating military virtues: faith, truth, vigilance, loyalty, chivalry, and sacrifice.[54] The death of Hentzi became a heroic myth that made sacred Habsburg rule in Hungary. The monument was strategically situated along the march route of St. Stephen's Day when the holy relic was carried to the Buda cathedral.

Attending the unveiling in the presence of the emperor were three archdukes, the Ban of Croatia Baron Jellačić, forty generals, and several hundred officers. For Austrian soldiers and Habsburg loyalists, St. George Square became a place of pilgrimage and a symbol of military triumph. But the presence of such a symbol on a main square in Buda became ever more contentious over time. The existence of the monument would plague Hungarian politics for the next forty-six years. It was a statue defended at high cost. Removal of the statue would be one of the central demands of the angry crowds during the army riots of the late 1880s. The Wekerle government would fall over the statue issue in 1892, and three years later Adorján Szeless, a journalist, would try to blow it up. In 1899 the statue would finally be removed from the square, with the figures placed in the cadet schoolyard in Buda. The edifice of the statue was destroyed in the revolutionary fighting in 1918, and the remaining six allegorical figures of military virtue were sold off in a museum auction in 1920.[55] Hungarians have so completely disassociated themselves from the statue that Endre Liber, in his otherwise comprehensive 1934 study of Budapest statuary and plaques, wrote, "This statue does not belong in the history of our Budapest statues."[56]

The strain of dealing with former "rebels" was evident as the tour wore on. Franz Joseph could become particularly prickly, for instance, he impatiently interrupted the Pest city council's statement of loyalty by slapping his sword and declaring that loyalty to him was guaranteed by his sword and the generals at his side.[57] The bureaucracy had aimed to convince Franz Joseph that the existing system was working and was becoming increasingly popular. The tour was remarkably free of untoward incidents; the raising of the tricolor over one church steeple, which greatly exercised the local police, turned out to be an act of simple ignorance.[58] The lower officials had generally managed to turn out the lower classes to hail the monarch. They manufactured crowds like Potemkin villages to welcome the sovereign on this first tour. They drummed up expectations any way they could in hopes of demonstrating the success of the bureaucratic system and their own hard work. Public hopes had soared at the outset of the tour. The official newspapers reported "frenetic, ecstatic jubilation," and commented that "Franz Joseph knows how to win hearts."[59]

But the Bach system was unable to suborn the rural elite.[60] Salutation of the sovereign was expected of all groups in Hungarian society. As towns and villages prepared for the event, a modicum of excitement was generated. But despite the momentary bursts of enthusiasm, basic unyieldingness on both sides characterized these initial, manufactured royal crowd events. Enforced hospitality brought out the officialdom, the subservient, and the curious in 1852. On state occasions the authorities could marshal the submissive crowd out of the lowly, but the nobility, able to make a political statement by their presence, often absented themselves. The gentry's presence was missed, for they inevitably provided one of the spectacles of such events, with their elegant carriages and unique holiday attire. Onlookers were very aware of which great families were missing. By the end of the tour, the populace came to feel they had been duped, conceding that the nobles had been right to boycott the tour. Even the bureaucratic pageant masters, especially among the lower grades, were ambivalent. Bureaucrats were not eager to have the emperor see the situation in Hungary with rose-colored glasses, for the rampant inflation was wreaking havoc with their living standards. In their correspondence with Vienna, the civil servants were constantly lobbying for raises and for some improvement of conditions in Hungary. The ambivalent result of the tour indirectly strengthened the hand of the Old Conservatives. Once Franz Joseph left Hungary proper, the tour proved even more problematic. The bureaucratic apparatus failed to make a respectable showing of South Slav crowds. The Croats had overthrown Hungarian supremacy, only to find they had traded it for German centralization. Their mood was so embittered that in May 1852 a general disarming of the Croat population was decreed.[61]

Yet, the tour of 1852 could be deemed a success for simply having taken place. Rather than the tour itself, the occasion of the tour could be celebrated as its main accomplishment. Appropriately, by far the greatest crowds to greet Franz Joseph gathered to receive him upon his return to Vienna. Sixty thousand assembled just at the Prater, the inner city was adorned with eight thousand portraits of the emperor and some twelve thousand banners, inscriptions, and other decorations. On one colossal pillar was the slogan "Franz Joseph I., the Victor over the Hearts of his Peoples." The reception, it was claimed, exceeded that given to Emperor Franz at the end of the War of Liberation from Napoleon. The mayor declaimed, "Not the defeat of enemy armies mark Your Majesty's train of victories, a far more beautiful victory, a victory over the hearts of your peoples, lends this day its high meaning."[62]

Despite Bach's hopes for the pacifying effect of the tour, the looming Crimean War incited international republicanism to new gambles. Mazzini's doomed landing of early 1853 in Italy brought a new vigilance. Hopes for a Hungarian rising were also dashed with the roundup of several hundred plotters in Transylvania soon thereafter. On February 17, 1853, János Libényi, a twenty-two-year-old tailor and former Honvéd attempted to take Franz Joseph's life in Vienna by stabbing him in the neck. Only the emperor's stiff collar saved him from being mortally wounded. For several days his sight weakened, and the Viennese public followed the news until it was clear that he had made a complete recovery. For the first time the emperor evoked public sympathy. On March 12, when Franz Joseph made his first public appearance since the stabbing to give thanks in St. Stephen's Cathedral, there were spontaneous street demonstrations on his behalf. A huge sum was pledged the first day of a subscription campaign in Vienna for the construction of the Votive Church on the site of the attempted assassination.[63] Hungarians residing in Vienna were conspicuously generous in their donations. A Hungarian attended one spellbinding Sunday sermon in Vienna imploring the flock to make large donations to the Votive Church building fund.[64] The church would serve the military garrison as a kind of Austrian Westminster Abbey, and became a final resting place for Austria's great men.[65]

In Hungary appeals were much less vociferous. A nationwide ceremony of thanksgiving was held four days after the attempted assassination, but people did not flock to the churches to show their gratitude for Franz Joseph's recovery. At the Veszprém Cathedral, for instance, attendance was sparse. In the evening, commemorative candles seemed to have been lit at only two sites in Veszprém, above the entrance to the Casino and in the synagogue courtyard.[66] It was clearly not an occasion that moved Hungarians. The assassination attempt was bound to lead to a new crackdown. Bach had been seeking to end the state of martial law, but Kempen, in charge of the police forces, announced this was now out of the question.[67] When news of the assassination attempt was first received in Buda, all the garrison gates were heavily manned. Six days after the assassination attempt, largely to combat the rumors that a riot was being planned, that some four thousand peasants were ready to rise, that the governor would soon be murdered, Archduke Albrecht marched the entire garrison onto the Danube bank for a great military review meant to intimidate the invisible rebels. In all, 379 persons were arrested in Pest. Former co-workers of Libényi were all tracked down, with one master tailor, sixteen tailor assistants, and one printer's apprentice condemned to various periods of hard labor.[68] Libényi's act intensified an already tense situation, fueling the regime's suspicions.

Strict passport controls were reinstituted to regulate movement in and out of Pest, again making visits over three days problematic.[69] A stepped-up campaign against guerrilla bands led to trials and executions in March. At the same time, the introduction of the Austrian legal code was used as an excuse to purge the legal profession of almost a fourth of all lawyers in Hungary.[70] The climate of fear penetrated deep into the provinces. A Veszprém barber deemed it too risky to keep the memorabilia of the revolution; after years of guarding his little stash, he proceeded to burn it. His wife still beseeched him to save the picture of Kossuth. On March 15,

1853, the very thought of any commemoration of the revolution was met with the response, "Let's not even mention it." A customer warned the barber, "they could easily respond with 'Kommen Sie mit!' if we mention our revolution too often."[71]

The specter of revolution was all but dissipated by this crackdown. On Franz Joseph's birthday, August 18, the *Wiener Zeitung* announced the emperor's engagement. The discovery of the crown of St. Stephen on September 8 was a last symbolic blow to Magyar feeling in the anticlimactic year of 1853.[72] Within four days of its discovery the crown arrived by steamship in Buda. Archduke Albrecht went out onto the Danube to meet the ship as it approached. He spoke of the significance of the moment. Primate Scitovszky and numerous officials were on hand as the pieces were carefully removed from the battered old trunk, inspected for authenticity, and logged into the record. The primate prayed, a military band played the "Gott, erhalte," and the ship fired its guns. These were answered by a round of gunfire from the fortress and citadel, and the ringing of church bells in Buda and Pest. The next day the ship arrived at the Pest dock, and eight aristocrats carried the iron chest to shore. An ornate carriage bearing the treasure set out through a swarm of people that had come to catch a glimpse. Again guns and bells rang out as the procession crossed the bridge to St. Stephen's Cathedral. There the bishops set out the crown and the accompanying regalia; a mass was said, punctuated by a volley of shots by the soldiers on St. George Square. Two imperial officers stood guard with unsheathed swords while the public filed past the treasured objects that remained on display for three days.[73]

Everything was then replaced in the chest, and Albrecht personally accompanied the treasures on a heavily armed train to Vienna. Franz Joseph hurried back to Vienna from Olmütz for the occasion. A ceremony was held in the throne room; mass was said in the chapel, and the objects were placed in the treasury for safekeeping. According to Hungarian lore, the crown would remain there as a hostage of neo-absolutism. But actually, the emperor ordered the crown returned to the Buda fortress the next day, and a banderium of Hungarian magnates escorted the crown from Pozsony back to Buda.[74]

Pilgrimage and Funeral

In the Bach system's new normalcy, the gregarious instinct of Hungarians found limited expression but could not be completely denied as long as it assumed religious coloring. The giddy carnival ball, the mass pilgrimage, and the moving funeral became outlets for the Hungarian crowd in a decade conditioned by the collapse of insurrectionary hopes, a resurgent monarchy, and a spreading prosperity. By dismantling Josephinism Bach freed the church and, by extension, religious festivity from state tutelage. Pope Pius IX was, like Bach, a liberal renegade, traumatized by the revolution of 1848. In exile the Pope injected the counter-revolution with the trappings of a renewed ideological crusade—the legitimist system of 1814 was to be defended at all cost, but this time legitimism was to be buttressed by a popular religiosity. For the Habsburgs, with their special relationship to the Papacy, cooperation between the two was more than second nature.[75] Franz Joseph was particularly scrupulous in performing the traditional rites of *Pietas Austrica*. He walked through the streets of Vienna on Corpus Christi Day, bareheaded, holding a lit candle, bent on his solemn purpose, while on Maundy Thursday he washed the feet of selected commoners.[76] The fit of Catholicism and dynasticism was snug in the Austrian half of the Empire.[77] Catholicism united Italians, Austrians, and Czechs; only Jews and the few Protestants stood outside. In the Kingdom of St. Stephen, with its substantial Protestant and Orthodox populations, religious pluralism had a greater claim to tradition, and the Roman Catholic emphasis would be more divisive.

Bach's efforts to regulate the veneration of Sundays and religious holidays became a case in point. Complaints that Jews in Kubin had held a Purim dance as a fund-raiser on a Sunday that fell during the Catholic observance of Lent prompted Bach to issue strict new regulations of October 1852.[78] The Sunday ban closed taverns, denied bakers and cafe owners the right to sell their wares on Sunday mornings; Saturdays also assumed the character of a day of abstinence. Orthodox and Greek Catholics complained that their religious calendars differed from the Roman Catholic. The constraints were resented as an intrusion into confessional and family customs in a country as religiously heterogeneous as Hungary. Police found the rules were hard to enforce and complained they had no counterpart in the other crown lands. By 1858 Bach was backtracking, ready to allow carnival balls on Saturday nights provided they ended at midnight.[79]

The hold of Catholic festivity, particularly on the rural populace, was evident at the onset of Lent, during Easter Week, occasionally at the New Year, on the local saint's day, at harvest festivals, on All Hallows. In addition to these festivities, on the night before the military induction of new recruits all villages indulged in festival abandon. These holidays were all important to village life, for only during these religious pilgrimages and the secular market fair did the village expand to incorporate a crowd of strangers. In Hungary the pilgrimage was a crowd activity rather than a private journey. It was a public representation of oneself as a Catholic and as a member of a specific village community. Organization and leadership of this annual event were in the hands of pious village elders (the *búcsúvezető*) who took charge of the pilgrimage and instructed those making their first journey. Everyone was expected to participate in at least one pilgrimage during his or her lifetime. Pilgrimages included the pious, marriage parties, marriage seekers, village leaders, rural clergy, tradesmen, and entertainers, as well as pickpockets, confidence men, and prostitutes. The pilgrimage seemed to portend a new social peace in the Catholic countryside, among Hungarians at least, and certainly played an important role in the fashioning of a new post-serf peasant culture.[80] With the flowering of the linden tree, the whole village left on a pilgrimage to the Lőcsei mountain church to see the miraculous picture of Mary, recalled one gentry historian lovingly of his boyhood in the fifties. "Like a long snake coming down the mountain," the crowd returned. "The wind carried the distant singing which seemed to stop when they reached the bottom of the mountain. I guess we did not imagine even a coronation procession being prettier" than the undulating procession, song floating through the air, and flags flying.[81]

Often the pilgrim's destination was a day's march away, and pilgrims were festively greeted in every village through which they passed, normally between two and ten different villages. In each, lookouts, usually in the belfry would spy the horizon for approaching pilgrims. When sighted the village bell was rung and villagers would gather to greet them. The pilgrims entered the village singing and praying, with flags pinned to their poles.[82] Organ music greeted them at the church. After prayers in the church, pilgrims mixed with villagers in the church courtyard for a brief festival. The pilgrim leaders were considered important representatives of their village. Village lore and village news were exchanged. Various village delegations would arrive from different directions carrying flags of their church before them with the cantor behind them singing songs. Upon arrival, those on their first pilgrimage would undertake the "pilgrim's baptism." The pilgrimage site, usually a small village, would quickly be overfilled and run out of lodgings, so most would sleep under the stars, in barns, and even in the church itself. The day of the actual festival would begin early with the attending clergy often conducting twenty, thirty masses, all in preparation for the high mass performed by the bishop or another high priest. This took place out in the open when the crowd of as many as several thousand could not be accommodated in the village church.

After High Mass, the festival took on the character of a county fair, where vendors sold religious pictures, prayer books, and religious paraphernalia. All sorts of goods could be acquired at the pilgrimage destination: clothes, household goods, children's toys, and holy pictures. The development of photography also fostered the growth of an international popular pilgrim culture. The same holy photograph could now be seen in peasant homes across the Continent. Other business was conducted. In some regions the crucial marriage market of the year took place during the pilgrimage. Parents would accompany their eligible children and make the dowry arrangements as the festival turned feast-like, musical, and lively.[83] The aura of piety lifted and the hour of scandal had arrived. Outsiders—curious Protestants, pickpockets, and the like—mixed with crowds as great amounts of alcohol were consumed.

The 1850s saw the florescence of the religious crowd in Catholic Hungary. The purge of the Catholic Church tended to diffuse religious energy away from the cathedral settings, away from Esztergom, Pest, and other ecclesiastical centers to the countryside. The dramatic expansion of the pilgrimage in mid-century stimulated traditional forms of devotion. The revival of pilgrimages, processions, rosary campaigns, and indulgences had already been felt throughout Catholic Europe in the 1840s. After Missionaries of Our Lady of La Salette spread the news of the 1846 vision of Mary throughout Europe, up to sixty thousand French pilgrims were taking the waters daily during the pilgrimage season at the new La Salette shrine in the Midi. Just as the European revolutions utilized the railroad to amass crowds in March 1848, the railroad could now also speed pilgrims to their destinations. Pius IX was actively promoting the Marian doctrine, and his enunciation of the Dogma of the Immaculate Conception in 1854 was the high-water mark of the papal campaign to make the nineteenth century the Marian century. The cult of Mary served as another impetus to the pilgrimage culture. The Bach system accommodated such gatherings, even when they became mammoth events. In September 1853 German Catholics congregated in Vienna to hear calls for mass pilgrimages to Maria-Weissenstein in Tyrol and other sites.[84] During Christmas 1853 the Zichy family summoned Jesuits priests to Gyulafehérvár (Alba Julia) where a large procession greeted them with song. The popularity of the pilgrimage reverberated through Hungary where martial law prohibited large gatherings. This focus on the pilgrimage led to a relaxation of the restrictions against crowd formations. The local pilgrimage gained a new vitality, serving as an apolitical outlet for the gregarious instinct and a stimulus of peasant culture.

Buda, with six major sites within its confines, became a center of pilgrimage activity.[85] Situated in the center of the country, easily accessible to those on both sides of the Danube, Buda could draw peasants from a wide area. While the provincial pilgrimage was important in the creation of regional identities wider than one's own village, the Buda-Pest setting enhanced the pilgrim's national identification.[86] The growing urban character of Buda-Pest made these pilgrimages a special magnet for an adventurous, more mobile peasantry. Eventually, the days that Buda was traditionally packed with villagers arriving to visit the shrines of Máriabesnyő (Maria-Eichel) and Máriaremete (Maria-Einsiedel) became a different kind of festive experience. After visiting the shrines, the people would enjoy the remainder of the day on the large, but crowded Leopold meadow in Buda. In coming years the new urban folk festival in the Pest City Park would even begin to overshadow the annual religious observances in Buda. The press began a long drawn-out campaign for a new urban holiday calendar that could appeal to a multi-religious urban population.

The religious and nationalist themes of the pilgrimage took on a political coloring in the urban funeral procession. When the Magyar romantic writer János Garay (1812–1853) died, the Pest funeral became a swollen public event. Garay is remembered today only for his character János Háry, immortalized by the Zoltán Kodály opera of the same name, *János Háry*. But the fate of the professor of Hungarian literature—ousted from his post by the counterrevolution, to struggle in poverty, tumble into apparent madness, and finally succumb at the age of forty-one—resonated in the oppressed atmosphere.[87] Theater benefit performances were held in Debrecen, Győr, and Nagybánya, and elsewhere, to finance a stately monument in Pest's new cemetery.[88] The funereal seemed to enshroud Europe in the fifties, with Victorian society pouring out its grief in ostentatious displays. The most well-known example was Wellington's 1852 funeral, grander than earlier rites of royalty. The crowds who turned out to watch the procession came in the deepest mourning or their "Sunday best." English Victorian funerals were showcases of opulent display. It was in the funeral that the romantic and realistic met. In Victorian society "the style of the funeral helped to establish social position, for it was with a funeral, even more than a wedding, that the wealth and power of a family could be publicly displayed."[89] In the funeral, liberal culture emphasized acquisition of goods. In Hungary, the material and political conjoined in these rites of death; in them bitter Hungarian nationalism displayed and acclaimed not only material wealth or family status, but the wealth of its culture.

In 1855 Hungarians seized on the death of one of their major writers to hold a mammoth funeral that was really more a political demonstration than a religious rite of mourning. The inhabitants of Pest turned out for the funeral of Mihály Vörösmarty en masse.[90] The Vörösmarty funeral was the most significant Hungarian crowd event of the Bach period. An archduke in his carriage, at least according to legend, found his way blocked by the huge crowd. When he was told it was a funeral, he asked which great lord had died, and the answer was: "Only a poor Hungarian poet."[91] In the unquiet wait in Hungary it was the poet who seemed to embody the best of the nation's values.[92] Vörösmarty was a genius of the pre-forty-eight literary revival. He had "fulfilled the literary expectations of a nation," writing the necessary national epic in 1825, *The Flight of Zalán*. His imaginative boldness had a "shattering" effect on "poetic language" and contemporary literary ideals.[93] He provided the burgeoning Hungarian stage with Magyar plays; in his themes and the beauty of his language had reverberated the concerns for the nation. His lyricism had provided solace and echoed the sadness. In his final years he gave voice to the bitterness of the aftermath.[94]

The ill Vörösmarty journeyed to Pest in search of better medical care, or perhaps to die amidst a recovering literary scene. He took up residence in a modest inner-courtyard apartment, but in the same building where the writer Károly Kisfaludy had died twenty-five years before. This building was on Váci Street, the first elegant commercial boulevard in Pest. Vörösmarty's last public act was a visit to the Korona coffeehouse at the busy five p.m. hour. He entertained the customers with Gypsy and Slovak tales until the pipe smoke proved too strong for him. The elegant Korona coffeehouse was a central magnet on Váci Street, serving 1,500 coffees daily.[95] The language battle was being nudged along over these coffee cups, with the *Gutgesinnt* making the necessary accommodations with their neighbors. The café had originally catered to Greek businessmen, then German speakers, but now the *Gutgesinnt* were increasingly fighting a rearguard action as the café was being taken over by the Magyar literati and students.

In 1908, a faltering liberalism would fill the square in front of the grand coffeehouse on Váci Street with an extraordinary statue of Vörösmarty, so large that it completely overwhelmed the square. Modernists of the *Nyu-*

gat found it "too cluttered, too folkish."[96] A monumental Vörösmarty in folk costume stood surrounded by a chorus of figures singing the "Szózat" while he listened. The first stanza of the poem was carved on the base. More than his individual literary genius, the statue memorialized Vörös- marty's success at mobilizing the chorus of voices. The image was of Vörösmarty as the patriot, the poet of the Magyar folk, who heard the peo- ple and evoked their words, evoked the procession, the national effort— filling the square so full that "it blocked the flow of air."[97]

By coming from the provinces to spend his last days on Váci Street, the dying poet facilitated the most imposing funeral hitherto seen in Pest. "The whole length of Váci Street was full of carriages and people participating in the funeral."[98] The transparently political demonstration of pent-up na- tionalist sentiments wound from Váci Street to Pest's Kerepesi cemetery. The *Pesti Napló* wrote that every class of society, from the aristocrat to the poorest artisans, joined the procession, and that the capital had never seen a more effective celebration of common lament. Vörösmarty's funeral would be remembered as the first time "the capital's society . . . was pulled together as a Magyar community."[99] The dignity of the event was espe- cially noted; not one voice, or one incident disturbed its solemnity. The outpouring for Vörösmarty would spill over to the other writers and states- men of this Magyar revival. Henceforth, deaths and centennials would fill a reservoir for the reawakening of national politics. Although obviously political, a "danger-signal" to the neo-absolutist authorities,[100] this was also forging something new. Here was the civilized crowd, capable of pro- found sentiment, acting together, but nonviolently and without fanaticism.

The Promenade and the Tour of 1857

Váci Street was a symbol of a new society. Petőfi's march had begun from the Pilvax coffeehouse around the corner from Váci Street, but to engender the revolutionary crowd he and his supporters moved to the university, to the printing house, and then to the museum steps and the city hall. Now the new shopping district served as a magnet of a new prosperity. With the de- velopment of an elegant thoroughfare and a promenade along the Danube, Pest seemed nearly as fashionable as the district around the cathedral in Buda. The regime had begun the decade seeking to limit Pest's growth, de- vising methods of undercutting its future. But these gave way quickly, and Pest proved to be the principal beneficiary of the increasing prosperity of the Bach era. Its growth far outstripped the other towns; quintupling in population, Pest moved from fifth place in 1785 to first. Pest counted over

100,000 residents in the census of 1857, while Buda and Óbuda had a population of about 50,000.[101] Only in Pest was economic growth tied in any significant measure to heavy industry. Aside from a few mining cities, the Hungarian economy remained resoundingly agricultural. Before the tendrils of a railroad system were complete, grain traveled by ship on the Danube and Tisza rivers and the connecting Ferenc Canal. This spurred growth in the Bácska and neighboring Alföld areas, and transformed Szeged from a middling-sized town to the third largest city, but left Debrecen, not connected to these waterways, behind. In the 1850s more grain still flowed into Györ's port than Pest, but Pest was smack in the middle of the country. It would become the hub of the railroad system, and taming the Danube and making it more navigable around the Iron Gates was a recognized priority since Széchenyi's infrastructure reforms. Pest's surrounding region was Catholic and German to the west, but the city was also a meeting ground for Protestants and Jews, with communities of Croats, Serbs, Romanians, Slovaks, and Greeks, as well. Pest also gained new importance for Hungarian magnates seeking an urban social base now that Vienna was less hospitable. With the suspension of constitutional rule, Pozsony, the seat of the Diet, lost its political significance.

Since the Chain Bridge had linked Pest and Buda events spilled from the cathedral square in Buda to the park in Pest. The promenade became a common greeting ground for Magyar, *Gutgesinnt*, and foreigner; the Bach Hussars frequented Váci Street, as did the apolitical burgher. Smoke-filled cafés, fancy hotels, fashion stores, expensive apartment buildings, and elegant restaurants lined the Váci Street promenade.[102] Couples strolled along the smart new thoroughfare where a new prosperity ran riot. The street became a showcase of a nascent capitalism, complete with new forms of display. To be sure Baudelaire's *flâneur* might have become bored with its attractions, but for Hungarians, particularly those from the provinces, the material display in booming Pest was all quite astounding. The Veszprém barber dreamed for years about one day seeing Pest for himself.[103] Above a watch store, the first public clock was lit by gaslight until midnight and window displays delighted and amazed. Novelties like soda water made their debut here.[104] "We went straight to Váci Street, the heart of the city where life now pulsates most intensely," wrote Károly Vadnai, a popular essayist and novelist. "At times the whole long street is an open salon where everyone can enter without an entry card or differences in rank. It is a living museum, lovelier than the prettiest picture."[105] Real genre figures in a kaleidoscope of color could be seen socializing on the street. Window displays dazzled. Váci Street became Magyar women's window into Parisian fashion. Mimicking French fashion was expensive, requiring yards and yards of fabric, flounces, and lace. Just the crinoline required about sixty yards of wire, and layer upon layer of underskirt.[106] One Daumier print proclaimed, "I would rather a whirlwind went through my garden than that accursed crinoline!"[107] The crinoline filled Váci Street with opulent splendor.[108]

The spirit of the revolutionary crowd was being displaced by the promenade of prosperity. On Váci Street a new urban, literary culture was also percolating. The opening of Mór Ráth's large bookstore on a prime corner was considered a major event by the newspapers. Ráth made available copies of such banned works as Széchenyi's attack on Bach, *Ein Blick auf den anonymen Rückblick* and Mihály Horváth's military history of the revolution. Ferenc Deák, emerging as Hungary's most important politician, lived two blocks away at the English Queen's Hotel, and he used the Ráth bookstore as a meeting place.[109] The absence of urban centers before the 1850s made Hungarian literature by definition provincial in character. But now the Deák literary party, headed by Zsigmond Kemény and Pál Gyulai, both of Transylvania, had taken up spiritual residency on Váci Street.[110] Kemény, an impoverished member of the Transylvanian gentry, had experienced the revolution's crisis as civil war. The peasant unleashed in his provincial world took on a sinister character. Revolutionism was dismissed as a pose or demagoguery. As a representative in the Debrecen revolutionary government of 1849, Kemény had organized against the "Jacobins," toppling the key street orator and "grandmaster of terrorism," László Madarász.[111] Kemény viewed his faction as the Girondins facing down Robespierre and his Jacobins. After a Kossuth speech was interpreted as an ultimatum against Kemény's club, Kemény had felt himself in personal danger during the last stages of the revolution.[112] Kemény despised Kossuth as a demagogue with a futile policy. He discounted as naive the assumption that "Europe" would have allowed Hungary to emerge from the revolution as an independent country.[113] Kemény recommended that Hungarians "hang a votive plaque on the church wall for our remarkable escape."[114] Kemény saw himself as the intellectual architect of the turn away from Kossuth, the "people's apostle" who had allowed the ship of state to capsize.[115] Kemény accepted the monarchy not as a holdover but as an instrument of modernity and change. He rejected the defeatism of the moment, arguing instead, "Everything is new, everything is untried, everything is unusual."[116] "Epimenides' long sleep is inappropriate for us in these eventful times."[117]

The arguments of the 1850s revolved around the options of moralism and aestheticism. In the writings of the Deák literary school, it became fashionable to mock the previous belief that literature and criticism were forms of transforming national life and that books could be held responsible for actions, that the writer could be the savior of the people. The new school turned vehemently away from romantic political verse of Petőfi and scorned the populist rhetoric of Jókai, insisting on a tight, refined style that scorned pathos and grand eloquence; sobriety and realism became the watchword of the new school. Verse, as such, was demoted and history and economics became the coming genres of those concerned with Hungary's practical future.[118]

As the decade dragged on, writers chafed under the forced isolationism of neo-absolutism, recognizing that nationalism was in danger of becoming parochial. They craved contact. We had "to struggle" just as hard to retain our "cosmopolitanism," to resist "lethargy," or "charlatanism in the guise of nationalism," Szilágy recalled.[119] Kemény's message was: let us work and prosper within the given situation; resentment could not "save the homeland." He was in search for balance. There was an alternative to passivity or resignation: realism, the need to belong to one's time. Love of country was no longer enough; Hungarian nationalism had to be brought into harmony with European developments and that of the Empire. In Hungary's restricted atmosphere, the Imperial state was the access route to a wider world. "Our horizons have widened," wrote Kemény.[120]

The Deák literary circle did share the earlier Hungarian assumption that the vibrancy of Magyar theater was a barometer of Magyar culture. While they disparaged the romantic hyperbole and idealism of the prerevolutionary literature, Gyulai fretted in his theater reviews about the effect of the disillusionment, political withdrawal, and cynicism of the age on the theater. "Now there is much behind us; exhaustion and disappointment weighs on us."[121] And he was nostalgic for a lost time when actors used to be driven by their mission, unlike neo-absolutism when no new leaven was being added to the mix; in short, the actors lacked the vision that came from political commitment.[122] Gyulai's lament that Hungarian actors were more cynical, self-absorbed, egoistic, and materialistic, signaled a new call for political theater, but most of all he worried that actors were less involved in the national project than in individual gain. Actors were forswearing their role as political missionaries and martyrs for wealth and international fame, made imaginable by the breakthroughs in travel and communication. "Once the Hungarian scholar, writer or artist starts falling into the sick desire to have been born in a country where one could have been famous in half the world, one does not sacrifice oneself to the common suffering, which substitutes for everything else here; if in the desire for wealth or pride one forgets, that one must live for the homeland: there will be tragic consequences and our literature will lose its center of gravity. Thank God, we are not anywhere near this point."[123]

While the 1840s had fostered a politicized high-culture, mid-cult theater flourished all over Europe in the 1850s. Newspaper's star-struck gaze at the actors of the stage was promoting a popular culture that could spread beyond the bounds of the attending audience and tended to obscure its partisan message. Since Hungarians had placed such an emphasis on their theater, German theater acquired a heightened political importance, as well. Bach officials took a proprietary interest in the theaters of their jurisdictions, and often became involved in overseeing the day-to-day operations of the provincial theaters. In towns with only one theater building, support for the German theater directly curtailed the scope of the Hungarian theater. Clearly the most important function of the German theater company was keeping the Hungarian company at bay. Bach's support of German theater was intended to defuse the political potency of the Hungarian theater. The censor's heavy hand promoted the frivolous tendencies in theater. "The audience acts quite peculiarly," wrote a reviewer of one operetta on the Hungarian stage. "They laugh a lot at the first act, even more at the second, and even more at the third, and then they leave the theater shrugging their shoulders that there wasn't much to that piece." "In today's sad world" such a comedy is about as funny as things can get, concluded the reviewer.[124] The *Pester Zeitung* commented in 1851 that the loges were empty for *Othello* but filled when a midget performed.[125] While the Bach system sought to depoliticize all theater, the effect was most evident in the German theater where it trivialized most of it. [126] The audience came to see the latest Viennese curiosities, but no longer patronized serious drama. Despite official encouragement, in this age of fussy censorship German theater in Pest and Buda did not find its footing. In 1851 the Pest German theater was moved into another interim wooden structure, but it turned out to be uncomfortably drafty. Public interest in the German theater declined, and financial difficulties proved unavoidable. The Pest German theater became ever weaker and increasingly reliant on foreign guest performers. [127] Consequently, theater directors passed through a revolving door of short tenures, bankruptcies, and interim closures.

Bach, for his part, wished to seize on the prosperity and civilized atmosphere exemplified by Váci Street to produce a second, successful, even splendid tour for the sovereign. But a tour could still lead to embarrassment. To go, or not to go on another tour became an issue. Except for a perfunctory visit in 1856, he had not made a formal visit to Hungary since the tour of 1852.[128] Too long an absence left the impression that the sovereign was afraid to show his face again, or that he had become indifferent to the fate of one of his peoples. Tours were vital in the maintenance of a unified empire, and therefore, could not be indefinitely postponed. Pope Pius IX would similarly make a tour the summer of 1857, anxious to show the world that he had the support of his subjects and that his rule was not simply based on foreign bayonets. Vienna was concerned that the Pope might make too many concessions in his eagerness to win back his lost popularity.[129]

The progress of the economy was an important validation of the neo-absolutist system. But the regime had reason to worry: The prosperity they were so anxious to highlight proved fickle. In 1857 a sharp international economic recession hit. The Bach Hussars, responsible for organizing the tour, were a poorly paid lot, whose morale plummeted even further with the dip in the economy. The Bach Hussars had taken credit for the boom, but their personal glory days were long gone. On fixed salaries, the bureaucrat had become one of the principal victims of the inflationary pressures accompanying the expansion. Civil servants in the countryside were particularly badly hit. Although Bach and his cohorts were aware of the importance of the social position and prestige of their administrators, they had been reluctant to improve the position of the lower civil service lest further resentment be aroused in the lower classes. Not only was the bureaucrat not entertaining lavishly as in earlier years, but many could not afford a servant and pressed their daughters into household work. Christoph Stölzl, in his study of Bohemia, found upper civil servants were dipping into their private savings to maintain their social standing, while in the lower ranks, there were even reports of pauperism and a proletarianization of the civil service.[130] This was equally true of Hungary, and the situation was, perhaps, most bleak for the politically-tainted Bohemian officials dispatched to minor posts in Hungary. When the novelist Božena Němcová left the "suffocating atmosphere" of Prague in 1851, she hoped that she "would recover a little in the Hungarian air." But by 1853, her husband had become suspect, and he "even has to sue the shameful bureaucracy for the money he was awarded." Traveling to rejoin him in upper Hungary (Slovakia), she wrote "whoever has never seen Hungarian mud, has no idea of mud—that is antediluvian mud." Her letters, very often beseeching her admirers for money, depict desperate poverty.[131] The Bach system was torn between the conception of a "strong" state with a powerful, proud bureaucracy and the declining economic position of the bureaucrat. This led to a general undermining of morale. Since the promise of the Bach system had been administrative efficiency in place of politics as usual, the status of the administrators was important. They were expected to mold public opinion and fill the gap between civil society and the state. The reform spirit, the take-charge mentality of the early years, increasingly gave way to a kind of paralysis and fatalism.

Franz Joseph launched his empire-wide tour in Lombardy and Venice in late January 1857. "I have forgotten the past!" he proclaimed.[132] But the Lombard nobility had not forgotten. They insulted Franz Joseph by sending their servants in their place to the gala opera performance attended by the emperor. The servants wore one white and one red glove, a local custom of servants attending funerals. But the official hyperbole about the event spoke of "a world historical day" in the history of the Lombard-Venetian kingdom that would be remembered for eternity. (The state would not exist within three years.)[133]

In Pest the carnival ball of the law students stepped well beyond the bounds of the previous years. Everyone wore Hungarian national costumes in what became a clear nationalist demonstration. In anticipation of the sovereign's tour, János Arany, living in bitter retreat in the countryside, wrote the condemning, "The Bards of Wales." The poem memorialized executed Welsh poets, who had refused to sing for the English King Edward I. The burden of the massacre drove Arany's King Edward insane.[134] It was clear that the tour would have to be orchestrated carefully. Unlike 1852 important estate owners received polite invitations, but they were still in German, and the gentry complained of the decided tone that "required" attendance at the imperial reception, prescribed their attire, and arrival in four-horse carriages.[135] Although preparations were hampered by the constant rain of late April, thirty thousand lights were strung in the City Park, a twenty-five foot tall palm tree was placed in one square, and a huge candelabra decorated another. Expectations were so high that some new political program was in the offing that the government felt obliged to semiofficially warn in the Augsburg *Allgemeine Zeitung* that no great political breakthrough was likely.[136] To underscore that point Countess Batthyány, widow of the executed prime minister, was expelled from the capital for the duration of the royal visit. Yet on the eve of the emperor's arrival, many pardons were granted, some émigrés were allowed to return, and restitution was made to the daughter of one of the generals executed in Arad.

At six a.m. on May 4, the cannons announced from the Buda fortress that the imperial couple had crossed the Hungarian border. A hour-and-a-half later two steamships filled with deputations of excited notables started up river. Their mood changed, however, when they were told that only the imperial colors were permissible. Many refused to wave "those unhappy pieces of cloth" when the imperial ship, bedecked with Imperial black-yellow and Austrian red-white flags, came into sight.[137] In Visegrád the ruins on top of the hill were decorated with flags. The banks of the Danube were decorated, and villagers were brought out to wave and cheer. The weather was good, and Budapesters were out in force. The pier was a forest of flags, and some one thousand people gathered around the receiving area. The official greeting party was led by Archduke Albrecht and several other archdukes, the primate and bishops, a few magnates and the mayor. The sight of the emperor disembarking in Austrian rather than Hungarian uniform prompted widespread disappointment. But, this was partially compensated by the sight of the empress in Hungarian attire with a brilliant diadem on her head. Thus began a drama around the royal couple that would define Hungarian-Austrian relations for a decade.[138]

A half-hour procession led to the Buda castle, seventy-four guilds formed the cordon; the parade included an exotic hundred-fifty-man mounted banderium of Jazyges and Cumans. However, the visit had a rocky start, for rain canceled the planned illumination and public anger turned against the organizer. When the illumination did take place two days later, it was an impressive spectacle with a parade of four thousand torches in four columns across the Chain Bridge. The whole city seemed to turn out with the largest crowds on the Danube banks. The hotels were illuminated with Bengal light, the city hall with gaslight. For the climax of the event Franz Joseph recrossed the bridge with fireworks exploding overhead.[139] Nothing similar had been staged over the Danube before. Yet dark facades were evidence of an undercurrent of opposition. Candles were conspicuously absent from the windows of some casinos. The royal receptions were poorly attended. Not until the sovereigns made an appearance at the National Theater for a performance in which Hungarian not German was the language of the hour, were they greeted with real enthusiasm. For the first time Franz Joseph had entered national ground. He underscored the concession to Hungarian feeling by appearing in a Hussar uniform. The audience burst into an extended ovation that lasted several minutes. When the curtain was raised, the entire theatrical company sang the imperial hymn.[140] Nothing so illustrated the decline in popular support for German culture than the Pest German theater's inability to perform for Franz Joseph during his 1857 tour due to its temporary financial insolvency.[141] He did receive an enthusiastic reception when he visited a ball held in the German theater that was attended by the bureaucracy and the German and Jewish middle classes.[142]

Elizabeth was clearly the attraction of the visit. When the imperial couple walked through a cordon of 2,600 workers when they visited the Óbuda shipyard, the sight of Elizabeth adorned again in red, white and green colors generated a wild enthusiasm.[143] Word spread that she could be seen riding her horse in the City Park; this snarled the carriage traffic in that direction. Her horsemanship at the military parades aroused rapturous enthusiasm and pleased her as well, since in Vienna she had been permitted to attend such events only in a carriage.

In addition to the attractive image of Empress Elizabeth, Franz Joseph sought to identify himself with the progress of the Hungarian economy. "I have always worked to advance the standard of living" of my Hungarian subjects, the emperor declared at the beginning of his tour. Neo-absolutism wanted to document and underscore the advances made under its tutelage, but the regime walked a tightrope between the previous use of the fairs by the radicals in the 1840s and the hope of the Bach system that it could convince the public that they had a better way of life. The counter-revolution's suppression of Kossuth's Industrial Association left a magnate-led National Agrarian Society to partially fill the void in the fifties and early sixties. Industrial fairs per se were not permitted, but agricultural exhibitions became one of the very few permissible arenas for public action.[144] Hungary's little six-day agricultural exhibitions of 1851, 1853, and 1857 were held in the shadow of the Great London Exposition of 1851. At first glance nothing could have better highlighted the disparities between Hungary's backwardness and the technological leader. The Crystal Palace was a triumph for British enterprise and technology. The exposition attracted world-wide attention, symbolizing the high noon of the Victorian era, underscoring English technological primacy.[145] But the Crystal Palace was also a giant greenhouse, containing the exotic goods of industrialism; it was an unconscious metaphor for a nostalgic ruralism, calling for a recovery of the forgotten garden that was England.[146] Hungary's peasantry, in contrast, was only beginning to be lured into the technological vortex. Expositions spread enthusiasm for industrial capitalism, fostered an industrial myth, and encouraged professionalization.[147] While the 1857 exhibition in Köztelek graphically reflected the chastened mood and modest post-revolutionary expectations, agricultural machines were the centerpiece of this exhibition. Machines would take up an increasing amount of space in every exhibition to follow, finally filling the great temple of Hungarian industrialism—the Industrial Hall of 1885. Bach tied the monarchy's future to progress, but by blocking Kossuth's vehicle for modernization, Bach exposed his system to the criticism that he was blocking economic development. Inadvertently, the emperor's tour highlighted this conflict between nationalist and administrative modernization programs when the busy sovereign was obliged to interrupt his Hungarian tour after visiting a Flower Exhibition in Pest in order to race back to Vienna to open a grander Agricultural Exhibition.[148] Of the 1,800 machines displayed, 1,300 were from the monarchy—a hopeful sign—yet of these only 97 came from Hungary. The Viennese exhibition seemed to dramatize Hungarian backwardness. Hungarian newspapers reported, "it is striking that Hungary is so poorly represented."[149] Official visits to the six-day agricultural exhibition in Köztelek or the sovereign's visit to a modest Natural, Industrial and Art Exhibition in Kassa could not undo the damage.[150]

Tragedy struck on the last leg of the 1857 imperial tour. Measles made the infant Princess Gisela seriously ill, how seriously, the royal couple who continued their tour did not realize. They proceeded through small and middle-sized towns: officials would greet the railway car as it arrived, the local military would be out in force, a banderium would accompany the party from the railroad to the market place or city hall for speeches before thousands of peasants and townspeople. Sometimes local celebrities, e.g., old Hussars who had fought Napoleon were presented to the emperor. Festive decorations with Hungarian, German, or Hebrew expressions of homage were common. The receiving lines in town after town, as well as the monarch's attendance at local exhibitions, banderiums, and the like, brought the rituals of official receptions and visitations into public view and were an integral element of the royal tours. The royal visit became the occasion for grand popular festivals, as well. Oxen were roasted and barrels of wine were made available to the town folk and peasantry. Gypsy and military bands competed and illuminations were staged. At Nagykőrös around twenty thousand gathered at the station to await the imperial couple and the great holiday that could then begin. For the sovereigns virtually every day presented the same festive whirl, only the size of the banderiums would vary from ten thousand riders in Kígyós to eighteen hundred horsemen of Jászberény who thoughtfully assembled in stages, since "all of them would create too much dust."[151] On some days four banderiums would be reviewed. It was as if the sovereign had come to see the whole Hungarian aristocracy pass by on horseback.

News of their daughter's worsening condition reached the imperial couple in Debrecen. The image of the empress distraught and in tears, rushing with her husband back to Buda was the strongest memory of the ill-fated tour. Three days later the child died and the couple returned with the body to Vienna.[152] Elizabeth would not return to Hungary for another nine years. The Hungarian public may not have known the full despair of the mother who had brought her sickly child to Buda despite her doctor's warning and her mother-in-law's pleas, but in this second dramatic event in Franz Joseph's tenure (the assassination attempt of 1853 being the first), the Hungarian public felt part of the family drama. This time they could be the sympathetic rather than the implicated spectator.[153] Elizabeth was disconsolate and melancholy. Mourning became public when she and Franz Joseph went on a personal pilgrimage to the Mariazell shrine in Styria, near the Hungarian border. By appending a pilgrimage to the funeral rite, the ruling family dramatized the event and accentuated the pious nature of the dynasty. Subsequently, the crowds seemed more sympathetic to his person if not to his policies.

The tour of 1857 had genuine drama and a beautiful, bereaved heroine. In the midst of neo-absolutism, a new celebrity monarchism was being born. And however skewed the crowd estimates of the time may have been, it is clear that several hundred thousand Hungarians gathered to see Franz Joseph and Elizabeth. Even more were swept up in the Habsburg family tragedy, for on this issue the official press was more than adequate. To a degree that most Hungarians, certainly Hungarian nationalists, were unwilling to admit, the tour had succeeded in bringing the monarch and the crowd together in a new connection that was to become the foundation of dualism. Nationalists had been waiting for the supra-nationalist values of the Bach system to recede. The bureaucracy had been active in the 1850s, but they, too, had been waiting for the pathology of a martyred nationalism to wane and for the people to love their emperor. The tour as an icon of pseudo-affection and hyperbole in 1852 had succumbed to a modicum of sincere affection in 1857. Franz Joseph had encountered and countered the passivity of his people; he had opened the door a bit toward a repopulating of the political arena.

After a two-and-half-month interruption, Franz Joseph returned to Hungary to complete the tour. Between twenty and thirty thousand greeted his train as it arrived in Sopron, but the crowd was quickly scattered by the rain.[154] The whole unfortunate tour of 1857 came to a fittingly macabre denouement when the emperor was greeted at the district border of Miskolc by the mayor at the head of a sizable banderium. After presenting his welcoming speech under the triumphal arch, the mayor joined in the boisterous cheers to the emperor only to fall from his horse, victim of a heart attack.[155] After presenting condolences to the family, the weary Franz Joseph returned to Buda and then Vienna.

In response to the dynasty's tragedy, the Old Conservatives organized a massive pilgrimage to Mariazell, the site to which the imperial couple had gone in their grief. Thirty thousand Hungarian pilgrims made their way to Mariazell. The event was full of mixed messages for the system. While seemingly a display of sympathy for the Habsburg family, the Old Conservatives would later flaunt it as a demonstration of their influence over the rural masses, one that underscored their claim of fitness to lead the nation.[156] Few actual benefits had accrued to Hungary from the official visit. No new illusions about power relations were engendered by the imperial visit. The one attempt by a delegation of aristocrats to broach the matter of a constitution with Franz Joseph was brusquely rejected. He deeply resented having to listen to an address by the primate requesting both the use of Magyar in local offices and the abolition of the five-part military and administrative division of the country. The emperor took that to be fresh proof of the bad faith of the Old Conservative party, with whom Primate Scitovszky was now aligned. The Old Conservatives channeled their disappointment into the pilgrimage. During the Hungarian mass procession from the border to the Styrian site, Primate Scitovszky also annoyed the nationalists when he made no objection to General Kempen's police escort of the pilgrims. The Hungarian tricolor banner was brought along, but the police made sure it was not unfurled.[157] Nevertheless, this was a clearly successful conservative-nationalist crowd demonstration.

The aristocracy had more than ever demonstrated its claim to symbolic leadership both when aristocrats presented themselves in homage to their sovereign in colorful banderiums and when they defied the local officials by staying away. Their reception of the sovereign in 1857 had been correct, but not overly enthusiastic. However, unlike the colorless tour of 1852, with its Potemkin village crowds, the sovereign had performed the rite of interaction with his public, and they with him. The imperial tour had resulted in a standoff. Insofar as physical presence and enthusiasm became a measure of political support in the 1850s, both nationalists and dynasts could take comfort. The tours forced the act of homage but also allowed for the demonstration of good will on both sides.

The Old Conservatives were emboldened to press for restoration of national privileges. Under the leadership of Count Emil Dessewffy they defined a new public politics by setting out on an aggressive pilgrimage to culture. Dessewffy, a self-assured, unyielding magnate, stepped in be-

tween the crowd and regime as a new pageant-master.[158] Through his base
in the academy, Dessewffy orchestrated the politics of cultural nationalism, eventually nudging Hungary out of the unquiet wait of the 1850s. But
first, he appealed to the sovereign for the restoration of Hungarian rights.
If he could have sold it to the emperor, then the Hungarians probably
would not have wanted it. This was the dilemma of Hungarian cultural politics. The more his memoranda were rejected, the more his claim on national leadership was validated. His program of conservative compromise
had an element of creativity about it. Dessewffy stepped forward with
"constructive criticism," a plan for "a constitutional coup d'état" led by the
emperor that would grant some constitutional autonomy, while retaining
the unity of the monarchy. The plan acceded to some of the social achievements of the revolution, while protecting the influence of the great estates
and shoring up the position of the estate owners as leaders of a resurrected
Hungary. Unable to sell his program to the emperor, he tried to sell it to his
countrymen, hoping to generate a ground swell of popular opinion that
would prompt the emperor to adopt the necessary policies.

In his presidential address in December 1858, the first general meeting of
the academy in eleven years, Dessewffy galvanized those in attendance
when he spoke what was widely heralded as the first unrestrained words
heard in Hungary in a decade. He exhorted the assembly to walk with their
heads high, because one could not expect Hungarians to be treated with respect if they acted subservient. He told the writers and academics that they
were "soldiers of the Hungarian soul."[159] As president of the academy, he
filled the many vacancies created by the purge of the academy at the beginning of the decade. The intelligentsia was again organizing, but with a difference. The seventy-four new members, often middle class, were also primarily post-48 intellectuals. This gave the organization a new dynamism.[160]

The Bach theaterocrats, by contrast, found themselves in a rear guard
battle. The case of the theater in Kassa is particularly illustrative of the cultural conflicts that bedeviled provincial towns as the decade wore on. The
town had two competing companies, a Hungarian and a German, vying for
control over the one theater.[161] Since Kassa originated as a "German colony," officials made it a matter of pride that the town not lose its German
theater, while the Hungarians never forgot that the nucleus for the first ensemble of the Hungarian National Theater had been recruited from the
local Kassa troupe. The Slovak peasant population in the hinterlands was
not yet a party to the competition, but neither the German nor the Hungarian potential theater-going public, about equally divided, was actually sufficient to sustain a year-long theater schedule. The town of seventeen thou-

sand had a sizable number only interested in the Hungarian theater, while the theater-going German public, made up mainly of officials, military, and the German commercial families, was so small a public that there was a limit to repeat performances. This made new productions particularly costly and exhausting for the actors. The Kassa bureaucrats were painfully aware that the German theater directors hardly lasted a season, making city authorities increasingly reluctant to extend generous leases and/or free heating to German theater directors.

Officials became alarmed when a shrewd Hungarian theater director in the neighboring town of Eperjes (Prešov) sought a six-week engagement in the middle of the lucrative winter season in return for splitting the profits with the German theater director of Kassa; such a marginalization of the German theater would be a most distressing precedent.[162] As one official wrote, "I must emphasize that the Hungarian theater has long waited to establish itself in the winter here; if the German performances ended in the winter or if in the summer a competent German company can not be put together for next winter season then the Hungarian side will see it as a perfect opportunity to get a concession which cannot be denied them on legal grounds. This would create an unfortunate precedent which would encourage the Hungarian theater to eliminate the German theater altogether," thereby, "a terrain would be lost which had been won through sacrifice, toil and money."[163] If the German theater went under there would be no legal way of barring the lease for the Hungarian theater as it would be "disadvantageous if the Hungarian public saw that one preferred to see the theater empty than to allow them any pleasure."[164] Ticket prices were kept the same for many years, despite significant inflation and the increase in wages of actors. To bring ticket prices in correct relation to costs, they would have to be doubled, one official noted. This, he quickly added, would be to throw the baby out with the bath water, for it would reduce attendance. He was unwilling to even support a moderate increase in ticket prices.[165] The de-Germanization of the Hungarian stage had become a process the Bach system could only delay, not stop.

The more neo-absolutism became routinized, impoverished banned Hungarian playwrights were elevated to the status of martyrs. The martyrology of its culture heroes blurred the gap between high and mid-culture. The funerals of legendary actors and playwrights became the focus of an outpouring of collective emotion. The death of a great matinee idol in 1858 was the occasion of another great demonstration, when fifteen thousand to twenty thousand people entered into the funeral procession for the fifty-one-year-old Márton Lendvay. Lendvay had delivered the first lines on the National Theater stage in 1837, when he recited the prologue of Vörösmarty's *Árpád Awakening*. His *Hamlet* and *Bán Bánk* epitomized the romantic stress on sentiment. He was stately and well built with a resonating voice such that he even sang in musical parts with success. He had secured his right to such national recognition by supporting and fighting for the revolution. His funeral procession was led by twenty-one writers and actors carrying torches as they made their way to the square before the National Theater. The eulogy was delivered by József Székács, a Calvinist minister so given to such passionate performances that he was dubbed the "national pope."[166] Jókai, the most popular writer of the age, gave the necrology.[167] Lendvay was a celebrity, and a fading one at that. But although his last performance had been in 1854, his death was an opportunity for the audience to play out the drama of patriotic mourning.

The Garay, Vörösmarty, and Lendvay funerals reflected the intense feeling the public of the 1850s had for the National Theater, seeing it as the place where national expression was still braved during a time of oppression.[168] The theater was one of the few permissible crowd experiences; it was as well a civilized forum where gestures of reconciliation could first be ventured. Once a primarily élite entertainment of the court, the theater had become a cherished institution of national liberalism with its elitist, reformist view of culture. By 1858 the square before the theater was inaugurated as the new gathering ground and as a stage for new democratic feelings.[169] The first Magyar statue in a Pest public square was erected that year on the site to honor the playwright József Katona. This statue was widely understood to be the patriotic response to the regime's statue of General Hentzi.[170] But patriotic or not, it was an artistic flop. The public was sorely disappointed. Jókai satirized it as such a poor likeness, that from time to time the name on its pedestal could be changed. The same patron commissioned a Lendvay statue, and this displaced that of Katona, with the Katona scooted further back in the theater garden. The field of plastic arts was in its infancy in Hungary, but the Lendvay work showed a bit of improvement over the Katona. The statues of Hentzi, Katona, and Lendvay were the first three secular statues in Pest-Buda, each erected for the recently deceased and each eventually to disappear from the urban landscape, an indication of the character of the political passions of the 1850s. Katona's inferior likeness was removed from the capital to the playwright's provincial town, while the Lendvay statue became in only a few years an embarrassment, an all-but-anonymous figure in bronze.[171] In the Horthy period, which was fascinated with ceremonial nationalism, there was talk of taking even the Lendvay statue out of storage and returning it to some square in Pest.[172] Today, it inconspicuously adorns

Marton Lendvay statue at the National Theater (Capitol's Ervin Szabó Library, Budapest Collection)

a shaded bench along a street in Buda. By the late 1850s it had become possible to erect statues to Hungarians, provided they were a minor playwright and an actor. Once the aspirations could be bronzed, the unquiet wait was coming to a close and the curtain was about to rise.

Kazinczy centennial celebration on October 27, 1859 (detail), at the Hungarian
Academy of Sciences in Pest. Drawing (Hungarian National Museum, Historical
Picture Gallery)

6

The Emergence of the Chastened Crowd

The balance between a conservative regime and an unquiet crowd changed forever once the regime stumbled into the Austro-French-Italian war of 1859. The three-month conflict politicized the population. Suddenly there was news that could not be censored. "Facts spoke."[1] Newspapers became interesting. The quality of journalism improved overnight. A new addiction was born. In 1848 the politicians in Pozsony were prompted to act by their ignorance and fear of what the crowd was doing in Pest, and a decade of rumormongering had followed. But now, thanks to the telegraph and the newspaper, the events impinged on Hungarian public opinion with a startling immediacy. Journalism had gained its lease on life and would become a central aspect of the political culture of the coming decades. Everyone wanted to know whether Austria was winning or losing and what Kossuth and the Hungarian Legion were doing.[2] The general European war scare of 1859 alerted conservatives and reactionaries to their vulnerability to public opinion. Now that newspaper coverage made it possible to not only follow events but be almost simultaneous with them, public response was much more immediate. The older connection of nationalism with revolution was being displaced with an association between nationalism and war. Hungarians began redefining the revolution of 1848/49 as the war of independence.[3]

"Now is the time for retaliation," Kossuth proclaimed.[4] For a moment the emigration defined Hungarian politics by forming the Hungarian Legion, establishing the Hungarian government in exile, obtaining the backing of Napoleon III, and creating the dreamy prospect of a Danubian confederation that would include Hungarians, Romanians, Croats, and Serbs.[5] Kossuthites demonstrated their willingness to retreat on the Transylvania issue somewhat, accepting the potential of a separate administration for

Transylvania. General György Klapka, commander of the Hungarian Legion, called on Hungarian troops to desert. His proclamation, printed in the *Kölnische Zeitung* of June 29, was banned. So long as local authorities could keep the existence and content of the proclamation a rumor and not fact, they hoped to contain its impact to the mutterings heard already among the newly conscripted volunteers, reservists, and those on furlough.[6] Kossuth issued a manifesto directed at Hungarians in the Habsburg army. Franz Joseph was a usurper. "He is not King of Hungary, according to our laws the Hungarian only owes allegiance to a king who is legally crowned. The power of Franz Joseph acquired by alien brutal force has not been confirmed either by coronation or by election." "Our country has been struck off the list of living nations." It was "time to unfurl the tricolor of Hungary banished from the earth for ten years."[7]

While Kossuth busied himself with negotiations with the Serbian Prince, inside Hungary walls were plastered with notices from the sovereign "to my people." Hungarians affected detachment, and defeatism was rampant. When, at the outbreak, an Italian delegation displayed its flag at a Szeged sharpshooter's festival, they were cheered hysterically.[8] The Habsburg defeat at Magenta on June 4 was a body blow to the Bach system. As the imperial forces were abandoning Milan and Lombardy, the Hungarian Legion was formed in Genoa. In the minds of the militant, the day of action was imminent. After dutifully producing bland, reassuring mood reports for five years, the Bach system faced a fatal crisis of confidence. In northeast Hungary, for instance, Nagyvárad officials reacted nervously at the end of May to anonymous warnings of a web of revolutionary insurrection being prepared in the county and presumably throughout the whole country as well.[9] Kassa district authorities passed along reports that the French government was spending millions to incite rebellion in Hungary, Croatia, and Transylvania, and that the uprising would follow the first decisive Austrian defeat.[10] Troubling as well were widespread rumors of imminent pogroms, which authorities suspected were being spread by revolutionaries to divert attention from their own violent machinations.[11] By the third week of June the public and regime were reeling from the news from Italy. Outlying towns such as Ungvár (Uzegorod), fearing that any spark might occasion an explosion, requested and received an additional battalion of infantry.[12] In Máramaros County, the Calvinist population was characterized as affecting indifference with a minority of individuals openly joyful at the news.[13] As elsewhere, the peasants were outside the newspaper culture, receiving only sparse reports. Their concern remained confined to the fate of local troops engaged in battle. Officials took comfort in this passivity.

Nevertheless, the defeats and émigré commotion aroused official anxiety about a still invisible crowd of rebellion and revolution. Recognizing that the immediate threat was more theoretical than actual, officials took steps to rally spirits. They elicited loyalty addresses and patriotic donations and summoned a stream of volunteer recruits. Authorities were granted more secret funds to pay off informers. Although the mood throughout Hungary remained worrisome rather than threatening, here and there troublesome incidents manifested themselves. On June 16 in one small town a group of animated day laborers ambled into the marketplace joyously singing antigovernmental songs, cheering Kossuth and Napoleon III. They did not restrain themselves in front of the gendarmes, who moved to arrest them. The peasants grabbed their scythes to protect themselves, and they taunted the gendarmes, cursing them as bandits and dogs. After much effort, a few were arrested on the spot and more were seized the next day. At their trial the eleven accused explained that a fellow worker had told them that the French had taken over all of Italy after beating the Austrians in several battles. Moreover, they believed that the Russians were about to enter Hungary and that Kossuth was to name the Tsar's brother-in-law king of Hungary. The little band talked excitedly about taking up arms to free the country from the Austrians, imagining that when Kossuth and Klapka arrived, they would kill the imperial officials. They also expected this would liberate them from their heavy taxes.[14]

With the reverses of Magenta and Solferino, the war came to a sudden end in mid-July, too rapidly for any dramatic benefits to accrue to the Hungarians. There would be no rising. By making a quick peace with Napoleon III, Franz Joseph had short-circuited both the danger of a general European war (in which Austria would have become dependent on Prussia) and an uprising by the Hungarians. The Habsburg experience had been that military defeat, if accepted at an early point, need not be fatal. Austria had been repeatedly defeated by the first Napoleon and survived. It was hoped that the same pattern would hold true again. The embarrassment of defeat, however, could no longer be convincingly explained away.[15] The debacle exposed both the weakness of neo-absolutism and the hollowness of Kossuth's plans to exploit such weakness.

The Bach system began to unravel. Habsburg diplomats seemed to have frittered away the years. The bureaucracy was already demoralized. No longer very feared but much mocked, the Bach Hussar knew his days were numbered. By the late fifties bureaucrats were just holding on. Bohemians no longer saw any professional advantage to a post in Hungary. There were more profitable things to do than serve the state in an inhospitable area away from their homeland. The indigenous bureaucrats showed a growing schizophrenia; the "imperial civil servant" in working hours was all-too-often the Magyar nationalist at home. They, too, were tired of the dead-in-the-water feeling of Hungarian politics during the fifties. The Habsburg defeat at Magenta prompted a mood of great expectation. The unquiet wait seemed over and the day of immediate action seemed to be approaching. It was clear that the invulnerability and rigidity that had been the strength of neo-absolutism in the preceding decade could no longer be sustained.[16] In August Bach was dismissed; Police Minister Kempen was also replaced.

Cultural Nationalism

By the fall of 1859 neo-absolutism began to leak like a sieve. Not one event, not one place in Hungary proved determinant, but authorities in place after place were confronted with demonstrating crowds. As the political crisis would unfold, it was inevitable that there would be an enlivening of public space. The ten-year-old order was breaking up; the crowd again became the wild card. On September 1, 1859, Vienna worsened the crisis when it foolishly promulgated the Protestant Patent for Hungary.[17] Two conflicts met in the patent issue, that of religion and that of the subject peoples. Historians are still puzzled as to why the government would allow Cultural Minister Leo Thun to bring up such an explosive issue at this unsettled time. In part, the government just stumbled into it, because after years of consultation the commission had completed its report. But the policy was a key element in Thun's agenda; he had assumed his post in the same year as Bach and Kempen, and he defiantly issued the Patent after his neo-absolutist colleagues had fallen from their posts. Thun's cultural politics was predicated on the need to curtail Hungarian nationalism by delimiting Hungarian Protestantism.

The government was unprepared for the fierce resistance the Patent would trigger. The regime seemed to have handed the Magyars an issue and an opportunity. Even Catholic Old Conservatives registered horror. In 1849 Count Emil Dessewffy had warned that Hungarian Protestantism was more dangerous than Magyars, but in 1859 he deemed the Patent "the most colossal idiocy that the government has done since 1848."[18] For Protestants who had felt threatened under neo-absolutism, the Patent revived fears. Rumors spread; some Protestant peasants believed the Patent required them to convert to Catholicism. Protestants were traditionally leery of the power emanating from the Catholic center, and the Concordat of

1855 had already heightened suspicion. "Simply the issuance of a patent," the very fact that a law was created for the Evangelical Church, was such a great "insult," declared Kálmán Tisza, curator of the Calvinist Church of Nagyszalonta, that even if the content of the Patent was flawless, it could not be accepted.[19] The Calvinist organization was the launching pad for Tisza's formidable political career. In the absence of politics in the 1850s, would-be politicians in eastern Hungary utilized the lay positions in Protestant church administrations. The Patent reorganized the Protestant Church structure to more closely resemble that of the Catholic Church, the goal being to reduce secular authority over church policy. Initially, many Magyar clerics supported purging the church of these secular-political influences. But the regime now also claimed jurisdiction over matters that Protestants had presumed were theirs to decide. For example, the Patent increased central authority over educational matters, including selection of teachers and textbooks. The Patent redivided the Protestant ecclesiastical map to add two new jurisdictions, one for German and another for Slovak Lutherans. The restructuring promised a more compliant Protestantism by reducing Magyar dominance. Protestant ethnic minorities were appreciative of the principle of equality within their own confession and, therefore, generally endorsed the Patent. This was particularly threatening to the Magyar elite in outlying areas, for it struck at their haven during neo-absolutism.

Magyar Protestants determined to confront the government. They hurried to a convocation in Késmárk (Kežmarok) on September 27–9, where the well-known Old Conservative Ede Zsedényi presented an uncompromising critique of the Patent and called for it to be rescinded.[20] With a noted conservative and Habsburg loyalist like Zsedényi as spokesman of the religious "Autonomists," their movement garnered support among monarchists. Zsedényi, Pastor Károly Máday who drafted the document, and a Professor Antal Pálkövi of Sárospatak, who had it published, were arrested. Lutherans convened in Sopron on October 5–6 and Calvinists in Debrecen on October 8, where Kálmán Tisza emerged as the principal spokesperson of the anti-Patent movement.[21] Although the agitation seemed, for the moment, to be innocuous, the remnants of the Bach system found themselves confronting an organized political campaign, ready to seize on the new vulnerability of the regime. Széchenyi feared that, as in 1848, once the agitation was in swing it would be hard to quell. The government in Vienna stubbornly refused to budge, seeing the opposition of the Autonomists as simply opportunistic, motivated by politics and Magyar nationalism, rather than pious anxieties. This was largely true; the Protestant campaign was reactivating politics.

In September the Patent had created a martyr of Zsedényi; by the beginning of October, it had brought forth politicians. Tensions were escalating. The Autonomists exploited the festering anger and posed the Patent as an attack on Hungarianness. The agitation expanded, gaining a wide base of support far beyond the confessional communities or the radical Kossuthites. The Catholic Dessewffy was quick to throw his support behind the Autonomists, neutralizing the confessional divisions among Magyars. His embrace of the Protestant gentry of eastern Hungary and Transylvania projected a powerful example of Protestants and Catholics, magnates and gentry cooperating, overcoming regionalism, and confessionalism to affirm a common Hungarianness. Dessewffy placed himself in a leadership role, standing above religion, using Magyar identity, instead, as his direct connection to the public agitation.

Dessewffy and József Eötvös began preparations for a Ferenc Kazinczy (1759–1831) centennial, at the same time that the Germans were planning a lavish commemoration of the Schiller centennial. Kazinczy was a poet and grammarian; he had broadened the Magyar vocabulary by unearthing forgotten words and rationalizing and ordering the grammar; his translations had elevated the prose, and perhaps most importantly, his lively correspondence with the young romantics buoyed their efforts to write in Hungarian. Kazinczy's biography also underscored the radical nature of this activity. Kazinczy had been one of those "philological incendiaries" threatening the dynasts and their order. The Enlightenment grammarian had been sentenced to death as a co-conspirator in the Ignác Martinovics Jacobin plot and was forced to serve six years of his sentence (1795–1801) before he was released.[22] The image of the persecuted man of letters resonated for contemporaries who had felt the threatening hand of a distant central power.

Gyula Andrássy had, initially, wondered about the efficacy of using the Kazinczy centennial as a national holiday, thinking it might have been better to have chosen one not so compromised. The holiday, he correctly reasoned, would gain its fullest expression among Protestants. It proved particularly propitious, however, that Kazinczy was a Calvinist member of the gentry. Comments about Kazinczy could still be understood in the narrower context of the Patent controversy, but they were nonconfrontational and nonviolent forums. More importantly, however, the local festivals surrounding the Kazinczy centennial reached beyond the exclusive ecclesiastical meetings in September, October, and November. The assertion was that all readers and speakers of the vernacular could gather around a Kazinczy bust or join in prayers "before the national altar."[23] The journalists fixated on the themes of cooperation, unity, and ecumenicalism, elevating "love of homeland above all differences." "Nobody asked: Was Kazinczy Catholic, Protestant, or Greek Orthodox? It was enough to know that he was the champion of the Magyar language and nationality." Nationalism was not just a secular faith neatly displacing traditional religiosity; religious struggles helped define nationalism.

This was a juncture when holidays were being "invented." Whether it was name days of patriotic individuals treated as holidays or an elaborate centennial for Kazinczy, these were overtly nationalistic and implicitly political undertakings. The new piety preached a fellowship in the vernacular. Central to that fellowship was the shared sense of victimization. The Kazinczy martyrdom had, moreover, been passed on to the next generation; one of his sons, Lajos, was remembered by many as "the fourteenth martyr."[24] The twenty-nine-year-old captured Honvéd general had been executed some nineteen days after the executions in Arad.[25] The Kazinczy centennial celebration in Arad would be particularly self-conscious; from the hallowed ground of the martyrs of 1848, the press reported, a message was sent forth to the nation that "we are not broken, not even captured."[26] With neo-absolutism in decay, the identification with an unjust humiliation was an injunction.

Hungarians would not claim Kazinczy was Schiller's equal, but they could claim in Kazinczy a martyr to their cause, who had prepared the ground for the nation as an "imagined community."[27] As a linguistic nationalist Kazinczy shared with Herder the belief that it was through the nation's tongue that God spoke, and not to cultivate the language in which one was born was to deny a moral obligation taken at birth. The vernacular had come to take on a spiritual life of its own. Magyar culture could now feel rivalry, suffer affronts, and even face the prospect of national extinction. Although the Kazinczy centennial provided another opportunity to invoke the rhetoric of self-protection, the defensive posture was giving way to the celebration of the rise of the vernacular and the decline of illiteracy. By 1859 almost a third of Hungarian speakers were literate and the end of mass illiteracy was in sight. The focus on Kazinczy as the hero of the Magyar revival was illustrative of this optimism. The preference for Kazinczy mirrored the shift in the 1850s from the fragile language of poetry to the honing of Hungarian as a professional and scientific language. Two years earlier the poet János Arany had asserted that Hungarians owed their cultural rebirth not to the fine romantic sentiments of a Kisfaludy but to the durable linguistic pragmatism of a Kazinczy. Arany hailed Kazinczy as a "flag-bearer" and urged the founding of a Kazinczy Society.[28]

Hungarian plans for the Kazinczy centennial grew ever grander as the academy sought to keep pace with the simultaneous preparations for the Schiller centennial in the German-speaking world. German liberalism would mark its political return in the cathartic celebration of Schiller's genius.[29] Eleven days prior to the Kazinczy celebration, Pest students circulated a petition demanding Hungarian become the language of instruction at the university and other institutions of higher learning. On the day that a student delegation was scheduled to depart for Vienna to lobby for this reform, the university authorities posted an announcement forbidding "student assemblies for other than lawful purposes."[30] The faculty senate pleaded with the students to observe the order. All were aware of the unpopularity of the language regulation. With the expansion of the student body in the 1850s, more students lacked the mastery of German, which had been a given with the previous generation of students. The German language requirement seemed particularly onerous at the agricultural institutes. Amidst the Kazinczy enthusiasm, these students were moved to an eloquent articulation of their demand for Magyar education. They confronted the argument used by some of the Germanizers that Hungarian was an inadequate language for learning. The cult of Kazinczy rested on the assertion that Kazinczy's generation had provided the discipline and precision to make Magyar a learned language, appropriate for modern expression and use in the sciences.

No Hungarian event could pass without a look over one's shoulder to see how one was being assessed in the Viennese press, which was invariably and often intentionally irritating. One such Viennese report discounted Kazinczy as a minor figure who had not even warranted mention in the latest *Brockhaus* encyclopedia. The Hungarian press immediately and bitterly countered that Kazinczy was in the *Brockhaus*.[31] But most deflating was Viennese dismissal of the Hungarian event as merely a sideshow of the Schiller festival planned for two weeks later. It was an invidious comparison. In the imperial capital tremendous preparations were being made for the Schiller festival, while of course, the oppositional Hungarian festival lacked the regime's patronage. Four days before the Kazinczy festival, Franz Joseph announced that the square before the Hofburg theater in Vienna would be renamed Schiller Square.[32] Hungary, with its large bilingual population, was involved in honoring both, with gradations of enthusiasm sometimes displayed within the same households, depending on generation and temperament. The Budapest press responded with the formula: While Schiller, the poet of freedom, was worthy of general European celebration, Kazinczy, "the poet of nationality," was worthy of special Hungarian homage.[33] The acrimony in the newspapers was one of the signs of a more open press in the fall of 1859. More was said, but Hungarians were also more affronted by what the Viennese did say about them. The politics of cultural celebration and competition resonated through the monarchy. In these weeks Serbs announced that they would be holding a comparable centennial for their "Kazinczy," Sebastyén Tököly.[34] In a period of rapidly rising literacy, pride in the strides of one's own vernacular alternated with the fear of being swamped by another vernacular.

To celebrate Kazinczy was also to proselytize the academy's agenda for Hungarian cultural development. The day of the gala the academy's rotunda and auditorium were packed. The Transylvanian delegation was particularly conspicuous amongst the several thousand who came from throughout Hungary. There and at the adjoining banquet and performance in the National Theater, the literary elite rubbed shoulders with the great families of the land. On display were commissioned objects, a marble bust of Kazinczy, as well as a painting of Kazinczy's first meeting with Kisfaludy. The watchword of the academy's observance was "the memory of the people is more powerful than the fashions of the moment."[35] Dessewffy began his address with a personal anecdote, a childhood memory of Kazinczy at the Dessewffy estate; the tie of the magnate and the nation's cultural life was underscored at the outset. Dessewffy then spoke of the "national death" so barely avoided. Having raised the specter, he continued on a positive note: "Today, I will gladly believe that my fear proved unfounded. . . . We are . . . here to bring our patriotic hearts together, and to allow the great example before us to prompt us into action. We suffer and sacrifice like him, without hope for immediate success, remaining true to high and noble goals. We do not shirk from conflict and are filled, as he was, with the same determination!" He concluded with the assurance that "the crown of laurels on Kazinczy's brow would never fade, if it is watered by the thankful tears of living and future generations."[36] Eötvös, the leading intellectual of the day, delivered a measured, classical oration, enumerating cultural achievements and political grievances. Additional orators stirred the crowd, amongst them Pastor József Székács, a Calvinist firebrand, who declaimed a poem written for the occasion.[37] But the climax of the whole event, most would later declare, was when the "silent Deák" rose at the end of the banquet. "We must pray. My prayer is brief, consisting of only four words: Long live the homeland!"[38] The long ovation that followed indicated that the assembly understood these words to mean there would be no retreat, that the demand for the April Laws of 1848 would not be compromised.

The banquet had been resplendent with Magyar music, interrupted continuously by toasts, buoyed by ample Tokaj wine. During the meal Dessewffy called for the creation of a Kazinczy Society and a subscription was taken up. The fund was to be overseen by Deák, Eötvös, a son of Kazinczy, and Kemény. There was a rush of pledges, some quite generous. The successful subscription campaign allowed for a conspicuous process of signing on, bearing witness. Newspapers dutifully recorded each contributor and contribution in the coming months, which incidentally provided an opportunity for burghers, amongst them Jews, to demonstrate their commitment to the national cause.[39] Commemorative coins were issued; streets were renamed "Kazinczy" in many provincial towns.[40]

Enthusiasm spread through the country, with people flocking to theater performances, city halls, schools, and fancy banquets. These events followed a fairly similar pattern. Festivities usually began at the local high school, festooned with tricolors, where it became an opportunity for student and teacher orations. Parents and local notables were in attendance. In larger locales, such as Debrecen, Kazinczy busts were commissioned for the foyers of the Protestant gymnasiums.[41] Theater performances provided the festive flourish. National flags were hung from the facade of the theater, flung across banisters and sewn into curtains to adorn the drapes of the box seats. Kazinczy's portrait was tacked to the pillars. Tricolored lighting gave it all a magical quality. Typically, as in Miskolc, the theater was filled to the rafters well before the performance began. "And what a crowd! In truth it was beautiful to look over the whole audience, elegant, in large part in national attire."[42] Among this decidedly elite gathering of wealthy citizens, gentry from the countryside, and literati, nationalist fashion was suddenly the rage. Crowds milled around outside, soaking in the ambience and peering at the privileged passing in their expensive Magyar costumes. The audience was what counted, not the performance. Every show began with the audience singing the "Himnusz" and "Szózat." Both songs had attained their permanent place in the Hungarian liturgy. In contrast to the vibrancy of the audience, the program was often heavily laden with long-winded addresses by notables and recitations of familiar texts, capped by a predictable theater piece.

The Kazinczy centennial produced repercussions in every direction. The Schiller festival was certainly a more intense moment, but it only involved one night. The excitement over Kazinczy resonated out into the provincial towns. Over and over again the centennial was reenacted and re-reported in the press for months. The extensive newspaper coverage of event after event produced a bandwagon effect, through which journalists attuned readers to an imaginary nationwide crowd. Kossuth called it the "holiday of the awakening of the Magyar national spirit."[43] As events proliferated, each catering to different groups and classes, the press delighted in the fact that the Kazinczy commemoration was "the true people's holiday." A potluck dinner in Miskolc for artisans and workers was a lively meal with lots of food and drink that collected twenty forints toward a Kazinczy bust. Although it began late, at nine in the evening, the dinner still contained a heavy quotient of poetry, speeches, and patriotic song.[44]

Bureaucratic "obstacles" drew out the celebration even further and added an element of struggle. The final event, the procession to Kazinczy's grave site in Széphalom, was repeatedly delayed and renegotiated. Finding themselves obstructed, the festival committee defiantly elected Andrássy as president. The bureaucracy held firm, denying the right to association by objecting to the bylaws of the society. In the course of the year the Academy raised enough money to purchase Kazinczy's Széphalom estate. The collapsing garden house was replaced by a neo-Greco mausoleum to serve as the Kazinczy museum.[45] Finally, the procession was sanctioned for the last day of the year.[46] Around five thousand people gathered in the little town of Újhely. The locals came out, indeed, "ran out in amazement" at the sight and the day's prospect.[47] Four huge trees were loaded onto a wagon waiting to be planted around the grave site, quite an oddity for a winter day.[48] The trees, steadied by ropes, seemed to suggest that this was an unusual event with its own rules. The tree-filled cart was harnessed to six oxen, all decked out for the occasion. An orchestra played as the torchlight parade set off for Kazinczy's grave. There was a stream of carriages, a profusion of carts, and thousands of people parading on foot through the mud and snow to Kazinczy's grave. Around five thousand people passed through Széphalom that day. Participants were "surprised to see so many new faces, nonofficials."[49] The road to the grave was strewn with tricolor flags. Wreaths were solemnly laid before the grave, and defiant speeches were made, peppered with reminders of why the holiday was being celebrated on the last day of the year. Students from Sárospatak led the singing of the "Szózat" and the "Himnusz." The final words and prayers were reserved for András Kalniczky, the old priest who had buried Kazinczy twenty-eight years earlier. The crowd filed back to town in as orderly a fashion as they had come.[50]

When seen within the context of the Magyar heartland, the Kazinczy festival was as uplifting as advertised, but moving toward the outlying areas, the event took on the qualities of an ethnic demonstration. In Pozsony, the Kazinczy celebration was limited to an exclusive gala banquet.

The magnate families of Pálffy, Zichy, and Esterházy were all in attendance at the exquisite ball. The hall was not only decorated in the national colors, but expensive exotica; tropical flowers ("a real American plant") decorated the entry staircase. The quotable toasts and notable donations were duly reported in the local press, but the press report was defensive about the event's exclusivity in a city whose burgher and peasant populations were mostly not Hungarian: "Those who think our city's inhabitants care less about the national question than any other area are much mistaken."[51]

The Kazinczy celebration in quasi-autonomous Transylvania raised questions dormant for almost a decade about the relation of the Magyars, Romanians, and Saxons. On the surface, the event was like any other. The public, in holiday garb, gathered on the street corners to watch the elegant carriages carrying ladies and gentlemen to the festivities. The newspapers claimed that the Assembly Hall was filled with Magyars "from the highest noble to the people's most ordinary son." The banquet for 150 men turned into a four-hour event, drawn out by repeated rounds of toasts. But most telling was the appearance of the pageant master Count Domokós Teleki in full Magyar regalia, as in the manner of the revolution, with sword at his side—prohibited since the bloodletting in the region in 1849.[52]

The opening of the Transylvanian Museum three weeks later revived the Romanian demand for an "academy," which had been denied them in 1852. The Orthodox Bishop of Transylvania Andreiu Şaguna would submit a petition on May 10, 1860, to the governor of Transylvania on behalf of 170 priests and intellectuals requesting permission to establish a cultural society.[53] The conservative Şaguna clung to a hope that an appeal to his "fellow Transylvanians" might succeed. His program, as spelled out a year later in a private letter, was "We shall not allow Transylvania to be turned into a Magyar country; we shall try to keep Transylvania as Transylvania. Just as Transylvania could not be Germanized, so shall it not be Magyarized. It must exist as Transylvania, that is, all its nations must live as nations of Transylvania equal in all things."[54] But unlike an independent Swiss confederacy, Transylvania was a multinational entity within a multiethnic system. Each of the three groups had been compromised by that relation. The group that would have benefited most from a Swiss solution, the Germans or Saxons, were compromised by their special relationship with the Habsburgs and the dominant linguistic group. For the Saxons the Schiller festival became an important demonstration of their resistance to Magyarization.[55] While the Transylvanian Romanians were the most downtrodden, the rise of a Romanian nation-state raised the prospect of

Transylvania becoming part of Romania. Romanians were "engaged in the most intense political activity that they had ever known."[56]

The dedication ceremonies for the Transylvanian Museum in Kolozsvár produced the largest assemblage in Transylvania since the revolution; the newspapers spoke of a crowd of ten thousand.[57] The governor attended. Museums were novel institutions. In the age of historicism, they gained special importance, and in ethnically disputed areas such as Transylvania, they were used to prove national claims. There was, and would continue to be, a very sharp political edge to the museum idea in this area. The establishment of a museum was an assertion of Hungarian culture and presence in Transylvania. In the era of neo-absolutism the issue of the future of Transylvania was put on hold, but the Hungarian elite was unanimous in their continued insistence that Transylvania be incorporated into Hungary. Eötvös delivered the key oration, a laudatory piece on Kisfaludy's poetry.[58] Eötvös understood liberty, equality, and fraternity as liberty, equality, and nationality, and embraced these as the three liberating ideas of the nineteenth century. But even as he set out to nurture Magyar culture in the borderlands, he trusted in liberal individualism to protect the other nationalities.[59]

By the late fall of 1859, many Old Conservatives thought things might be getting out of hand. They wanted to appeal to Franz Joseph for a change in policies toward Hungary before the impetus shifted back to the crowd-driven politics of 1848. With Primate János Scitovszky's support, Széchenyi prepared a petition to be presented at the primate's fifty-year jubilee in early November 1859. At the banquet a magnate made an easily understandable reference to the crowning of the emperor as Hungarian king, expressing his hope that "the primate would soon perform the constitutional role expected of him."[60] The Archbishop of Eger echoed these sentiments. Archduke Albrecht, representing the emperor, was indignant at the "nationalist and constitutionalist expectorations" uttered in his presence.[61] A displeased Albrecht left by steamer and telegraphed Vienna that with the exception of his own and the primate's speeches, none of the toasts could be published in the newspaper. Anger was fierce in the government, but the time had passed when such speeches were reason for imprisonment. For his part, Széchenyi was discouraged by the low turnout of the aristocracy at the ecclesiastical jubilee and grumbled about the faint-heartedness of those who did attend the elite banquet. He felt the aristocracy had failed to meet their responsibility to act. The emperor would be extremely irritated with the nobility for their action, which he viewed as a sign of disloyalty.

The conflict over the Protestant Patent also boiled over in Pest at year's end.[62] When Protestant church leaders met in December and drafted a statement announcing their rejection of the Patent, a delegation was dispatched to convey this message directly to the sovereign. The Pest meeting produced a crowd dynamic; tensions escalated immediately. When delegates found police had locked them out of the Calvin church, their meeting place, an angry crowd clashed with police in Calvin Square. The Pest incident revived international interest. Protestant Forty-Eighters in exile publicized the sensational trial of Zsedényi on December 28, 1859. Kossuth proclaimed, "The clergy, both Catholic and Protestant, are not simply patriots, they are apostles. And if they have to be, they can be martyrs."[63] A defense committee formed in Glasgow presented Hungarian Protestantism as an isle of freedom threatened by the dark power of Catholic Austria. For one last time, Hungarians successfully played on the conscience of the English; German Protestantism, more cognizant of the ethnic issues, took a more jaundiced view.[64] Zsedényi and Pálkövi were sentenced to four months in prison, and their accomplice Máday received two months. The trial created bitter debate within the government, but the emotionally charged atmosphere, in the end, only hardened attitudes. When Zsedényi appealed his sentence, the highest court doubled it to eight months and also stripped him of his title and pension.[65]

That winter the academy launched a campaign to erect an imposing Hungarian National Academy building.[66] When the Szeged-Csongrád savings bank donated a substantial sum toward construction of a palace for the academy, both city and county councils rushed to do the same. The Magyar elite also launched a major charity drive, ostensibly to aid Croatia after the disastrous harvest of 1859. But the underlying message was clear. Under Austrian rule Croatia was suffering, but under Hungarian rule Croatia might again prosper.[67] Noble ladies from the best families took to the stage of the National Theater or the Academy of Music to recite patriotic poetry, perform skits, or sing Magyar folk songs. The "Rákóczi March," "Himnusz," and "Szózat" were standard elements in these programs. The provinces followed Pest's lead, but by then the administration was wary and created obstacles to these supposedly philanthropic events.

During the carnival season of 1860 there were repeated confrontations between the police and young men. Soldiers even had to be brought out to suppress demonstrations and the singing of songs. Carnival could also be contentious in the hinterlands. When a district head canceled a ball in tiny Lőcse at the last minute without apparent cause,[68] Count Tivadar Csáky, a nationalist magnate, invited the guests to his home, instead, whereupon troops raided his home, disbanded the merrymakers, arrested two men, and brought the rest of the elite party-goers in for questioning.[69] One excitable guest published an account in the *Breslauer Zeitung* and remained so agitated about the matter that while discussing the case in the local casino, he had a stroke and died within the hour. His death was widely viewed as a consequence of official bullying and much sympathy was shown to his widow and two children. His funeral of March 4 brought out local residents in force.[70]

"Looking out my window," one provincial wrote on Easter Sunday 1860, "I was watching the people come out of the churches. I was fascinated, not by them, but by their clothing. The Magyar outfits have multiplied in such large number that they have become the general fashion."[71] Not to be in Hungarian attire was defying the fervent mood of national display. Male fashion was particularly striking. They wore hats with feathers, thickly embroidered atillas (braided gala cloak), decorated pants, boots, topped off with a pipe. The most radical wore Garibaldi shirts.

The Crowd in the Cemetery

Since the fall of 1859, the cemetery had been a scene of politically charged incidents. The Kerepesi cemetery in Pest opened during the revolutionary war. It was Hungary's first large public cemetery, and more importantly, it became the pantheon for its favorite sons and preferred burial ground for its wealthiest citizens.[72] The funeral of a leading soprano from the National Theater in September 1859 became a mini-demonstration when mourners interrupted an Austrian monk conducting the burial service in German by breaking forth with a Hungarian prayer.[73] They did so to protest the monopoly of German-speaking clergy in what was now viewed as a national Valhalla. The memorialization of heroes focused on the cemetery. Hungarian liberalism would use the cemetery as an arena to air its most defiant sentiments. For several years the press had been publishing proposals for a pantheon of Hungary's great men.[74] Law students in November 1859 took the initiative by dedicating a new headstone for Kisfaludy in the Kerepesi cemetery. All afternoon a stream of humanity made its way to the cemetery bringing wreaths in tribute to the poet who had died almost three decades earlier.[75] A few weeks later the distinguished writer and editor, Ferenc Toldy, Toldy's son, and a friend of his son, stole into the old Pest cemetery one night, transferred Kisfaludy's remains into a new coffin, draped it so it would look less conspicuous, and surreptitiously carried it in the dark to rebury the poet under a new gravestone.[76] Perhaps, only at

the apogee of cultural nationalism could one imagine an establishment figure acting in such a manner.

The "cemetery question" was high on the press agenda. Journalists fretted that it was disgraceful that graves in the Pest cemetery were in a state of
chaos. There was no wall to keep out rummaging animals, few paths, and
above all no sense of piety for the nation's dead.[77] The mid-nineteenth century scorned the chaotic and largely perfunctory burial practices of earlier
times. Drunken gravediggers, the stench of corruption, and the sight of scattered bones thrown up from yawning graves, such a part of Gothic sensibil-
ity, were repugnant to the realists of the late-Romantic decades. The new
funereal aesthetic demanded pleasant, leafy surroundings, sentimental statuary, and significant inscriptions. The late nineteenth-century cemeteries
were to be oases of quietude in the city, elaborate funeral gardens with imposing statuary, to which grand funeral processions would slowly make their
way. Once people were disgusted by the older form of burial, haphazard
resting places for political heroes seemed a patriotic affront. The cemetery
question became laden with political emotion. In the funereal, neo-absolutist
taboos could be challenged, and historical memory could be fostered.

On March 15, 1860, the Kerepesi cemetery became the site for a revived
public politics. The prostrate crowd had not been permitted to lament publicly the defeat in 1848. In 1860, university students challenged the ban on
assembly by calling for the public commemoration of the outbreak of the
revolution.[78] Police sought to forestall the demonstration by arresting presumed and actual planners of the event, but students gathered anyway at
the university church on the morning of the fifteenth. They were a chastened crowd, daring authorities but frightened of repeating the experience
of the revolutionary crowd. Faced with armed police squadrons, the small
student crowd of several hundred stood mutely, then set off for another
sanctified ground, the Buda cemetery, where those who had stormed the
Buda citadel in 1849 lay buried. Ordered to disperse, they moved back
across the bridge to another presumably safe gathering place, the Kerepesi
cemetery in Pest, where the repeated order to disperse was met with jeers.
The police moved in to arrest, shot a volley of rifle fire into the crowd, and
fatally wounded a nineteen-year-old aristocratic law student. Out of the
gunshots the chastened crowd gained conviction, hailing the revolutionary
memory, and causing officials great concern.

The worsening condition of Géza Forinyák was monitored for the next
two weeks.[79] Censorship restrictions allowed rumors to run riot, so that officials were forced to publicize what actually happened to stem the stories

of even greater violence and loss of life. Authorities shut down the university for the remainder of the school term—the first time the university had been closed since the revolution. The funeral procession for the dead student on April 4 brought out perhaps fifty thousand people, according to press estimates. (The official estimate was thirty thousand.)[80] Forinyák's friends and university classmates carried the casket to the Kerepesi cemetery accompanied on both sides by youths in Magyar attire carrying torches. Stores were closed; people stood on the sidewalks with heads bowed. Memorial services were held in most of the cities in the country. With the burial of a student martyr, the Pest cemetery became the pilgrimage site of the chastened crowd. Henceforth, students and veterans made March 15 their symbolic day of protest. March 15 would become a mock ritualization of 1848, in which the apprentice members of the political elite were joined on the speaker's rostrum by gnarly veterans of the revolution.

March 15 could represent the ideals of revolution in their purest form, and, thereby, elevated the martyrology of the revolution. András Gerő has conjectured that the evolution of a holiday around March 15 rather than April 14, the day Hungary proclaimed its independence in 1849, reflected Hungary's condition as an "occupied" territory subjugated to "a foreign power."[81] But celebrating April 14 would have highlighted Kossuth, rather than the crowd expressing its will. April 14 reflected a breakdown in consensus, the moment of defection of many indisputably patriotic Magyar leaders. March 15 spoke in the rhetoric of inclusion, precisely what was necessary for a liberal strategy of compromise. To recall March 15 was to operate as a chastened crowd, while the choice of April 14 would have been to opt for revolution once again.

Patriotic feelings were running high when the shocking news arrived that Count Stephen Széchenyi had committed suicide on Easter Sunday, 1860. One historian recalled hearing the news as a seven-year-old, "I, too, could understand that some big, mournful, terrible blow had hit the country."[82] The despairing Széchenyi had gone mad in 1848 and remained sequestered in an asylum thereafter. Széchenyi's bouts with madness were intermittent, but the asylum was his retreat from a public role that had become too demanding. During his long lucid periods, he continued to be involved in Hungarian affairs, remaining, in fact, one of the most fearless critics of the regime. His long, rambling response to Bach's self-serving evaluation of the system after the royal tour of 1857 became the most important statement of the Hungarian conservative position.[83]

Many refused to believe that the "greatest Hungarian" had committed suicide and remained convinced that a police agent had shot Széchenyi at close range. This was a minority view, but there was a general sense that the authorities had driven the patriot to suicide. The accusation gained greater credence later that year with the publication of Aurél Kecske-méthy's sensational *Stephen Széchenyi's Last Years and Death (1849–1860)*.[84] According to Kecskeméthy, the authorities had harassed the hypersensitive, paranoid Széchenyi after the magnate demonstration at the primate's jubilee. They had badgered him into believing that he was to be publicly tried and then imprisoned for violation of the censorship laws for his anonymous commentary on Bach's anonymous treatise.

The family and clergy agreed to bury the suicide as quickly, quietly, and with as little fanfare as possible. The local Catholic priest administered last rites, and Széchenyi's body was placed in the family crypt. To avoid a crowd, the funeral was held a day before the announced date, leaving thousands stranded *en route*. All ostentation was avoided with the coffin adorned only by a simple cross. The casket was followed by his widow, two sons, and some of the academy's delegation: Dessewffy, Deák, Kemény, Toldy, and Arany. About fifty magnates were there, as well as some members of the Jockey Club and the Pest National Casino. The local lords and neighbors carried three to four hundred torches, and peasants of the area came in their holiday dress. The procession was quiet, devoid of any music or singing. While eight young Széchenyis carried the casket into the crypt, the five or six thousand mourners stood quietly outside. Loud crying interrupted the last prayers. At the end of the service, the crowd sang the "Szózat."[85]

Still the public refused to be shut out, and each new train from Sopron brought more and more people to pay their respects. Within a few days over forty thousand had gone to the Széchenyi estate. Mass was said continuously in the chapel. To stem the flow the Sopron Benedictine church held a celebratory mass. People gathered for requiems in cities, towns, and villages throughout Hungary.[86] The events of the preceding six months—the agitation against the Patent, the Kazinczy centennial, the Croatian relief effort, the riot of March 15, and the Forinyák funeral—all culminated in the great outpouring of emotion for Széchenyi.[87] But unlike the events that mobilized the Protestants, intelligentsia, or the students, this moved the entire population. Even the simplest peasant felt the need to express the appropriate sentiment. Commentators took pride in how united the nation was in mourning. That solidarity itself was an important step; thus, it was noted that even in death, Széchenyi moved the nation forward and bestowed his blessing upon it.

With everyone hurrying to pay his or her respects, a business in Széchenyi mementos flourished. Newspapers ran advertisements for Széchenyi portraits.[88] For six weeks community after community lamented and venerated in public. Ecumenical mourning became typical, as in one small Transylvanian town where a crowd of several thousand gathered in the city square, proceeded to a requiem mass, then to a sermon in the Reformed Church, another in the Unitarian Church, before finally gathering at the synagogue, where since the building was too small, the mourners conducted their devotions in the courtyard.[89] Mourning Széchenyi was a galvanizing experience, possible for all classes, conservatives and radicals; even the minorities showed no particular animosity toward his memory.[90]

Some Catholic clergy balked at conducting services for a suicide. When the Catholic Bishop of Kassa refused, a large crowd of parishioners silently commemorated in the cathedral.[91] In marked contrast, Primate Scitovszky decided to officiate at the Széchenyi requiem in Pest. It was an important political gesture and increased the popularity of the Slovak primate immensely. In a profuse statement of gratitude to the primate Dessewffy said, "With the news that Your Eminence was sick, we were ready to give up hope that a great Magyar was to receive his last rites from the leader of the Catholic church in Hungary, which was customary for the nation's greatest sons."[92] Some eighty thousand people gathered at the church, so that the whole area around the church, the large market square in front of it, also the City Hall Square and the streets opening from there were all thickly filled with people. There was no unrest; solemnity marked the hour. At the conclusion of the service, Dessewffy was profuse in his thanks to the primate. The tens of thousands in the square sang the "Himnusz" and the "Szózat" and greeted the primate with cheers when he showed himself at the window to bless the throng. The fit of faith and nationality seemed snug that day. Crowds headed to the English Queen Hotel where the Széchenyi sons were staying. Around the hotel they again sang the first verse of the "Szózat," the sons appeared at the window to acknowledge the unabating cheers. Schools and stores were closed. Black flags were everywhere, and the funereal display on Váci Street was particularly striking.[93]

The massive mourning emboldened. Pest students rented a steamboat for three hundred to travel to Vienna for a memorial service, but authorities banned the trip, fearing its repercussions. When students still made the trip, the Viennese police bluntly informed them that they were under surveillance and had better keep away from any demonstrations.[94] The Széchenyi funeral became a watershed, for the mourning of Széchenyi was an event that the officials did not and could not boycott. It proved impossible for the regime to resist the tide of emotion; even Habsburg officers made their appearance in the church pews. On April 26 when Szeged held its memorial service, the local Bach Hussars attended. The Széchenyi wake produced such an uplifting mood in the city, that it seemed to help the public deal with severe flooding in early May. Personal problems and losses were placed into proportion when compared to the "nation's wounds."[95] To be was to lose oneself in a throng whose patriotic feeling argued its inherent virtue. From this point on, officials began flirting with the nationalist movement. While the course of events in 1848/49 had been indicted by many as leading to madness, the funereal crowd of 1860 also seemed to comprehend that the despair of inaction could lead to suicide.

The ecumenism of the nationalist movement spilled into all areas. The Catholic hierarchy and a committee of Catholic magnates joined the clamor for revocation of the Protestant Patent.[96] The regime was forced to back down. Gen. Lajos Benedek replaced Archduke Albrecht. Benedek, a Protestant, convinced Franz Joseph to rescind the Patent on May 15, 1860.[97] The same day in Kassa, patriots were to gather with boxes of soil from all over Hungary to create a Széchenyi Hill. Seen as an antigovernment demonstration, the police banned the meeting. Count Ede Károlyi, organizer of the event, was placed under house arrest, and the military occupied the county hall. Meanwhile, Benedek was advising the emperor himself to take the lead in raising a Széchenyi statue.[98] The crisis was defused in Kassa when the two leading "Patent martyrs" were released from prison. Protestant Hungary began celebrating. Youth of Kassa wearing Magyar attire rode out from Késmark to greet Benedek; the town erected three triumphal arches and held a torchlight parade in his honor.[99] A formal letter of appreciation was sent from Protestant Hungary to the primate for his support in the campaign to rescind the Patent. The primate, in turn, made a point of inviting a leading Protestant church leader to the December 1860 convocation of bishops in Esztergom.[100]

The revocation of the Patent led to a triumphant demonstration of thirty thousand Calvinists, ostensibly gathering in Sárospatak to commemorate the three hundredth anniversary of the Protestant college. Deputations arriving from thirty-four different places swamped the small town and the castle ruins. National flags flew from every house; clinking swords marked men's stride, and everyone seemed to be sporting a *dolmány* cloak. There was spontaneous singing of the "Szózat" on the streets, and at night students staged a torchlight parade through the triumphal arches decorated with Hungarian insignia.[101] "We have never heard the 'Szózat' sung by a more impressive mass of people with the exception of the Széchenyi requiem in Pest," wrote a reporter.[102] "The festival was magnificent and moving in its national significance."[103] The procession to the church was so large that less than a sixth of the crowd was able to gain access. All the leading Protestant magnate families were represented, with Andrássy, Dessewffy, Kemény, Mikó, and Vay prominent. Despite its confessional character, it was the ecumenical feeling that was stressed over and over again. Among the guest speakers at the college was a representative of the Újhely Jewish congregation, who conveyed his community's appreciation to the school "where so many of our youth have been educated and enjoyed friendly treatment."[104] So long as the issue concerned relations to Vienna, the triumph of the Protestants could become that of the Hungarian Catholics and Jews, as well.

Each took advantage of the new associational freedom, with Christian clubs and other such societies springing up in the towns. When the reconstituted Kisfaludy Society held its first meeting on May 24, 1860, it had ten members, but it seemed as if all of Pest's citizenry appeared on the streets to honor the society. Five days later the alarmed authorities insisted on an early morning ceremony to keep the crowds away from the dedication of the bust of the romantic poet Dániel Berzsenyi in the museum garden.[105] But the newspapers, on this, as other occasions, maintained the sense of participation. They recorded Pál Somssich's speech that rejoiced at the "holy enthusiasm." Somssich observed that "the young join with the old to respect the feats of our nationality, one after the other we have statues of Kazinczy, Kisfaludy, Berzsenyi. The death of our great Széchenyi is bewailed by the whole nation in one voice and with one great, deep sigh from our hearts."[106]

Symbolic events occurred throughout the land. June was high season at Lake Balaton, not only for summer vacationing, but also for patriotic contemplation. An obelisk to Berzsenyi was unveiled in Nikla the same week as a statue to Kisfaludy was dedicated at his native village of Balatonfüred. All rooms were booked, deputations arrived from all over, and conspicuously present were veterans of 1848/49. The academy delegation arrived on a lavishly decorated steamer to the sound of the "Rákóczi March" and the singing of the "Szózat."[107] Peasants and vacationers joined in celebration, which included a mass, a procession, and a choir of school children singing a mixture of patriotic folk songs and funeral dirges. The weather was glorious, "the wreaths seemed greener, the grass straighter, the fields of flowers bowed, and it was as if from the grave the heart of the dead beat again," wrote the press.[108] The nationalist discourse spoke of "honszerelem" (adoration of the homeland) rather than "hazaszeretet" (love of country), the phrase in usage today. After the speeches, participants all embarked on decorated boats to the Tihany church where four hundred banqueted and others picnicked. Donations were collected for a Széchenyi statue, and a statue for Vörösmarty received endorsement.[109] The next day a procession of two to three hundred carriages, accompanied by peasants on foot, made its way to the village of Nikla. A coach deposited the academicians into the center of a crowd of people waving national flags or torches.[110] A Protestant church service and rites at the cemetery followed.

In the summer of 1860 the proliferation of voluntary associations created meeting grounds for the agrarian elite. Numerous new chapters of the National Agrarian Society, headed by Dessewffy, spread the message of economic modernization under their leadership. Activists in the National Agrarian Society were those who had been prominent in the agitation of the preceding months.[111] A special train carrying some four to five hundred luminaries from Pest traveled to an agricultural exhibition designed to honor a new chapter in northern Hungary (Slovakia). Some five thousand attended. These meetings were still carefully monitored. One speaker in Szekszárd urged that the organization be used to spread word that the nation was not dead. For this he was rebuked by the county chairman and hauled before a court in Sopron to answer for his words.[112]

Street Theater

On the street Hungarians had armed themselves against the authorities with the power of song. Song galvanized everyone, noble and commoner, man and woman, old and young. Folk songs, not necessarily explicitly nationalistic ones, when sung in unison by pedestrians had the effect of turning the pedestrians into a crowd and song into a form of demonstration.[113] New songs were constantly springing up. They were heard in church, in the theater, and on the street. The nation saw itself spilling out its pain in song. In the German theater of Temesvár, the audience sang Hungarian songs between acts.[114] After the song, "My dear homeland why are you so sad?" frenetic clapping broke out, and the audience asked for the "Szózat." The director came out and reminded the audience that it was prohibited. In Szeged, Kassa, and Kecskemét musicians were not allowed to play the "Himnusz" in the theater. All over the country authorities struggled to keep control of song.

On May 15 in Debrecen a riot erupted when authorities sought to stop students singing. Two youths were bayoneted and several warning shots fired into the air.[115] Anything seemed possible on the streets. Traveling actors and a Gypsy band arrived in Szeged one Sunday in June.[116] They marched from the theater to the front of the city hall to music and waving flags. In a few minutes more than a thousand people gathered. The actors read nationalist orations and dramatic soliloquies, and sang the "Himnusz" and "Szózat" with the crowd. As the crowd grew and grew with no one wanting to disperse, the actors, caught up in the crowd's enthusiasm, began leading the crowd through the main streets of the city to the refrains of the Rákóczi, Klapka, and Kossuth marches. By the evening the whole city was excited and caught up in the happening. In crammed coffeehouses and restaurants, the stooges of the hated system were denounced.

The Pest promenade became an avenue of political theater with the authorities the intended audience. On a dare three young lawyers strolled down Váci Street in broad daylight wearing theatrical Magyar costumes. One noble lady paraded down Váci Street hand-in-hand with her four-year-old son, whom she had dressed in a scaled-down version of the banned Magyar outfit.[117] Foreign newspapers began sending correspondents to Pest to follow the ferment. Defiance in Pest turned into rioting on July 20. A rumor that a torchlight parade was going to be held to honor József Székács, one of the Patent martyrs, on the occasion of his election as superintendent, brought out thousands of celebrators.[118] But no such parade had been planned, and the disappointed crowd began roaming the streets shouting, "Éljen Kossuth! Éljen Garibaldi!" Demonstrators were cleared from one area, only to regroup in adjoining streets or in another part of the city and continued their singing. The police turned to the army, but they proved no more effective. For three nights, crowds gathered and became assertive, ready to pelt advancing police and army with rocks and verbal abuse. The arrest of twelve artisans and a student on one night suggests the composition of the crowd. Each night brought new arrests.[119]

General Benedek was determined to bring demonstrations to an end; he banned all public "ovations."[120] The police announced stern punishments for those arrested and their families. If fifteen to twenty people came together in a pack, the police were ordered to respond immediately; inevitably, when force was applied, crowds grew larger and denser, as the curious gathered, the demonstrators rallied, and the floating population on the street joined the fray. Dispersal typically developed into scuffles and regularly ended with injuries. A lawyer described being trapped in a crowd that was being dispersed. When a line of infantry approached, he found himself jammed into the crowd with the army cutting off all avenues of retreat or flight. He and some three to four hundred others sought refuge in a narrow inner courtyard where the danger of being crushed to death seemed as perilous as the threat from the army outside. The shoving, screaming, and fainting caused panic in the courtyard. Such rioting seemed to no longer fit the term demonstration that had been in vogue up to the summer of 1860.[121]

Benedek was increasingly inclined to share in the terrified conservative appraisal of the situation. The policy of arrests, floggings, and forced conscriptions were having little effect. Benedek's travels in June confirmed that the provinces were equally inflamed. Torchlight parades with singing of the "Szózat" and cheers for Kossuth and Garibaldi were a repeated occurrence in Eger.[122] A rash of violence over peasant land claims in the countryside exacerbated Benedek's concern. The peasants of Magyargyepes in Bihar County reacted with violence to a land survey.[123] Troops were deployed, and three villagers died. When authorities tried to redistribute land at Leányvár in Zemplén county, rioting began, and both a cavalry squadron and an infantry company had to be called to aid the gendarmerie; women were whipped and men were flogged before the rioting was squashed.[124] Benedek sent ever more anxious reports to Vienna. In case of war, he said, "the quiet revolution" would quickly turn into a bloody insurrection, and "Hungary, women and children included, would go over to the foreign power."[125]

St. Stephen's Day, 1860, became yet another effusion of national feeling that was impossible to suppress. It was a key Catholic calendar holiday and therefore was celebrated in some way under any circumstance. The Buda procession focused on the first king, made a physical part of the ceremony through the relic of his hand. Once but a local religious holiday of Buda, it had grown in significance, receiving imperial sanction in 1818. Peasants of the area around Buda had been drawn to the event in the early nineteenth century. The holiday enjoyed special status in the revolution but had been suspect since 1848. In 1860 St. Stephen's Day regained its popular dimension. General Benedek initially sought to inhibit a large Buda gathering for the holiday. He distributed edicts prohibiting travel to Pest-Buda but was forced to yield. Hungarians were determined to make this St. Stephen's Day unlike any before, a truly national holiday.[126] It was celebrated not only in Buda, but all over the country, including Protestant regions. In Arad the Calvinist ceremony at 8:30 a.m. drew an elite but fairly large crowd, while in Temesvár they celebrated in the Greek Orthodox Church, as well as the cathedral and the Protestant Church. The Governor of Transylvania was conspicuous in his attendance.[127]

The primate had not officiated at any St. Stephen's Day since the revolution, but in 1860 he led the procession down the streets of Buda, filled with enormous crowds of peasants, city folk, and nobles. The march moved in a slow shuffle, with each gesture defined by ritual, with each of the marchers in the procession in his or her clearly delineated place, defined by status, guild membership, and the like.[128] The number of people who crossed the bridge that day was 88,577, larger than any previous St. Stephen's Day crowd.[129] On the return from the cathedral, two students climbed on the primate's carriage and waved a Hungarian flag.[130] Police were uneasy as youth gathered in the City Park for the folk's festival that followed the procession.[131] Occasional cheers to Garibaldi and singing of the "Szózat" could be heard. Some ventured that even though the time was not yet right, since they still did not have weapons, the moment of insurrection was near. Individuals gained courage from the crowd in the park. At eight in the evening two to three thousand people headed out onto the streets toward downtown. A few women walked at the front of the demonstration flanked by men in national attire with unsheathed swords at their side. All walked bareheaded and demanded that passersby remove their top hats, as well. According to the police report, burghers did not join the march; participants were primarily students, literati, journeymen, and apprentices.[132]

With St. Stephen's Day, 1860, the emergence of the chastened crowd was sanctified and given a clear political direction. György Szabad, in his account of this day, stressed the disconnect between the conservative message about ancient rights and popular defiance in the singing of the "Garibaldi song." But rather than a clash between Hungarian aristocrats and commoners, in 1860 the chastened crowd and chastened elite were singing from the same songbook. Civil society was empowering itself. Potential leaders and a potential political public were both asserting their presence.[133] Doing honor to St. Stephen, the first crowned king of Hungary, was also a nationalist way of rebuking the uncrowned king in Vienna. The desire for a crowned king and the end of neo-absolutism were both pointing toward compromise. King Stephen was a political figure who accepted Christianity and was later canonized; the holiday in his honor was a political one with religious overtones. In this holiday the political argument could be validated on religious grounds. In the St. Stephen's Day rite, there was also a recognition that recovery would be bound up with traditions that Hungarian radicalism had forsaken. The chastened crowd would aim at a just restoration, which meant steering toward a new political system.

St. Stephen's Day was wedged in between Franz Joseph's birthday two days before and the Lajos (Kossuth) name day four days afterwards. The holiday could draw on one or the other. In 1860 it drew a new synthesis, while it fed on the charged atmosphere. Six days after St. Stephen's Day, during the biennial fair on the outskirts of Pest, crowds of demonstrators marched into the city, full of anger that the performance of a historical drama, *The Siege of Szigetvár*, had been banned. Rioting continued until the army appeared. Benedek had painted a bleak picture of Hungarian conditions in a memorandum presented to the ministerial conference of August 9, and by the end of the month, a discouraged Benedek submitted his resignation, which would be accepted only after the October Diploma was issued.[134] When the editor of the *Szegedi Hiradó* (Szeged Gazette) was arrested on September 7, a crowd of young people responded by marching through the streets cheering "Éljen!" and singing subversive songs. Singing continued to run riot through the month of September. On the ninth the officials were driven to issuing a proclamation, "To Szeged Youth," asserting that the singing of forbidden songs on the streets was a "disturbance of the peace." They attempted to marginalize the participants as not representative of popular sentiment.[135] Civilians and soldiers clashed in Nyíregyháza, with the riot dying down only when additional military was called out to force the rioting soldiers back into their barracks.[136] But the rash of demonstrations was infectious. Boisterous spirits spread the slogan of the hour: "Él magyar, áll Buda még." (The Hungarian lives, Buda still stands.)[137]

In the course of a few months the whole nation, men as well as women, had donned the national costume conscious of its symbolic political message. The defiance of the decade-long ban on Hungarian attire now became universal; fashion and prudence dictated that every woman appear in embroidered apparel, adorned with a Hungarian hat. Men splurged on silver-spurred boots to pull over their skintight pants. A decade of petty commands and restrictions was flaunted as the political emotions quietly harbored in the home discharged themselves onto the streets. Barbers watched their business plummet when beards became a patriotic fashion. To speak German on the streets was no longer politic, to look German on the street was no longer fashionable. Formerly German-speaking guilds began to cultivate their bilingualism; several hundred Pest typographers celebrated the name day of Gutenberg by carrying pictures of Széchenyi, and Kazinczy, as well as Gutenberg.[138]

"The costume of Hungarian gentlemen" was "*de rigueur,* by way of demonstration against the Viennese Government," observed a visiting Englishman in the early sixties. "I could hardly help smiling: the attire thus worn by all the guests made the place look to me like the supper room of a costume ball, from which the ladies were somehow unaccountably absent." But when he returned at the end of the sixties, he noted that "the Hungarian gentry, at any rate in the capital, have to a great extent adopted 'German,' i.e., European, attire. As one of the extreme Nationalists said to me, 'Civilization is getting too strong for us.' "[139]

Dániel Kászonyi, the radical Forty-Eighter, sourly recalled the months when Hungarian attire, Gypsy music, and the *csárdás* were "demonstrations" defying Austria. What Hungarians were unwittingly doing, Kászonyi sardonically argued, was declaring a war on "civilization, on fine taste and aesthetics."[140] Kászonyi felt estranged from Hungarian cultural politics after a decade in England. It seemed to him that Hungarians were showing the effect of having been isolated from western Europe since 1849. The *népi* (folk) costume made the Hungarians seem quaint and removed. Kászonyi predicted sympathy for Hungary would slip away. Gaining credibility, he feared, was the oft-repeated Austrian assertion that the Hungarians were "a raw, barbarous people incapable of any kind of civilization, not yet ready for freedom."[141] The dilemma of cultural nationalism was that the more strident a people's unique voice became, the more problematic were its claims and grievances against other nationalities, and the greater the barrier to international sympathy. The cult of the national costume made it seem that Hungarians were no longer melding into a western idea of progress, but rather creating obstacles to that progress by a cult of tradition.

Historians have followed Ferenc Deák's lead in focusing on the limitations, irrelevance, even wrong-headedness of this politics of dress and demonstration, and thus, have not drawn attention to the significance of this display that pointed to a compromise in the rural world. The demonstration of Hungarian attire may have been a hay fire quickly extinguished, but the Magyar costume was a rural look that enveloped the whole country in 1860. Creating a national costume was a parallel effort to the canonization of a national literature, and the expansion of a national political calendar. The national costume was as novel as the fabricated epic. These were the decades of the self-conscious creation of national traditions. The utopian ideal of this moment in which everyone would wear Hungarian attire disintegrated, but Magyar attire became a permanent feature of Hungarian ceremonial society. The gentry would continue to wear this ritualized clothing at all ceremonial functions of the Dual Monarchy and the Horthy period.

The chastened crowd had emerged from the shadows of neo-absolutism in a series of spontaneous demonstrations, which embraced the overwhelming proportion of the population, defied the police bureaucracy, and threw the regime on the defensive. However, the agitation spent itself well before it had become a true revolutionary threat. For this was a chastened not prerevolutionary crowd; there was much posturing and the hint of charade in its acts of defiance. When the demonstrations became unruly, each of the protagonists stepped back. Demonstrations wound down, replaced by an era of negotiations.

King Franz Joseph slashing his sword in four directions in the public coronation ritual in Pest, June 7, 1867 (BTM Kiscelli Museum, Budapest)

7

The Celebration of Compromise

During the period of neo-absolutism, when Austrians felt free to say what they wished about Hungarians, not a few Austrians commented on the Hungarian's laughable fixation with a formal ceremony of coronation. One anonymous pamphlet mocked the Hungarians for chasing after coronation as if it were the Holy Grail. The author deemed the Hungarian claim that all Magyars were members of the Holy Crown as mystical nonsense and suggested that there was something barbaric and superstitious in this fetish about the crown.[1] Yet throughout the 1850s a sustaining myth for Hungarians was that Joseph II's uncompromising power had partly been undone by the mystique of the crown of St. Stephen. As a youth in 1764 Joseph had undergone an elaborate coronation in Frankfurt to become Holy Roman Emperor, but he saw no reason to foster the sectionalism and decentralizing implications of a Hungarian coronation, and so refused to have himself crowned king of the Kingdom of St. Stephen. He inflamed Hungarian hostility and challenged noble power further by removing the crown to Vienna.[2] Hungarians, for their part, dismissively referred to their sovereign as the "hat king" rather than the "crowned king." At the end of Joseph's ten-year reign (1780–90), mortally sick and politically broken, he yielded, dispatching the crown back to Buda and allowing crowds to celebrate the object on its return route. Although Hungarians were aware that Joseph was on his deathbed, a joyous crowd came out at the crown's arrival and partook in a lavish and raucous holiday.[3] As it happened, the crown had arrived in Buda the day after Joseph's death. The consequences of the reign of the "uncrowned king" carried a foreboding message heeded by Joseph's brother Leopold II, who marked his accession with an immediate coronation in Pozsony. Upon Leopold's death two years later, his son Franz went so far as to accede to Hungarian wishes that his coronation be moved from the border towns of Pozsony or Sopron to Buda in the center of Hungary. Franz later arranged that his son Ferdinand be crowned Hungarian king during Franz's lifetime.

Coronations had ceased to be part of Austrian political life since the demise of the Holy Roman Empire. Consideration had been given to staging an imperial coronation in Vienna in 1804 and 1849, but in both cases the idea was scrapped.[4] Max Falk, editor of the *Pester Lloyd*, was one of many seeking to convince Austrians of the seriousness of the "apparently childish game" of the Magyar coronation.[5] Hungary's coronation, he asserted, was the most original, antecedent to all others, and the peculiar Hungarian theory of the coronation had kept its inner meaning more central than anywhere else. Hungarians had clung to two medieval traditions: the mass assembly and the mystique of the crown. The coronation of King Stephen in the year 1000 with a crown donated by the Pope marked both the mass conversion of the Magyars to Christianity and the integration of the Magyar horde into Western Christendom. The crown is actually two crowns—one Byzantine, the other Roman—fused, reflecting the degree to which the Magyars had initially been tugged and pulled by the worlds of Roman Catholicism and Eastern Orthodoxy. When Stephen's Árpád dynasty passed from the scene, the Anjou dynasty clung to the symbol of the crown, fostering the legal fiction of "the lands of the crown of St. Stephen" to anchor themselves in Hungary's founding myth. Vassals were obliged to swear fealty to the crown itself rather than to the new dynasty. A material object became the sacrosanct cornerstone of an ethnically disparate kingdom. During the Investiture Crisis, when the Pope and the Holy Roman Emperor were at loggerheads, oaths in Hungarian legal proceedings included swearing fealty to "the kingdom of St. Stephen." The legend of St. Stephen grew ever more elaborate.

Prior to coronation the crown and connected regalia were taken on an elaborate procession through the country.[6] The accompanying Crown Guards were joined at almost every stop by a festive banderium, a mounted procession of noble deputations from counties and towns of the area. The village bells were rung and people would gather and cheer the crown and nobles on parade. The coronation ritual itself had two phases; the first took place in the church before the magnates. Inside the church the election or acclamation of the king was performed by king and nobles. The public was excluded from this first act, announced to them with a blast of cannon fire at its conclusion. The coronation oath was seen as the key constitutional element that made it not simply the transference of power to the new king, but also the affirmation of the nation's legal code. The king promised obedience to the mission of the church, to be righteous and merciful to his subjects, to rule justly and preserve internal and external peace, and to request similar behavior from his vassals. The symbolic acts signified that the crowned king was not just the protector of the nation's church but much more: he was their king.[7]

The second act was a public one, developed over time in acknowledgment of the publicistic and validatory role of the crowd of the cathedral city, border town, or capital. A procession had carried the crown through the streets to the cathedral. After the ceremony coins, usually minted especially for the occasion, were thrown out to the people gathered outside the church. This ensured a large crowd, and almost inevitably resulted in an unruly melee. In 1563 the crowd fought over pieces of the coronation carpet as well as the coins. Various strategies were employed to include and restrain the crowd.[8] At subsequent coronations burghers stood in a tight cordon to inhibit the peasants from racing into the procession for the silver. The public ceremony became an expected rite that could only be curtailed, as in 1715, when fears of a raging epidemic overrode the importance of having a crowd.[9] Atop an especially constructed platform, the sovereign appeared before his people. The competing contentions of the powerful about what indeed was the nation, who or which institution was entrusted to represent and defend the people—the king or the gentry—added the political subtext to the second phase of the coronation as a crowd event. During the public ceremonial the sovereign could appeal to the "people" over the heads of the nobility. The administrator of the oath would acclaim, "Long live the king!" three times. The assembled throng watched, cheered, and thus assented to the coronation.

The king was invariably mounted on a stunning steed, and rode with the unsheathed sword of St. Stephen, symbolizing that his first duty was to care for the nation's military might. Before the public he or she, in the case of Maria Theresa, had waved the sword in four directions defining the corners or boundaries of the territory of St. Stephen and recited the "world oath." In the oath the king indicated that he would protect the nation no matter from where the onslaught might come. The identity of the Hungarian state was thus tightly defined by a geographic notion of boundaries. The Hungarian kingdom was conceived of as having corners, and in other contexts, seven sides; its geographic dimensions were thought to be fixed. The Habsburg relation to this ceremony was inherently problematic. Unlike previous dynasties the Habsburgs had multiple interests that transcended their concern with the Kingdom of St. Stephen and created a more conflicted relation to the coronation. But for the Habsburgs the notion of boundaries was organic, familial; boundaries expanded, divided, and shrank with the ebb and flow of inheritance and political fortune. For Hungarians, the homeland of St. Stephen, in contrast, conflated an imperium with a nation, and later a nation-state—which, of course, placed it in direct confrontation with the peoples who straddled the boundaries, with homelands or imperiums that fell partially inside and outside the boundaries of the Habsburg Monarchy. Two of the four borders of the kingdom lay next to other Habsburg crown lands. The coronation rite of the Kingdom of St. Stephen implied the undivided attention of the monarch. But a problem of the Habsburg empire was that it was not simply a multinational but a multi-state system as well. If Franz Joseph agreed to a Hungarian coronation, should a Bohemian coronation follow? Vienna had good reasons to hesitate and backtrack. The coronation would, in any event, be the concluding not the opening act of compromise.

Opening Moves

General Benedek warned the Pest press on the eve of his fall 1860 departure, "Tomorrow on October 20 our gracious Lord and Emperor will issue a constitution from Vienna. I know all too well that even if God himself created a constitution, you would bellow against it . . . he who agitates against it will be locked up!"[10] When news of the October Diploma arrived in Veszprém, a national flag was hung from a city hall window. Bells were rung, trumpets blared from a near-by hilltop, and people streamed to the cathedral to hear the announcement. An illumination was held that evening, drawing a huge crowd to the market square. Around eight p.m. a torchlight procession departed the casino for the fortress.[11] People rejoiced at the concessions of the October Diploma. The October Diploma formally dissolved the post-revolutionary order: Magyar was again an official language of administration and education; the Austrian ministries of interior and cults (religion and culture) lost jurisdiction over Hungary; Baron Miklós Vay, who had been imprisoned for sedition, was appointed to head the reinstituted Buda Court Chancellery; and elections were scheduled for a new Hungarian Diet to meet within six months. The Diploma fueled hopes of further concessions, including a rumor that Franz Joseph was on the verge of agreeing to a coronation in Hungary.

However, disillusionment was immediate. Franz Joseph clung to a vision of himself as the head of a unitary state rather than as the king of Hungary. He not only retained control of foreign and military policy but through concessions had avoided constitutionalism. The Old Conservatives regained local rights and privileges, but the Diploma created a central parliament where Hungarians could be outvoted and carefully limited Hungarian influence on the center. The Hungarian public quickly grasped the narrow range of concessions in the October Diploma. In provincial towns, such as Eger, Szeged, and Pozsony authorities staged illuminations that were greeted with some excitement but each was marred by incidents of dissatisfaction. In Pozsony windows were broken that evening, and the next day troubles escalated. Emboldened street youths broke more glass and dared to "knock off people's top hats" on the street. The crowd had to be turned back by the military when it threatened the Jewish quarter.[12] By the first week of December, Bach officials and some Jews began leaving towns that seemed poised for riots.[13]

In Pest an illumination was announced for the twenty-third. The mood was volatile and unclear. People were uncertain about what to do. Should they illuminate or smash in the windows of those who did illuminate?[14] At the last minute the event was canceled for fear of violence. Even so street crowds came out that night, smashing the windows of those houses where candles had been lit. There were many arrests; twelve wounded were taken to the hospital, and one person died.[15] Benedek growled, "You do not know Benedek by half. Next time I won't ask how many fell."[16] The official *Pest-Ofener Zeitung* reported window smashing in Sopron, Pozsony, and Pest and took the people in the capital to task for being "too cowardly" to illuminate their windows and allowing themselves to be "intimidated by an irresponsible, incited mob." When the commanding officer of the police action made his customary visit to a coffeehouse in Pest, all the customers got up and left, leaving him alone like a leper. The coffeehouse crowd waited on the street until he finished, then they returned to their seats.[17] Intended to mollify, the October Diploma had barely brought a temporary respite. Thousands attended the funeral of the Pest victim of the October 26 rioting. This procession paused in front of the National Theater where the chorus sang a funeral dirge.[18]

The political drama continued through the winter. On December 3 several hundred artisans marched in a funeral for another riot victim; windows were broken, provoking military action that left yet another wounded.[19] Szeged was caught in turmoil for several weeks, with milling crowds not only breaking windows, but also marching on the police station where the insignia of the two-headed eagle was pulled down and burned. Plaques and other insignia on official buildings became targets. Surprised by the huge crowd, the Szeged police stood by and did nothing. The army was only brought out of its barracks around midnight to disperse quietly the few remaining demonstrators. It was now open season on the imperial eagle.[20] By December 6 imperial insignia were ordered removed from all public buildings, except the military and tax offices. Even the stone eagle chiseled into the facade of the Pest City Hall was effaced.[21] When a provincial judge ordered a Hungarian flag lowered from the Szatmár City Hall, he himself was removed from office. On December 30, 1860, a boisterous crowd of young men marched through downtown Pest yelling "Long Live Kossuth" and "Long Live Garibaldi." They gathered in front of the military police building, loudly demanding that the imperial insignia be removed. When ordered to disperse, they brazenly ignored the gendarmerie's authority. Their persistence was shocking to police and the press, who reported that demonstrators bit two of the military police before fleeing the scene. Four tailors, an upholsterer, carpenter, journeyman lathe operator, and seven apprentices were arrested; three had also suffered slight injuries.[22]

The violent turn spelled the end of festive politics and marked a political move away from street tactics. Magyar moderates who had been praising the crowd throughout 1860 began expressing misgivings at year's end. Crowd politics had degenerated into a kind of routinized disorder and was in danger of upstaging the upcoming electioneering mandated by the October Diploma.[23] Seasoned politicians like Ferenc Deák, naturally suspicious of the crowd's staying power and political reliability, warned that crowd politics could become an emotional distraction. His party newspaper, the *Pesti Napló*, was raising the standard of the April Laws of 1848 as the basis of a genuine compromise. This mediating position was widely embraced, undercutting both street activism and the electoral prospects of the Old Conservatives. Since limited concessions to the Magyars did not seem to be working, Franz Joseph changed his tack once again. This time he turned to the liberal *grossdeutsch* centralism of Anton Schmerling.

Neither the Diploma nor centralism brought relief to beleaguered official circles. The situation had become more openly polarized, and concern about potentially subversive organizations was growing.[24] A few oppositional counties defied the Schmerling government by electing unacceptable candidates, such as Kossuth, Klapka, Garibaldi, and Prince Napoleon. Nationalists used their new visibility to demand restoration of the constitution of 1848, and that the sovereign reside in Hungary and come to know his people. Franz Joseph expressed his annoyance in a manifesto to the Hungarian people on January 16, 1861, in which he remonstrated against the misuse of the new county autonomy to elect subversives. Franz Joseph could count on little support even from the Hungarian Catholic hierarchy, since the bishop's conference in Esztergom that December had itself become a protest gathering. And Old Conservatives who remained supportive had been left even more isolated from Hungarian public opinion.[25]

Ostensibly to supplement the October Diploma but actually to change it fundamentally, Franz Joseph issued the February Patent. It hit like a bombshell right on the eve of "the new dawn of our constitutional life."[26] Hungary's representation in the planned Reichsrat would be further diminished.[27] The real locus of power, Hungarians feared, would be in the Cisleithanian parliament from which they would be excluded. But the Patent preserved a separate Diet for the lands of the Kingdom of St. Stephen, and so the immediate consequence of the Patent was to charge the elections for the Hungarian Diet held between March 1 and the first week of April 1861 with nationalist intensity. Any parliamentary arrangement, even this one, may have been a step forward toward constitutionalism, but Hungarians felt challenged. The *Magyarország* provocatively asked who would be better suited for the post of palatine, Kossuth or Deák, and then weighed in, it seemed, on the side of Kossuth. The police authorities impotently complained of the all-too-common invocation of Kossuth.[28] Émigrés or former revolutionaries who had often not been on their estates since 1848 won in district after district. Lipót Imrédy, for instance, was chosen to the Mosony County seat precisely because he had lived in French exile since holding local office during the Batthyány government. János Nedeczky, the notary of Magyaróvár during the revolutionary period, was swept into office with the support of disaffected Protestants.[29] The appearance of Honvéd aid societies posed a stark nationalist challenge.

In contrast to the largely perfunctory if often symbolic electioneering in the hinterland, the Pest campaign of Deák's lieutenant, József Eötvös, was seized upon by the press as an exemplary campaign. Although notable politics of 1859–61 was politics by acclamation, the newspapers chose to describe these events in the idiom of crowd politics. Commentary emphasized the thousands of people cheering the decision outside the building and relayed in detail the actions and mood of the rooting sections inside. The election took place in an auditorium packed with Eötvös's supporters wearing pictures of the candidate on their hats. The mayor convened the assembly on a stage decorated with flowers, flags, and city insignia. When Eötvös's name was announced, cheers shook the walls, fashionable women in the balcony waved their handkerchiefs, and several thousand people outside echoed the cheers inside. The election was over in a few minutes, then Eötvös spoke.[30] Henceforth, even politicians holding "safe seats" would at election time feel they had to go to their stronghold and produce a crowd that could acclaim them. And at this moment, in particular, the liberal nationalist elite needed to validate the claim that they should be the just rulers of a resurrected Kingdom of St. Stephen.[31] "What innocent times they were back in 1861, when it did not cost anything to get elected," Kálmán Mikszáth mused in 1887.[32]

When parliament convened in Buda on April 6, 1861, a cordon stretched from Pest to the Buda palace. The crowd was so dense at the castle entrance that there was only the narrowest passageway, and all but the most intrepid ladies found it unmaneuverable in their unwieldy crinolines. Opening two days before the anniversary of Széchenyi's death, editorial writers lamented the fact that Széchenyi was not able to witness what was still hoped to be the turning point in Hungary's fortunes. "While in all the corners of absolutism's house the edifice began to creak, crumbling piece by piece, how often it has been said, "If only he had seen this! Why did he have to die just now!!!" "Precisely from the date of his death. . . . Hungary's fate turned for the better," it was claimed.[33]

Many deputies boycotted the opening session, because it was held in Buda and not in Pest. There was also a generalized irritation at the sovereign's absence. Deputy factions divided on the question of how the monarch should be addressed. The moderate, so-called Address Party, forming around Deák, wanted simply to address Franz Joseph as the real king, while the oppositional Resolution Party of László Teleki, Ignác Ghyczy, and Kálmán Tisza, clung to the principle that Franz Joseph, although de facto king, would not legally become king until he was crowned. On May 8, 1861, the parliament gallery was packed in anticipation of a hard-hitting exchange between Deák and Teleki. The gallery was humming, and an excited crowd swarmed outside in the museum garden. When Deák rose, he announced instead that Teleki had committed suicide that morning and adjourned the session, declaring that in this hour of mourning, "wisdom has no voice."[34] There were screams and sobs. The crowd outside was paralyzed by a sudden quiet. In the streets all smiles were wiped from "the people's face," Jókai wrote in his weekly column.[35] Teleki's suicide on the "thirteenth-month anniversary" of Széchenyi's suicide had a dispiriting effect. A rumor that Teleki was murdered in order to hinder the radical program was widely believed.[36] Teleki, one of the three leaders of the emigration, had just been captured in Dresden in December 1860. After being extradited to Austria, he had negotiated an amnesty in return for a promise that he would not engage in further revolutionary activity. In the stalemated politics of would-be compromise, he apparently felt himself compromised. It was assumed that Teleki was planning to stake out a more radical position for his party that day, but instead, took his life. The theaters were dark and the pool tables of the coffeehouses were covered. The mayor of Győr came to loggerheads with his fellow officials when he refused to hang a flag of mourning at the city hall for a suicide.[37] But people found Teleki's death bewildering, and consequently, this mourning did not galvanize the public as Széchenyi's had the year before. Ten thousand people attended Teleki's funeral, but exasperation seemed to underlie the expressions of sadness.[38] "We have so many memorial days, that in these last days one does not even know which ones to commemorate."[39]

Still, masses assembled. In Szeged, the mayor staged an open air commemoration attended by about thirty thousand people.[40] A crowd followed the hearse to the cemetery in Kunszentmiklós.[41] The preacher had to stop the burial service several times because of the "general sobbing." According to the Hungarian news report, local Romanians also "collectively took part, rang their church bells, and let it be known that they also felt the shock."[42] All around the country people gathered for church services dressed in black, carrying black flags. During a memorial procession in Győr, mourners became so outraged by the sight of four Hussar prisoners being transported that day laborers and journeymen among the mourners broke down the gate to the military prison and smashed the windows to free the prisoners.[43] At the conclusion of a ceremony in Újhely, the Calvinist preacher declared, "as the torches burned out so should the Austrians be extinguished."[44]

Police warned of the potential for unrest.[45] Clerics were now as likely to inflame as mediate public sentiment. "In Szabolcs county the Calvinist pastors are fomenting the public against the government from the pulpit," an official complained.[46] In particular, the romance and martyrology surrounding the Honvéds of 1848–9 began resounding openly in the churches. Officials were reluctant to ban these memorial ceremonies for the fallen, because the mood was too "volatile to permit the suppression of demonstrations," especially ones of family or community grief.[47] But they did stop one memorial service in which the names of the Arad martyrs were displayed on the catafalque,[48] but permitted a Honvéd aid society in Debrecen to erect a tombstone for those who fell fighting the Russians. It was placed on a hill where patriots had left flowers during the Bach era. According to legend a Honvéd had collapsed, died, and been buried there. Local peasants considered it a memorial hill protected by angels.[49]

In May 1861 Vienna was particularly exercised by a requiem officiated by both a Catholic minister and a Calvinist preacher on the twelfth anniversary of the battle of Nagy-salló. The emperor personally expressed his anger, and an inquiry was launched. County officials were asked the following questions: Did the forty-two men on horseback who appeared at the religious services represent a revolutionary demonstration, or were they there to prevent disorder by the crowd? Did sermons contain any insulting remarks toward the royal house? There was also official disapproval of the town's decision to erect a gravestone and commission a painting of the battle, including a lithograph reproduction meant for popular distribution.[50] The new lithograph technology was facilitating the spread of the iconography of protest, with the Honvéd aid society having just ordered two thousand reproductions of the Arad martyrs.[51]

What worried authorities most was a growing tax revolt. By June 1861 89 percent of Hungarian taxes were in arrears, more than double that of the previous year.[52] Those who paid or collected taxes were accused of being traitors. Local officials found it politic to obstruct, or stall, or even to refuse to assist the tax collector. On the other hand, those who were not paying their taxes for economic rather than nonpolitical reasons, received harsher treatment than usual, because authorities could not distinguish between those who could not or would not pay. The exile Bertalan Szemere saw the tax revolt jolting the "stagnant, dead masses" out of their apathy of the past decade; he visualized a populace "alive, aroused, ready to act like a crowd"—ready, in other words for revolution.[53] Nationalists closer to home evoked the rhetorical bluff of revolution.

The atmosphere of general disaffection emboldened the Hungarian Diet to send an address to the emperor rejecting both the October Diploma and the February Patent. The sovereign, in turn, refused their address, which the Diet followed with a correspondingly intransigent response. Thereupon, on August 21, 1861, the sovereign dissolved the parliament and three months later suspended the constitution. The so-called Provisorium that now followed resembled a chastened neo-absolutism, eager to reassert authority yet leery of any confrontation. Deák assured his supporters that it was only a matter of time before Vienna would have to yield, because the confrontation with Prussia was coming to a head. Deák's strategy of waiting for the inevitable reversal of policy set the tone from the fall of 1861 to the spring of 1865. Hungarians had made their terms clear; it was now up to Vienna to discover that there was no alternative to negotiations with Hungarian nationalists. "The Hungarian mood," wrote Zsigmond Kemény, "is quiet and peaceful, because we trust that the 1848 laws will sooner or later be recognized by the hereditary Magyar king."[54]

In the limbo of the Provisorium, unrest was really more latent than actual. Deák consolidated his authority over what now became known as the "Deák Party" and its affiliated press organs. Hungarian parties had emerged out of the casinos. No parties had been permitted after 1849; instead, there were just two gravitational poles located in Vienna and Turin. The Pest National Casino had stood as the demonstrative building where a statement could be made by it remaining dark during illuminations. Party cliques reemerged in the Diet of 1861, transforming the informal "literary Deák party" into the Address Party. This vehicle for would-be constitutionalism would evolve into the formal governmental party after 1867. Oppositional party politics was correspondingly formalized in the process.

Deák did not practice a notable politics of sterile, bureaucratic stasis but rather a dynamic legalism to promote change. Although the undynamic Deák personally treasured his private space and shunned the politics of the street, he utilized the dashing style of attractive lieutenants, such as the recently amnestied Gyula Andrássy. Andrássy's name had been nailed to the gibbet in 1849, but now he was the magnate spokesperson for the moderate nationalists. The era of festivals helped define and publicize the Deák · ists' tactics and goals. Andrássy, in particular, was adept at fostering cultural nationalism as a substitute politics during the four-year Provisorium. Andrássy worked on two fronts, to calm the fears of Viennese authorities and to paper over divisions within the Hungarian opposition. Deák and Andrássy's authority rested, in part, in their success at quieting the crowd, in seeing to it that the demonstrations of 1859–61 were not repeated. Deák was unwilling to justify, dignify, or animate crowd politics, but his notable politics dignified the essential demands of the crowd.

Deák and Andrássy were cognizant of mass public sympathies and channeled this crowd politics.[55] Andrássy took charge of the planned Széchenyi monument, deciding its placement at the Pest bridgehead, the "most elegant square of the capital."[56] The site was appropriately adjacent to the Hungarian academy building, then under construction.[57] Andrássy insisted on a simple, realistic design, so as avoid the mistake made with the recent statue of Palatine Joseph, which had posed him in a historical costume he would never have worn.[58] Provincial towns followed with their own statue raisings. When the Kölcsey statue in Szatmár was unveiled in 1864, the Transylvanian town was described as "transformed into a little Pest." With fifteen thousand gathered for the event, the crowd spilled into the streets of the city and into its restaurants and taverns in the evening.[59]

The government nervously monitored such expressions of cultural nationalism. Officials warned that banquets of the Kisfaludy Society and other philanthropic and literary associations had all the earmarks of political rallies.[60] But since bureaucrats were no longer guided by Bach's supranational ideology, they found themselves vacillating between policies of renewed repression and appeasement. Arany, Jókai, and Eötvös delivered addresses at the annual Kisfaludy Society meetings, and the fulsome press reports of these "fashionable," passionate keynote addresses kept Hungarians in a perpetual mood of expectation.[61] These banquets were also the forum for signing on to politicized collection efforts for statues of Hungary's great men.[62] There was much said about statuary giving guidance to a new generation. Much official effort was spent curbing the more radical manifestations of the civil society emerging around them. The government dissolved various societies, particularly voluntary fireman's associations, which bore disturbing resemblance to paramilitary organizations. Officials suspected these, not without reason, of acting as fronts for illegal radical groups. But even when authorities took action, such as their order to dissolve the Zips voluntary fireman's association, the group reconstituted itself—without approval—as a choral society.[63]

The public was unmoved by the government's overarching definition of unrest, but public sympathy and involvement in demonstrations seemed on the wane, leaving demonstrations looking like feeble acts of bad behavior. When some twenty students sought to interrupt a March 15 theater performance, they found little support in the audience and were drowned out by the orchestra playing the can-can as loudly as possible.[64] Urban demeanor was being defined by the participating public. On March 13, 1864, an agitator with a Napoleon III-like beard rallied a crowd outside a Pest coffeehouse prompting a small demonstration, mainly of youth. When passers-by refused to chant "Éljen Kossuth," the event escalated into a melee, in which an apartment superintendent was knifed.[65] These isolated incidents seemed to violate the canons of civilized crowd behavior valued in the growing urban complex.

Pest had been committed to creating a secular holiday worthy of a burgeoning city since the first such festival in 1845. While in 1845 between

12,000 and 15,000 attended the festival, in 1859 it was closer to 30,000, and in 1862 it had reached perhaps 50,000.[66] The influx strained the city's resources; hotels were filled to capacity. The novelty of the 1862 folk festival was the arrival of tourists on trains from Szeged in the south and Temesvár in the east. Just as international exhibitions owed their existence to the railroad, the railroad was making it possible to transform local Pest events into regional and finally national ones. The press took the opportunity to promote Pest as a future capital and wanted to compare it with Vienna, but while they had hoped for 3,000 Viennese visitors, only 422 arrived.[67] Group tours were the new rage, and when thousands of Hungarian pleasure-seekers took part in an excursion to Trieste that year, a crowd saw them off at the Pest railway station, and well-wishers filled railway station platforms along their route. When they arrived in Trieste, Archduke Maximilian had a military band play in their honor.[68] Thousands of people now were traveling to distant reaches of the monarchy and experiencing a bourgeois version of a royal tour.[69]

The content of the folk festival had also changed. It was no longer dependent on the pilgrimage or the fair to draw a crowd. The people came to the park for entertainment. Revelers in 1862 were beckoned to the festival by wall placards and cannon fire at three in the afternoon. The City Park filled with music; five military and three Gypsy bands played. There was a taste of the exotic, the bizarre, and the erotic: four camels, tableaux depicting Hercules with his club, and a parade of athletes; entertainment of all types, including comic skits, boxers, and donkey races. Free food, cheap drinks, and low entrance fees added to the carefree spirit. A hot air balloon, fireworks, and a finale of all the bands playing in unison satisfied the desire for spectacle and fantasy.[70] To counter the argument that the event was too commercial, a portion of the profits was given to charity. In 1859 proceeds were donated to Honvéd aid societies; in 1862 a significant sum was used for improvement of the City Park's water system.[71]

On holidays it was still most common for urban dwellers to return to their native villages. But in August people gathered in Buda to watch the primate lead the procession on St. Stephen's Day. The Sacred Hand was borne aloft in a new gold and glass reliquary in 1862.[72] At the St. Stephen's Day banquet Count Pálffy praised the day as "religious, dynastic, and national," and dangled the pleasing prospect of coronation and compromise before his listeners. "In Hungary all of us are filled with the strong desire that we will find the means to achieve the goal of seeing our great king wear the crown of our first king and patron."[73] The need for a Hungarian coronation was becoming a central axiom in the agitation for dualism. The Schmerling government, however, relegated the Hungarian problem to the backburner, hoping that its diplomatic offensive in Germany would produce a better bargaining position vis-à-vis the Hungarians. When Prussia refused to attend the 1863 Frankfurt Congress of Princes convened by Franz Joseph, the *grossdeutsch* diplomatic offensive began unraveling.[74] Moreover, a Russian Polish rising that year prompted closer ties between Russia and Prussia, and raised Habsburg apprehension about the impact of refugees fleeing into northern Hungary. There was concern that Hungarian sympathizers might assist the Poles, either as individual "freedom fighters" or in Hungarian units, or that Hungarian émigrés would recruit Poles into their own clandestine networks. Warnings of female couriers at work in the border areas made the task seem even more daunting. Local bureaucrats received a flood of requests for mood reports, to which subordinates replied with supposedly reassuring formulas: The residents are "more inclined to inhibit than to assist the Polish movement," one official from Liptó county reported. "The Polish unrest has had no effect; politically the people accept the official position." Yet, at least two, maybe five, individuals had fled the county for Poland, and it was reported that sympathy for the Poles extended from the "half-educated" and "artisans" to "the coffeehouse crowd." The sheriff of Sáros County voiced "concern about the county's priests and intellectuals being in sympathy with the Polish revolution." Officials warned against Pest becoming a "point of refuge," for this "would provide an opportunity for demonstrations and other unpleasant consequences." Preventative measures, such as quartering refugees in provincial towns, did not keep revolutionary manifestos from appearing on city walls. Ferreting out the authors involved countless hours and numerous memoranda, followed by complaints of over-zealous police tactics.[75]

But even before the Polish rising was fully suppressed, Austria found itself allied with Prussia in a war against Denmark in the spring of 1864. This new era of short wars brightened the Kossuthites' prospects for overthrowing Habsburg rule. Uncovering the Almásy conspiracy confirmed the worst official fears, for it implicated members of parliament and other politicians. Police also had reason to worry about "public dissatisfaction" with the harsh sentences handed out to the conspirators: several death sentences, commuted to twenty years; fourteen years for a number of others, and six-year terms where the evidence was weak.[76]

The monarchy's efforts on the diplomatic front were as frustrated as radical hopes for a revolutionary breakthrough. On Easter Sunday, 1865,

Deák electrified the nation by publishing in the newspapers an open letter indicating his readiness to negotiate. Deák's timing was exquisite, appealing to the "father of the country" to redeem his fallen people on the day of resurrection and the fifth-year anniversary of Széchenyi's suicide. Franz Joseph responded to the Easter Letter by offering to attend the Pest Agricultural Fair.[77] The backroom dealings toward compromise would always have a vital public dimension. What had begun in the newspapers—the printing of the Easter article—was now feverishly sustained by the Deák party press. Mood in the country had become "more settled, they sincerely desired settlement," wrote Ferenc Toldy.[78]

The Uncrowned King and Would-be Capital

Pest would be the arena of the celebration of compromise, with all important gestures made in Pest (June and December 1865, February 1866, May–June 1867). It was to Pest that Franz Joseph had to go to make his first overture of his readiness to compromise.[79] That this process have an urban dimension was critical in the era of the chastened crowd. It also suited Franz Joseph's monarchist ideology to visit the Pest fair. For a decade he had stressed the progress of the economy as a validation of his system.[80] Habsburg monarchism and Hungarian liberalism could find connection at such exhibitions. The National Agrarian Society was a quasi-political body containing much of the leadership of both conservative and Deákist camps.[81] The formal invitation welcomed the monarch to see "all the most important branches of agriculture; your personal visit would bring joy to Budapesters as well as bestowing a blessing on what would be a brightening dawn of a better future."[82] It seemed evident that the monarch wanted to resolve the crisis, and the invitation from the agrarian society became an excuse to stage publicly a festival of reconciliation as the first public step toward that goal.

Since there was no Hungarian government to provide the formal greeting, citizens' committees were formed in Buda and Pest. Although it was important to give the sovereign an enthusiastic welcome, there was only a little over two months to prepare. The committees settled for the standard torchlight parade, voluntary illumination, folk fest, and citizen's ball. What became crucial was involving the public and turning out the crowd; public fervor was to compensate for the lack of spectacular display. The city newspapers thus became a critical element in agitation aimed at convincing the public that it had become possible and necessary to join a "loyal" crowd. The newspapers printed their manifesto, "On the reception of His

Majesty the Emperor," with instructions for participation.[83] As many windows as possible should be decorated with flags, carpets, and flowers. The populace should line the streets from the Pest railroad station to the Buda castle in impressive numbers. On the nights of his arrival and departure, illuminations should include virtually every residence, particularly in those parts of town through which he passes.

On June 6, the day of Franz Joseph's arrival, the *Pester Lloyd* struck the theme of the Deák party when it wrote that, "after four years of silence . . . the silent nation rediscovers its voice" in greeting Franz Joseph. "As a blind man who regains his sight is surprised by the color of the yearned-for-light, greeting it with a cry of rapture, so the first word that comes from the breast of this loyal people is a festive greeting to the prince who has the power to bring language to the tongue."[84] Never before has the "nation been so hopeful, so in touch with its deepest purposes, as today when we greet our royal guest."[85]

Franz Joseph crossed over into Hungary before dawn; the telegraph sent the message, and cannons soon sounded from the Buda fortress.[86] Along the route he breakfasted with four hundred notables, arriving several hours later in an overcast Pest wearing a Hungarian general's uniform. After reviewing the honor guard on the platform to the accompaniment of the "Rákóczi March" and the singing of the royal anthem, Franz Joseph passed through the crowds lining the streets to the castle. Here and there groups awaited him: the amassed school children in uniform, guilds with their flags, the various corporations. All told perhaps as many as 60,000 lined the route. The castle square was packed with an enthusiastic crowd. The primate and other notables awaited the monarch in the Buda castle. Both the grand staircase and the room in which Franz Joseph's baby daughter died during the tour of 1857 "had been filled with flowers, in many instances brought by the wives and widows of men who had fought against him in 1848." Franz Joseph was moved when he entered the room.[87]

After a few hours rest Franz Joseph set off for the City Park and the exhibition. It was a modest affair, taking up a small area, most of it occupied by agricultural machines. Already at a distance one could hear the thrashing of the new threshing machines and the whistle of the steam engines. Most of the machines were British. One entered through an unimpressive entrance gate and faced a festive pavilion surrounded by a landscaped garden and shaded by thickly leafed trees. Right and left from the entrance were protective shelters housing sheep. For the urbanite the display of sheep, pigs, and cattle; the iron furniture, mill stones, terra cotta objects, sewing machines, and the like were hardly crowd-drawing sights. Indeed, attendance on opening day (just three days before) was an embarrassing eight hundred.[88] After the papers reported that Deák had toured the fair, attendance jumped to a more respectable, if not impressive, 6,200 and 6,300 respectively for the next two days. A steady stream of items were still being added to the exhibition in those opening days.

But on the day of the royal visit, the fair was filled with deputations from local, provincial, and Transylvanian chapters of the National Agrarian Society. In greeting the monarch, the society's president, Count György Festetics, delivered a homily on the importance of culture to the modern state and to Hungary in particular. He warned that a decline in agriculture would not simply weaken Hungary, but rob it of everything it possessed. He then underscored the modesty of the fair, offering this as a rebuke of the difficult, oppressive times of the recent past.[89] The society had served as a cover organization for magnate politicians for a decade. Its main agenda was to foster an agrarian intelligentsia by promoting technical agricultural institutes with instruction given in Hungarian. The society had founded a Buda school of viticulture in 1860, a credit bank in 1863, and agrarian exhibitions in the 1850s.

Franz Joseph, for his part, praised the society's efforts to improve the agrarian economy. Eötvös and Deák joined the society's magnate leadership in the receiving line to greet the emperor. The tour of the exhibition was brief, with the monarch stopping to look at a streetcar and a printed leaflet that announced: "The land which has been quiet for four years, begins again to speak and it raises a cheer to your majesty much as a child learning to speak says 'father.' Long live our king." It concluded with the hope "that the memory of this joyful day will have a profound impact upon our public life."[90] The monarch also presented a monetary contribution to the society. The visit was an act of homage to the liberal elite in which the urban crowd was only tangentially involved, but to which the newspaper crowd became a voyeur.

Gypsy music and a large crowd awaited the emperor on his return to the castle. While the tour of the fair may have been the pretext of the trip, it was swallowed up in the three-day ceremonial calendar. The public saw Franz Joseph dressed as a Hussar colonel on his way to a regatta where magnates joined the emperor on a steamer. Large crowds followed Franz Joseph's movements. The next morning at seven the emperor arrived at the Buda meadow on horseback in a Hungarian Field Marshal's uniform for the grand parade, but the rain was so heavy that the parade was canceled. On his way back to the castle a wet monarch received the cheers of those who had also been caught in the downpour. That night four thousand flickering torchlights snaked up the hill, followed by a crowd of ten thousand.[91] The square in front of the palace filled; the crowd spilled out into the adjoining streets and squares. When Franz Joseph appeared with the primate, commanding generals, and other dignitaries, a Gypsy band played the royal hymn and the "Himnusz" to the repeated cheers of the over fifteen thousand gathered there. After fifteen minutes Franz Joseph left, and his Hungarian deputy made a speech that few could hear.[92]

The next day was filled with a flurry of early morning visits: to the Ganz iron foundry, Buda polytechnical high school, the academy, and the construction yard at the Danube docks. Visits to the National Museum, an orphanage, and the military hospital were delayed so the monarch could return by ten a.m. for a five-hour reception of county deputations. A formal dinner was held at five o'clock; he then attended a portion of a performance at the National Theater and briefly visited a citizen's ball. The final day of the hectic festive schedule began with tours of a military hospital, the Josephine orphanage, the institute for the blind, followed by visits to the Buda choral society, and the university, where two thousand had gathered. Public attention focused on the illumination that evening. Eleven thousand lamps had been installed at the railway station and the whole of the king's route was lit. The newspapers estimated the evening crowd to have been between eighty and ninety thousand. An elite assemblage of some four thousand were at the railway station to see Franz Joseph leave on his eleven o'clock train.[93] The unflappable Eötvös scrawled in his diary, "The emperor has left . . ." and Eötvös could get back to the work, which had accumulated during the "wasted week."[94]

The concrete gesture that would follow this visit was the regime's formal abandonment of the October Diploma. That summer as an Austro-Prussian war scare darkened the horizon, Franz Joseph removed a principal stumbling block to dualism by accepting a union of Transylvania and Hungary.[95] Romanians followed the political reversal with alarm. Archbishop Şaguna left his audience with the emperor complaining that the Romanians had been "handed over to the Hungarians."[96] For their part, Transylvanian Hungarians were conspicuous in their celebration of Franz Joseph's birthday on August 18. In Kolozsvár some 200 nobles attended a banquet to honor both the uncrowned king and the union with Hungary.[97] Budapest pageant-masters promoted Franz Joseph's birthday as a "national holiday" so that "mass participation" can be a sign of "reconciliation" for "all of Europe to see."[98] Many prominent Hungarians went to Vienna to personally pay their respects.

Celebration followed celebration. "We are living in holiday times, we move from holiday to holiday."[99] But what made that August particularly memorable was the first Pest music festival that brought together more than a thousand singers and commensurately large audiences both in the halls and on the streets. A crowd lined the streets and leaned out of windows to see and hear a parade of choruses.[100] The five-day event concluded on St. Stephen's Day, August 20, featuring Franz Liszt and showcasing his oratorio, *St. Elizabeth*.[101] It was a triumphal moment for Liszt. Richard Wagner marveled at the success of his friend, rival and future father-in-law. Eighteen sixty-five was the high-water mark of musical nationalism in Europe—the great, final summer of the cultural festivals that had been building in Central Europe since 1859. They were largely seen as a demonstration of middle-class culture and its claims on the future. With this prominence, composers for the first time began to use their celebrity status to advance political positions. Wagner in Munich had the ear and support of the young Bavarian king, Ludwig II, and Liszt arrived in Pest after a nine-year absence to play his role.

Although he never completely mastered Hungarian, during this final phase of his career, his Hungarian identity surfaced as an ever greater factor in his music and his life. He discovered Magyar and Gypsy melodies and rhythms (often embarrassing Hungarian nationalists by not carefully distinguishing between the two). Liszt committed himself to drawing Pest into the urbane, musical circuit, and he succeeded in establishing Budapest as a musical center by the 1870s, with the founding of the Academy of Music.[102] Liszt's endorsement also bolstered Hungarian liberal confidence that they could make Pest a worthy partner in a Dual Monarchy. As a child virtuoso, Liszt had been spirited out of Hungary at an early age to assume a prominent place in the cosmopolitan world of European high culture. In the 1840s he and Chopin had been stars of the Parisian musical world. In the fifties he held court in Weimar, and with Richard Wagner, he became the exponent of "the music of the future." In the sixties he became the Abbé in Rome, but like Wagner, Liszt was "a great man" taking up his people's cause. He did so with an enthusiasm that at times was amateurish but always cosmopolitan. Liszt's patriotism represented a reconciliation with Germanic, Catholic Austria.

Elizabeth and Cassandra

Although Liszt's oratorio *St. Elizabeth* was not a great crowd pleaser, then or later, it took on a special significance in Pest that summer. The Oratorio reinforced the acceptance of monarchism, and more importantly, it became identified with the reigning Empress Elizabeth. Elizabeth would herself, in the following months, foster the identification with the martyred medieval Hungarian queen of German extraction. Liszt and Elizabeth played complementary roles. Although both had only visited Hungary once in the fifties (within a year of each other), they returned nine years later as champions of the Hungarian cause.

In the summer of 1865 Empress Elizabeth presented Franz Joseph with a "your-mother-or-me" ultimatum. She mobilized herself around the issue of Rudolph's "future," insisting that his tutor be dismissed and that the Emperor sign a statement giving her "complete autonomy in everything which concerns my children." And "all matters which affect me personally will be determined solely by me."[103] While her hated mother-in-law headed the anti-Hungarian party at court, Elizabeth became the linchpin of Hungarian strategy behind the scenes, and she was its visible champion to the masses. Her Magyarophilia turned into a Magyaromania.[104] At a formal dinner she attracted attention with the statement that, "If the emperor's cause goes badly in Italy it pains me, but if it goes badly in Hungary, it is death to me."[105] Every concession wrested from Franz Joseph would be credited by the Hungarian public to her influence, as every setback was blamed on her mother-in-law. Elizabeth's study of Hungarian intensified when she included Ida Ferenczy in her entourage in the fall of 1864. By the following year she purged her retinue of all those who could not speak Hungarian.

For the one-and-only time in her life, Elizabeth assumed the role of heroine of the crowd. This was all the more striking, coming after her virtual abandonment of her public role as empress after 1859. When Franz Joseph returned to Pest on December 14, 1865, effusive crowds greeted him. He had come to convene parliament in person and delivered a conciliatory speech in Hungarian, but what generated the greatest excitement was his promise to return soon with Elizabeth at his side.[106] On January 8, 1866 Elizabeth, in Hungarian dress accompanied by her eight new Hungarian ladies-in-waiting, received a Hungarian deputation. Elizabeth replied in Magyar to their formal invitation that she visit Buda-Pest, saying she had no "dearer wish than to return to that beautiful city."[107] She was most taken by the interest shown her by the dashing, dark Gyula Andrássy. Elizabeth would strike up a warm personal friendship with Andrássy who called her "our lovely Providence." Andrássy became stuck with the nickname of "providenciális," spoken respectfully by his partisans but most ironically by his critics.[108]

In any age Elizabeth's beauty would have been legendary, but in the new age of photography and the lithograph it seemed palpable. Her beauty was memorialized in Eduard Winterhalter's portrait of 1865. Wounded soldiers would hang her picture above their beds; inexpensive reproductions allowed the portrait of the beautiful young queen to adorn peasant homes as an icon. Elizabeth filled the public sphere with the glamour of a new monarchism and gave royalty a human face. We now know how much daily energy, exercise, and misery went into keeping Elizabeth one of the wonders of the age. But we sometimes forget how she helped define something new in the 1860s—a celebrity monarchism that fed a love-hate relationship with the crowd.[109] Celebrity monarchism was, in part, pioneered by the glamorous Bonapartist Empress Eugenie. But Elizabeth began to displace the French empress in public fascination, and a meeting of Eugenie and Elizabeth became legendary. Queen Victoria's melodramatic, unrelenting public mourning for Prince Albert in these years diverted public interest further onto Elizabeth. Dubbed Hungary's "guardian angel," she was also assumed by much of the populace to be the supreme protector of feminine virtues.[110]

In Elizabeth shone the new, human face of Habsburg royalty. Citizens clamored for a glimpse of her. Elizabeth made herself the model of Hungary's role in the unique personal union that was established: if dualism was acted out as a marriage, the Hungarians clearly played out the role of the wife. The "hereditary royal couple"—to use the Hungarian phrase of the moment—arrived in Buda-Pest on January 29, 1866, adding an element of drama and public appeal to the negotiations. On February 1, Elizabeth addressed the parliament in Hungarian.[111] During this visit she confirmed Hungarian impressions of her partisanship, of her public role as Hungary's advocate. Indeed, she could be ruthless about this issue within her sphere of ceremonial politics. During a visit to a convent school, Elizabeth spoke in Hungarian to the Mother Superior, who being Italian did not understand her. The empress retorted in her coldest and haughtiest manner that next time she expected to be answered in Magyar. True to her word Elizabeth returned, only to find that the Mother Superior had taken to her bed with a sudden illness. Undaunted, the empress went to the Mother Superior's room, said something in Hungarian, which the woman did not understand, and left abruptly. Shortly afterwards the unfortunate woman resigned her post.[112]

"The ice is breaking. We are full of hope," wrote Nándor Zichy in February 1866.[113] A month later he jotted down in his diary that "Time is flying, and we're just bustling, preparing, listening to everything."[114] "Deák and the emperor are now like two men standing at a door, each wanting to thrust the other through, so as not to be the first to step into unfamiliar territory."[115] Elizabeth's last words on the train platform after her six-week Pest visit were, "I hope soon to return to my dear, dear Hungary."[116]

During the war crisis of the spring of 1866, Franz Joseph turned to Elizabeth for help. It would be the one and only time in Franz Joseph's long reign when he permitted his wife so much political sway. Elizabeth's great achievement in these critical months was to upstage Kossuth.[117] Kossuth's proclamation of June 23, 1866 concluded with the words, "I embody a principle called 1849." Hungary had been isolated then, he said, but now, as an ally of Prussia, "we are neither alone nor abandoned," and will reap the fruits of Hungarian efforts in 1849.[118] In the sloganeering of that moment, political positions were encapsulated in terms of years. While 1849 was the rallying cry for the radicals, the laws of 1848 were the touchstone of the moderates, and 1847 was the year of restoration for the Old Conservatives. The monarchy, in contrast, was faced with the dilemma that neither the concessions of 1860/61 nor the renewed negotiations of 1865 could serve as a rallying cry for Hungarians.

In the months preceding the war, largely moribund nationalist underground organizations were suddenly resuscitated. The prospect of insurrection resurfaced. Exiles again met to draw up plans. Bismarck assumed the role Napoleon III had played in 1859, funding insurrectionary nationalist movements in order to weaken the monarchy. The Kossuthites' plans called for General Türr to march up from the lower Danube and General Bethlen to move in from Transylvania, while General Klapka's Hungarian Legion would descend from the north with the Prussians and Garibaldi would lead another expedition from the Adriatic. Together the various columns were to ignite an explosion that would bring about the final collapse of the monarchy. Both General Moltke and Kossuth were convinced in May 1866 that a revolution in Hungary would bring this end. This would be the decisive moment for Hungary, Kossuth believed, for another Austrian victory would be Hungary's death. The choice, in his view, was between Hungary as a mere Austrian province, disappearing as a state, or again seizing the flag of 1849 that had been torn from the hands of the Honvéds. Eighteen sixty-six was to be the year 1849 was restored, and an independent Hungary would assume its place as the sixth most powerful nation in Europe.[119] General Klapka's manifesto addressed Hungarian soldiers in Habsburg service, urging them to defect: "Lajos Kossuth will be with us, so united we chase the Austrians out of our land. We reconquer what is ours—the land of Árpád. In the years 1848 and 1849 we earned great glory, now we await the victory laurel and the crown of peace when we liberate the homeland." Archduke Albrecht ordered executions of anyone distributing these leaflets.

The Prussian Blitzkrieg inflicted a lightning defeat on Austria at Königgrätz on July 3, 1866, but like a lightning bolt the sharp jolt passed quickly through the monarchy.[120] While Klapka's Legion was assembling in Prussian Silesia, Elizabeth was dispatched to Buda by Franz Joseph: "Take the children to Buda and be my advocate there. Hold the people in check as best as you can, and we shall find a way."[121] Only Ida Ferenczy accompanied her and the children, but she was received in Pest on July 10 by tens of thousands of cheering people. Deák and Andrássy were there to greet her, and the six kilometer drive from the station to the castle of Buda was triumphal.[122] In 1859, after the defeat at Solferino, Elizabeth seemed to have withdrawn completely, but in the crisis of 1866 she became active, directed, and single-minded. Elizabeth consciously played on the legend of Maria Theresa calling upon the Hungarians to save the monarchy in its struggle against Prussia. She appealed for public support and promised reconciliation.

It was a curious circumstance: the anti-liberal Bismarck was the ally of the liberal-revolutionary Kossuth, while the compromisers of the Deák camp opposed Bismarck and Kossuth in the name of liberal constitutionalism.[123] Ironically, Kossuth lost because the Hungarians won, and because his allies won, i.e. Prussia triumphed. The speed of victory brought the undoing of the insurrectionary fantasy. The Hungarian Legion of fifteen hundred men was never employed in the war. Desperate to display the flag, the Legion made a ludicrous incursion into the Kingdom of St. Stephen during the final days. The inhabitants of the Slovak border village observed the demonstration with little enthusiasm and some antagonism. So ended the 1849 option.

Ensconced in Buda, Elizabeth bombarded Vienna with her solution: appoint Andrássy Minister of Foreign Affairs and thereby keep Hungary attached. She was in daily consultation with Andrássy. Franz Joseph criticized her "exclusively Hungarian point of view" which he felt "slight[ed] those lands which have endured unspeakable sufferings with steadfast fidelity." She responded by begging him "in Rudolph's name not to lose this one chance at the last moment" and insisted that he see Andrássy.[124] When Elizabeth returned to Vienna in the fall of 1866, she responded to the court's hostility to her Hungarian partisanship by defiantly engaging in her service the liberal Hungarian Jewish journalist Max Falk and adding five more Magyar ladies-in-waiting to her retinue.[125]

Elizabeth was central to the pageantry of Compromise during the year-and-a-half between her 1866 visit to Pest and coronation day, June 8, 1867. She would be remembered in the decades to come as a "lyrical child-woman," who understood little about the art of political intrigue, and yet for those critical weeks stood sentry, caring about every detail. "And besides the fact that she was as good as an angel, she was beautiful too, like a Goddess," one nostalgic historian wrote at the turn-of-the-century after her martyrdom.[126] The compromise was enacted publicly as a drawn-out courtship, a pseudo-romance highlighting Elizabeth and Count Andrássy.

In defeat Franz Joseph made rapid moves to effect the Compromise. While not precluding a policy of revenge and reversal of 1866, he appointed the expelled Saxon Minister President Friedrich Ferdinand Beust as his imperial minister president on October 30. Beust was a conservative liberal, a Protestant, and as an outsider had little sympathy for the minorities in the monarchy. However, Beust and other Saxon *grossdeutsch* partisans believed that the failure of the monarchy to resolve the Hungarian issue before the confrontation with Prussia had been a fatal lapse. Soon after he took office, Beust declared a willingness to appoint a responsible Hungarian ministry, and on December 20 Beust made a surprise visit to Pest-Buda where he established personal contact with Deák and Andrássy. In the following weeks, he moved energetically to formalize a Compromise. A few Austrian politicians would speak of the compromise as an "internal Königgrätz," but the new regime in Vienna was out to stress the positive.[127]

While Deák was negotiating behind the scenes, he also played to the crowd. When students marched before his headquarters, he addressed their exuberant display of patriotism with "heartfelt words."[128] The threat of disruptive, Kossuthite crowds loomed in the background in the weeks preceding the coronation. Eighteen days before the occasion Kossuth published his "Cassandra Letter," condemning the Compromise as a surrender of national independence. Kossuthites began a press campaign and launched a new weekly, alternately called *March 15*, *Freedom*, *Equality*, and *Fraternity*. By changing the title, the weekly circumvented some of the censorship laws. Its pages presented a progressive vision, highlighting such events as the opening of the Paris Exhibition. Kossuth's sons' visit to the French world's fair seemed to be everything the coronation was not: "modern" in contrast to the "feudal," clerical rite of coronation. Although the Kossuthites disparaged the agreement as a betrayal, they skirted making a direct call for demonstrations against the coronation. Crowds shouting "Kossuth" and singing defiant songs did not materialize in the weeks preceding the ceremony.[129] "The national revolutionary spirit has been broken," József Madarász stated bitterly. "The era of concessions (*megalkuvás*) has arrived."[130]

While Kossuth's mournful prophecy may not have brought out angry crowds, it did have a certain resonance. A dark shadow already hung over the coronation. The unfolding Habsburg family tragedy in Mexico threatened to upstage the Pest ceremonials. While Emperor Maximilian, Franz Joseph's brother was under siege and then imprisonment, his wife Empress Carlotta, in critically worsening health herself, frantically toured Europe in search of help for her husband, only to suffer a mental breakdown in the Vatican. In the weeks preceding the coronation his fate was in the hands of the "rebel" Benito Juarez. The drama of 1849 seemed to be replaying itself in the New World but with a new script. With about a ten-day news lag between events in Mexico and word reaching Europe, Franz Joseph was unclear whether his appeals and gestures on behalf of his brother were succeeding or not. Various governments were pleading with Juarez to pardon the brother of the Austrian Emperor, but to no avail. Archduke Maximilian had been popular in Hungary, and many had hoped for his appointment as Hungarian palatine in 1860. When the Republic of Mexico shot Maximilian that same summer much in the same manner as the Austrian Empire had once shot Batthyány, it became more problematic to see 1867 overcoming 1849. This act, memorialized in Manet's painting, remained a troubling portent.

The Coronation of Celebrity Monarchism

The terms for the 1867 agreement, *Ausgleich* in German, *kiegyezés* in Hungarian, and Compromise in English, each carry different connotations. The German word, *Ausgleich*, suggests equalization, that is, raising the Hungarians to the level of the Germans. Those Hungarians supportive of the agreement preferred the more legalistic concept of settlement, which emphasized their concern with transfixing the agreement in time, in making it legally binding, and creating a firm foundation on which to build a Magyar polity. The English word compromise contains an element of regret that captures the disappointment of the Kossuthite opponents and the distance of the bystander outside the process. The German term, connoting a leveling, suggests flexibility toward the other ethnic groups, and thus a process which could include a future agreement with other ethnic groups in the monarchy such as the Czechs. The Hungarian legalistic image was more static and finessed the internal resistance. The word compromise recognizes the existence of unresolved issues, but privileges political stability.

Coronations generally involved three questions of rulership: who, when, and how. Only one, "when," was specifically answered by the coronation moment.[131] In 1867, however, the coronation's purpose was not to answer the question "when." The date of the coronation had virtually no impact on the daily running of the system, and unlike previous coronations, did not coincide with the convening of the parliament. Parliament was already in session; its calendar was not beholden to Franz Joseph's willingness to be crowned. Similarly, "who" was addressed only peripherally. On June 4 fourteen members of parliament presented a formal protest on the floor in an attempt to embarrass Franz Joseph by declaring the coronation invalid, because Ferdinand V was still alive and had not formally abdicated his Hungarian kingship in 1848.[132] This forced a prologue to the coronation ritual in which Ferdinand and Archduke Karl Ludwig, Franz Joseph's father, formally disavowed the office. The function of this coronation was not the introduction of the sovereign; it was already quite clear that Franz Joseph was the ruler of Hungary. Rather, the rite demonstrated that the sovereign recognized limits to his authority, that he was "king" of the kingdom rather than a conquering "emperor." Franz Joseph's coronation was designed to address the question of "how." It was an announcement of a changed commitment, a pledge to uphold the Hungarian constitution.

For the Hungarian gentry the coronation of Franz Joseph was a command performance if one ever expected to participate in the government or move in the highest circles. Written excuses seemed necessary for any absences, including the elderly or infirm requesting exemption from "exhausting duties."[133] The quarter year given to staging the coronation became a frenzy of protocol.[134] The privileges and obligations of nobility traditionally revolved around such grand moments, when favors, honors, and privileges were distributed, and displays of homage were rewarded.[135] For noble participants it was an expensive occasion. Some were literally wearing their wealth, and relative standing could be measured by the outfitting of carriages and person.

If one disregards the crowd and the setting—the largest crowd ever assembled in the budding metropolis—the coronation might appear an archaic rite. The mighty of the nation assembled in the cathedral were prone to consider themselves "the nation." But in 1867 they were well aware that the audience was a much expanded public, the "nation" a much larger entity. When one takes the throng into one's view, one sees the novelty and strangeness of this occasion. The distinctively Hungarian feature of the coronation was not what occurred within the church but what took place outside. The spectacle of coronation was an urban crowd event. What seemed like the most incidental question a coronation posed was "where" it would be held. But the answer in 1867, Buda and Pest, was novel and represented the most significant change in the coronation rite. Franz Joseph's coronation would be the first to be performed in Pest-Buda; it simply had to have a Pest dimension. The coronation sealed the would-be capital's claim to be the hub of the system. For a month the eyes of the nation, the monarchy, and to some extent Europe came to focus on the approaching ceremony in Pest-Buda. Hungarians thrilled at the exposure of their burgeoning city. Construction of the rostrum, stands, and triumphal arches along the parade route began many weeks before.[136]

"Today is the day óf festive joy and national pride," declaimed the newspapers at the arrival of Franz Joseph and Elizabeth in Pest-Buda on May 8. Several thousand people of all classes jammed the railway station to greet the "crownable" regal couple.[137] Forty to fifty young girls waited with bouquets. Front and center were Andrássy, Eötvös, and other notables. There was complete silence when the train arrived, but cheers rang out as the king disembarked in a Hussar uniform. After the brief speeches, the sovereigns proceeded to Buda. The royal couple moved along the route from the railway station to the Chain Bridge through a thick cordon of people. They were showered with flowers, filling their carriage and turning the roadway into "a colorful carpet where every step and movement was silenced."[138] Persian rugs were draped across the balconies. At the Pest bridgehead, a huge banner declared, "Long Live the Royal Couple and the Homeland," and at the Buda bridgehead a banderium of nobles and two thousand Hussars awaited the royal couple to escort them the final distance to the castle. The citadel commander extended the key to the city to Franz Joseph on a velvet pillow,[139] and the city fathers, in accord with tradition, "became [the sovereign's] bodyguards at the entrance into the popular sphere; in the streets of the city the king received the shouts of joy."[140] Elizabeth wrote Rudolph that she had gotten "a really big éljen," that the cheers were so deafening they almost blew the roofs off the houses, and that she was buried under the flowers.[141] The royal entry thus initiated a month of coronation festivities.

The impact of the coronation had to be felt directly in Pest. In 1867 Hungary's villages had to come to the metropolis. Since April 26 every county of Hungary had been sending soil to be added to the coronation mound in Pest.[142] The mushrooming city drew everything to it. For the first time representatives from foreign countries arrived in Pest in significant numbers. No other location would have provided the publicity and legitimacy of public concurrence in Franz Joseph's reign as king. The competing contentions of the powerful about what indeed was the nation, who or which institution was entrusted to represent and defend the people—the king or the gentry—required the affirmation of a crowd.[143] Old rituals would be altered, and with them the relations between the king and his subjects would be transformed. Eötvös likened preparations for the coronation to rehearsals "for a theater performance," but the masquerade of Hungarian kingship would be altered by the chastened crowd who would gape and stare as tradition itself seemed to perform before them. "Tomorrow we have the coronation . . ." Eötvös wrote in his diary, "The people will try out whether they can like the sovereign. That they learn this, is much more important than any ceremony."[144]

Magyar radicals and minorities were still attempting to obstruct, divert, or modify the agreement, or simply threatening to disrupt the celebration itself. The Croats worried that they would be forced back under Magyar tutelage, and determined to make their presence at the coronation contingent on a successful outcome to the internal Hungarian-Croatian Compromise. But negotiation broke down, and the Croatian Diet voted to boycott the ceremony. The bitter bone of contention was the ethnically Italian city of Fiume, Hungary and Croatia's access to the Adriatic. After two decades of administrative rule from Vienna, Fiume was claimed by both Hungary and Croatia. The Italian population favored the more distant rule of Pest-Buda over Zagreb, and the city would ultimately be represented in both the Hungarian and Croat parliaments.

Only the semi-autonomous Croats were able to register an effective protest over the coronation. Within Transylvania, the Saxons were the great losers. Having been the most conspicuous beneficiaries of Austrian centralism, they now found themselves without recourse. Five days before the coronation a dispirited Transylvanian-Romanian deputation presented their grievances to Deák in his hotel room, gaining a sympathetic but unwavering response. Although Deák sought to reassure them that Hungarian liberalism would guarantee the minorities certain liberties, he also made it clear that resistance to Transylvanian union was pointless. But Romanians would continue to hold mass protest meetings against Transylvania's integration into Hungary. On May 15, 1868 a mass rally was again held in Balázsfalva, the site of rallies in 1848, and its organizers were arrested.[145] Beyond the Transylvanian mountains, the King of Romania pointedly ignored the coronation.

The Czechs registered the greatest displeasure and moral indignation. František Palacky, the leader of Czech nationalism, undertook a much publicized tour to Moscow in the weeks before the coronation. It was one of the most effective demonstrations of Pan-Slavism. Palacky would issue his own jeremiad, prophesying that dualism would bring down the monarchy. He comforted himself with the reflection that "we Slavs were here before Austria, and we shall be here after it."[146] The Bohemian aristocracy lobbied for a parallel compromise between Prague and Vienna. The Archduchess Sophia would sympathize with this, viewing dualism as rewarding the disloyal, sacrificing the loyal, and violating tradition, especially since no Habsburg had ever been crowned in Hungary without also being crowned in Bohemia. Elizabeth remained deaf to the pleas from Prague. The Czechs would assume the former role of the Hungarians as the slighted and embittered opponents of the status quo. In 1868 they would boycott a visit by Franz Joseph to Prague, and the situation became so tense that between October 1868 and April 1869 Prague was placed under a state of siege. There were also arrests of Slovak nationalists who called for a boycott of the coronation. Despite the injury inflicted on the ethnic minorities, they did not take to the streets. Neither the Serbs, nor the Transylvanian Romanians or Saxons, Slovaks, or even Croats were able to confront Hungarian authorities with vigorous mass demonstrations against the coronation. Thirty years later such passivity would no longer be presumed.[147] Still, a specter of Magyar republican retaliation hung over the event. Deák received a death threat, and Andrássy's wife worried greatly on the day.

By five a.m. on June 8 people in their Sunday best were streaming into Pest. Parliamentarians in "Magyar gala" rode through the crowds in their carriages toward the Mátyás Church. When the festivities began at seven, the streets were thick with people. Shop windows were packed and people climbed ladders and rooftops to watch the notables on their way to Buda.[148] The crowd was fascinated by the foreign dignitaries, clerical hierarchy, the royal retinue, and especially the aristocrats, bedecked in gold embroidery and precious stones, in high boots, with heron feathers in their caps, and the parade of hundreds of exquisite carriages, many even decorated with gems and covered with gold leaf. A crowd hero that day was Liszt, who was fêted with emotional ovations everywhere he went.

With a one-hundred-and-one-gun salute the procession in Buda set off, passing the Hentzi statue on its way to the Mátyás Church. The marchers moved at a slow gait between a double row of soldiers.[149] At the forefront were courtiers, pages, and various knights, then recipients of the Order of the Golden Fleece, followed by Prime Minister Gyula Andrássy. Thereupon, came palace guards, women bearing the coat-of-arms, heralds, the Lord Steward of the Royal Household with the staff in his hand, then three Archdukes, together with a Bishop and Acting Master of the Horse, bearing the "sword of the nation." The ruling couple rode in a carriage drawn by eight white horses. The monarch was dressed in a Hungarian Field Marshal's uniform, while Elizabeth wore national gala dress complete with Magyar headdress. Captain of the Guards, the Head Chamberlain, and First Adjutant followed. Flanking them the city council marched bareheaded on one side and the queen's pages on the other.[150] Nobles carried flags of historic Hungary and regions connected to the kingdom. Trailing behind were five carriages carrying bodyguards, palace guards, and military officers. Power paraded before the public on coronation day. Oceans of people were everywhere. Even the rooftops were crowded with daring youths, who from early morning waited and watched.

The primate greeted the ruling couple, who rested briefly in the lull while the coronation regalia were prepared and the last honored guests and participants took their places.[151] Liszt's *Hungarian Coronation Mass* resounded through the vaulted hall. The coronation procession to the main altar of the Mátyás was accompanied by a rousing fanfare. Magnates, lords-in-waiting, barons, keepers-of-the-crown, were followed by the bearers of the coronation symbols, the coronation robe, and traditional attire.[152] The Grand Cupbearer carried the sword, the Lord Chief Treasurer carried the cross, the Bán of Croatia the gold imperial orb, the Lord Chief Justice the scepter, finally Andrássy brought the crown. The Primate, Court Chancellor, and Court Treasurer presided over the presentation of the coronation artifacts, maintaining the symbolic confluence of lay and church authority. Once all symbols were in view, the Habsburg Archdukes filed in, followed by the ruling couple. In the ceremony, Franz Joseph swore on his knees that he would maintain peace and truth. He also demonstrated his faith and obedience to God's laws by kissing a crucifix, and accepting the anointment with consecrated oil by the Primate. With these acts, the king demonstrated his obedience to the mission of the church, but also that as a crowned king he was not just the protector of the nation's church but much more: he was their king, preserving the nation's legal code.[153] Franz Joseph could then be adorned with the coronation robe and mass was celebrated. The sovereign was offered the sword, which he grasped and swung in various directions as ruler and protector of the nation. At this, the cannons were sounded.[154] The king then kneeled down before the Primate, who girded the king with the sword. Thereupon, Andrássy as acting palatine, placed the Crown of St. Stephen on his head. "Long live the crowned king!" was the collective shout, and a volley was discharged outside. It was Andrássy who was the instrumental person in Franz Joseph's coronation, thus acknowledging the revival of Hungarian magnate prominence in the monarchy. But this was coronation by acclamation not election. It was Franz Joseph who had finally allowed himself to be crowned, not the Hungarian nobles who had selected him or even agreed to his assumption of kingship. The Hungarian medieval tradition had incorporated the English idea of election. The palatine asked the assembled crowd, "Do you want X to be crowned king?" To these perfunctory questions, the nobles were by custom to reply in unison: "We do!"[155] The Habsburgs had reduced this aspect, and in 1867 it was dispensed with altogether, replaced by acclamation of "Long live the King!" As Franz Joseph was led to the throne by prelates and notables, more volleys, now cannon fire, and then bell ringing resounded from without. The crowning of the queen followed; this was a unique addition, for queens had customarily been crowned apart from the central ceremony, often the following day. Franz Joseph turned to the primate and made the ceremonial request that his queen be crowned before the assembled officials. She was anointed by the primate, handed the staff and orb, then her shoulder was grazed by the crown.

The coronation ritual had two phases. The public was excluded from this first phase; its progress was announced to them through the blasts of gun or cannon fire. But the public was recruited for the next phase. Gold and silver commemorative coins were thrown among the people as the newly crowned king made his way back to the garrison church. After conferring knighthoods in the garrison church, he mounted his steed for the final act in the ceremony. This was to be performed across the river in Pest. At the head of a gala procession, the sovereign rode across the Chain Bridge and along the Danube bank to the square facing the Pest parish church where a platform had been raised. At what would henceforth be called Oath Square, the king took the constitutional oath to great public cheering. The queen watched from the balcony of the Lloyd building. The whole procession circled the coronation mound and Franz Joseph galloped onto it; there he made the four slashes with his sword toward North, South, East, and West, which brought more cheers and renewed cannon fire. Andrássy was to have proclaimed the "éljen!" cheer three times, as custom dictated, but before he had the opportunity, the crowd yelled the chant instead. The crowd had assumed their authority to acclaim the king. The emergence of the chastened crowd was finally sanctified and ritualized in Pest-Buda that day.

Distributing coins during the coronation procession in Buda, while a coronation flag is being ripped apart for souvenirs (detail), 1867. Etching by Vilmos Katzler (Capitol's Ervin Szabó Library, Budapest Collection)

1848 into 1867?

After two decades of demystifying monarchy, Hungarian nationalists found themselves ready to venerate it. An appearance of the sovereign couple, however brief, would inevitably produce tremendous excitement. For instance, when they passed through the town of Zala in 1869, it produced the largest crowd gathering ever seen in the area.[156] The legitimating crowd had become a participant, separating itself from the principles of its symbolic leader, Kossuth, without abandoning its emotional tie to him and the myth of 1848.[157] The threat that the Kossuthites might disrupt the coronation or put a pall on it dissolved when faced with the presence of a skeptical, but also buoyant, celebratory crowd. In the aftermath of the coronation, the new Andrássy-led government launched a vigorous campaign against "Kossuthite subversion" in certain Kossuth strongholds, such as in Heves county.[158] The government also staged a show trial, targeting the publicist László Böszörményi for publishing Kossuth's "Váci letter," in which Kossuth restated his repudiation of the Habsburg Monarchy and insisted that there could be no compromising of a free Hungary. With the Böszörményi trial the "Kossuth cult" was, in effect, placed on trial and convicted of being impractical. While stalwart Kossuthites mobilized the old martyrology, the Andrássy regime succeeded in marginalizing Kossuth and his supporters as fanatics.

Co-opting the Honvéds was a more sensitive issue. Within a week of the coronation, *Alföld*, a newspaper based in Arad, had called for public commemoration of the Arad martyrs. This proposal had been floated in the early sixties, but rejected as too provocative. Compromise made such an event possible. But when it seemed the Honvéd aid societies would be bringing large crowds to Arad on October 6, the Day of the Arad Martyrs, the Andrássy government banned their meeting.[159] The day, which had been celebrated as a "big anniversary only in our hearts" before 1867, would, nevertheless, become a civic event of larger and larger proportions. In 1868 black flags hung from Arad's houses and public structures. The city elite attended a special service with thousands gathered on the church square. The religious service was ecumenical in tone, including singers from the synagogue and a National Theater chorus. Everyone was united in the religion of patriotism.

The veterans of 1848/49 had been awkward spectators at the celebration of the Compromise, and they remained embarrassing reminders of past conflict and suffering. During a March 15, 1868 rally of the Buda-Pest Worker Association, an amputee created a "painful incident" when he evoked the misery of the poor Honvéd, displayed his amputated arm for all to see and then broke into reminiscences.[160] Pál Somssich, a leading conservative, warned Andrássy that the Honvéd problem threatened the regime with "dangerous outbreaks," and urged the government to appease the Honvéd aid societies by establishing ten Honvéd regiments within the army. Although Andrássy wrote in the margins that this was typical conservative politics—making a revolution out of fear of revolution—he made settlement of the Honvéd question among his highest priorities.[161] In March 1868, three of Kossuth's former allies, the Generals Mór Perczel, István Türr, and György Klapka toured the country visiting Honvéd aid societies in support of the Compromise. When Perczel arrived in Veszprém peasants from the countryside filled the streets, and it seemed that the whole city was lining the thoroughfare through which he passed. Despite a few minor incidents (on March 15 rocks were thrown at the railroad carriage carrying General Klapka), the touring generals denounced Kossuth's intransigence to packed halls. Counter-demonstrations failed to impede their triumphal progress. One audience listened breathlessly as Perczel successfully out-dueled Madarász in debate. On March 15 the editorials reflected on the painful memories that remain in the hearts of the generation of Forty-Eight but were unknown to the younger generation. In its place Hungarians were creating a legal fiction that reconciled the symbolic years of 1848 and 1867, that coupled the new celebrity monarchism with national sentiments. On March 15, 1868, the goals of 1848 were "largely reality," it was claimed. Absolutism and the "aristocratic state" were gone. "Prejudice is smashed; not pedigree but work—spiritual as well as material—is the key. . . . Culture and effort are the certificates of nobility today."[162] The visual rhetoric of the royal ceremonial was so persuasive that the very idea that there might be other constitutional arrangements than a monarchy became unthinkable for most Hungarians in Austria-Hungary.

Yet the undercurrent of repudiation and paranoia was never far from the surface. The greatest crowd event in the post-coronation years was the reburial of Lajos Batthyány in 1870. The public was startled to learn that the corpse of the principal martyr of 1849 had been secretly diverted from its intended grave and that, instead, for twenty-one years Batthyány's remains had been entrusted to a Franciscan monastery. This set the stage for an elaborate reburial service. Huge crowds flowed into Pest from the countryside the day before the ceremony. Portraits of Batthyány, biographies, and occasional poems were hawked for sale outside. At the center of attention was the mournful figure of Batthyány's widow. She had played the stern, disapproving apparition during the celebration of the coronation. Now she and her daughter, who had worn black for twenty-one years, held the limelight and received the cheers of the crowd. In attendance were worker delegations, such as the Óbuda boat factory, leading unions, and guilds. The Franciscan church was so crowded that it was difficult to move. Students, officials, an aristocratic banderium, firefighters in uniform, the Pest city fathers, representatives from parliament, the academy, and the Kisfaludy Society were present, and of course, particularly prominent were the Honvéd veterans. In short, the establishment and counterestablishment gathered in apparent unanimity, perhaps in a display of a more unanimous settlement than three years before during the coronation.

The commemoration of revolution and monarchy could not be disentangled. The same ambiguous pattern would repeat itself during the twenty-fifth anniversary of 1848–49. Nor could Austrian and Hungarian commemorations be coordinated. In Austria the anniversary of the emperor's accession came in 1873, while in Hungary the jubilee for the king would be celebrated in 1892. For Austrians, Franz Joseph was the monarch who arose out of failed revolution—the Man of 1848. Austrians studiously ignored June 8, Hungarian coronation day. Hungarians, for their part, were loathe to pay homage to December 2, the day of Franz Joseph's accession in 1848. Kossuthites would thunder against any Hungarian celebration of Franz Joseph's jubilee in 1873, and five hundred of the 2,500 guests invited by the royal couple did not attend the palace soirée that Jókai described as "an occasion when former prisoners and former jailers congratulated each other on their mutual successes."[163] In 1873 there was no taste for celebrating. March 15, June 8, and December 2 were less than low key in Budapest. Even the key symbolic royal gesture of the year, the official unification of Buda, Óbuda, and Pest into one capital city, Budapest, was experienced purely in bureaucratic terms: a change of stationery, reclassification of civil servants, and so forth.[164] In contrast, the Honvéd aid societies demonstrated their organizational and agitational prowess on October 6, 1874 for the twenty-fifth anniversary of the Arad executions. Hundreds of bouquets with long ribbons formed the backdrop to a fiery sermon delivered by a cleric who had spent years in prison. An actor from the National Theater recited the poem Jókai wrote for the occasion, with the refrain: "You aren't dead, you heroes!"[165] The event was focused on the widows of prominent Honvéds. The crowd of several thousand watched as the procession, four abreast with flags and torches, made its way to the site of the executions. Several bands accompanied them, playing funeral marches. The spot was encircled by flags.

Neither the defenders of the Compromise nor the unreconciled would have the last word. Or rather, a Janus-faced system spoke simultaneously out of both mouths. Lajos Mocsáry, at a March 15, 1874 banquet, first toasted Lajos Kossuth, only to follow that up with another toast where he voiced the hope that in time all of Hungary "would turn into a large banquet for the March 15, 1848 memorial holiday," and its toastmaster would be Franz Joseph.[166]

March 15 celebration before the Sándor Petőfi statue in Budapest (BTM Kiscelli Museum, Budapest)

8

The Exhibition of Liberalism

The era of Franz Joseph's greatest popularity as king of Hungary coincided with the high point of Hungarian liberalism, Kálmán Tisza's premiership, from 1875 to 1890, the longest continuous administration in the period of Compromise. Tisza was, indeed, the perfect Hungarian counterpart to the stiff, equally colorless monarch who awoke early each morning and attended to the paperwork, much in the same fashion as a faithful servant of the bureaucracy. No one worked more shrewdly within the restricted field of internal politics or more effectively manipulated the parliament and bureaucracy than Kálmán Tisza. Tisza's understanding with Franz Joseph lay in their identical ages. Both men were born in 1830, and both had come politically of age in the revolution: one as a counter-revolutionary autocrat, the other as a Hungarian revolutionary, too frail to fight, but for all that, the more resolute Kossuthite. It was Tisza in 1867 who persisted in raising last-minute legalistic objections to the coronation, pointing out that Ferdinand made no reference to Hungary in his abdication. As Franz Joseph had shed absolutism, now Tisza dispelled the dream of independence. Tisza, a gangling, dour Calvinist party boss, fended off Kossuth's influence by relegating the self-styled hermit of Turin to an older generation already transfixed in time, consigned to the role of the idiosyncratic conscience of 1848.[1] In sharp contrast to the flamboyant Gyula Andrássy and the oracular Kossuth, Tisza's political style was decidedly bland. He was content that Franz Joseph and Kossuth would cast long shadows, so long as he might stand between. Kálmán Tisza emerged in the vacuum left by Andrássy's departure for Vienna in 1871.

The writer Kálmán Mikszáth likened Kálmán Tisza to a "sphynx bird, mysterious and mute."[2] Tisza ostensibly remained in the background as the third man, the compromise solution to the question of Lajos Kossuth or Ferenc Deák. Unlike Deák who found it a burden to be a party leader, and unlike Andrássy who was glamorous and removed, happier in court circles, the man with contacts rather than the organization, Tisza thrived in the give-and-take of factional politics. Tisza was neither a Hungarian Bismarck nor a Hungarian Gladstone, nor even the Hungarian Boss Tweed; or rather, he was all and none of these. He was not a Bismarck, because he had at best indirect influence on foreign policy. He also did not control the monarch, since the bifurcation of dualism enabled Franz Joseph to play Austrian and Hungarian politicians off against one another and to emerge himself as the unifying figure. Tisza would affect Hungary's place in the world through internal rather than external policy. For that reason, his means to further Hungary's standing in Europe was to showcase Hungary as a triumph of European liberalism. Tisza's government financed a profusion of statue raisings; the building of monumental state buildings, such as the parliament; and grand events, such as the National Industrial Exhibition of 1885. However, Tisza was not a Gladstone, because his liberalism was mitigated by his agrarian gentry roots, and he continued to operate in the shadow of Kossuth, so he would never become "Mr. Liberalism" to his generation. His power rested on his control of the rotten boroughs in the hinterlands. For this reason, Tisza was also not a Boss Tweed; he remained a man of the provinces, never fully at home and never quite allowing himself to be identified with the metropolis. Tisza's rise was as surreptitious as would be his hold on Hungarian politics. Nonetheless, over time Tisza came to seem an inevitable element of the political landscape.[3]

The clear divisions of the 1860s between Deákists and Kossuthites broke down in the early 1870s, especially when the economic crash of 1873 exposed the frayed edges of the Deákist camp. Their governing party had remained a loose organization, because Deák, the uncontested leader, was a loner accustomed to playing his cards close to the vest. With József Eötvös's death and Andrássy's departure for Vienna as foreign minister, few of the makers of the compromise remained in Budapest to reform the system. Deák's underlings, moreover, busied themselves expanding the bureaucracy to widen the net of sinecures; scandals soon followed. Deák, to paraphrase Marx, insisted he was no Deákist. The ailing Deák grew ever more disillusioned with his tarnished party. The economic downturn led to a paralysis that forced the political class to look for some new solution. The one aspect left fluid in the Compromise, the economic and financial clauses, had to be renegotiated at ten-year intervals. The approaching deadline spurred political realignment, as would the subsequent ones of 1887, 1897, 1907. Tisza fused Deákists with his own Kossuthite left center into a new synthesis called the Liberal Party in the spring of 1875. This "fusion" involved reconciling the 1848ers with 1867ers. The nationalist opposition formed the Party of Independence, and a smaller, but vocal minority clung to a Kossuthite intransigence, calling themselves the Party of 1848.

In 1875 the "fusion" was celebrated in the new Liberal Party caucuses around the country, but not elsewhere. Neither did Tisza's elevation to prime minister six months later stir public acclamation. On New Year's Day, the prime minister traditionally held the political spotlight as he received the homage from his amassed party and delivered his primary address of the year. On January 1, 1876 a procession of wagons rolled from the Liberal Party's headquarters to Deák's home and then to Tisza's official quarters in Buda. Three weeks later Tisza was faced with his first major public event, the ceremonial burial of Deák. In the mourning of Deák, there was a wider sadness about the passing of an era and its great founding leaders—a sentiment that has persisted in the historiography. Tisza donned the mantle of the grieving heir and prepared to defend the Compromise against the Left Opposition. In memorializing Deák, it was Queen Elizabeth who melded the national grief into an identification with dualism. The lithograph by Mihály Zichy of Elizabeth kneeling before Deák's casket in homage to the architect of dualism would become a central image in the iconography of the monarchy, familiar to virtually every Hungarian. Despite its dark, somber colors, a hopefulness seemed to generate out of the lofty, albeit funereal theme.[4] It was for all practical purposes also her last political act.

The Liberal Party press praised Deák for his simplicity, reflected in the unadorned coffin and stark funeral ceremony. However, within a couple of weeks there were expressions of uneasiness that not enough had been done to memorialize Deák and his principles. Legislators scrambled to find the correct gesture that could define Deák's legacy. "Kings can give successors titles, the church can make men saints, how, however, does a free people, an adult people, represent its deepest piety and gratitude?" asked a Liberal Party editorialist, and answered, by creating a memorial in law, the "Deák law," commissioning the raising of a Deák statue.[5] During the debate over this symbolic legislation, one left opposition member dared to object "lest every majority apotheosize its men." The usually aloof Tisza "became pale from excitement," the newspapers reported. "His hands trembled, and at first, his words were halting. . . . He unleashed 'holy anger' on Ernő Simonyi's head" and vociferously defended the Compromise and the wisdom of its architect.[6]

Mihály Zichy, *Queen Elizabeth Praying at Ferenc Deák's Catafalque,* 1876. Lithograph (Hungarian National Museum)

Within the month a letter from Kossuth reminded the Hungarian public that Kossuth, "an exile from the fatherland, was also exiled from Deák's heart."[7] Kossuth would have the last word. The fusion was not complete. Yet, although, some political wounds were still unhealed, March 15, the holiday of revolution, a day feared by the authorities in the early 1860s, now passed without concern. Had it been a day of tension, the National Mourning Commission would not have chosen it to wander around the Kerepesi cemetery determining the appropriate site for the Deák mausoleum.[8]

Liberalism in Hungary was connected to a small political class. The 1874 electoral law reduced the electorate to 5.9 percent, a shocking figure to the twentieth century, but a respectable one at the time. The problem was not that the percentage was low but that it would remain low. András Gerő argues that the 1874 law caused a fateful rigidity in the system and became the major impediment to subsequent democratization.[9] Tisza's Liberal Party would rely on the rotten boroughs in the borderland districts which, despite non-Magyar majorities, returned pro-Tisza liberal Magyar deputies. These districts served as a balance wheel against the more militantly nationalist, Kossuth-leaning Magyar core areas. The Liberal Party advanced the "fusion" of the new metropolis and rural counties. It also promoted a convenient secularization of politics, enabling eastern Calvinists and western Catholics to embrace a common nationalism.

The peculiar success of Hungarian liberalism was also not its liberal legislation, which was sparse, but rather its ability to counter conservative fatalism that presented two dreadful alternatives to the nationalist imagination: that Hungary could disappear like Poland or that it would become a mere Austrian province. Hungarian liberalism identified its conservative rival with the alien royal court and thus discredited conservatism as a viable alternative. Conservatives had accused liberals of taking the nation through the disastrous adventure of revolution. But by orchestrating a martyrology of revolutionary defeat and projecting an economic program of modernization, liberalism sustained its hold on the Hungarian political imagination. With the repoliticization of Hungarian life in the 1860s, liberals were poised to emerge as the architects of the Dual Monarchy. They were rewarded by uninterrupted Liberal Party rule from 1875 to 1905. Although Tisza himself remained obscure abroad, his regime benefited from Hungarian liberalism's appearance to others as a consolidating, integrating, and rejuvenating force. This was a welcome contrast to the divided and rattled liberalism of the new German and Italian nation-states, or the growing political paralysis of generational and ethnic tension dividing liberals in the other half of the monarchy. Hungarian liberalism would so dominate political life that every party but the most extreme would consider itself or call itself liberal. For the younger age-group the "fusion" would eventually come to seem like a second Compromise; midway through Tisza's fifteen-year tenure as prime minister his contemporaries began accustoming themselves to the thought that they were living in the Kálmán Tisza era.

The Nationalization of the Fairgrounds

Exhibitions were the great minstrel shows of an approaching capitalist breakthrough, which promised to legitimate the liberal oligarchy. With the Compromise lending economic issues a special political character, exhibitions should not be underestimated as simply a prop in the Hungarian liberal program. In anticipation of the inevitably drawn out and contentious negotiations for the decennial ratification of the Compromise's economic stipulations, the liberal pageant masters lobbied at home as well as in Vienna; they lobbied behind closed doors and also by staging demonstrations at national fairs. As advertisers of a liberal capitalist future, liberal politicians sought—differently in every decade, to be sure—to reconcile the claims of national identity and imperial loyalty, to assert the national market while ensuring international credit. Hungarian liberals were determined to turn the Dual Monarchy into a dual marketplace and fairgrounds.

The nineteenth-century exhibitions staged by Hungarian liberals—the modest Pest industrial fairs of the 1840s; the agricultural exhibitions of the counter-revolutionary 1850s; the Pest agricultural exhibition in 1865; the three provincial industrial exhibitions of the 1870s in Kecskemét, Szeged, and Székesfehérvár; the successful national exhibition in Budapest in 1885, and the lavish Millennium Exhibition of 1896—conformed to the wider European and American pattern of exhibitions. Between 1876 and 1916 some one-hundred million Americans attended exhibitions; over 20 percent of the U.S. population attended Philadelphia's Centennial Exhibition of 1876. Over 48 million people passed through the turnstiles of the Paris Exposition of 1900. The three million who attended the Hungarian Millennium Exhibition were well aware that they were participating in a distinct rite of industrial civilization. Although the Hungarian numbers were far smaller, Hungarian national fairs were not copycat undertakings but had their own distinctive character.[10] To be sure, it was the distinct sense of being handicapped that gave the first Hungarian exhibitions their distinctive character, and in 1896 success was measured by the distance traversed in that half-century. Of all the societies engaged in the exhibiting of industrialism, Hungarians felt that theirs was coming from the greatest deficit, from the most backward place.

The message of the first Pest industrial fairs in the 1840s had been the political-economic refrain of backwardness and political inferiority. The new rhetoric of the boom of the 1850s and 1860s was supposed to advertise Hungarian success. But the centralist principles of neo-absolutism allowed little play for Hungarian pride. Typical was Hungary's humiliating presence at the London Exhibition of 1862, where the Austrian organizing committee incorporated Hungary's exhibits into an Austrian-dominated display. The refusal to permit a separate Hungarian exhibit provided an insatiable source of newsprint, because it seemed to encapsulate the problem of the Provisorium, that Hungary had been relegated to a subservient position. This left the impression, one newspaper sourly observed, that nature may be bountiful in Hungary, but human productivity was meager.[11] But even Hungary's wine tasting booth was a fiasco; the featured Hungarian wine arrived turned.[12] Although most Hungarian items were scattered amongst the Austrian ones, one small room within the Austrian exhibit was devoted to distinctively Hungarian objects. Still, superior quality goods, such as Hungary's flour, were upstaged by more professional presentations of inferior products of other nations. Clumsy design and a lack of salesmanship left reporters grumbling about lost opportunities. What drew any interest in the Hungarian exhibit was the addition of photographs of native costumes above the raw materials of a region. This was also the first exhibition at which photographs were incorporated into the displays. While ethnic promotion was a cherished goal for the Magyars, the subtext in the London context was of Hungary as a rural, exotic other.[13]

With the achievement of dualism in 1867, the banned National Industrial Association could reconstitute itself, and within two years the society proposed a general exhibition to be held in Pest combining agricultural, industrial, and decorative art exhibits. Since Hungary had now "rejoined" the independent European states, the association sought to engage in "the peaceful contest of peoples toward the noblest goals of humanity."[14] A national exhibition was meant to be more than a material display; it was to be the first report card to the nation and the world of Hungary's progress and promise since the Compromise. Habsburg legitimacy had rested nervously after 1849 on economic viability. Now allied, the Hungarian political elite found themselves in a similar position, but they had grounds for optimism. The display of wealth, enthusiasm, and civic pride at the fair would be yet another option to widen the liberal public consensus and fashion an urbane crowd. Kossuth and his followers came to view these exhibitions with ever greater distress as they became forums for the legitimation of the compromisers rather than a platform for independence.

Nationalists were annoyed that a proposed Hungarian national exhibition had to be delayed in deference to the upcoming Viennese World's Fair of 1873.[15] Instead, an industrial exhibition was held in the provincial town of Kecskemét in 1872. The "pinnacle of interest" at this exhibition, much like a county fair, was the food bazaar, organized by local women's organizations. The *Pesti Napló* delighted in recounting the awkwardness of a visiting Pest emissary, a bachelor, when "besieged" by the local matrons, proffering their bounty of pastries, numerous glasses of liqueur, and a stream of welcoming banter.[16] Rather than machinery, it was high-quality crafts, especially cabinetry, that garnered most interest at this exhibition. Commentators were encouraged at the prospect of a "maturing" national aesthetic.[17] Local fairs helped engender and standardize a new regional style of folk art—a melding of traditional local motifs into a regional commercial style, while also acquainting the local craftsman with the innovative materials and the fashions emanating from Budapest.[18] National identity and liberal purpose was being built out of and from the local. Exhibitions were facilitators in the process of combining folk cultural fragments, infusing the traditional with the modern, and out of the mix forming and articulating a national culture.

The invention of the folk (*népi*) tradition coincided with the transportation revolution transforming the rural landscape. The railroad played havoc with the old system of county fairs, and where the railroad went the county fair soon suffered. Peasant commerce now concentrated in peasant villages near the traffic lines, especially around the capital.[19] Peasants began more consciously to wear clothing that demarcated them from peasants of other regions and accentuated the difference between their look and that of the gentry or the city. Magyar peasants became more involved in developing ostentatious variants of their traditional garb, which under serfdom had been strikingly plain and modest. Serfs had been tied to a definite dress code with rules governing color and types of materials that could or could not be worn. As these restrictions fell into disuse, peasants adapted lavish materials paralleling the new urban culture. Peasants began using manufactured cashmere, cotton, and even silk and velvet, favoring textiles dyed in brilliant colors. The conspicuous folk culture also distinguished Hungarian from German, Slovak, Serb, Romanian, and other peasants. The Magyar peasantry invested more in items of dress, and their household goods and textiles tended to be far more lavish and colorful than, for example, the Germans, who seemed puritanical in comparison.

Romantic nationalism had long championed the peasant as the force of independence, attributing a collective creative capacity to the peasantry. Just as nations had mother tongues, the argument went, so a people had a nurturing peasant culture from which their native "genius" sprang. The Germans were the first to celebrate the folklore, folk music, and folk art of peasant culture, praising it for its introspective, moral, and aesthetic character. Mid-century Magyar peasant culture was not unaware of this "ideological" prompting, but such ideas had never been more timely than when foreign occupiers ruled in Pest-Buda. The economic expansion, beginning in the 1850s, had allowed peasants to redefine local culture in material forms, stimulating a new aesthetic in the East-Central European village.

Folk culture had since sunk its roots. The peasants had come to think of their place in society in a new way. They had made the sacrifice and demonstrated their patriotism in the revolution. The abolition of serfdom, the revolutionary experience, as well as the sufferance of defeat made the Magyar peasant feel more a part of the civic culture. It was no longer possible to imagine, as in 1848, the mobilization of tens of thousands of peasants in Pest as sufficient to prompt a revolution from above in Pozsony. The expectation of rural uprisings had passed. Instead, the lure of an urban alternative for peasants and the spread of folk dress to the burghers and elites in the 1860s became an expression of reconciliation among classes and/or the decline of the agrarian order.

In the dualist era there could be commercial value in employing the motifs of the regional costume in product decoration, serving as a kind of trademark for special village crafts; hand-painted furniture, for instance, typically utilized a motif from the regional costume. Provincial fairs with national coverage would, it was hoped, stimulate commerce and propel an economically based national identity. Pageant masters and reporters for national and international fairs made themselves arbiters of taste, providing visitors with a one-day technical and aesthetic education. But this project required an audience, and at the Kecskemét exhibition of 1872 there were no crowds. The exhibition's limited draw was a disappointment to boosters and journalists. It had become clear that the urban setting was as important as the objects themselves. Those who made banquet toasts at the Kecskemét fair turned their attention turned toward the opportunity the coming Viennese World's Fair would afford Hungarians to "make evident our progress."[20] But the Viennese World's Fair was a fiasco. Attendance was abysmal; technological wonders were no longer a sufficient draw to justify the enormous state expenditures. The Viennese municipality was strapped for funds when the fair began, and a week after the opening, Viennese bank failures set off the worldwide crash of 1873. The deficit was to be staggering. Fair organizers were ill equipped to handle a stock market collapse. Instead of a showcase of liberalism in ascendancy, the Viennese exhibition became a symbol of liberalism in crisis.[21] As it was the first exhibition in the German-speaking world, German liberals in Austria had hoped for its promotional value. The German Empire had accounted for 8,000 exhibitors and generous financial support. France sent 5,000 exhibitors, Hungary 3,500. The Czech nobility had been hostile, but eventually participated.[22]

The May stock market crash was followed by a cholera scourge in June. The literary critic Ferdinand Kürnberger called the exhibition "our second Königgrätz," and the *Neue Wiener Tageblatt* proclaimed the "death of World Exhibitions."[23] Vienna 1873 became the chilling example of the dangers that might befall a Hungarian national exhibition were it to be staged prematurely. Hungarian journalists took some ghoulish pleasure in revisiting the exhibition site to watch its demolition and moralize over false pride.[24] The expansive economic mood of the preceding quarter century dissipated in a new gloom. In this chastened atmosphere the provincial industrial exhibitions of Szeged in 1876 and Székesfehérvár in 1879 could alternately critique or reinforce dualism. The Szeged fair was termed a "universal exhibition," meaning it combined agricultural and industrial exhibits to bring the "economic life of the whole country together." The stated political goal was to accentuate the need for "an independent tariff area and protection of our industry."[25] The economic renewal of the Compromise was completed just prior to the opening of the exhibition. The Trade Minister used his public address to vent his frustrations with the outcome of the negotiations, which he declared inhibited Hungary's ability to meet its own economic needs and redress the import imbalance with Austria. He urged visitors to use the exhibit to verify this lack of progress. In the spirit of the Kossuth trade fairs, he hoped the exhibition would be an "impetus" to complete emancipation of Hungarian economic life from Austria ten years hence. He punctuated his statement by resigning that same day.[26]

In 1879 at the opening of the Székesfehérvár exhibition, journalists focused on the "cry of pain" from the depressed Hungarian artisans.[27] The exhibition rhetoric remained that of an uplifting international contest, but it was supplemented in the newspapers by a grimmer vision of a struggle for economic survival. Of Hungary's economic policy, the newspapers wrote, "There is no policy, let alone a good policy."[28] Count Jenő Zichy, head of the organizing committee, declared that in the "hard days" that had befallen Hungary the Székesfehérvár exhibition would be "no victory festival."[29] A nation that gives up on itself, he warned, would be abandoned by the others to its fate. The press highlighted this fear: "A country that just exports food ends up exporting people."[30] This fear was premature, for mass emigration from Hungary would not occur until the turn of the century. However, population in the countryside was not keeping pace with that of the cities. In retrospect, we can see that Hungary still experienced economic growth and weathered the European economic crisis of 1873–9 more successfully than most of its neighbors.[31] Hungarian industrial production and Austrian investment continued to flow into the ever-expanding food-processing industries, so that in Hungary the major repercussions of the Great Depression were muted. However, those living through the depressed decades were not consoled by their relative status, by not doing as badly as others. The gentry, long the stabilizing force in the countryside, clearly lost ground. Gentry holders of middle-size properties felt the sting of declining land values and suffered most from the international long-term decline in grain prices. The result was a polarization of land ownership. While the number of peasant holdings remained stable, this camouflaged a constant turnover. A mere 321 holdings absorbed an additional 11 percent of the land, a territory approximating the size of Massachusetts and Connecticut combined, between 1867 and 1914.[32]

Gentry economic distress was all the more critical to the health of the regime, for the gentry had replaced the magnates as the dominant political voice since the fusion. Yet, the more regional a fair, the more it highlighted the local magnates rather than the gentry. This was especially obvious at the Székesfehérvár exhibition of 1879. Count Zichy garnered praise from the national press; his father boasted that his son Jenő had shot a "bull's eye" for Székesfehérvár. The city mushroomed in size for the duration of the exhibition. But "an exhibition in Székesfehérvár is a light under a barrel," some complained.[33] Once visitors had toured the exhibit, there was nothing to do in this small town (population 23,000, in a sparsely populated county). Székesfehérvár was first of all a commercial fair, packaging Hungarian goods to attract Hungarian consumers, hoping to convince them that buying quality Hungarian manufactured goods was a viable alternative to French-made furniture and the like. The exhibit proved itself a popular weekend outing from Budapest, but mid-week a depressing emptiness dominated the event. An exhibition as the handiwork of a magnate was fundamentally at odds with political and economic ambitions of national fairs. These exhibitions were meant to link the provincial and urban crowds to nationalism. But an exhibition that claims to speak for the nation, the mantra became, has only one natural and justified place, and that is the capital.[34] The Székesfehérvár exhibition did succeed in revealing a commercial resourcefulness and a diminishing political resentment. Unlike the previous exhibition, when Budapest and Vienna were at loggerheads, at Székesfehérvár both monarchy and Hungarian elite seemed to be facing down crises together.

Policing the Budapest Crowd

While the Kálmán Tisza era has been neglected, the transformation of Budapest that took place in the liberal period was profound. Budapest was the fastest growing European city between 1801 and 1891.[35] In part this was because it began from nothing. In 1787 Buda, Pest, and Óbuda had a combined population of only forty-seven thousand.[36] By the time of the Compromise, Budapest's population was a little over 250,000. "The most remarkable social phenomenon of the present century," Adna Weber wrote in 1899, "is the concentration of population in cities." Berlin, Rome, Vienna, Munich, and Hamburg all experienced similar, even equally dramatic growth during the nineteenth century.[37] But unlike the German cities, Budapest was the only Hungarian city undergoing this dramatic transformation. And it did so, at least in part, at the expense of the other Hungarian urban centers. Literary, intellectual, and political life had come to revolve around Budapest. "The love of the Hungarian for the capital of his fatherland can only be compared to the 'sacrilegious reverence' the Frenchman holds towards Paris," a Viennese reporter remarked in 1885.[38] Of course, the French provinces periodically turned on Paris, and so too, the Hungarian provinces could display both admiration and hostility toward its dominating city. Yet while Budapest was the sixteenth largest city in Europe at the time of the Compromise, Budapest was far from being a metropolis. Of the 9,351 housing units in the city only 750 were two or more stories high. The intercity transportation system was still severely limited, and no water or sewer system existed in Pest. In 1866 a cholera epidemic ravaged the city, finally prompting measures for sanitation control. Andrássy had lived his exile years in Paris while Georges Hausmann and Napoleon III redesigned the city. As prime minister, Andrássy made the elevation of Pest-Buda into a dignified, modern city a first priority. The cornerstone for his plan was a grand boulevard, modeled on a promenade like the Champs Elysées in Paris that would connect downtown Pest with the City Park. In 1868 the urban planning commission ratified Andrássy's vision, turning away from its earlier plan focused on the corso along the Danube and the development of the Pest dock.[39] After fourteen months of construction, the wide, spacious promenade opened in 1870. Wide boulevards were intended to deter barricades, but they facilitated gathering to stroll or march. From the Budapest City Park a series of townhouses surrounded by gardens fed into an unbroken row of multistory residential blocks, interrupted by a large square, the Octagon, ideal for the gathering urbane crowd. It was lined with elegant shops and cafés and became a transportation nexus.[40]

Budapest was the central arena of politics. Elsewhere, crowds, no matter how large they might be on occasion, were still far from the symbols of power. Only in Budapest could a sufficiently massive crowd be assembled that contained within it the latent but controlled power of revolution. In Budapest huge crowds were in the position of seizing the symbol of power (the crown) and the instruments of power (the citadel or parliament). Oligarchic politics, even if its political base was in the countryside, had to be able to rally a mass public in the capital. The ability of the liberal oligarchy to restrain and orchestrate crowds validated its leadership. Indeed, to assert the strength of Hungarian public opinion internally and to outsiders on whom Hungary was dependent (the Austrians and Germans), the liberal elite fostered a legitimating crowd.

The urban crowd was at the center of what was new, arresting, and off-putting about the future. For a quarter century the control of this crowd was in the hands of the colorful, corrupt Elek Thaisz, police chief of Pest from 1861 to 1873, then head of the capital police force from 1873 until he was finally driven from office in 1885.[41] Thaisz was the archetypal rascal, the fitting exemplar of a booming metropolis, who ultimately eluded investigators by escaping into a monastery (so as to be protected from testifying against himself). Thaisz saw to it that Budapest would be one of the most open cities in Europe with a red light district second to none. He had his fingers in prostitution, gambling, and other forms of corruption. How he survived scandal after scandal has led to much speculation. But there is no question as to the efficacy of his street-cleaning methods. From his investigation of László Teleki's suicide in the spring of 1861 to a calamitous Opera House dedication in 1884, Thaisz was among the most powerful figures of the capital. He saw his job as primarily a political one, suppressing street demonstrations, strikes, and maintaining security. Thaisz made it possible for the political capital to coexist with the urban crowd. He assured the security of the powerful. This made him indispensable to the oligarchy, and so they looked away from his rough and ready tactics. When foreign dignitaries were in town, or at moments of royal or oligarchic festivity, Thaisz accomplished his security duties by mobilizing the underworld to his assistance. When a respected mayor staked his career on dethroning the corrupt Thaisz, it was the mayor who would ultimately be forced to resign. Thaisz emerged triumphant, for he not only remained in office but was freed from city authority, reporting henceforth directly to the minister of the interior.[42] When Franz Joseph arrived in Pest in 1872, awaiting him on the platform alongside the mayor and ministers was Police Chief Thaisz.[43] Thaisz played the role of the liberal Magyar nationalist, but there was something of a sham in this, too; a half-century later it became known that he had been a police informer during the Bach era.[44]

Thaisz's ascendancy coincided with that of the chastened crowd. He was willing to cut the crowd some slack, but not too much. The cynical Thaisz could only have reigned in an era of liberal fear of the crowd. After the rising of the Paris Commune in the spring of 1871, Thaisz wielded his baton in the shadows that hung over street politics in Europe.[45] Thaisz determined that no ripples from the Commune were going to spread to Budapest. He did a police sweep of foreign agitators, and in the process, arrested the entire leadership of the Hungarian Socialist Party.[46] The specter of the Commune and a fear of the crowd was cemented into liberal politics until World War I. In an era where the "glorification of the Commune" was a punishable crime, the holiday of March 15 withered as a liberal celebration. Still, a few diehard antidynasts celebrated the Commune even in its defeat. The angry, polemical poems of Sándor Petőfi became fashionable again for the first time in a quarter century. The novel *Szegények harca* (War of the impoverished) landed its author, a veterinarian in the Hungarian hinterlands, in prison for a year. The very word "Commune" provoked a violent reaction. *The Communist Manifesto* became known for the first time, and the International conjured a far-flung conspiracy. Yet even as the radical style revived (on the right as well as on the left, as it turned out), the new fear was tied to the rise of the metropolis. The 1848 panic was occasioned by fear of peasants rallying in the city; after 1871 the concern was with the urban masses as a demanding mob.

Fear of outside agitators had been a preoccupation of the pre-Compromise era. With conservatives across the Continent viewing the Paris Commune as the ultimate consequence of 1789, Thaisz had the green light to move against outside agitators, that is, largely German-speaking socialists who were following the lead of their Berlin comrades. On March 18, 1873, twenty thousand demonstrators, the largest protest since 1848, marched in

Berlin to celebrate the Commune and the failed revolution of 1848.[47] In Budapest that day, Thaisz prevented any street demonstration, but Mihály Táncsics, the worker's hero of 1848, took to the podium alongside Leó Frankel and his younger generation of Hungarian social democrats. The new revolutionism argued that 1871 was more of a herald than 1848, because the workers were now fighting for freedom and equality rather than just for freedom. For the generation that had grown up in the quarter century since 1848, the Commune made revolution visible, and for the following generation, the Commune would remain what Lenin called a "festival of the oppressed." The image of the red republic as the coming political system, one that repudiated the nation and denigrated religion as the upholder of morality and tradition, sent shivers down the spine of liberalism in Hungary as elsewhere on the Continent. The socialists, though small in number, did manage to project an alternative historical vision; the defeated Communards now competed with the defeated Honvéds of 1849 as the lost cause that would ultimately triumph.

The first direct challenge to Thaisz's control of the streets in the Tisza period came in October 1876 when nationalist students took to the streets. Russo-Turkish tension brought the threat of war to Hungary's borders and fear of Pan-Slavism stirred up jingoism among students. They organized rallies in ostensible support of the government's pro-Turkish policies, with an aim of pushing Tisza into a provocative anti-Russian posture. First four hundred, then six hundred gathered. As the agitation grew, a student deputation met with Tisza. He banned their proposed torchlight parade, reportedly remarking, "Students don't understand politics. . . . If one allows them to smoke a cigar, they at once want to burn down houses."[48] Stunned at their rebuff, a thousand students stomped off noisily toward Jókai's house. Jókai was warmly greeted by the singing crowd who then carried him on their shoulders. He praised the students for their sentiments but rejected their jingoist agenda, warning them that, "There is something that we must still hold higher than the fatherland and the tricolor, and that is freedom. If you demonstrate the world will say you are following selfish interest so please don't." He added that other nations would only read partisan motives into further demonstrations and urged them to desist. Surprised and angry, the students hooted and jeered as Jókai retreated into his home.[49] The following day students congregated at a café to decide their next move; as the meeting dragged on, the crowd outside swelled to ten to fifteen thousand. Workers, artisans, and the curious had joined the throng.[50] A picture of confusion ensued. Student leaders asked the crowd to disperse, but mounted police, personally supervised by Thaisz, charged anyway. Those demonstrators who dared to hurl invectives at Thaisz himself were promptly arrested. The quashing of these pro-Turkish demonstrations (and thereby anti-Serbian ones) left no lasting memory, except as another demonstration of the speed with which Thaisz moved against illegal crowd formations. During the Russo-Turkish War the following year, Tisza would ban demonstrations altogether. The Habsburg Monarchy's controversial occupation of Bosnia-Herzegovina in 1878 inflamed a paranoid Magyar chauvinism that left a lasting stamp on Hungarian politics.

Tisza's own government almost collapsed the next year—but for a bailout from Franz Joseph. Tisza saved his bare majority in parliament by pursuing an aggressive Magyarization of the elementary schools. This recourse to forced assimilation worked like a charm. The *Pesti Hirlap* declared, "Let us hurry! Let us hurry! Let us Magyarize the Croats, Romanians, and Saxons, or else we will go under!"[51] Suddenly all the Hungarian parties backed the government, but, of course, the government exacerbated the ethnic tensions of the kingdom. When a Serb deputy objected to a general tax benefiting the Hungarian National Theater but not the Serb theater of Újvidék, Deák had agreed with him. A decade later, Tisza was brushing aside this precedent. He insisted that Hungary was a Magyar entity, a national rather than a multinational state.

Such chauvinism reflected a general crisis of liberal nationalism in the region. During the era of good feelings of the early 1860s, liberal politicians such as the Slovak János Bobula or the Serb Vladimir Jovanović, and other moderates, such as the Romanian Bishop Şaguna, had envisioned a move from a unitary state to a state of nationalities. While the actual provisions of the compromise disappointed and alienated all the nationalities, Deák had no interest in a policy of repression for which the Hungarian state lacked the means in any case. To avoid breeding resentment, Deák chose the liberal solution of curtailing the state to its minimum.[52] In the 1870s when the Serbs represented the greatest challenge and the Slovaks the least, Tisza moved against them both. The dissolution of the Slovak literary society, Matica Slovenska, prompted wealthy and educated Slovaks to send their children to Czech schools. In the pathology of liberal nationalism, the liberal program was being confused with the will of the nation. While this proved helpful to national liberals in the short run, it proved corrosive to their ideals in Serbia as well as in Hungary.[53] The illiberalism of national liberalism came to equate opposition to their programs with opposition to the nation. But although Tisza launched the new confrontational phase of Magyarization, he did it with a characteristically half-hearted manner. The regime would periodically crack down and harass—dissolve associations, suspend charters, and deny permits—only to relax restrictions again. Such a strategy kept the Magyar heartland and Budapest, in particular, largely in the dark about the seething feelings of resentment and grievance developing in the hinterlands. Major incidents might come to the attention of the metropolitan public, but typically they captivated attention but for a moment as evasion of the public was an essential aspect of the Magyarization policies.

Dualist Loyalties and the Magyarization of the Crowd

The king had adapted to the party system in Hungary, carving a central role in it for himself. In March 1879, a great natural disaster permitted Franz Joseph to project an image of the concerned father of his country. The government received a telegram reading, "Szeged was. We are saving what can be saved."[54] The catastrophic flooding of Szeged, the second largest city in Hungary, created a mood of hysteria. A false rumor that Székesfehérvár had also been destroyed by fire ripped through the capital. Amidst the sorrow, Franz Joseph arrived at the flooded-out provincial city with words of comfort and promises of aid. A high drama ensued without orchestrated ceremonials and fanfare. Face to face with the immensity of the tragedy, the king wept while making his address, which prompted Kossuth to write, "I, who don't recognize the power of your king, who view with complete indifference the glitter of purple luxury, bow myself in tribute and respect at the sight of the king in whose eyes the tears of human involvement shimmered."[55] The traditional relation between the monarch and his subject found its voice. This would be remembered as the high-water mark of Hungarian monarchist feeling, when the king had succeeded in playing the role of the "*Landesvater* consoling his unhappy children."[56]

Royal festivity had a special function in Hungary under dualism, that of articulating something intangible, the physical manifestation of the entity called the Austro-Hungarian monarchy. Franz Joseph fared best in his role at groundbreaking ceremonies, gala openings of exhibitions, theaters and state buildings, or at military reviews. He was constantly traveling, but developed a clear, matter-of-fact pattern to his annual movements. He utilized the punctiliousness that was his genius in playing out the exacting role of king to some and emperor to others, a nominal distinction perhaps, but one which at the very least required a change of dress and language, and adherence to two festive calendars not infrequently at odds with one another.

Franz Joseph's inability to be in both residential capitals at the same time inevitably compromised the festivity of dualism. Vienna took precedence, while Budapest ceremonials in the king's absence suffered an invidious comparison. The equal status that dualism purported could not be festively delivered. Monarchic holidays as a rule were celebrated in Vienna; the simultaneous Budapest fêtes had a hollow echo. For example, an awkward ritual replaced the celebration of Franz Joseph's fiftieth birthday in Budapest. The mayor of Budapest led a deputation to the prime minister, conveyed a formal speech of congratulations to Tisza, who then in turn relayed it by dispatch to the king. Flags were hung on state buildings, and there was an evening illumination; but it lacked the splendor of the one in Vienna. "Let us openly admit," that the festivity of Vienna "has been viewed here with a sort of envious displeasure," one Budapest editorialist wrote, rescuing Hungarian pride by adding that St. Stephen's Day, coming just two days after the king's birthday, amply "demonstrated what life there is in our festivity."[57]

A solution was to expand the appeal of St. Stephen's Day by making the holiday as inclusive and widely based as possible. The liberal regime packaged it as a national patriotic holiday, as a celebration of national and state resurrection. Some minorities in the hinterland resisted this nationalist move. In 1875 in one Saxon Protestant town in Transylvania, St. Stephen's Day was not celebrated, and the local newspaper asked: "Are not those who pay homage to the holy king really only the Catholics? Or should we celebrate, if not the saint, then, at least, the king? But Stephen never ruled in this region, and he would be amazed to be celebrated as a founder of Hungary. Hence, we have no special reason to celebrate our state or its founding in an exaggerated manner."[58]

St. Stephen's Day was the only religious spectacle that drew provincials to the capital rather than producing a mass exodus from the city to the villages. In Budapest, therefore, the holiday became ever more irresistible as the occasion when church and state linked themselves with the metropolis. It was the ideal opportunity for displaying the growing metropolis of Budapest, the showcase of the Liberal regime. A great many Budapest residents still felt themselves to be peasants, slowly shedding their peasant costumes and habits for city ways. The pageant masters visualized a great urban holiday, with the capital attracting tens of thousands of provincials. In 1880 forty thousand people crossed the Chain Bridge in a rainstorm and after the event sought refuge in the museums and other public buildings. The next day's newspapers were filled with descriptions of peasants' "naive surprise and undisguised pleasure" as they "examine everything with wonder, which for us from the great city hardly warrants a cursory glance."[59]

The Magyar liberal vision was unquestionably paramount in Budapest with its grand facades, wide boulevards, squares, and public facilities. As mausoleums in cemeteries were intended as objects of pilgrimage, so the raising of political statuary in the city squares ensured liberalism's presence at all large urban gatherings, if only in bronze. Shrines and monuments to cultural and political leaders focused the political feelings of the disenfranchised, exacted passive homage from the urban population, and implicated resident and visitor alike in the political tradition made manifest before them. The Tisza regime reaped the harvest of the politicized statue-raising campaigns of the sixties that had become an "obligation of the intelligentsia and patriots."[60] This is not to say there were not some glitches. After ten years of fund raising and anticipation the Széchenyi statue was finally completed, but not to artistic acclaim. An attempt was made to hurriedly redesign the statue, with the sculptor trying "a lot of last minute drilling and carving" to meet the criticism.[61] However, even the impediments were rationalized as part of the patriotic process of creating a school of world-class sculptors. Unveilings of the Széchenyi, Eötvös, and subsequent statues were staged as major festive events to which the prime minister, Liberal Party officials, and Budapest city fathers came bedecked in the now mandatory Hungarian gala dress.

Adolf Huszár was the young sculptor who filled the void. Huszár began his career in Vienna with a bust of Franz Joseph, gained Hungarian attention in the Eötvös statue competition, and would complete the Petőfi statue in Budapest. In choosing Huszár to memorialize Deák, the new regime expressed its confidence in its ability to present publicly the symbols of both 1867 and 1848, and its ability to control the demonstrations that would coalesce around them. In the attendant publicity, Huszár expanded the possibilities of cultural politics. He forged the statue of the revolutionary General Bem, whose unveiling in distant Marosvásárhely prompted patriotic demonstrations in Budapest. Similarly, his monument to the Arad martyrs of the revolution rang a warning note in Vienna and helped consecrate October 6 in the festive calendar of the nationalists.[62]

The regime prepared to monumentalize the liberal vision, with Tisza's grandiose plan for a gigantic parliament on the Danube. And finally, in 1882, the statue for Petőfi was ready for unveiling. It was a necessity that the regime integrate the myth of 1848 and make it its own. No Hungarian government could claim full legitimacy or gain a meaningful consensus without identification with this powerful legacy. Adolf Huszár's portrayal of Petőfi as the histrionic orator corresponded to the theatrical character of the dedication that began in the academy. Jókai, toastmaster of the regime, came bedecked with the Order of St. Stephen and beguiled the elite audience with his impassioned address. Tisza and the official party then struggled through the crowds to the monument square where Mayor Károly Ráth claimed the fruits of 1848 were now being enjoyed, that Hungary now possessed the freedoms of press, assembly, and parliament that the revolutionaries had sought.[63] March 15 was now sanctioned, revised, ritualized, and tamed. Instead of the student pilgrimage from university square to the graves of the revolutionary martyrs in the Kerepesi cemetery, students amassed in the heart of the capital, first at the university and then at the monument of the fallen poet. They tried out their oratorical skills and acted out the gestures of Petőfi and the students of 1848 as women watched from the surrounding windows and waved encouragement. March 15 had lost its subversive liberal edge; what was still subversive in nationalist cultural politics focused more narrowly on linguistic issues.

Hitherto, cultural Magyarization had been voluntary and relatively calm in the capital city. The exemplar of this process had been Franz Liszt. His exchange of a German identity for a Magyar one had set an important example in the late 1860s and early 1870s. Liszt had bestowed his cultural blessing on the creation of the Music Academy, and in return public gratitude poured out from the concert hall to the streets during his jubilee in 1873. Liszt became (like his friend, rival, and son-in-law Richard Wagner) a "Dichterfürst," poet-prince, whose regal-like arrivals in Budapest from Rome were accompanied by festive receptions at the railroad station. Meanwhile, the Buda city authorities ended their contract with the German theater in Buda in 1870, and the Buda Várszínház became a Hungarian theater. These changes had produced little public reaction, but the mood turned acerbic after the move to forced Magyarization in 1879.[64] The sword of Damocles now hung over the German theater in Pest. In April 1880 Pest ordered the closing of the theater rather than allow a Viennese bank to finance a renewal of the lease, a decision the Budapest city council ratified by one vote amidst a fire storm of controversy. The *Pesti Napló* spoke of "traitors" who supported the German theater, while the German-language newspapers denounced the sacrifice of "liberalism" in the name of "patriotism."[65] Budapest in 1880 was still 33 percent German, some 120,000

Germans, including a sizable number of recent immigrants from Austria.[66] In absolute numbers Germans in Hungary had actually increased. In 1840 there were a little less than a million and a quarter, forty years later there were a little under two million.[67] Bitterness grew among the German-speaking middle class who felt threatened by "national terrorism."[68] Prominent liberal Forty-Eighters, such as Dániel Irányi, called for the Hungarian nationalists to retreat, insisting that their actions were illegal, and in any case, the idea that the Germans could absorb the Hungarians, least of all through the theater, was ridiculous.[69]

Despite a ban on any further performances, the German theater opened again amidst threats of demonstrations. The city authorities chose not to block the performance but did fine the theater director. Given the fear of violence, few women attended. Demonstrators, mostly students, were quickly removed, and when the curtain was raised the actors were greeted with fifteen minutes of applause. In any case, the theater had run out of money and could not have afforded any further defiant performances. But what had been a local cause célèbre had by now become an international incident. The pressure came less from Vienna than Berlin. One German business canceled a contract with a Hungarian insurance company; a Berlin newspaper called for a boycott, and the Berlin-based Schulverein rallied the liberal academic elite behind a "threatened German culture." Disgusted that "our chauvinists have excited Austrian and German chauvinists," Jókai attacked the ban. He pointed out that the German theater was stagnating in the provinces and would be ruined in the capital eventually without any bureaucratic harassment.[70] When the Hungarian ambassador in Berlin warned that the incident was damaging German-Hungarian relations, Tisza finally reversed his endorsement of the ban. But when the German theater was granted its reprieve, a band of thirty to forty smashed the windows of Jókai's house. They moved on to the *Pester Lloyd,* screaming "we don't need a German newspaper." But when someone yelled, "Let's burn down the theater!" the others shouted him down, saying "We are not *petroleurs* [arsonists]!"[71]

In the ensuing year-and-a-half, the Schulverein's passionate support for the Transylvanian Saxon's resistance to Magyarization compromised the largely bilingual, assimilation-minded, German-speaking community of Budapest. A further upsurge of anti-German sentiment placed the capital's German-speaking community in crisis. It was especially disturbing to the German-speaking Jews faced with the rise of antisemitism in Germany, pogroms in Russia, and the unfolding of a sensational blood ritual trial at home. On April 30, 1882, the German-speakers came out onto the streets in a mass demonstration to protest the anti-Hungarian propaganda of the Schulverein. Calvin Square was filled with protesters who then marched to the City Park to hear speakers declare that their demonstration of loyalty had no parallel in history. They described themselves as the mass of German-Hungarians who, although they had previously shied away from all patriotic demonstrations, now felt compelled to declare publicly themselves as free Hungarians.[72]

The cause of the German theater was marginalized, and though it would linger until the end of the decade, the end was clearly in sight. In 1887 the critic Adolf Silberstein, a prominent voice of the Jewish bilingual community, reviewed the Hungarian National Theater jubilee for the *Pester Lloyd.* "Fifty years ago Pest and Buda were so-to-speak foreign colonies. . . . Pest was a suburb of Vienna. The German muse dominated, she had her palaces, her repertoire, her public, her artists." Hungarian theater existed "only as a dream."[73] Silberstein's sentiments were in tune with the monumentalizing Hungarian rhetoric of the time, and it was remarkable for its disinterest in the threatened presence of the German theater. Silberstein viewed the jubilee as a "political-patriotic celebration," rather than a literary-cultural one, since in his view Hungarian theater was also in decline, as a consequence of its lost political role.[74] Instead of the theater as a catalyst of the political, the talent of the theater had been sucked into the political; parliamentarianism had drawn the talent to itself.[75]

The end of the German theater came on December 20, 1889, when a fire demolished the theater building. The police blamed a foyer heater on the first floor, but there were also rumors of arson. It was said that it had been set by a Hungarian chauvinist infuriated by a Christmas guest appearance of the Burgtheater star Adolf Sonnenthal, who had just exchanged his Hungarian for Austrian citizenship. Anonymous letters had warned that his guest performance would be disrupted, and the manager had been sufficiently concerned to promise Sonnenthal police protection.[76]

The battle against the German theater was but a benign reflection of the angry politics of the 1880s. Ethnic politics had hit Budapest with a vengeance. Chastened crowd politics had been upstaged by clashes in the streets against which Thaisz's street-cleaning methods proved wholly inadequate. A furiously impotent rage came out of the shadows and threatened liberalism at its core. During the spring holiday season of Passover and Easter, 1882, a servant girl was murdered in the village of Tiszaeszlár. The village of 2,700 turned on the twenty-five Jewish families, accusing some of its members of ritual murder. The case became infamous, receiving worldwide press. The *Times* of London reporter wrote, "England is separated from Hungary by three hundred years."[77] It troubled liberals throughout Europe and the United States as more than simply an example of backwardness at the periphery of Europe. Rather, Tiszaeszlár foreshadowed the antisemitic attacks on liberalism in the coming two decades. In the Tiszaeszlár affair an antisemitic demagogue, Győző Istóczy, and the antisemitic press gained celebrity, an antisemitic party was created, and most obviously, the angry disenfranchised public attacked liberalism and religious tolerance on the streets and in the villages. Massive newspaper coverage split the society, with Tisza's opponents hoping to use antisemitism to bring to power an anti-liberal coalition.[78] Kálmán Mikszáth, the most talented of the liberal reporter-novelists of the period, covered the trial that began in mid-June 1883, producing a powerful defense of the accused in the name of religious tolerance and legal justice, much the way Émile Zola would in the Dreyfus affair in France fifteen years later. As the trial progressed, violence spread to other parts of Hungary.

On August 3, 1883, the Nyíregyháza court acquitted the accused. Four days later the principals of the trial arrived in Budapest. Thaisz's police seem to have done nothing to disperse the unruly mob—some armed with clubs—awaiting them at the train station and before their hotel.[79] The crowd cheered its antisemitic demagogues, became more and more boisterous, broke the windows of the hotel tavern, and with nightfall, was transformed into a looting and plundering mob. On the evening of August 7, and for the next five nights, the Tisza regime lost control of the streets of Budapest. Areas of the city were plunged into darkness as rioters smashed gas lamps. Certain streets turned into battlefields, first with the police, then the army. Uhlans with lances patrolled the city while gangs violated the curfew.[80] The rioting in the heart of Budapest was a severe blow to the regime. The image of the city representing progress to the benighted provinces was now challenged by the sense that the metropolis itself was breeding a new and dangerous neo-barbarism. Budapest was no longer exempt from what liberals and Budapest Jewry, in particular, had wanted to believe were "medieval" feudalistic remnants that prosperity and cultivation would dissipate. It planted a permanent fear of the crowd, for the perpetrators of violence had not been uneducated, but largely semi-educated artisans and apprentices. No sooner had the Budapest rioting subsided than the army was called upon to quell pogroms in western Hungary. In Somogy and Zala counties they ordered a state of siege.[81]

Jewish editorialists first labeled it an anarchist revolt. Police Chief Thaisz denounced it as communism masquerading as religious persecution, while

Tisza latched on to: "The formula is antisemitism, the result is robbery."[82] These definitions were all struggling with the same desire to fit these riots into familiar patterns, while fearful that they were the expression of a different, dangerous new force. One German-language newspaper that catered to the Jewish population catalogued the previous demonstrations since 1860 to underscore this difference: the Kossuthite demonstrations of 1867, the frequent antigovernment rallies of the early seventies, the demonstrations over tariff negotiations in the late seventies, all were arguments over the correct political path towards progress. It was the proudest claim of Hungarian liberalism that the old power relation between sovereign and subject was being replaced by the distinction between the cultivated and the uncultivated, and that the liberal elite was entrusted with cultivating the unenlightened. Liberalism was elitist to the present and democratic to the future, projecting political inclusion to all who were educated and owned property. In the Hungarian context this had provided a path for assimilation of Jews who were willing to matriculate through a Hungarian school system, but remained exclusive to other language minorities who wanted to develop their own language cultures. On the danger of this antisemitic nihilism, Franz Joseph, Tisza, and Kossuth were in full agreement, struggling to check it in their own domains. Against the liberal strategy two avenues of resistance lay open to the disenfranchised of the eighties: one leading to the forming of a distinctive socialist subculture or in the case of the minorities an alternative identification, and the other leading to an ultimately nihilistic attack on the liberal concept of culture. Magyarization built on expansion through absorption. The chastened crowd had been open to those who embraced the martyrology of defeated revolution. It involved a certain solidarity among loser groups. The antisemitic crowds, by contrast, repudiated such openness; they represented the exclusivist resentment of the losers from industrialization.

The riots, the ordeal of the trial, and the presence of an antisemitic party and press left liberalism shaken. The peculiar consensus of Hungarian politics that made most everyone liberal and in favor of industrialism was unraveling. Ágoston Trefort, minister of culture, worried about the infiltration of prejudice within the educational system, and directed schoolteachers to take greater vigilance in their mission.[83] The incident left Kossuth disheartened. "As a man of the nineteenth century, I am ashamed by this antisemitic agitation, as a Hungarian it embarrasses me, as a patriot I condemn it."[84] But the Kossuthites were wrenched by division, with some of their numbers attracted to the exclusivist nationalism of the antisemites.

At their March 15, 1884, rally in Cegléd the antisemitic faction stoned Gábor Ugron, one of their principal critics in the Independence Party.[85] But the political effectiveness of the antisemitic political party would deflate in the coming years.[86]

Stung by the criticism of police ineffectiveness during the riots and muddied by yet another corruption scandal, Thaisz deflected his problems by arranging for an award to be presented to him at the opening night of the new Budapest Opera House in 1884. Franz Joseph was to attend. Thaisz dressed for the event in his finest Magyar gala, which was decorated with gems. The public gathered to watch the elite file into the theater, but the crowd got out of hand and pushed its way into the foyer. Many were injured in the shoving, and a wealthy Budapest burgher was crushed to death. Franz Joseph witnessed the melee, and reported his displeasure to Tisza.[87] Thaisz fell, and the police force of Budapest was restructured soon thereafter.[88]

The National Universal Exhibition of 1885

The pageant masters of the liberal regime were able to patch up the facade in time for the National Exhibition of 1885, the first real celebration of Hungary's economic boom and Budapest's rise. Manufacturers could exhibit to "the whole mass of consumers," but the liberal pageant masters saw their task not so much to be staging a celebration of a capitalism that was, but a capitalism that might be.[89] The exhibition was to have a broadened vision. Named a "universal exhibition," it was to encompass culture and the arts, and include exhibits on public health, transportation, and infrastructural development. The move shifted the focus from the complaints of the periphery to the accomplishments of Budapest in "the constitutional era," the period since the Compromise.[90] But when planning and preparations finally proceeded for the exhibition, conflicting urban and rural interests became manifest. Competing industrial associations, one representing provincial industrial-agricultural interests, led by Zichy, the other speaking for Budapest burghers and industrialists, led by Mayor Ráth, found themselves at loggerheads. The rancor became public in 1883 over the proposed Animal Pavilion to be built next to the Industrial Hall. Budapesters viewed it as an assault on urban hygiene to have livestock housed in immediate proximity to the Industrial Hall. In the name of preservation of green space and trees, city activists sought to block construction.[91] The Kálmán Tisza government weighed into the controversy, with Sándor Matlekovits, minister of agriculture, manufacturing and commerce, forcing a resolution. For the government, prestige rested on a successful, imposing exhibition. The agrarians got their pavilion, but on a reduced scale and at some remove from the Industrial Hall. Urban, liberal interests established their preeminence when Matlekovits, the one Jewish member of Tisza's cabinet, was appointed president of the National Industrial Exhibition Commission, while Zichy was consigned to sharing the pageant-master role with Matlekovits as "Second President."[92]

What economic equilibrium existed lay in the convenient convergence of agrarian and manufacturing interests at a time when international economic stagnation underscored Hungarian advances. The assumption was "The domestic audience will discover that we produce many of those products which . . . out of prejudice . . . they purchase from abroad. It will be a potent toxin against foreign competition, but it will also point out that we have remained behind in significant areas."[93] The industrial myth was fueled by an ideological symbiosis of business interests and nationalism, as well as growing interdependency between the newly Magyarized commercial classes and the Hungarian nobility. The nobility, ruling through a Hungarian plurality rather than a majority, were driven to enlarge their economic and political base, while assimilating groups acquired a rise in status from Hungarian identity. The coming national exhibitions were to be a showcase for the newly Magyarized. Assimilated Jewish industrialists were prominent in organizing the exhibits, while German Magyars were conspicuous in their exhibition cafés and restaurants. They were, also, the principal architects and designers of those gingerbread creations that strained to evolve a mythic Hungarian style of architecture. Hungarian liberalism promoted a Magyarization that absorbed virtues associated with the principal groups being assimilated—the industriousness and urbanity of the Germans and the Jews. As long as industrialism was uncomplicated by economic reversals, as long as it seemed the great hope to escape backwardness, the most visible carriers of the industrial myth—the Magyarized Jews—were accepted for economic and nationalist reasons (the need for more Hungarians). Preparation for the 1885 exhibition took place in the wake of the Tiszaeszlár trial and antisemitic rioting in Budapest.[94] The rioting in 1883 had been a portent, raising the theme of the 'contamination' of Hungarian nationalism by alien influences from the city. Still it shook rather than shattered the promise of Hungarian industrialism. Exhibitions now became more self-consciously a tool in the liberal pedagogic arsenal against such resentment.

The exhibition venture was fraught with danger. Crown Prince Rudolph, the protector of the exhibition, toured the site repeatedly during its construction, reminding planners to stay within their budget constraints.[95] Yet momentum was toward impressive, more costly structures, and as the Industrial Hall went up in its splendor, the Budapest pavilion adjoining it became more formidable and decorative by coming in at twice its initial budget.[96] The specter of cholera almost led to a delay of the exhibition in late 1884. A severe housing shortage fed the resentful subculture of discontent and violence.[97] Yet nine thousand exhibitors and two million visitors would come over six months to partake in the drama of overcoming backwardness. The exhibition was the quintessential celebration of the accomplishments of the period since the Compromise and reflected well upon the Habsburg crown and the Tisza regime. On opening day Crown Prince Rudolph was the darling of the crowds and jointly conducted the opening ceremonies with the king. Rudolph's reception demonstrated the popularity of the ruling house. This was the era when celebratory monarchism could enjoy triumphs on the street. Large crowds gathered to catch a glimpse of the three Crown Princes Edward, Wilhelm II, and Rudolph when they toured the exhibit together. A smaller, but still formidable twenty thousand people had mobbed the Hungaria Hotel to catch a glimpse of the Prince of Wales in 1873. This was quite different from the earlier visit of Prince Jerome Napoleon, the "red prince," in 1868, when a huge crowd had gathered in front of his hotel, only to be chagrined when he referred to Pest as "un beau grand village." At its high point in the 1870s and 1880s, liberalism developed strategies to mold the new urban crowd into a civilized crowd.[98]

The aristocracy assembled on opening day on the steps of the Industrial Hall in all its finery; some who were so elegant "wore their entire worth." Or to pose it in their own framework, standing before the king "was the whole nation." Already by early morning a "swell of people, rippled up and down the streets" broken only by street corners and the distraction of "shiny carriages rumbling by." A recurring metaphor on opening day was that of a "wall." From Buda above it looked like a "wall of people" awaiting the processional. For late arriving notables the crowd surrounding the City Park seemed like an impenetrable "wall."[99]

It was that urban crowd that marked the character and hope of the fair. Although 74 percent of the population was attached to the agricultural sector, Hungary wished to present its own success as a triumph of technology and industry.[100] The grandest building, at the center of the National Universal Exhibition of 1885 was the Industrial Hall. A working brewery was at the center of the hall, surrounded by such machines as seed drills, reaping machines, and steam-driven threshers. Hungary's economic and political strength derived from its healthy agrarian sector, the marriage of agricultural technology and export-oriented latifundia. Exhibitions were emporiums of the latest technology, displaying improved scythes, plows, and other tools, as well as artificial fertilizers, and the like. The brewery was a refreshing demonstration of the wonders of modern industrial machines. The exhibition was stocked full of the latest consumer goods and fashions. While an initiation into the liberal-consumer vision, highly technical public health displays received a centrality they had never assumed in the earlier exhibitions. Clean water and infrastructural developments—sewers, streets, and transportation—were new elements in the fair. Electrification was the latest technology on display. It anticipated a bright future. A fountain in front of the Industrial Hall seemed to dance in the artificial light at night. The Radial Street and path to the Industrial Hall were lit by the Ganz factory's new incandescent bulbs.[101] The results were dazzling or illuminating, but how they worked was mysterious.

"The site looks like the sixth day of creation," reported a newspaper as it followed the construction: "A completely new world" has been created in the City Park . . . with more than "American speed."[102] The result was the creation of a wondrous miniature realm of some hundred buildings and structures. "The impression" of the eclectic mix was "overwhelming," observed an architectural journal. "It appears as if the architectural styles of all times are placed next to each other. The Oriental and the West, the Renaissance and the Byzantine forms are in these buildings." The Industrial Palace evoked the Renaissance, while the Croat pavilion was in a "Slavic style," and the Ganz's iron foundry copied itself. "The Oriental pavilion, with its Byzantine domes, wooden railings, and beautiful arcades is like a magical piece of painted east."[103] There was also an anthropologically detailed composite village, including a tavern and crafts fair, as well as three beer halls, four coffeehouses, and restaurants. This was a place to stroll and discover what was suddenly indispensable.

The capital's boosters hoped for a steady stream of tourists bringing "great material gain and prestige."[104] Foreign tour groups, delegations, and important personages were followed avariciously by the press, which was interested in their dress, their impressions, and their movements through the city. But the striking achievement of the exhibition was not in its ability to lure foreign tourists, but rather in its success at enticing over a million peasants to make the journey to Budapest and to saunter through the vast, high-ceilinged, and ornate Industrial Hall. The Hungarians were following Napoleon III's 1867 exhibition policy of free travel and free lodging, bringing a flood of peasants into the capital who could not have undertaken such a visit otherwise. The *Times* of London reporter was taken by "the merriment of all these women from far-off villages with unpronounceable names . . . as they passed the turnstiles—and these very turnstiles make them laugh as half-impudent inventions for squeezing the waist, [but] by the time they have gone the rounds of the central pavilions there is no spirit of mockery left in them." Amusement and entertainment shared the stage with the pedagogic and commercial purposes of the exhibitions. "The Hungarian government, which has given [the peasants] every facility for making this excursion cheaply—and in many cases gratis—has really done more thereby toward advancing rustic education than had been accomplished in a hundred years previously by books and preachers, wars, and lawmaking," the same reporter commented.[105]

The streets were more tightly packed than anyone could remember on St. Stephen's Day in 1885. "Who knows how many there are in this city, which for two days has been so loud that one just about goes deaf?" Food and drink prices soared. One "can't get a carriage for money," and "the world is turned upside down," complained a Pest burgher.[106] The peasants came to participate in the ancient rite of the procession of the right hand of St. Stephen; they came to see the national exhibition, but the real marvel was Budapest itself, with its facade of mammoth new buildings, modern thoroughfares, and political statuary in the city squares. The official Hungarian tour guide recommended visitors plan two days to visit the exhibition, but also reserve at least two days for sightseeing in Budapest.[107] The *Times* reporter described it as "two poor towns" transformed into "one magnificent model city, with all the beauty and bustle of a capital." It was clear from the outset that Budapest would be the greatest exhibit. The city's breakthrough had come in the preceding decade-and-a-half; a population of 280,000 kept it from the rank of a metropolis, but as the fastest growing city in Europe its dynamism was apparent to all. A tour guide for English visitors enumerated the relics to be found in Buda, but focused on the construction of a booming Pest, where few traces of the city of 1848 remained. An opera house, a railroad station, and 419 apartment buildings were completed in the year prior to the May 2, 1885, opening.[108]

For the Hungarians it was an extraordinary event, the statement of their arrival, and they presented their remarkable economic development as a model for the region.[109] An editorial declared, "The foreign countries that looked down upon Hungary, mocked her," will see that "in one leap she has jumped to that pinnacle which much larger and richer nations reached only after decades."[110] And even one Viennese columnist wrote, "No country in Europe has achieved so much economically in the last half-century as Hungary."[111] The exhibition demonstrated the remoteness of the goal of modernization as well as its accessibility; the road to modernity was hard. The history of the journey was documented in ethnographic exhibits of peasant life, in keeping with the anthropological trend in international exhibitions.

The exhibition seemed to confirm Hungary's role as a stabilizing and modernizing force in the region. Despite the fears of 1883 and 1884, Hungary would represent during the six months of the exhibition a hopeful isle of peace and prosperity. "Budapest must develop the character of an emporium for the traffic flowing to the east," asserted one editorial.[112] Through its importation of Romanian wheat, Hungary had also established itself as the economic broker and model to its eastern neighbors. The rhetoric of peace used in the exhibition reflected the anxious faith being placed at that moment on diplomacy and capitalism in forestalling war. The Budapest National Universal Exhibition opened as the Bulgarian crisis (1885–7) threatened to touch off a general European war. War would in fact break out in November, and Hungary, bordering on the warring states of Serbia and Bulgaria, became a place of importance to the great powers who seemed on the verge of being sucked into the conflict. Unlike the crisis of 1914, when expansive capitalist economies, a pervasive short-war illusion, and a sense of optimism encouraged risk-taking, the depressed 1880s was much more fearful of the economic penalties of a general European war. The Oriental Pavilion of the exhibition was a testament to this position: exhibits from Serbia, Romania, and Bulgaria were represented, and the sovereigns from each of these countries paid the exhibition a formal visit.[113]

Within the economically depressed mood of the eighties, which half-expected exhibitions to fail or be redundant, the Budapest exhibition was an unqualified success. Its modesty reflected the general economic stagnation and deflation, without having been stymied by it. It turned Hungary's secondary status, its role as a backward and developing country to its advantage, and dramatically counterpoised itself to the Balkan War as a peaceful option to Eastern European economic and political development. There were, of course, Viennese cynics, who noted, "The epidemic disease of the century, exhibition fever, has raged for several weeks in Hungary's capital and claims its victims."[114] But success of the exhibition was not measured by western reaction or embodied in the pose struck by the aristocrats on opening day. The defensive liberalism of the Tisza regime had made its point.

Opening ceremony of the Millennium Exhibition, 1896. Franz Joseph presiding in a "replica" of Attila the Hun's tent (BTM Kiscelli Museum, Budapest)

9

Memorializing

The fragility of the success of the National Exhibition, rather than its permanence, became apparent in the half decade that followed. The underpinnings of the ideological consensus had begun to wobble and crack, and it became difficult to celebrate both dualism and Hungary's economic arrival. On January 1, 1888, Kálmán Tisza's traditional New Year's address to his Liberal Party was particularly gloomy. The prime minister lamented that movements hostile to liberalism seemed to be in the ascendancy throughout the world.[1] What especially worried him and everyone else was that the European war scare, gathering steam since 1885, seemed ready to explode in a general European war, if (as was feared) General Boulanger would seize power in France. While that threat evaporated in the coming year, Hungarian liberalism was stuck in a spectator role during the succession crisis in Bismarckian Germany. The Berlin funeral of Wilhelm I overshadowed the fortieth anniversary of March 15 in Budapest. Kossuth's traditional telegram to his followers was heavy with a mournful sense of the end of an era. He mused about his fellow Forty-Eighters who had passed from the scene beckoning him to join them.[2] Jókai was toastmaster to a more buoyant commemoration for 1848 at the Redout Hall, where two thousand students, some young women, and a sprinkling of workers gathered. But here, too, the rhetoric was overwhelmingly nostalgic, with Jókai recalling once again the heady days of his youth.[3] The death of Wilhelm I was followed by the agonizing ninety-nine-day reign of the cancer-stricken Friedrich III and then by the accession of the young, headstrong reactionary Wilhelm II. The confluence of a dynastic and an international crisis made uncomfortably clear the degree to which Austria-Hungary had tied its future to the colossus to the north. Dualism in the monarchy rested on a trialism in the region with Budapest a poor third after Vienna and Berlin. Symptomatic of the dependent status of Hungarian liberalism was the willingness of the Tisza government to lead the international boycott of the Paris Exposition of 1889, refusing to be a party to a celebration of the revolution of 1789, a curious undermining of the Hungarian myth of 1848.[4]

At year's end with a lessening of the war scare crisis, Tisza faced a new round of street politics. Students challenged the requirement that they know German to be army officers and took to the streets to protest the military bill under debate in parliament.[5] They gathered at the Hentzi statue to rail against the system. They demanded a national army with Hungarian banners and, most importantly, Hungarian as its language of command. Demonstrators had desecrated the hated Hentzi statue in 1886; once again the Hentzi statue became a magnet for strident nationalism. In what may be an apocryphal story current at the time, Franz Joseph was engaged in a conversation with Andrássy while standing in view of the statue. "This old piece of bronze could be taken away to the arsenal in Vienna," Franz Joseph allegedly conceded. "But let it just stay here awhile longer! This will illustrate whether others can forget as well as I."[6] Both the statue and the army issue dragged on for years, tearing at the fabric of the Compromise by pitting the Austrian high command against the potential Hungarian officer corps. The fact that students rather than antisemitic apprentices organized this street violence made opposition respectable. Although their numbers were typically in the hundreds rather than the thousands, they were unceasing, and they captured the public's attention.

Crown Prince Rudolph's suicide on January 30, 1889, came in the midst of anti-Habsburg rioting over the army; the demise of "the great liberal hope" caused hardly a ripple. The embarrassment and/or indifference to Rudolph's passing was a sign of how dramatically the mood had changed in just four years. Franz Joseph told Tisza days after Rudolph's death, "I have lost all my hope and all my faith which I had placed in the future. All that is left to me is my sense of duty to remain loyal as long as my old bones permit. On that you and my peoples can be sure."[7] Hungarians went through the motions of mourning; there was some indignation (but not much) that at the Estergom Basilica bells were not rung and no flag of mourning was flown and the primate absented himself from the Viennese burial of the royal suicide. Habsburg dynasticism seemed as tired and frail as Hungarian liberalism. In February a requiem was said for Rudolph in Buda by Bishop Lórinc Schlauch. The public lined the streets and squares from the railroad station to the Buda fortress to watch the king ride by in an open wagon. The queen, darkly veiled, followed in a closed carriage.[8] She had become the *mater dolorosa* of liberal monarchism, convinced that the monarchy would not outlive her husband. She decided it was an "expensive ornament," which would soon enough bore the crowd and be discarded.[9] In her poetry she was Titania, the fairy queen, with the admiring crowds as the jackasses of a midsummer night's dream. Elizabeth had long tired of public adulation. It was as a disappointed, withdrawn figure that she would live out the rest of her life.

Student protests and arrests continued, with visions of 1848 dancing in their heads. "The present Hungarian youth is ready to enthusiastically follow the example of the youth of 1848 and to sacrifice everything."[10] Student demonstrators and their supporters targeted parliament; they gathered at Parliament Square and hurled invectives at government deputies. At one point police had to extricate Tisza from a mob on the Budapest Museum Ring. Tisza's son, István, the future prime minister, acted as an unofficial bodyguard for his father's safety on the streets, arming himself with an iron cane.[11] A new pattern developed, with demonstrators routinely gathering in front of parliament in the coming decades. István Tisza's obsessive hatred of parliamentary obstructionism and scorn for mass demonstrations dated from these experiences. His father proved more adaptable. There was a clear symbiosis between the demonstrating crowd and the deputies inside. The crowd was an instrument of the political policy of a political faction. In this crisis Kossuthites could use the demonstrations to their advantage inside parliament.[12] Kálmán Tisza was able to wrest a concession from Vienna, permitting the officer's exam to be taken in Hungarian or Croatian. With this he managed to finesse the army issue. The crisis dissipated, but much bitterness remained.

Tavern owners sourly reported that between the student riots and the state of mourning for Rudolph they had suffered one of the most miserable carnival seasons on record.[13] Public festivity swung back and forth between the old dynastic, and sometimes stale, sometimes rousing nationalist festivity. For years city officials and boosters, their eyes on tourism, proposed new festivals for Budapest. St. Stephen's Day continued to draw the largest crowd of peasants into Budapest, even when conditions were not ideal. Fifty thousand people braved the murderous heat and the foul, ochre-yellow, eye-smarting haze on August 20, 1890, to go out to the City Park. Mayor Károly Gerlóczy suggested two new Budapest festivals, one connected directly to St. Stephen's Day, the other around May Day. Previous private-for-profit festivities, such as a ludicrous loincloth procession down

Andrássy Avenue, ran deficits and were embarrassments beside. City-fostered festivity had tended, also, to be boring and unsuccessful. Gerlóczy argued, however, that the most serious impediment to a peasant influx was the high cost of railroad travel. Railroad tariffs were 25 percent higher than in Germany, and only in Hungary was an additional 15 percent transportation tax added, as well. Even when special discounts were offered for holiday travel, they did not offset the basic disparity in transportation costs.[14] Sheer growth would resolve the problem of drawing the public into Budapest; in the meantime, crowds were drawn together by controversies, anniversaries, and funerals.

In contrast to the tepid response to Rudolph's death, the death of Gyula Andrássy in February 1890 shook Hungary as no death since Deák. The city fathers were eager to celebrate Andrássy as one of the architects of modern Budapest and bury him in the Kerepesi cemetery in a mausoleum similar to those of Deák and Battyhány. The grand seigneur of liberal Hungary, however, would be buried on his family estate with little fanfare. Unable to claim the body, the capital was still determined to memorialize its benefactor, and Tisza's last political act before surprising everyone by resigning on March 8, 1890, was to shepherd through the bill allocating funds for an Andrássy monument.

Tisza resigned over the most symbolic of issues, refusing to take responsibility for a law that, in effect, would deprive the eighty-seven-year-old Kossuth of his Hungarian citizenship.[15] The act of burying Kossuth, which for so long seemed a looming responsibility for Tisza, passed to his lieutenants in the Liberal Party. Tisza made his formal exit at a crucial turning point in European history, with Bismarck's dismissal following his departure by ten days. Symbolically, at least, the "long" twentieth century, 1890–1989, can be said to have begun. Tisza's departure was generally greeted with a certain relief. Still, it was hard for Budapesters to gauge the significance of his resignation, since he would remain a power behind the scenes. On March 15 the thousands of demonstrators who packed the squares before the university and the Petőfi statue denounced him as roundly as if he were still in office.

From May Day to Crown Jubilee

Press attention in the capital soon shifted to the launching of a new, possibly subversive holiday for workers to be held on May 1. The call of the Second International in 1889 for workers throughout the world to celebrate May Day 1890 as a worker holiday replaced an idyllic, naive holiday with a day of troubling seriousness. May Day had been the traditional day "in the green" for city folk. However, since the law prohibited rent increases or evictions in the first four months of the year, the first of May was also the most active moving day of the year. The new epoch of street politics launched in 1890 would be the first great symbolic triumph of the international workers' movement. In the six weeks after March 15, tension and excitement built. Throughout the 1890s workers and police would jockey over the ground rules for the massive parades and demonstrations planned for May Day.

Labor unions held meetings that first spring on whether and how to participate. The book printers were told by their leadership that even though they had hitherto held aloof from the workers' movement, it was now their "moral duty to participate in an action involving all of Europe."[16] The slogan that year was a work-free Sunday, an eight-hour day, and a May Day holiday. Their banners displayed the three eights for eight hours work, eight hours rest, eight hours sleep. The police stuck by the position that "the government could not allow foreign workers from Paris to dictate holidays, and if the workers gained their holiday today, another class would want another tomorrow."[17] The police did permit a rally in the City Park, but the proposed festive march down the central boulevard was banned on the grounds that it would disrupt traffic. This led to a flurry of worker convocations and protest deputations descended upon the police and mayor's offices. The authorities rescinded their ban but rerouted the march to side streets. Unlike the Austrian government, Hungarians also permitted municipal factory workers to participate.

Fearful rumors swept the city. Shopkeepers braced themselves for a repetition of the student rampages in the riots of the preceding year.[18] Workers, however, were out to demonstrate their earnestness by preventing any violence on May Day. Organizers distributed 50,000 leaflets beseeching workers to be orderly. Theirs was to be a legitimating demonstration, focused on concrete issues. If May Day remained peaceful workers could expect public support, they argued. As May Day approached alarmists feared the end of the world; optimists, on the other hand, expected only a harmless form of mass entertainment. Army reservists were called up. The police insisted that marchers would not be allowed to unfurl their banners or play music until they reached the City Park. Tension built until the day itself.

May Day was something new and frightening. Unlike the antisemitic riot of 1883 that flared up suddenly, without a center, these socialist-led demonstrations had a clear vortex, and thus were, perhaps, a tornado that could sweep away the existing system. But since the demonstration was structured and hierarchical, it was also possible to negotiate. The Budapest workers would underscore their peaceful intent by marching behind a white flag—a flag of peace. Monitors wore red arm bands; about sixty thousand demonstrators gathered at factories and then marched in columns to the City Park. Trades grouped together, not unlike the traditional processions of occupations collected under the banners of their guilds. The workers were in their Sunday best and on their best behavior. In Hungary, May Day 1890 was an almost exclusively Budapest event, but Budapest was conscious, thereby, of having joined the ranks of the other major cities across Europe and North America. Worker grievances loomed larger, since they were internationalized and intellectualized, subsumed within a wider system of ideas.

Nationalist celebration found its strongest voice that October in Arad, where a monument was unveiled to the Arad martyrs of 1849. The monument Hungaria, begun by Huszár, then substantially modified by György Zala after Huszár's death, included portraits of the thirteen martyrs on the base relief and highlighted four virtues: freedom, sacrifice, struggle, and patriotic abnegation.[19] Several thousand spectators, notables, and the families of martyrs gathered at the unveiling. The declamations were peppered with inflammatory images of "holy soil drenched in blood" and the "eternally burning wound of the nation" that alternated with endorsements of the spirit of "upright reconciliation" with the monarchy. As a precaution, officers and soldiers of the Arad garrison were ordered not to appear on the streets and remain in their barracks the whole day.[20]

Two weeks later about a hundred thousand Budapesters streamed to the cemeteries on All Saints Day. Although this was essentially a religious and family holiday for paying respect to ancestors, five hundred students, waving black flags of mourning marched in the early morning from University Square to the grave of Géza Forinyák, the student martyr of 1860. Socialists arrived at the cemetery around two in the afternoon singing the "Internationale," an otherwise forbidden anthem, but the day passed without police intervention.

Facing the third May Day, the capital had lost much of its apprehension. "Two years ago one feared the day. Today there is no such fear."[21] May 1, 1892, happened, also, to fall on a Sunday, which precluded the problems of absenteeism, strikes, and lockouts. Preholiday publicity had encouraged women workers to attend, but bad weather inhibited turnout. The press did take note of contingents of 50 to 150 women from a box factory parading along the wet streets. The news that day, however, was of a huge arson fire at the Nicholson agricultural machine factory. Smoke filled the sky over Újpest. Arson rather than a peaceful, self-controlled march became the main topic of conversation. Demonstrators were incensed at the inevitable accusation that they were responsible for the fire. There had been a strike at the factory on the preceding May Day. In 1892 workers again vowed to march, this time as a 600-person mass; management threatened retaliation and brought in police to guard the factory. Still there was a fire. Now a huge crowd gathered at the blaze. Some foremen and workers were "sobbing loudly." But facing the crowd, "not a muscle on his [the owner's] face twitched." He said only, "May 1" as he turned to leave.[22]

With May Day behind them, preparation proceeded for the Crown Jubilee. While the solidity of the past twenty-five years had succeeded in generating loyalty to the system,[23] Hungarians were not particularly in the mood to celebrate. A crisis over compulsory civil marriage, state registration of births and deaths, and recognition of an "Israelite confession" was pitting liberals against Catholics (including Franz Joseph himself).[24] Tisza's successor, the colorless technocrat Count Gyula Szapáry, fell in this confrontation over church-state relations, but his replacement, Sándor Wekerle, the first middle-class prime minister, continued the anticlerical crusade. In this frayed atmosphere the king's jubilee seemed a kind of benevolent anachronism. "On the day of the Crown Jubilee the whole city should publicly express the happiness and good feelings held by the population," read the parliamentary authorization.[25] Effusive pamphlets and magazine essays were filled with reminiscences of the pomp and ceremony, and radiant crowds in 1867,[26] but this only seemed to highlight the changed circumstances of 1892.

The Austrians either affected indifference or viewed the commemoration of the Compromise as an occasion to denounce dualism. The up-and-coming Viennese Christian Socialist demogogue Karl Lueger denounced "Judapest," the two-capital arrangement, dualism, and Vienna's loss of primacy in the monarchy. He also made ostentatious expressions of solidarity with the Romanians in their ethnic struggle against the Magyars. Once again Budapest was on display. "Budapest embodies the Compromise," wrote a Viennese reporter, and perhaps Budapest was the only one to benefit from the Crown Jubilee. The king's one gesture to the Hungarians was the announcement that "henceforth I permit the capital city Budapest, as my Hungarian city residence, to use the name 'Budapest capital and residential city.' "[27] The squares, streets, and buildings along the coronation route were again decorated more or less as they had been for the corona-

tion in 1867, with arches, banners, and carpets. Flowers were used lavishly: strung along bridges, balconies, boats at harbor, and strewn through
the streets. But what was to mark the 1892 festivity was the illumination,
which for the first time truly demonstrated to all in the capital the extraordinary breakthrough of electric lighting. In a last hurrah of gas lighting, a
five-meter-wide and four-meter-high Magyar gas crown, glowed in color
above the old city hall tower. Budapest shimmered in gas lamps and the
new electric glow.[28]

The king had arrived in Budapest alone on the morning of June 6 to participate in the banderium, the central event of the jubilee. Elizabeth absented herself. Three hundred thousand people lined the streets to catch a
glimpse of Franz Joseph. The king's carriage moved slowly through the
amassed humanity to the parade grounds. For the next hour aristocrats
filed slowly past the king in their resplendent costumes. The procession
went off smoothly except for two mishaps: one aristocrat fell off his horse
and another nobleman's horse kicked a policeman. Some foreign newspapers treated the display of medieval and ornate costumes and coverings for
the mares and stallions as further reminders of Hungary's Oriental aesthetic heritage. A Viennese reporter conjectured from the magnates' ostentatious display that "exclusive tendencies" were being "more aggressively
displayed" than in 1867, when, "In the enthusiasm of the new freedom,
they had sought to include all strata of good society in the brilliant caval-
cade."[29] The jubilee organizers had distributed only forty thousand tickets
for the parade. This absurdly low number probably reflected what this reporter sensed to be an underlying tension between the aristocratic display
and the urban crowd. The city leaders and notables from the upper bourgeoisie were but spectators rather than participants in the jubilee events.
"The unchallenged possession of power has made the gentlemen more
conservative," the Viennese observer concluded.[30] The most noteworthy
aspect of the 1892 Crown Jubilee was, perhaps, that it had been gotten
through without incident.[31]

The elite pageant was followed by a carnival-like folk festival. When
night fell military bands played in the parks. Free food, beer, and wine
brought the festivity to the public. The one jarring note was when drunken
soldiers seized a dispensing area and fought off civilians. The confrontation led to a melee. Soldiers drew their swords, wounding fifteen civilians
and sending three unconscious and gravely wounded to the hospital.[32]
Lower classes caroused in the parks, higher society attended a *tableau vi-
vant*, "The Holy Crown," at the National Theater. The three living pictures
were the 1526 defeat at Mohács, the 1686 victory over the Turks, and Buda-

pest in 1867.[33] The following day, the prince primate conducted High Mass followed by an official reception at the castle attended by fifteen hundred people. The king received representatives of all political parties, including, for the first time, the extreme left.[34] After a perfunctory speech to parliament, the bequeathing of a scholarship fund, a torchlight parade of students across the bridge, and a serenade by a three-thousand-person choir, Franz Joseph left for Vienna after his three-day stay.

In the following twenty-one months, the liberal campaign for civil marriage kept religious passions at a fever pitch, with large Catholic Day rallies of aristocrats, lower clergy, peasants, and politicians polarizing the public in what seemed to be a showdown between clerical and liberal ideals. Under Count Albert Apponyi's leadership a popular Catholic party vociferously linked Magyar identity to Catholicism. Hitherto, the Catholic hierarchy had often shared the liberal state's unease with spontaneous peasant religiosity. In May 1889 when an apparition of the Virgin Mary with child appeared at a farmer's well, the village of Szentpéter turned into a potential new mass pilgrimage site. The church had nipped this development in the bud by filling in the well.[35] But three years later the church mobilized the pious crowd in a challenge to the liberal, chastened crowd. More important than the occasional massive Catholic Day rallies in Budapest, were those in the countryside, where they more effectively combined the aspects of pilgrimage and political demonstrations. Eight to nine thousand Slovaks, for instance, mostly elderly or middle-aged, walked from a 120-village area to partake in such a Catholic Day celebration.[36] These rallies transcended ethnic divisions, much like the workers' movement, but produced other divisions. These peasant crowds of believers in the countryside provoked a nervous, massive response from the liberal crowd in the city, and from Orthodox Catholics, Protestants, and Jews.

During the six days of debate over civil marriage in March 1894 the liberal crowd impressed itself on the debate. A liberal newspaper crowed, "Only in the history of England can one speak of comparable popular assemblies, of comparable monster meetings."[37] The culmination of the liberal agitation came with a significant march of perhaps 60,000 on March 5. Liberals may have felt they had trumped the Catholic Day rallies, still none of the government ministers thought it politic to appear. Instead, Munkácsy and Jókai oversaw the crowd that day.

Fifteen days later, Kossuth's death set the stage for the most mammoth event of the liberal era. His funeral on April 2, after forty-five years of exile, brought forth the old schism and the old unity. Kossuth had refused to accept the Compromise, and now Franz Joseph forbade the Hungarian government from accepting the body and giving the dead insurrectionist a hero's burial. The government was painfully embarrassed by the king's insistence that members of the cabinet, government officials, and army officers not attend the funeral of Kossuth. But the municipality of Budapest claimed the body and held a "private" funeral attended by millions in a moment of great collective emotion. The whole nation mourned Kossuth's death and embraced his son Ferenc, who had accompanied his father's body from Turin. Jókai delivered the emotional funeral eulogy to the man he had followed in his youth, but with whom he had broken in his maturity. With the Magyar hero dead, his banishment ended, the tension between the leader in exile and public politics at home was removed. The chastened crowd had played itself out.[38]

Ferenc Kossuth was so moved by the outpouring that he would stay in Hungary and assume the titular leadership of the Party of Independence. A Kossuth had returned, and moreover, he would prove to be a very different personality from his father, a conciliator rather than a revolutionary. With the elder Kossuth's passing, the liberal regime lost the goading presence of the left-liberal opposition, whose challenge had contributed to the dynamism of the liberal regime and to the illusion of democracy. In its place a new socialist opposition confronted the liberals with a new street politics and demands for real suffrage reform. To this juncture, the factions of the political elite, however disparate, had agreed on the restricted electoral system. The Kossuth radicals had wished the exclusion of the minorities, and neither the Compromise liberals nor the conservatives had desired to include workers or peasants. The Liberal Party clung to power but with an increasingly aging hierarchy that found itself on the defensive. The very success in urbanizing Hungary rendered the rotten borough system on which the Liberal Party had manufactured its majorities indefensible, and the prospect for a mass base for liberalism began to dim. In reaction, the liberal elites, as the last representatives of the revolutionary tradition of 1848, as well as the generation that had fashioned the liberal compromise, sought to memorialize their achievements by anchoring liberalism in a thousand-year past. Statues to Hungary's liberal leadership and other great men proliferated on the urban landscape.

The Hungarian Millennium

The impetus for the Millennium Exhibition was no longer marketing industrialism but memorializing itself. In 1881 the Budapest city council began planning an immense monument to the arrival of the Magyars on the Pannonian plain.[39] This statuary in Heroes' Square would be the entrance gate to the Millennium Exhibition. Its mighty symmetrical pillars were ornate, but still presented a rather blank facade, not yet the pantheon of great leaders. The project would take a generation to complete; only in the 1920s were the final figures added, then removed, replaced, and restored again as the heroes in Hungarian history have been reinterpreted by successive regimes.[40] The presence of this monument has reinforced the importance of the Millennium Exhibition, but for our purposes, it stands as a reminder of a reorientation, from the ephemeral activity of projecting an industrial future as in 1885, to the exhibit as museum, the act of collecting and preserving its past and engraving its present onto the future.[41]

For a decade and a half, liberal politicians had been planning and building great public buildings and infrastructural projects in the name of the millennium. The public spectacle to mark the millennium had, above all, to be mammoth, awe-inspiring, and a monument to their rule.[42] Since the precise year of Árpád's arrival was a question of debate among experts, the politicians operated with the assumption that any year between 1888 and 1900 could be used to mark the thousand-year Hungarian presence on the Pannonian Plain.[43] They attempted to set a date to coordinate with the completion of major building projects, for instance, the Large Ring Boulevard, which would gird the city and bordered the City Park; the Comic Theater; the new parliament, a large neo-Gothic structure that would dominate the Danube bank like a massive Westminster, as well as large-scale renovation of Mátyás Church, the site of the coronation.[44] Aristocratic aesthetes, in such organizations as the Club of Art Friends, came forward with plans that extrapolated from the banderiums. In 1890 they had broached the idea of a great eighteen-day millennium celebration, one which "would put in shadows all that had preceded it," and which would draw the whole population to the capital.[45] They proposed a grandiose costumed procession, depicting the preceding nine centuries, with the tenth presented in a tableau as a glorious apotheosis. Skeptics remained unconvinced that a retrospective celebration would be financially successful in the modern capital, pointing to the financial shipwreck of various Budapest folk festivals with a historical theme.[46]

An alternate concept was promoted by the National Industrial Association, which had been considering holding an exhibition of its own in Budapest to mark the fiftieth anniversary of the first Kossuth industrial fair in 1842.[47] In recognition of the new consumer age and the great advance of industrial arts, they had toyed with the idea of a modest, pedagogic fair focused exclusively on consumer items. They feared, however, that excluding displays of luxury goods would diminish its popular appeal, and such tight-fistedness might backfire, with repercussions on their association's treasury. Industry no longer expected great financial gain from an exhibition, but it could be a magnet for Budapest tourism. So they decided to scrap the idea of their own exhibition, and sought to interest the government in a large-scale exhibition. Such an exhibition, they argued, could bring "a flow of gold to the city," as the 1889 Paris exposition, and on a more modest level, the Hungarian 1885 exhibition had done.

The planning commission began mulling over various options in earnest at the end of 1892, once the Crown Jubilee was behind them. The commerce and trade ministers responsible for the millennium celebration were replaced several times in the governmental shuffles of 1892.[48] Committees organized and reorganized; indeed, the millennium planning itself took on a memorializing aspect with the frequent deaths of its liberal elite who had come to power with Tisza. With the past millennium as its theme, liberal Hungary had to draw beyond its own genealogy to the conservative pillars of church and aristocracy. The aristocracy was also anxious not to rest solely on historic birthright. The success of the 1885 exhibition made aristocrats eager to bedeck themselves with honorary posts in an exhibition fostering capitalism.

The World's Columbian Exposition in Chicago that opened in the spring of 1893 presented the planning commissioners with new possibilities for a world's fair format. Chicago had raised a "white city" upon the mud flats of Lake Michigan. The latest technology was not used simply to overwhelm the exhibition-goer, as Paris had done with its Eiffel Tower in 1889. Nor did it invoke the more solemn, businesslike atmosphere of the Philadelphia Centennial Exhibition of 1876. Chicago, instead, introduced a lighter, more fanciful air, transporting the visitor to a fictional, magical city. This "white city," with its whimsical, romantic facades and pleasure-seeking crowds was unlike the "black city" whose buildings—bold, modern, and permanent— loomed above it. The "white city" had been purposely created and was meant also to disappear at the close of the affair. It was a nostalgic flutter, grasping at the architectural forms of the Old World, just as it commemorated the discovery of the New World by Columbus four hundred years before. But whatever ambivalence the white city revealed in the attitude toward the modern, the fair was first of all a powerful announcement of the arrival of a new major city, Chicago—the city of the American agricultural plain.[49] The comparisons between Chicago and Budapest were obvious to Budapesters: both were booming cities whose economic dynamism depended upon agrarian-driven industrialization.

The planning commission decided to emulate Chicago's approach of a combined exposition, pleasure garden, and amusement park. Some lobbied to have the celebration moved from the site of the 1885 exhibition to a larger space somewhere outside the city, so that the Millennium Exhibition might indeed become a world exhibition, so that it might "excite interest" in Hungary "throughout the world" and "for a little while" Hungary would be the focus of attention in Europe.[50] For a moment it even seemed that the first modern Olympic Games would be held in Budapest in conjunction with the millennium celebration.[51] Proponents of a world's fair argued that Hungary might be "festively brought into the rank of world cities."[52] But reality proved more modest, and the commission retreated from the full implications of the Chicago model.

The Millennium Exhibition remained at the same site as the National Exhibition of 1885 after officials cautioned that too much time had elapsed to complete a large-scale project at a different site without inviting possible disaster.[53] Too many world exhibitions had become economic failures requiring large expenditures of state funds. "The international exhibitions are today not so much exhibitions as markets," and they "assume such dimensions" as to become prohibitively expensive, argued the architect of the historical exhibit. Of course, markets and masses of tourists crowding its turnstiles and hotels was just what city boosters and entrepreneurs were dreaming of, but architects and planners lobbied for a smaller scale. They employed a backhanded nationalist argument that a world exhibition would detract from the Millennium Exhibition's national character. With the 1885 exhibition as Hungary's common experience and most important model, the government could say "a national exhibition in its narrower framework would require effort but promised success, while still being large enough to awaken the interest and sympathy of foreigners."[54] The Industrial Hall was to play the same role in 1896 as in 1885.

The traditional consumer-industrial fair would remain at the epicenter, but the exhibition was permitted to grow around it, spreading as far as the park's land would accommodate.[55] Like a Gulliver pinned down by a swarm of Lilliputians, the Industrial Hall of 1885 would be surrounded by pavilions, restaurants, cafés, and champagne bars. Hungarian Victorian social conventions were double-knotted: aristocratic and gentry rules of etiquette, power, and status laced with Victorian social fashions. This normative behavior also provided the patina for a parvenu urban elite that aped the still resilient aristocratic ethos and dreamed of inheriting an aristocratic way of life.[56]

The liberal oligarchy had a blueprint for the creation of a civilized, urban capital, but they did not have one for a consumer society. The year 1896 would, in fact, not represent an advance over the 1885 exhibition of consumption. The decade 1885–1895 saw no great prosperity or consumer breakthrough, and the business community, the producers of the consumer goods, was not the driving force behind the exhibit. Between the 1850s and the 1880s, Hungarians had "caught up" in certain key sectors, such as the milling industry, and Hungarian exhibition-goers had little difficulty understanding the general principles of steam engines. Incandescent lights had provided a glow over the showplace in 1885, but now electricity was the dominant technology on display. The telephone, phonograph, electric light, loudspeaker and electric railway were exciting innovations, yet their inner workings remained mysterious, not accessible to the fair-goer in the same way as the clanking steam engines still highlighted in 1885. The 1896 exhibits on chemicals, bacteria, and microbes marked extraordinary advances with immediate impact on the health and well-being of the crowd, but the displays were inevitably abstract.[57] A delegation scouted the Chicago world's fair for ideas, returning with a bag full of tricks for sedate entertainment, improved security, and profit. Smoking would be prohibited in all buildings of the fair, excluding restaurants and taverns. A million millennium coins were minted, and in imitation of Chicago, postage stamp vending machines were placed inside and outside the exhibition grounds.[58]

The new realms of technological innovation left Hungary once again at a relative disadvantage. Focus for the exhibition shifted from the displays of goods for sale to entertainment in a museum-like setting, from the consumer fair to the idea of a living museum. The Chicago example of the theme park as a world contrasting sharply with the cityscape surrounding it, licensed the already overheated memorializing impulse of the Hungarians and the eclectic age. Within the recreational fantasy land of a retrospective, they could incorporate the three strands (aristocratic aesthetics, industrial arts, and political posturing), adding a fourth, the historical. The focus of the Millennium Exhibition was a historical reconstruction of Hungarian architectural styles through the thousand years. The centerpiece of this exhibit was a mock Vajdahunyad Castle. This was not a new icon to the future, not an Eiffel Tower, but an assertion of history. Crossing a bridge over the moat of the island, the visitor passed into the neo-Gothic

Vajdahunyad Castle, painstakingly re-created to comply with historical lore. Sharing space on the island was a Renaissance structure with a Romanesque facade and a modest wood dwelling, representing a Magyar fishing village in primitive times. Setting the historical display apart on its own island, surrounded by moats and courtyards, was meant to dignify the historicist enterprise. The liberals were determined to create a retrospective affair, to substitute for the didacticism of 1885 a historicism of equal potency. The presentation of "the complete past, the struggles, the cultural level of the nation during the past millennium, in short the whole history," was to be this Magyar exhibition's unique contribution to the exhibition idea.[59]

A Magyar architectural heritage had to be pieced together, for pre-eighteenth-century structures had been ravaged by time and the Turkish occupation. The millennium would be the climax of this historicist effort. As the millennium celebration approached, historians and journalists filled the literary market with histories, historical novels, art histories, and the like. But what was re-created often relied as much upon wishful thinking, imaginative descriptions and western models as accurate reconstructions.[60] While this architectural historicism was supposed to spur the creation of an indigenous Hungarian architecture, what it actually did was mimic the eclecticism that was fashionable at the time. Liberal culture was stale, and the 1896 celebration made no connection with the modernism that was to burst forth in Budapest within a few years.

Mihály Munkácsy played a role comparable to that of Franz Liszt in 1867. He was the reigning national artist who had enjoyed decades of international acclaim. He was commissioned to paint *The Conquest* (Honfoglalás) (1893) for the new parliament. His *Ecce Homo* would be the featured work of the Millennium Exhibition, displayed in the new Fine Arts Hall at the entrance to the park. These two paintings as well as *The Strike* (1895) are crowd scenes, but each presents quite different images of the crowd. Árpád was the clear focal point of the mammoth canvas of *The Conquest* in which the warrior crowd—women included—is in the act of homage. Melodramatic and stiffly Victorian, with the crowd kept at some distance, its message is clear: the Magyars are a strong and united people. *The Strike* has two focal points: the radical orator encircled by his fanatical supporters and, to the side, a dispirited crowd of the long suffering. They are poor, old—losers, but a community nonetheless, one perhaps to be visited by more misery because of the extremists in their midst. *Ecce Homo* (1896) was an odd, even disturbing portrayal of Christ as a madman at his trial standing before a hysterical crowd. The crowd is half-bloodthirsting, half-lamenting. Munkácsy's

Mihály Munkácsy, *Ecce Homo*, 1895–6. Oil on canvas, 403 x 650 cm. (Debrecen, Déri Museum)

crowd has progressively encroached on the leader until both are mad. The three works reflect Munkácsy's waning talent and increasing instability (from advancing syphilis). If Munkácsy embodied historicist art become unstable and pessimistic, the other artistic endeavors at the exhibition remained safe, conventional, and predictable. None approached the artistic value of Franz Liszt's *Hungarian Coronation Mass*; instead, they served as sitting ducks for the burgeoning avant-garde. Ultimately, what the pageant masters succeeded in doing was convincing contemporaries and succeeding generations that 1896 was a symbolic year of closure.

Opening festivities for the exhibition were pushed back to May 2 to avoid May Day demonstrations. The growing presence of workers in Budapest meant that tension ran high on May 1, 1896. The government had called for a political truce for the Millennium Exhibition, but long columns of workers marched out from their suburbs anyway. Waving banners and sporting insignias in their hats, they made their demand for an eight-hour day and universal suffrage. The government did not use force against the marchers, but police did attack a crowd of strikers. However, one worker died, and at least thirty others were injured. In another factory a bloody confrontation took place between Magyar and Slovak workers.[61]

Meanwhile, trains were arriving with Magyar notables and foreign ambassadors from England, France, Germany, Russia, Italy, Spain, and Turkey. The city they encountered was festively decorated with flags and banners, and symbolic arches. Budapest was jammed; hotels were filled. Between 80,000 and 100,000 people flowed into Budapest to watch the festivities. For the opening ceremony, foreign dignitaries, Magyar notables, Viennese politicians, and Habsburg ministers assembled at the exhibition site around a garish tent of wild colors, weird tassels, and lavish ornamentation. The spotlight was on King Franz Joseph and Queen Elizabeth. But even the House of Habsburg had reason to feel slighted. For what distinguished the plans for the opening celebration of this festival from that of 1885 was the show of indifference to the monarch. The Habsburg sovereign had to deliver his address in front of a replica of Attila the Hun's tent. Few efforts had been made to include the royal house in the planning, and only after repeated requests for a new regal pavilion was the king allotted acceptable space in the historical exhibition.[62] What had been the King's Pavilion in 1885 was turned into an elegant restaurant specializing in fresh fish "dropped alive and kicking over burning coals."[63]

Queen Elizabeth still evoked sympathy from the Magyar elite who tried to recall her beauty as she sat there shielding her worn face behind a thick black veil. Her husband stood at attention in his Hussar uniform and listened to the commerce minister drone on. When the king finally spoke, his voice was so soft that even a correspondent seated in the front row could not understand him. While he mumbled on bells rang and the gigantic choir at some remove, thinking this its cue, burst forth in song.[64] After the ceremony the queen left immediately, and the king dutifully proceeded through the crowded park of pavilions, taking special note of some, such as the naval building, with its boatlike shape, and Archduke Joseph's personal pavilion. This was to be the last major public festival in which the Compromise between king and Hungarian elite was publicly acclaimed.

Ős-Budavár (Ancient Buda fortress) was Hungary's original answer to the whimsical amusements of the Chicago fair. It was set off from the rest of the exhibit and run by an independent company. Here food, drink, and entertainment were everywhere. It was "the kind [of place] where the pine tables are constantly wet with beer, and the same mugs do for all day with but a single dip in water."[65] Pest citizenry could come down to the exhibition for an evening at a carnival, without the pretext or expense of attending the actual exhibition. If gate receipts are the determinant of success, all three facets of the main fair—commercial exhibition, historical monuments, and aristocratic banderium of June 6—would be upstaged by the Ős-Budavár pleasure dome.

The segregation of communities so apparent in Hungarian society was re-created in miniature form within the exhibition grounds. Separate entrance fees made returning to the formal exhibition from the amusement park costly.[66] But even the amusement park was meant to replicate the ancient Buda fortress. Guides, costumed as army officers "in faultless uniform and white gloves," escorted "peasants . . . in their rough homespun" in groups of ten or twelve, explaining to each the several objects of interest. A "package deal" had been created to enable mass peasant attendance without undue disruption. Barracks and canteens were built, so that peasants received lodging, meals, transportation, and guided tours of the grounds and buildings for two days and nights. In the months before the exhibition opened, the city moved to facilitate travel to the exhibition site by provincial craftsworkers, their apprentices, and business owners of modest means. Schools were shut down in April and transformed into hostels.[67] Classrooms were outfitted with an iron bed, chair, shelf, clothes hook, sink basin, and writing set for each visitor. These more upscale tour packages included reduced rates on second-class tickets, modest restaurant meals at the fair, and a free tour.[68]

Within Ős-Budavár there were games and thrills, Turkish smoking rooms, and a mosque with "make-believe Orientals squatting on mats."[69] A "marvelous Polish beauty" and an Austrian contortionist entertained, while sideshows concealed by a carpet curtain tried to entice the thrill seekers. The most popular sensation cost one florin to witness: inside a glass box lay an Indian fakir asleep. He would sleep uninterrupted for a week in this box while everyone gawked. Hungarians had scrapped the old straightforward display of industrialism and marched from mid-century didacticism to fin-de-siècle exoticism.

While the pleasure fair freely manipulated ethnographic stereotypes to tantalize and transport visitors into distant, dreamy realms, the ethnographic exhibit of the kingdom tapped the most intense emotions of the time. It stirred up nationalist tensions to a fever pitch both inside and outside Hungary. On three dirt lanes nineteen villages exemplified the "Hungarian," the "Nationalities," and the "German Corner." Either guides or life-size wax figures clothed in peasant costumes occupied the different quaint whitewashed, thatched-roof cottages. It was assumed that the cottages would be a source of pride for the natives of these villages who would be pleased to see themselves reflected at the fair. The cottages were replete with "instructive drawings and models" for crafts or remodeling projects, such as how to dry out walls, the latest floor coverings, and protective foundation designs tailored to conditions in different regions.[70] The whole was presented as a complete community, with a church, school, tavern, and a marketplace.

Ethnographic exhibits had long been a part of international exhibitions, but by the 1890s they were the primary tourist attraction. An English visitor to the Millennium Exhibition thought the ethnographic and the Bosnia-Herzegovina exhibits the only ones worth mentioning, for it was only here that the "eastern flavor" of the kingdom was captured. The simulated villages were too clean, it was conceded; but that aside, some of the cottages were such "dreams of picturesqueness" that he "long[ed] to go off at once and buy their originals."[71] The Paris Exposition of 1889 had set the pattern, including a display of native villages from the French empire on a street of thirty-nine houses, each representing a culture and a stage in world housing from prehistoric times to the present.[72] In these western fairs Magyars played contradictory roles. In the ethnographic exhibits they were yet another quaint folkish people in the entertaining display of the "other," while at the industrial-consumer pavilions Hungarian aristocrats were often noted for their ostentatious investment in modern equipment for their enormous estates.

These anthropological exhibits were particularly provocative, because they raised the most volatile issue facing the Hungarian regime, that of its treatment of ethnic minorities, who represented over 50 percent of the population. The small, quaint, sentimentalized ethnographic exhibition inevitably angered Romanians and Serbs, as well as Czech students, and Austrian antisemites. For it implicitly defined and circumscribed the place of the minorities within the empire, legitimating a hierarchy of peoples. While Magyarization was triumphing in Budapest, a fierce resistance was developing in the outlying regions. Although the Millennium Exhibition was being held in Budapest, its ramifications were felt in the provinces in more immediate ways, as well. In Pozsony, above the Danube on the Dévény fortress hill, a new statue extended its right hand in defense of the Hungarian side of the Hungarian-Austrian border. Six other such monuments were erected marking the Magyar hold on Pannonia.[73] Most noteworthy among them would be an equestrian statue of Saint Stephen commissioned for the city square in Kolozsvár, Transylvania.[74] The Magyars had managed to antagonize almost everyone. The militants in Serbia chose active resistance; the Romanians divided over the issue. The Romanian king arrived as the first monarch to view the exhibition, but the Romanian metropolitan of the Greek Orthodox Church called for a boycott. Forty thousand Romanian students in Bucharest signed a manifesto against the Hungarian millennium festivity.[75] In Belgrade, Serbian students burned the Hungarian flag and rallied before the royal palace and Russian and French embassies. "We are like the elephant vis-à-vis tiny Serbia," one Budapest paper commented. "It has hardly more inhabitants than we soldiers. . . . Should we fight a war with Serbia? That is not compatible with our honor."[76] But the Hungarian army amassed along the border, fearing disturbances, even insurrectionary incursions.

University students in Vienna joined with Serb, Croat, Romanian, Slovene, Slovak, and Ruthenian students to denounce the Magyars, creating solidarity with minorities by organizing a boycott of the Millennium Exhibition.[77] In Prague, Czech students were warned that participation in similar demonstrations could bring dismissal. But the Czech newspapers pointedly ignored the millennium celebration in a silent form of protest. German student nationalists at the University of Vienna denounced the Judo-Magyars, the Jews, and the political establishment in Vienna as well as Budapest. Their hero, Karl Lueger, denounced the millennium as a *Judenwerk*. The future mayor of Vienna took the occasion to launch another attack on the Compromise in the Austrian Reichsrat. Seeking to sow dissension between Austria and Hungary, he made another show of solidarity with the minorities.[78]

That the Millennium Exhibition brought forth besiegers was inevitable, for it formalized a new chauvinism. The paternalistic hope of persuading the disparate nationalities to join them had faded; the pageant masters were left sentimentalizing a polarized polity instead. By documenting Hungary's place in the last millennium, Hungary was supposedly solidifying its nationalist claims to the Pannonian Plain in the next millennium. Since history was to turn in an opposite direction, with Hungary consigned after World War I to relative insignificance among the European states and to a linguistic and cultural isolation even in its own region, the Millennium Exhibition remained in Hungarian historical consciousness as a monument to past greatness. The goal of creating something that would live in history was at odds with the ephemeral quality of a fair. The commission's instructions that these be temporary buildings would be retracted at the close of the fair and was half-anticipated by the architect as design flourishes were hurriedly added or removed to meet deadlines and fulfill an ever grander scheme. Key buildings on the historical island were preserved. Precisely because the retrospective event offered no new vision for the future, the exhibition became a Hungarian symbol of "the world of yesterday."

The exhibition was, in a sense, the calcified "black" city, while the city it was meant to showcase was the vital "white" city. The progressive aspect of the millennium was inescapable, just a step outside the exhibition grounds. Construction crews at work had been ever present in the city since the coronation. The impressive Large Ring Boulevard swung around the city to two new bridgeheads. The Margaret Bridge had been dedicated in 1876, while the Franz Joseph Bridge opened for the Millennium Exhibition. Coronation day, June 8, 1896, began in Buda with an hour-long banderium of 995 horsemen under ethnic, city, and regional banners, wearing a blend of different costumes and followed by an endless train of carriages parading before a crowd estimated at 200,000.[79] An even larger crowd amassed before the not-quite completed Parliament building to see the king and politicians formally inaugurate what would become the landmark monument of Budapest. The Hungarian liberal elite inside the parliament could feel pride while a huge supportive crowd filled the square outside. With Austrian liberalism in decline, they also seemed to represent what future liberalism promised for the monarchy. Over half-a-million spectators lined the streets and one hundred thousand visited the exhibition that day.[80]

The millennium documented the degree to which Europe's periphery as a whole was experiencing the most dramatic surge of urbanization. The eclectic-historicist fashion had the virtue of unpredictable differences in each facade. Citizens of Budapest were accustomed to continual and constant change. This new urban reality heralded an exhilarating sense of possibility. The disconnect between a historicizing fashion and the new reality beyond the exhibition grounds would explode in the coming years into a confident Hungarian cultural modernism. György Lukács would remark that Hungarian modernism was the most modern of the modern.[81] The new cultural institutions arising in urban centers—coffeehouses, clubs, reading and language societies, lending libraries, concert halls, opera houses, theaters, publishing companies, lecture halls, museums, journals, and newspapers—were all distinctive products of a swelling verbal and written culture.

For the tourist, the futuristic aspect of the exhibition was experienced in the transportation to and from the City Park. Entrance to the first Continental underground was just beyond the exhibition entry gate. "Every passenger has a wide and comfortable seat, cushioned with velvet. The cars themselves are of mahogany or hardwood; the lights are brilliant; the roadbed as smooth as a floor. Each car starts as gently as a yacht with loosened sails, and slows down without a tremor. . . . The ventilation is perfect for there is no smoke, and consequently no smell. In fine, it is the poetry of motion on wheels, smooth as a gondola, and almost as noiseless,"[82] wrote an American journalist. The subway stops have "twice as many people" strolling along their walkway "at night as the Champs Élysées; is altogether more beautiful than the Ringstrasse, and infinitely gayer than the Unter den Linden." The last stop of the new underground was Váci Square, the old heart of Budapest's elegant shopping and apartment district, and around a nearby corner was a new elegant department store opening at the end of the millennial year. The American reporter was surprised to find that he could sample the luxuries of the "plutocrat" or the aristocrat in what he had expected would be a backwater. "In almost every block" the visitor stumbled on yet another "spacious café ablaze with lights and thronged with gaily dressed people," alive with Gypsy music and conversation.[83] Budapest had become the daring new addition to the European grand tour. The now quaint yellow tramcars have been renovated and continue to carry passengers below Andrássy Boulevard, a wistful symbol of Hungarian modernism stopped in its tracks. There are some who insist that innovative liberalism went underground that day and has been trying to dig itself out ever since.

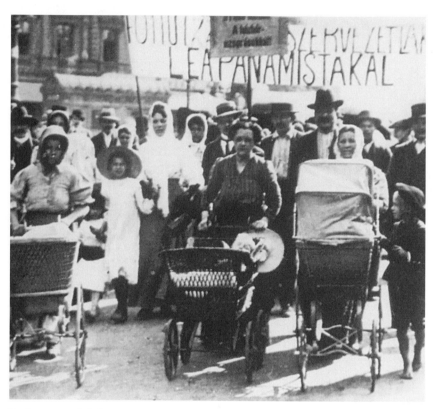

Budapest social-democrats protesting rent increases, 1910. Photograph (Hungarian National Museum, Photo Gallery)

10

The Loss of the Streets

Modernists yearned for a break with the liberal culture of the preceding half century. They were tired of the aesthetics of storytelling, and repudiated, in particular, the passion for tracing the nation's teleological development from its existence on the steppes under the barbarian chieftains. Modernists mocked the eclectic historicism and the aggrandizement of self-important individuals at the core of the memorializing project of Hungarian liberalism. There was outrage in the Budapest art world when Ferenc Kossuth tried to sway the jury deciding the design for the Kossuth mausoleum in the Kerepesi cemetery. An amateur painter and sculptor in his own right, he indicated his support for the layperson desiring a traditional design against the experts open to a modernist one. Kossuth's son, well-educated and mannered but lacking in imagination, seemed to epitomize the banality of late Victorian culture.[1] While the modernists demoted the politician with a capital "P" they placed in his stead the artist with a capital "A." While the lead roles were changed, the assumed role of the mass as a passive but impressionable audience remained much the same.

The modernist critique would dismiss the era between Petőfi and Endre Ady, i.e., 1849 and 1896, as a period of political advance but cultural decline. The modernist avant-garde and the Marxist vanguard converged in dismantling Victorian liberalism. Both targeted liberalism's missionary calling to spread higher culture down through the middle class and into the more reliable and sober working class. The lower classes were to be "prepared" for the suffrage. This was a notion rooted initially in a progressive optimism, ready and willing, in theory, to expand its base. But with the liberal oligarchy hiding behind a weak parliament and dependent upon a scandalous electoral system, they were attacked for a dearth of ideas but plenty of tricolors on dis-

281

play. Marxism challenged liberal historicism by unmasking its class character and offering an alternative teleological vision that turned the proletariat into the educators of tomorrow's society. Modernism reacted to the blockage in Victorian culture. The anti-Victorian rebellion hit Budapest especially hard, for it was an attack on both existing practices and a yet unrealized icon. Hungarian liberalism was elitist in practice, less so in theory, while turn-of-the-century modernists and Marxists were the opposite. In practice they were welcoming to outsiders, but in theory they were elitists addressing a vanguard—a narrow, highly selective, esoteric audience. Given Hungary's narrow and beleaguered political class, the claims to inclusiveness seemed disingenuous; their modernist critics were not reaching a mass base either. Yet as the population swelled into a metropolis in Budapest and the liberals retreated from the streets, modernists, socialists, and nationalists would all have to address the unchastened crowd of the new century in one way or another.

As the fiftieth anniversary of 1848 approached, there was widespread skepticism toward the aging March holiday. The rhetoric at the podium in the 1870s and 1880s had been triumphant, insisting that all but two of the Twelve Points of March 15 had been realized, and those two had been compromised for the higher good of the settlement. But by the turn of the century, March 15 was more likely to prompt reflections on how little of the parents' ideals had been achieved. The dialogue between liberal revolution and multinational dynasticism, fostered and sustained by the chastened crowd, seemed to lack anything new to say. However, all the impatience of the modernists and socialists aside, the postmortem on liberalism was still premature. As all the signs of the political collapse of Hungarian liberalism seemed to mount, the success and prosperity of Hungarian capitalism was solid and sustained. The Marxist theorist Ervin Szabó wrote no fewer than three articles in 1902 attacking the idolization of Kossuth, suggesting the extent to which memorializing Kossuth remained a popular passion.[2] Even as Szabó railed against the historicization of the hero of the liberal crowd, he was forced to acknowledge the Kossuth cult's peculiar staying power in Hungary. "The history of Hungary is a classic example of a vanity fair of obsolete traditions," Szabó snorted.[3] In 1904 he asked, "Who shall bury the dead haunting us? Who shall expel the ghosts and the specters? There is a mighty force in all of them."[4]

Fading Traditions

Aside from steering Hungary through its Millennium Exhibition, Bánffy's tenure would be notable for its aggressive response to growing Romanian militancy and his contemptuous air toward the burgeoning suffrage reform movement. Under Bánffy a camouflaged censorship, a sense of liberalism withering in a police state where rights depended on the whims of the bureaucracy, and the ritualistic conjuring of the revolutionary crowd of yesteryear reached its apogee. His heavy-handed tactics in the 1897 elections made them by far the most corrupt of the liberal era. The prime minister told a delegation representing a crowd of demonstrators: "Your 30,000 people do not impress me! There are another 100,000 who do not want to have anything to do with universal suffrage. When you have more supporters then I will talk with you!" Within six months, demonstrators had doubled their numbers and would not stop multiplying until 1914.[5]

Bánffy, a Transylvanian magnate, was particularly alarmed by growing Romanian nationalism. He intensified the Magyarization of the schools, and unleashed the considerable administrative powers of the state against Romanian politics and culture. What became known as the Bánffy terror cost fifty-one lives, primarily by police repression of rural Romanian rallies, and marked the beginning of a publicistic campaign appealing to Europeans on the "Romanian question" in Europe.[6] Under pressure to meld into a Magyar state, Romanians became ever more conscious of themselves as victims: victims of an electoral system that disadvantaged them because of their poverty and victims of the political illegitimacy of the union of Transylvania and Hungary. Transylvanian Romanians viewed May 15 as the holiday of national liberal freedom. This was the day that the Transylvanian Romanians had asserted their own claim in 1848.

Wishing to rid himself of the old divisions, the aggressive and brash Prime Minister Dezső Bánffy in 1898 established a new national holiday to commemorate 1848. The only possible day when king and nation could in theory celebrate 1848 together was April 11, the day King Ferdinand V sanctioned the March laws. The nationalist opposition wanted none of it. Ferenc Kossuth insisted that "not April 11 but rather March 15 be declared the national holiday."[7] The April Laws were the basis for the Compromise of 1867, and the Kossuthites who had balked at the Compromise were, of course, incensed at the attempted confluence of these two dates, which they, not unreasonably, saw as an attempt to efface the revolutionary tradition. Ferenc Kossuth declared April 11 and March 15 antithetical holidays. He insisted that March 15 was the only authentic holiday of the revolution, and April 11 was a day without meaning to the mass of the populace. Many of the freedoms were secured before April 11, he reasoned; April 11 connotes the formal sanctioning of the laws rather than the struggle to achieve them.

The parliamentary opposition succeeded only in deleting the phrase "for all times" from the enabling legislation. All state and religious schools were ordered to hold annual commemorations on April 11, in which a member of the faculty would deliver a speech on the 1848 laws, the ideals of March 15, the achievement of press freedom, and equality before the law. Students, the directive declared, were to be inspired by patriotic songs and declamations. University students were the first to call for a boycott of April 11. As the two rival holidays approached, student organizations defended the integrity of March 15 as the holiday both of freedom and of student activism. When university authorities used disciplinary procedures against student organizers, student anger grew. Police intervened to prevent a student protest demonstration in front of the Liberal Party headquarters; the rift between the Liberal Party and the champions of 1848 was undeniable.

On the fiftieth anniversary of March 15, the tricolor seemed to fly from all buildings, except the official ones. Although not a sanctioned work-free holiday, numerous stores were closed, and those that did open tended to close by 10 a.m. By noon all normal commerce had stopped; the downtown was packed with women in colorful national dress. Many men sported red insignia indicating that they were social democrats. Between 8,000 and 10,000 gathered at the national riding school, where the liberal politician Barnabás Holló allegedly told the social democratic leader Max Grossmann, "We can also rally masses, not only you." To which Grossmann replied, "Yes, you are right, but only so long as I allow it. There are so many of our people here that at a nod from me this will become a socialist demonstration." And, indeed, when orators praised the achievement of press freedom, they were heckled by social democrats waving an issue of *Népszava* confiscated just weeks before.[8] For socialists the 1848 demand for press freedom was becoming an epithet against the reigning liberal authorities. As the meeting closed, socialists began singing the "Internationale." As more and more joined in, the refrain grew louder and louder.

A more distinguished public met in the Redout Hall where the Petőfi Society listened to two of the last living legends of 1848, Jókai and József Madarász. But in the public procession to the Petőfi statue, socialists joined in as a large compact mass. They carried copies of that day's confiscated *Világszabadság* (World Freedom) hoisted on placards; hundreds of copies were distributed. When the marchers sang the usual patriotic songs, socialists countered with protest songs. At the Petőfi statue, liberal orators delivered their speeches, but a worker with a powerful voice interrupted the scripted proceedings, took to the tribune, and proclaimed a set of social-democratic principles, which he called "The Twelve Points of 1898." His words were met with icy silence by the largely liberal audience near the platform, but the socialist supporters ringing the liberals broke into frenetic cheers and refrains of the "Internationale." Socialists drowned out all attempts of the chorus to sing the liberal musical repertoire. The inability of liberals to make themselves heard at their own public rally left a lasting impression.

Later that day 35,000 gathered at a socialist rally in the City Park under the banners "Down with Censorship," "Long Live Press Freedom," and "Hurrah for Universal Suffrage." The socialists had changed the character of the fiftieth anniversary from a resplendent celebration of "Hungarian freedom" to a demonstration of the fissures in the social alliances that were forged in the liberal era. Socialists disrupted the Folk Theater performance of "1848" by throwing leaflets from the gallery. The Opera House ignored the holiday altogether, prompting the remark that if the Viennese Gustav Mahler had still been in charge, he would not have dared to be as cavalier as the present Hungarian musical director. Liberal cultural institutions were chided from all sides for a lack of passion in their artistry and in their politics. The National Theater was accused of having fallen into the doldrums of a subsidized institution.[9]

In the run up to April 11, the government courted favor by announcing its intention to move the offending Hentzi statue from St. George Square.[10] The weather was inclement on the day, but the prescribed agenda was followed nonetheless. This included special sessions at the Budapest City Council and a torchlight parade from Petőfi Square to Buda in the evening. A minimum of three thousand torchbearers crossed the bridge and ascended to the castle to honor the king. The press took note of Franz Joseph's formal declaration, which credited April 11, 1848, as the foundation stone of present-day Hungary. His words carried some weight, since the date both affirmed the basis on which dualism was justified and implied a formal sanctioning of 1848. But the Independence Party boycotted the functions, and the social democrats seized the spotlight with a counter-demonstration of 20,000 in the City Park. While April 11 resonated with almost no one, it still was a day off for workers. Its status as an official holiday underscored what March 15 was not—a holiday from work.

The new holiday did nothing to alleviate the edginess of authorities in the weeks preceding May Day. In anticipation they began ferreting out subversives, breaking up socialist meetings, and arresting socialist leaders.

When a crowd of 20,000 socialists gathered on April 21 at the Eastern Railroad Station to welcome the return of an expelled socialist, police moved in, inflicting many saber cuts and arresting 122 demonstrators.[11] Police measures far exceeded the actual threat. May Day, 1898, fell on a Sunday, causing no work stoppages. What violence there was happened out in the provinces where such demonstrations were frightening novelties. This was a tumultuous year in the countryside, with socialist agitation and land seizures by peasants on the Great Plain. On May Day four died in the village of Bóka, followed by further violence the next day in the same county of Torontál.[12]

Left-leaning sociologists labored to give dignity to the masses, but police directives and burgher angst zeroed in on socialist crowd action. For the unchastened crowd of the new century, the crowd image of 1848 was no longer a liberating one dominated by a lyrical March 15. The historiographical tone was set by György Gracza's four-volume history, *The Hungarian Struggle for Independence in 1848–49* (1894–98). Overwritten and splattered with historical inaccuracies, it dramatized the Lamberg lynching of September 1848 in the style of the new crowd literature of Le Bon that criminalized the crowd. Pál Angyal appropriated Gracza's lurid account of the revolutionary lynch mob directly into contemporary Hungarian legal sociology of crowd behavior.[13] Although the urban calendar was filled with a steady stream of predictable crowd events, the fear of the irrational crowd was so dominant that it obscured the generally controlled quality of these crowds: the mass gatherings of the urbane and religious crowd, the disciplined crowd that marched on May Day, and the patriotic crowds that came out for statue raisings. The assassination of the Empress and Queen Elizabeth that September on a public quay in Geneva at the hands of an Italian anarchist seemed to confirm all the liberal and conservative fears of the dark forces lurking in the urban landscape. Elizabeth became a target even though she wielded little power. Real grief was felt at the murder of the frail, unhappy recluse.[14] The shattering of the old icon of the chastened crowd further underscored the shifting templates of Hungarian social and political life. Celebrity monarchism faced the new threat of terror, and she had become an early victim in the politics of violence to which the monarchy would succumb.

By the beginning of the new century, March 15 had become an antiliberal holiday, significant mostly as an occasion for nationalist or radical crowds to vent their frustration. Shopkeepers scrambled to cover their windows as they heard the shattering of glass and a howling crowd approaching on March 15, 1900. They targeted storefronts without the tricolor on display. A crowd of fifteen hundred to two thousand people gathered to jeer at the liberal National Casino, shouting "Down with the traitors!" "Down with the aristocrats." Mounted police charged and dispersed the crowd in front of the National Theater. One police officer was seriously wounded.[15]

It was a discouraged liberalism that reflected upon itself at the death of Kálmán Tisza in March 1902. Eight days before on March 15, editorialists had denounced the Liberal Party bosses and hacks as the "winter patriots" of the Compromise.[16] Now there was a lack of generosity in the obituaries of the former leader. Kálmán Tisza had been strong, but journalists predicted that he had carried liberalism to its grave by tying liberals to reaction. The *Neues Politisches Volksblatt,* the champion of left liberalism's need to regain the streets for its cause, warned its largely Jewish German-reading audience that with Kálmán Tisza had died a kind of liberalism. What remained was the "swamp of present-day liberalism."[17] The figure who had presided over so many memorials was given a scant salute on his departure. There was no capital city commemoration. The Budapest mayor justified the decision with the officious reasoning that Tisza had never been a city official. That same year hardly five hundred people had shown up to listen to the traditional orations at the Petőfi statue on March 15. Liberal worthies barely went through the motions, delivering speeches with hardly anyone listening or anyone believing in the integrity of the declamations. Only the socialists injected any passion into the remembrance of 1848, when six thousand gathered that afternoon before the Petőfi statue.[18] With the Liberal Party ceding the streets, there was a growing conviction that after a quarter century liberal, one-party rule was decaying and on the eve of collapse.

The more socialists found access to parliamentary representation blocked, the more incentive they had in demonstrating their control of the streets. Strikes including hundreds, sometimes between one or two thousand workers had become a familiar sight. By the turn of the century, marches of the unemployed, at times ten thousand strong, signaled a new use of the streets to further economic as well as political claims. These, plus small but equally frequent rent strikes blended together in a new street theater. The blue-collar working class rather than students and journeymen assumed the principal roles. This brought them in constant competition with the Kossuthites, the last liberal force willing to contest their dominance of street politics.[19]

In 1903 several hundred liberal students left the university on a march to Ferenc Kossuth's residence and to the Independence Party headquarters only to find several thousand socialists had overwhelmed their march. Ferenc Kossuth appeared on the balcony, but was so startled by the chants for universal suffrage that he lost his train of thought, and what remarks he did make were drowned out by the "Internationale."[20] He lacked charisma or a common touch, but no other party leader possessed the charisma to overcome the Kossuth name.

The Kossuth cult was boosted still further by the discovery of the remains of Ferenc Rákóczi II (1676–1735) in Turkey. The identification of Kossuth with Rákóczi, grafted homage toward Rákóczi onto the martyrology of Kossuth. Planning began for an elaborate reburial. Reinterring the heroes of the Magyar past was becoming a new obsession. In order for Rákóczi's remains to be officially buried in Hungary, Franz Joseph was forced to acquiesce in the annulment of the 1749 law declaring Rákóczi a traitor and accept the political cult of an anti-Habsburg rebel. Nationalists celebrated "an injustice purged," as if Kossuth himself had been rehabilitated. Ceremony after ceremony followed in rapid succession for three years, primarily in Transylvania and the outlying areas, but eventually in Budapest, as well. In 1903 Kolozsvár was illuminated for a Rákóczi festival, a Rákóczi exhibition was held in Kassa, and a Rákóczi statue was unveiled in Nagykároly. Budapest held a banderium, but misfortune befell the event, when one of the tribunes, full of spectators, collapsed during a speech by Ferenc Kossuth.[21]

Kossuthites were in possession of the most evocative symbol in public discourse. Kossuth statues popped up all over Hungary in the decade-and-a-half before World War I. The unveilings were invariably attended by Ferenc Kossuth and the Independence Party establishment. The monarchist qualms about erecting Kossuth statues in consideration of the king had been brushed aside. What passion a Kossuth statue could stir was evidenced in Szeged in 1903.[22] The commanding officer of the Szeged garrison ordered the removal of a wreath placed by some soldiers at the Kossuth statue on the Day of the Arad Martyrs—a holiday which still underscored the gulf remaining between Hungarian nationalists and the dynasty. When the situation escalated, police occupied the square, and 10,000 demonstrators angrily confronted the army in front of its barracks. Two civilians were wounded when troops opened fire.

Marosvásárhely, the capital of the Székely lands bordering Romania, erected one of the first Kossuth statues, placing it directly across from a statue of General Bem in the town square. The message to the Romanians and Saxons could not have been made clearer. In pouring rain 20,000 Székely marched four abreast in village companies, with military-like bearing under distinctive village flags. In this borderland region that had experienced ethnic warfare in 1848–49, nationalism remained most raw. It was an unveiling with heightened patriotic pathos, from the sculptor eschewing payment for his labor of love to the subscription campaign underwritten largely by small donations by Székely villagers. The maladroit Ferenc Kossuth appeared in a garish yellow travel jacket that looked incongruous amidst the Magyar gala of the Székely dignitaries. An occasional poem, recited by its author, had Lajos Kossuth provocatively predicting Austria's disintegration. It was so enthusiastically received that a tumult ensued when copies were distributed. Less than twenty years later, when the monarchy did shatter, this area became part of Romania and the statue was torn down.

The Kossuthites faced a dilemma. Their radical-liberal struggle in the name of "the nation," it had been presumed, was synonymous with "the people." But if "the nation" could not accommodate universal male suffrage, then "nation" had to be redefined negatively in relation to the nationalities it opposed. The Kossuthites had supported an expanded suffrage in theory, even expansion into the national minority communities. However, in ethnically mixed regions they found themselves banding together with the government party. They feared the nationality vote playing Magyar factions against each other, and thereby, forcing concessions that might weaken the Magyar state. In parliament the Kossuthites would maneuver themselves into a policy of incessant filibustering, which spoke to their own impotence and that of the parliamentary institution as a whole.

Suffrage Battles

In the last peaceful decade of the compromise, the clash over suffrage reform between the liberal oligarchs and the socialist battalions on the boulevards would become more than a class conflict, more than a political test of wills. It marked an increasingly bitter cultural war between a liberal sense of law and order and the syndicalist vision of a mythic general strike. The socialists held onto the hope that a political strike might paralyze the capital and shake or, perhaps, break the establishment's control over parliament. They were operating in the abstract, with visions of a demonstrating crowd sweeping away the old order by the exertion of passion on the streets. The advocates of law and order would seek their remedy too readily in martial law and the state of siege. This would easily degenerate into a contest between numbers and weapons. In this struggle the dynasty and the nationalities would play crucial supporting roles.

The thirty-year Liberal Party hegemony was finally undone by the confrontational tactics of Prime Minister István Tisza in the fall of 1904. István was as different in his political style from his father Kálmán as Ferenc Kossuth was from his father. While Ferenc was compliant and out of his depth, István was so unyielding that he frightened his supporters as much as his opponents. Kálmán Tisza's strong-willed son had been waiting for at least five years to challenge the politics of obstruction both in the parliament and on the streets. Tisza suddenly dissolved parliament, and called an election, transforming what one newspaper had just been celebrating as an unusual period of "political calm" into, perhaps, the most intense electoral campaign season in the liberal epoch.[23] Tisza was convinced that his political aims—an effective parliament, continued support of the Ausgleich, and support of industrial growth—were sound positions, and that his disgust with the endless filibustering, in particular, was a view shared by the majority of the country's population. Filibustering, Tisza told parliament, was an import from Austria where liberalism was weak. As Bánffy's lieutenant, he had watched the obstructionist tactics bring down the Bánffy government in 1899. But unlike Bánffy, Tisza was out to reestablish the Liberal Party's moral legitimacy by running the least corrupt election of the liberal era. This lost him the votes of the magnates in the borderlands and opened the floodgates to reform in the Liberal Party bastion of Budapest.

His opening campaign rally in the Redout Hall was a portent. Despite an army of Liberal Party monitors, five to six hundred young men managed to gather in the back of the Redout Hall, creating a small disturbance before police moved them out to the street. Once outside they joined another 800 to 1,000 people shouting anti-government slogans. The crowd, according to the press, was made up of "various immature elements," but most of the twenty-three arrested were white-collar workers and students. They were either Kossuthites, or more likely supporters of Gyula Andrássy, Jr., who had just defected from the Liberal Party over the obstruction issue.[24] The next day two hundred students marched off from their classrooms at noon to the National Casino, calling for Andrássy, their man of the hour. Before Andrássy could appear, police arrived and cleared the square. During the coming weeks, it became commonplace for hundreds of students to march through downtown denouncing Tisza.[25]

In the capital's electoral districts there were some high profile campaigns in which party leaders and cabinet ministers squared off against each other. On January 1905 crowds of the disenfranchised gathered at the Budapest polling places of close elections, seeking to affect the razor-thin majorities amongst the narrow electorate. They cheered and jeered as voters appeared and made clear their preferences. In the contest between Andrássy and Tisza, newspapers reported women were beseeching voters to endorse Andrássy. When, to the consternation of many Andrássy supporters, Tisza squeaked out a victory, there was crying on the streets. In the heavily Jewish sixth district mounted police rode into one excited crowd, wounding five. They then formed a cordon that allowed only fifty voters an hour to vote, dragging out the contest well into the early morning hours. Results were tabulated on an on-going basis, with crowd emotion intensifying through the evening. When the democrat Vilmos Vázsonyi was declared winner at 2:30 a.m., with 4,034 to 3,812 votes, thousands of the disenfranchised celebrated in front of the Democratic Club.[26] In the 1905 election, the "Coalition of National Parties," i.e. the united opposition of Kossuthites, Catholics, conservatives, and a scattering of democrats, reduced the Liberal Party vote to just thirty-eight percent. Tisza took the defeat as a personal rebuke, announced his retirement from politics, and the Liberal Party dissolved.

Ferenc Kossuth declared on March 15 that for the first time in thirty-eight years Hungarian public opinion had effected a change. But that same day socialists lambasted, "the great patriots, who always have *hon* [the homeland] on their lips but never in their hearts."[27] On May Day worker columns loudly booed and called for universal suffrage as their march route passed the headquarters. The Kossuthites remained adamant on the army question. Franz Joseph was also intransigent and refused to allow the new Kossuthite-led majority to form a government. Instead, Franz Joseph appointed a caretaker government under General Baron Géza Fejérváry charged with negotiating a coalition headed by the sons of Kossuth, Andrássy, and Apponyi. The nationalist parties sought to rally the country against Habsburg "absolutism." The parliamentary paralysis created a crisis atmosphere in which even a military occupation of Hungary seemed possible. Fejérváry put forth a plan for radical electoral reform to undercut the Hungarian nationalist elite. He argued that expanding suffrage was the only way to stop "those elements—arrogant oligarchs, lawyers, clerics, petty nobles—who have for about one-hundred-and-fifty years made up the Hungarian parliament, and who have these many years thrown up these

sterile constitutional questions. Over the long run no Hungarian government can deal with these elements. Through universal suffrage at least part
of this group can be removed." He went on to declare that "the socialists
are not as dangerous as commonly believed . . . one can work with them."[28]
Interior Minister József Kristóffy proposed expansion of the franchise
from one million to 2.6 million voters. Franz Joseph followed up by slight-
ing parliament's coalition leaders with but a five-minute interview; this
was time enough for the king to inform them that he supported the increase
in suffrage. One hundred thousand socialists and liberal suffrage reformers
rallied before parliament to hail the royal initiative on September 15, 1905.
Remembered as "Red Friday," the size of the demonstration made it in-
stantly legendary.

A furious Andrássy accused the regime of inciting class conflict and tol-
erating working-class violence.[29] Workers began besieging coalition newspapers when they editorialized against universal suffrage. A frightened nationalist middle class bemoaned the "street scandals."[30] The coalition could
still rally supporters. On October 6, the day of the Arad martyrs, some
100,000 pilgrimaged out to the Kerepesi cemetery in what was billed as a
massive middle-class demonstration against Vienna and socialism. The
Hungarian coalition might dig in its heels, but it was boxed in. The Russian
revolution of 1905 obliged the Tsar to issue the October manifesto granting
constitutional reforms. In the face of massive Viennese demonstrations, the
Austrian government had also reversed course and embraced universal suffrage.[31] The Hungarians had always posed themselves as the liberal, more
progressive half of the monarchy. (Even the opposition to Franz Joseph's
intervention in the appointment of the Baron Géza Fejérváry government
had been posed as a defense of the principle of a parliamentary system—
and as a patriotic protest.) Now the reactionary character of the Hungarian
national coalition's parliamentarianism was hard to deny.

The Kossuthites had perceived themselves as the spokesmen of opposition. But the more socialists focused on universal male suffrage, the more
they denounced Kossuthite ambivalence toward democracy.[32] Socialists
demonstrated in the name of the "people"; the Kossuthites demonstrated in
the name of "the nation." Both sought to upstage the pageant masters of
the liberal regime. Nationalities had often supported Kossuthite candidates
in elections, since they constituted the most vocal element of the opposition and maintained a liberal notion of Magyarization, that is, in theory democratic to the future although not to the present. Embracing a liberal faith
in progress, they could assume that one day their efforts would produce an

expanded Magyar polity based on consent. However, in the meantime, inequities and resentment were inevitable. The Kossuthites found themselves more and more identified with the dualist parliamentary system they had so long derided. The Hungarian oligarchy was unwilling to take the Austrian gamble that reform would parliamentarize the radicals rather than radicalize parliament. Instead, in Hungary the street became shriller and any minority nationalist demonstration became magnified while the parliamentary debate became more vacuous.[33]

By early 1906 obstruction had so intensified that on February 19 the military dissolved parliament and physically evicted infuriated nationalist deputies. The coalition needed to mobilize street crowds, but only students responded in significant numbers, and even then demonstrations were easily spoiled. One gathering of two to three hundred found itself competing with a workers' assembly nearby, with its songs, chants, and suffrage slogans. The students traversed the metropolis singing the Kossuth Song at the Honvéd Statue and paying respects to Kossuth's grave. Police claimed students used flags as a weapon in a scuffle with the police.[34] In preparation for another election, the Fejérváry government cracked down on the rights of assembly. Nationwide press censorship became stringent; street sales of newspapers were banned; oppositional rallies were closely monitored or also banned. In early March a nationalist crowd threw rocks at a royal commissar in Debrecen and even at someone only suspected of being a county official in Szeged. The new sheriff in Ungvár was pelted with snowballs by women, including his sister; officials retaliated by imposing a state of emergency in the town and dismissed the police captain, who had been on vacation during the incident.[35]

For March 15, 1906, the government prohibited all public festivities, except in taverns with police monitors. One exception was made for Budapest. At this strictly controlled meeting, speakers lamented that never in the past fifty-eight years had the commemoration been held under such inauspicious circumstances. Still, it seemed to many observers that more houses were beflagged than usual. Amidst the contentiousness, March 15 seemed to those participating to have rewon its claim as the most important national holiday.[36] On the anniversary of Kossuth's death five days later a huge crowd braved a cold rain to make the pilgrimage to the gravesite. The Independence Party won a smashing national electoral victory, and Franz Joseph finally accepted a coalition government under Sándor Wekerle.

The new government took advantage of the long-awaited reburial of Rákóczi's remains to demonstrate the coalition's role as the pageant masters of Hungarian nationalism. On October 28, 1906, the newspapers enticed Budapest residents with full-page photo spreads. The railroad station and parade route were draped in royal purple. Flag staffs alternated tricolor, Budapest, and Rákóczi flags. The train slid into the station without sounding its whistle, but outside the church bells of the city began to ring. Although hundreds of thousands of people filled the station and lined the route, there was a respectful silence, and the click of thousands of camera shutters. Men doffed their hats and police saluted as the hearse passed. It took two hours for the elaborate funeral procession to reach the Basilica. It was Minister of Commerce Ferenc Kossuth who received the seven caskets of Rákóczi, his family, and followers in the name of the Hungarian government.

As the casket-bearing train moved on, it was the object of countless torchlight vigils and town celebrations. In Miskolc, for instance, fifteen thousand people waited at the train station, entertained by Gypsy music, speeches, and song. When the train arrived, the carriage doors were opened and illuminated with electric lights, and a minister led the crowd in prayer. At the train's final destination in Kassa, a banderium was painstakingly planned. Banderium participants wore elaborate and rather costly uniforms that were meant to replicate *kuruc* uniforms of yesteryear.[37] Historians had dug through the archives attempting to verify the pro-Rákóczi sentiments of upper Hungary (present day Slovakia) two hundred years before. The holiday was an opportunity for city boosterism. However, since a *kuruc* identification was both provocative toward the minorities and the Habsburgs, city pride and antagonistic chauvinism were not far apart.

Minority representation in the parliament had just risen from ten to twenty-seven.[38] After the 1906 victory a crowd of Romanian voters, their hats doffed, paraded down the streets of Szászsebes celebrating their candidate. Assembling in the market square they heard fiery speeches and sang the anthem, "Awake, Romanian, from your slumber."[39] The suffrage issue made evident to the minorities the obstacles before them, but at the same time fostered a commitment to greater involvement in parliamentary life. The suffrage question provided a national platform. The grievances of the nationalities could now be framed within a national debate in which they became potential players. The Romanian National Party began to hold regular mass rallies. Election rallies, victory parades, and reports from deputies became a convenient forum. The Romanian-language press urged that such gatherings be held once a month; hundreds of such rallies, with suffrage reform and nationality grievances as their central theme, were held between 1906 and 1911.[40]

While freedom of assembly was written into Hungarian law, granting of demonstration permits was clearly arbitrary. Efforts were made to retard minority organization, particularly amongst the Slovaks, whose organizations were the most rudimentary. The Kossuthites in power were proving to be more repressive than their Liberal Party predecessors toward anti-government demonstrations, whether in Budapest or the ethnic borderlands. The most infamous example was the "massacre of Csernova" on October 27, 1907. "In two carriages the false apostles of Magyar culture," reported R. W. Seton-Watson, entered the long narrow street where a crowd of several hundred Slovak peasants had gathered for a church dedication. "A solid phalanx blocked the way, the cortège was greeted with cries of 'Turn back.'" After a shower of stones, the gendarmes, without any preliminary warning, fired into the crowd, killing eleven, seriously injuring nine more, and inflicting wounds on scores of others. Hungary would be excoriated by European public opinion, especially liberal intellectuals. Most notable was the Norwegian poet Björnson Björnstjerne's emotional open letter which contrasted his youthful sympathy for an oppressed and martyred Hungary to his present disgust with Hungarian chauvinism. The incident provoked Seton-Watson to study and publicize Hungary's "racial problem."[41]

Hungarian social democrats distanced themselves from Hungarian nationalism, in theory, by proudly proclaiming their "unpatriotic" stance. However, while they embraced a multiethnic cosmopolitan vision, party strategists quarreled over the possibility of creating a broad suffrage reform front when the leaders of nationality parties were often clerics or conservatives. More often, the social democratic party's hopes swung between two options: many followed Szabó who interpreted the Russian revolution of 1905 as a sign that the day of the mass strike had arrived; others hoped for a suffrage revolution from above promised by the dynasty in the summer of 1905.[42] The third alternative, that of a united front, depended upon a tactical alliance with left-liberals in the suffrage struggle. Oszkár Jászi argued that to deny nationalism would hamper socialism. But in these years, in the futile hope of gathering mass support by allaying the nationalist intellectuals and middle class fears, he settled for a moderate program of reconciliation with the nationalities, e.g., native language schooling and administration. This neither allayed the minority problem nor cemented an alliance with the socialists.[43]

The elections of 1905 and 1906 might have shown that "1848" had defeated "1867," as nationalist editorialists were fond of proclaiming. But the consequence was that the street upstaged parliament as the key political arena. Street demonstrations aimed to prove that the crowd represented the true public, unlike the rigged parliamentary system. In an increasingly ritualistic conflict, suffrage reformers accused the coalition of new depths of hypocrisy. Ferenc Kossuth now celebrated the artificial national holiday, April 11, 1907, which he had previously denounced. In the topsy-turvy political world, the very Kossuthite patriots who were throwing rotten eggs at police earlier were now ordering the police to stifle suffrage demonstrations. Coalition leaders equivocated: Ferenc Kossuth declared support for electoral reform, but only if it could be done without diminishing the role of the intelligentsia or strengthening the nationalities. Andrássy came up with a plural voting system; it would expand the suffrage but also multiply the votes of the privileged.

The ethnic hatreds of nationalist struggle crystallized earlier in the monarchy than elsewhere, Robert Musil reflected. But monarchic festivity had engendered a "form of a sublimated ceremonial" which provided a kind of ethnic peace "that might have become of great importance if its evolution had not been prematurely cut short by a catastrophe."[44] Hungarians added a peculiar tension to the "sublimated ceremonial" of the Monarchy largely absent in the Austrian half. The fortieth anniversary of the Compromise would intrude like an unwelcome overnight guest. After the turmoil of the preceding two-and-a-half years, Franz Joseph expressed his reluctance to attend the jubilee. But when Franz Joseph arrived in Budapest after all, he experienced, perhaps, his most unusual reception. Social democrats decided to stage a monarchist demonstration of their own for their king who continued to dangle the threat of expanded suffrage before the reigning coalition. Forty thousand workers formed a cordon along his route on June 6, 1907. There was no subject-like waving of hats; rather the public raised their hats politely and cried out "Long live universal, secret suffrage." They also cheered, "Long live our King!' and even "Long live our people's king!"[45] The unperturbed monarch saluted gratefully over and over again as his carriage sped to the Buda castle.

This would be his last jubilee but just a stage in the escalation of the suffrage agitation. Socialists were on the verge of calling a general strike for the end of June. They delayed this extreme action, but the agitation for suffrage would reach new heights by September. A mass demonstration was called for the opening day of parliament, October 10. The coalition responded harshly to this "act of terror against the sovereignty of parliament," while socialist orators proclaimed that "We stand on the eve of revolution just as in 1848."[46] On what would be remembered as "Red Thursday," 100,000 people marched in disciplined rows. Yet like the workers who demonstrated that they owned the streets on May Day in the 1890s, the suffrage reformers seemed doomed to success. It became an annual ritual that on parliament's opening day the socialist legions would amass in Parliament Square to once again express their anger. In September 1908 the reconvening of parliament brought another predictable round of mounted police attacks on crowds, subsequent rallies honoring the victims, and ominous calls for the urban populace to arm itself in self-defense. Since authorities feared growing political street demonstrations were antecedents of revolution, they launched a preventive war on the potentialities of the crowd. Police were given the task of disciplining the working class, but this infused political crowds with a charged symbolic character. Budapest again seemed to teeter on the precipice when workers defied the ban on demonstrations and took to the streets. Police assembled at major intersections, under the Elizabeth bridge, and in many buildings. But on this occasion a bloody confrontation was avoided. Clashes between the lower-class public and the police became daily skirmishes in what seemed like a small guerrilla war. With the increasing number of work stoppages and recurrent clashes between strikers and strike-breakers, syndicalism continued to spread within the Hungarian left. The improving economy expanded the number of members in unions and socialist party organizations, which, in turn, prompted a counter-offensive on the side of the authorities.

The Hungarian polity cannot be divided into a simple dialectic of contesting forces. Amidst the heated rhetoric and physical confrontations, both sides were also consensus driven. The urban working class mobilized its troops for suffrage reform not the disintegration of parliament. When the Kossuthite dream of controlling Budapest dissolved, an alliance of democrats, led by Vázsonyi and the old liberal district bosses, elevated the reformer István Bárczy to power. Bárczy, a talented centrist, was able to realize the reform program that Vázsonyi would later term "liberal Luegerism." "I learnt from the Viennese example that if big business was not driven from city hall by the liberals," he reflected, "the storm would blow in from a reactionary direction."[47] The Budapest liberals carried out formidable municipal projects, including the construction of more living quarters than any other metropolis on the Continent between 1906 and 1914.

Crowding had become a cultural reality, and as the masses were necessarily molded into a civilized crowd, constituency and reform politics also turned on the ability to contain one's crowd. The drama of socialist and suffrage demonstrations became a dramatic narrative carefully told and re-told for the past half century. Hungarian communism nurtured its historic roots in an indigenous movement that had seized the streets. Yet even during this high-water mark of the clashes between crowds and police, there were counter-trends. Consensus crowds celebrating the modern also assembled. The Budapest authorities were not unsuccessful in eliciting the participation of sizable crowds in celebrations where the police would assume the role of facilitator. At the occasional moment when the society could demonstrate its integrative capacity, it did so with an excited gusto. The technological breakthroughs of the age offered one such moment.

Throughout the summer of 1909, Europe seemed transfixed by the possibilities of flight. The French pilot Louis Blériot received a tremendous reception in London after his flight across the English channel, and about a million assembled on squares, roofs, and boulevards on August 28 to see Count Zeppelin fly his airship into Berlin.[48] On October 18 almost 250,000, a fourth of the population of Budapest, made their way to Rákos field, the military parade ground on the outskirts of the city, to see Blériot fly his plane. Such a crowd dwarfed the familiar political events, whether socialist, nationalist, or religious, including May Day, the return of Rákóczi's remains, and Catholic Day rallies. Organizers had not expected such a reception in Budapest. Grandstands were set up for paying visitors, while everyone else assembled spontaneously behind a hastily drawn cordon on the field. The massive crowd seemed deathly still when Blériot began his first flight that lasted six minutes. A second flight of ten minutes went higher than the first. After the third four-minute flight, the police could not contain the crowd that surged through the lines, encircling the pilot and his machine.

Technological progress could appeal to the imaginations of all; its promise was integrative; the crowds that gathered to behold its wonders were peaceful. Crowds could be uplifting, as they could be violent and threatening. Historians have become ambivalent in their assessment of street politics in the last decade of the prewar era. Most have focused on the violent incidents, stressing a resurgent crowd, indicating an ascendant revolutionary trend between 1905 and 1914. Some have projected the war enthusiasm of August 1914 back into the previous decade to suggest an underlying longing for nationalist integration. Recently, interest has shifted toward what one might call modernist crowds, such as those for Blériot, who were drawn to a planetary vision of progress and plenty. The participants in all three types of crowds overlapped.

Within a year, the politician the Budapest crowd most loved to hate, István Tisza, was back at center stage. The coalition government, weak at its core, had brought little noticeable movement toward resolution of Hungary's suffrage, ethnic, or army questions. This enabled István Tisza's Party of National Work to come to power in 1910, with Tisza as speaker of the Lower House. The Kossuthites were again in opposition, but split internally, with a Gyula Justh faction supporting expanded suffrage. This made tactical alliances possible again (in the name of suffrage reform) between obstructionists in parliament and demonstrators on the street. The socialists launched a third, climactic onslaught on the suffrage question in the spring of 1912 and 1913. Parliament Square became the focus of an intense street politics that was paralleled by the turmoil within parliament. The split of the Kossuthites made possible tactical alliances over expanded suffrage between demonstrators on the street and obstructionists in parliament. At times it seemed like a castle under siege from the square below.[49] The parliament building provided a perfect site for symbolic confrontation between the grand fortress of Magyar legalism and "thousands upon thousands of raised fists." Cordoned off by military guards and filled with hecklers, the huge structure could seem a bloated facade masking rule by a recalcitrant illiberal oligarchy. The expensive, ornate edifice was supposed to assert liberal confidence, power and solidity. Its neo-Gothic design, a larger-than-life Westminster looming over the Pest bank of the Danube, suggested that Hungarian liberalism was neither modern nor indirectly derived from antiquity; rather, like the English, Hungarian constitutionalism supposedly could trace itself back directly to the thirteenth century.[50] In contrast, the Viennese liberals had erected a neoclassical parliament on the Ringstrasse evoking the Hellenic polis, thereby revealing their lack of historic roots, but also affirming their primary commitment to liberalism. The Hungarians had, instead, chosen to stress the historic traditions of Hungarian constitutionalism, underscoring their commitment to aristocratic traditions rather than to liberalism.

On March 4, 1912 in gray fog and continuous rain between 80,000 and 100,000 workers wearing their Sunday best marched or gathered at the Millennium monument. The disciplined socialist demonstrators, many women amongst them, and joined by students and liberal clubs, all marched four abreast. A contingent of bicyclists, their bicycles all decorated in red, led the columns, while other monitors wearing red arm bands patrolled the flow of the march. The crowd sang the "Internationale" on queue. Three weeks later, on the last Sunday in March, Budapest liberals led by Oszkár Jászi organized an electoral march of their own. Much smaller, with only about 10,000 participants, it proved much more violent, in part because the numerous socialist participants were freed from party discipline and were quick to respond to police provocations. Instead of dispersing when ordered, the crowd broke through the police cordon to reach Parliament Square where they were driven back by a mounted saber attack. Later, roaming contingents, largely of youth, vandalized and battled police who fired warning shots. The climax of the suffrage campaign came on Bloody Thursday, May 23, 1912, when the socialists called for a total work stoppage and mass demonstrations to protest Tisza's alteration of parliamentary rules. Tisza responded by banning all demonstrations and used the police to physically remove obstructionist deputies from the House of Deputies. By eight in the morning Budapest was filled with all available troops and police. Demonstrators still took to the streets *en masse*. By half-past ten in the morning, street fighting had become intense in scattered locations throughout the city center. It was evident that neither warning salvos nor the mounted charges were going to have their intended effect. Crowds might scatter and disperse, but within minutes they would regroup and return to reclaim lost terrain. One central square was cleared by the police ten times to no avail. By noon all ten thousand troops in Budapest had been dispatched onto the streets without bringing the fighting to an end. Yelling, running crowds seemed to be everywhere. Troops surrounded the stock exchange and the Austrian-Hungarian Bank. The conflict was unlike anything seen in the city since 1883. Demonstrators systematically smashed street lamps (977 by the city's count) to inhibit police at night. The darkness would make mounted police and cavalry vulnerable, because they could not detect wires strung across the streets. Demonstrators also systematically destroyed streetcars and attacked private cars and carriages to bring traffic to a standstill. Telegraph and telephone lines were cut, and barricades were erected.[51] In outlying districts police outposts were attacked and trashed.

The police estimated that forty-five percent of Budapest workers had participated in the riot and put the number involved at between 80,000 and 85,000. Fighting even extended to the City Park where a crowd was dispersed by cavalry. An amateur photographer photographed the corpse of a fourteen-year-old boy, then had the seven-man police detachment responsible pose for their own photograph. On March 5, the *Népszava* expectantly reported, that "the huge crowd displayed its strength, but has not yet used it."[52] However, in the confrontation between revolutionary syndicalism and martial law, the crowd, rather than Tisza, blinked. The following day, troop reinforcements arrived from the neighboring cities of Esztergom, Vác, and Székesfehérvár. Fearing a blood bath, the social democratic leadership called for an end to the strike. There had been some eight-hundred arrests. The hospitals reported 192 seriously wounded and six dead, one of them a policeman who had been shot. On Monday, May 27, 20,000 accompanied the bodies of three of the "suffrage martyrs" to Kerepesi cemetery. Soon thereafter a parliamentary deputy fired three shots at István Tisza, who sat pale but unflinching. The deputy missed each time, then wounded himself.

Nine months later, in March 1913, another parliamentary consideration of the suffrage bill triggered the last great spasm of crowd confrontation. Socialists once again raised the expectation of a great cathartic general strike. The suffrage league distributed several hundred thousand leaflets: "Citizens! Female citizens! During the general strike hang out flags, decorate your windows, close your businesses! The workers struggle for you, not against you!"[53] Shopkeepers scrambled to place the white placard with the bright red lettering: "Long live universal, secret suffrage!" in their windows. The government proclaimed a state of siege and urged the populace to buy two days supply of food. The city announced it would sell bread in the twenty-seven city schools. Papers reported two thousand gendarmes and police and as many as sixty thousand soldiers were amassed in Budapest. The capital had taken on the features of an occupied city. All apartment house gates were ordered closed after seven in the evening for the duration of the strike.[54] The city was filled with rumors, but at the last minute, the social democrats stepped back. They delayed the general strike for fear that they might be left in the lurch by the parliamentary opposition. Without a successful parliamentary confrontation, the mass strike was in danger of merely becoming a strong but still unsuccessful demonstration. The 200,000 leaflets distributed by the social democrats to explain their decision only spread a feeling of shame and anger among the hundreds of thousands who had prepared for the great showdown.[55] The air was let out of the general strike threat, leaving bitterness among a great part of the working class. Fifty thousand would still come out on May Day 1913, yet the revolutionary mood of the crowd had ebbed.

The War Festival

Nineteen fourteen began in an anticlimactic mood. The great demonstrations of the preceding years had yielded nothing. The massive suffrage demonstrations had, in a sense, proven too successful, too easily repeatable, too prone to routinization. The reformers could on any chosen day demon-strate their awesome control of the streets, yet the prospects of any victory in the suffrage question had not improved. After March 1913 reformers were thrown on the defensive. Even the opposition's success in driving one prime minister from office amidst scandal had backfired, for he had been replaced by István Tisza. This meant that both the crowd and the parlia-mentary opposition were out maneuvered. With the Party of Independence languishing, Ferenc Kossuth had become a forlorn figure, a fixture at the ritualistic commemorations of his father. On the morning of March 21, uni-versity students would make a pilgrimage each year to the Kossuth mau-soleum, completed in 1909. Independent Party deputies would gather for Lutheran services at Deák Square Church, and then members of the family, the Kossuth and Justh factions, and aging Honvéds would proceed to the cemetery, and end the day with a banquet at the Hotel Hungaria. The twen-tieth jubilee of Kossuth's death in 1914 was especially elaborate.[56]

The Kossuth cult continued gathering funds for statues. The most im-posing Kossuth statue raised to date was dedicated on Sunday, May 3 in Debrecen. The city's commanding general ordered barrack inspections in order to keep soldiers and officers away from the gathering. Ferenc Kos-suth's worsening health had prevented him from attending. His death three weeks later became an occasion to reflect on the disappointed hopes placed in the son. His limitations had diminished the standing of the Kossuthite cult. For the suffrage demonstrators, he had become one with the enemy, a patrician-plutocrat who had betrayed the democratic charge from his fa-ther. But his death, after years of ill health, provided a moment of nostal-gia for what could have been, and one last hurrah in what would become the last great public funeral of prewar Hungary. In death, Ferenc Kossuth was, more often than not, depicted as an innocent whose "Europeanism proved an unalterable obstacle in ever finding his way in the twilight of Hungarian politics."[57] Prime Minister Tisza wrote the widow that he dared not attend the funeral lest his presence touch off demonstrations that would interrupt the occasion.

Two hundred thousand spectators came out on the streets for Ferenc Kossuth's funeral. Mourners in their amassed cylinder hats and black suits along the long boulevards maintained a pious stillness; the police rode black horses. Yet it was clear to all that one was carrying the son of a great man to his grave. The crowd was a fraction of the size of the 1894 Kossuth funeral; still, people wanted to see how the son of the great man was buried next to his father. The name Kossuth had lost little of its wondrous ring.

There was also the sense that the funeral marked the end of an era. Ferenc Kossuth's name had been his program, a name that evoked faith in his politics. For the last time the name Kossuth stirred up the metropolis, and many made this the final opportunity to express their pain publicly over the loss of everything for which the name Kossuth had once stood.[58]

A week later, on June 5, Budapest newspapers reported Franz Ferdinand's planned visit to Bosnia scheduled for later that month.[59] June was a slow news month, still there was little coverage of the archduke and his upcoming Bosnian tour. In mid-June, Franz Ferdinand's two-day visit with Kaiser Wilhelm drew only passing attention, for the archduke was not a popular figure in Hungary. It was news, however, that Corpus Christi Day attracted an especially large Buda crowd to the Mátyás church and the Dísz Square where both a regimental and a Honvéd band performed. The city also contended with a pharmaceutical strike.[60] On the twenty-fourth newspapers played up a genealogical discovery of a fifteenth-century Hungarian ancestor of the heir apparent. This was a hurried replacement for a previously claimed Hungarian ancestor of the archduke, who turned out to be Romanian.[61] Coverage of the Archduke's Bosnian trip focused on the terrible weather that was being visited on the region as a whole. What commentary there was centered on the failure of the monarchy's Balkan policy, the unrest in Albania and a Dalmatian letter threatening Franz Ferdinand. However, assurance was included in the report that the archduke was protected by many police agents.[62] On the day of the Sarajevo visit, a Budapest rainstorm and an ethnic clash between Germans and Czechs in Bohemia topped the local news. There was scarce mention of the heir apparent's doings.

Garbled news of an assassination attempt reached Budapest by telegraph at 1:30 Sunday afternoon, June 29. Rumors spread through the taverns and wine halls. Huge crowds assembled in front of the leading newspapers feverish for news. By three in the afternoon the deaths were public knowledge in Budapest. At five o'clock the Sunday blue laws were suspended, allowing newspaper offices to open and publish extras verifying the deaths of the archduke and his consort. Mourning flags were hoisted on public buildings. Music ceased in public places.[63] The next day Budapest was in full mourning: Black flags hung from all public buildings, and there was hardly a house in the city center that did not display some sign of mourning. Shop windows posted black-bordered pictures of Franz Ferdinand and Sophie, and occasionally, their children, as well. The city announced its intention to rename an important street after the deceased. The death was formally announced to a packed parliament draped in black.[64]

Yet, public mourning remained perfunctory in the days that followed. Vienna, not Budapest, was the site of the funeral, and the ceremony itself was widely perceived as unworthy of the heir apparent and insulting to the memory of his wife. The court's rigid adherence to the Spanish ritual decreed the morganatic wife of Franz Ferdinand would be denied a joint burial with her spouse. Instead, she was given a slipshod funeral in Bohemia at two in the morning amidst a downpour of rain. A Viennese street demonstration of the members of the Hungarian and Austrian high nobility critical of the handling of the funeral aroused comment in a largely passive Budapest. As Count Albert Apponyi complained, "The funeral did not reflect the piety of the population and the tragedy of the terrible catastrophe."[65] But in death Franz Ferdinand had become primarily a question mark. The time had passed to dwell on his anti-Magyar stance and his partiality toward the Czechs. Instead, his contradictions, his opposition to the continued rule of the old Hungarian oligarchy, and his support for universal suffrage were balanced against his imperialist dreams.

Within a week the assassination crisis seemed to have passed, and the consensus of the Budapest press was that no reasonable person thought of engaging Serbia in an armed conflict. The current wisdom was that Hungarians did not need a war, for even a great victory could prove burdensome by bringing unwelcome annexations that would only further exacerbate internal ethnic imbalances.[66] The capital settled into the summer doldrums. Pistol shots and a wild tumult on July 2 between some sixty to seventy socialist workers who invaded a working-class tavern on Kőbányai Street to disrupt a meeting of a "yellow" union seemed to suggest a return to the old soured internal normality.[67]

At the end of the month, a red-and-green placard suddenly went up on Hungarian walls announcing mobilization. Dramatic days returned with a vengeance. The outbreak of the local war against Serbia prompted incessant playing of the patriotic songs, the "Rákóczi March" and the "Gott, erhalte" in the coffeehouses on both sides of the river. Crowds gathered at the railroad stations, in front of newspaper offices, or before wall placards to follow the momentous events. The call for mobilization threw Budapest into total commotion.[68] "There is no point in the city where one can't see hurrying people."[69] Excited and exultant inductees and demonstrators milled before the Pest City Hall, while inside frantic activity went on day and night. In Budapest, as in the other capitals of Europe, people seemed to interact in public with an unusual sense of community. "Let us admit that we had wondered," whether patriotism was but a bygone emotion, whether our complacency was just too deeply buried for it to ever be lit. "But like light Baroque patina, this coldness peeled away."[70] The barriers between the classes and age groups seemed unimportant. Everywhere there was an intoxicated bustle as civilians hurried to their units. The appearance of military bands touched off spontaneous processions snaking through the centers of provincial towns, such as in Szabadka where parading crowds stopped to make catcalls in front of Serb homes and then continued on their way cheering the war. One worker heard justifying the Sarajevo assassination was arrested, and there were scattered incidents where the unenthusiastic were pilloried or the unlucky Serb was hounded before being rescued by police.

During the day not any particular Budapest square or street was the focal point. And when night fell "the noisy demonstrating battalions take over." "A teeming horde" moved about the streets that Friday night, August 1, 1914. "The crowd engulfed Octagon Square" and hopelessly mired traffic.[71] Once the square belonged to the crowd, in a giddy procession, singing patriotic songs, they moved toward the inner city, and then up to St. George Square in Buda.[72] The crowd's intoxication with itself and the nation reached a crescendo on August 2 when local war turned into a continental war and Archduke Karl and Archduchess Zita, the new heir apparent couple, arrived in Budapest. This was the first time the Budapest public had ever seen the couple. Riding in their motorcade, they gave a human focus for those "living heroic days" to the fullest. Police in dress uniform began heavy patrolling of the streets well before the arrival of the train, but they were stretched thin. Military units were unavailable. In addition to fifty police on foot, four mounted police, even police detectives were walking the beat. A pale and tired István Tisza greeted their train at the Eastern Station. But the youthful Karl in a Honvéd Hussar uniform and the pretty Zita in black silk at his side seemed dispatched from central casting, delighting the mammoth crowds, especially the women and girls in festive clothing. Two hundred thousand Budapesters filled the streets on the cloudless summer day. The cliché of the hour was that great times removed great misunderstandings, that dualism had proved itself, and that a common danger had shown what the many peoples of the monarchy had in common. The sentiment of the young was expressed by the statement, "We want to demonstrate what our ancestors showed King Maria Theresa when they sacrificed blood and property for the beloved queen. We, too, are ready to make this sacrifice!"[73] Rarely had the House of Habsburg been cheered so lustily in Hungary as on that day. Dualism, it seemed, had withstood its test of fire. It took two hours before the procession reached the castle.

Fear of a copycat assassination was obvious, and maintaining order was also a great anxiety. No serious problem disturbed the procession. But as the car passed, the crowd swarmed onto the bridge behind the vehicle. The crowd ignored the toll booths and headed across the bridge. Many ran up the steps of the Buda hillside in hopes of getting one more glimpse of the crown prince couple. About a thousand people were soon at St. George Square. The crowd continued to swell until there "was not a single place to stand. One could not move to the right or left." Here, too, the crowd broke the cordon, and the police watched helplessly as they filled the palace courtyard. But once inside, these rambunctious celebrants removed their caps and sang the "Himnusz." Karl and Zita quickly came out to the balcony to thank the crowd. The throng continued to sing patriotic hymns well after the couple retired back inside.[74]

On August 3, under the heading, "The street speaks," the *Neues Politisches Volksblatt*, told its readership that the past week has brought us so many enthusiastic street demonstrations that it appeared nothing could top the last, and yet today's overwhelming demonstration has put everything in its shadows. "This was no longer the street alone, this was all of Budapest that let itself be heard today." With the outbreak of war, the chastened crowd seemed to come back for one last hurrah. They gathered at the War Office and recruitment halls. When the crowd swelled and swelled it did so at the castle and St. George Square, where they could pay homage to the monarchy for whom they would possibly lay down their lives. Or they gathered at Octagon Square on Andrássy Avenue where patriotism mixed with youthful urban pleasures. Like its chastened predecessor, the war rally desired that an inaccessible normality and a unity be restored. In this grotesque parody of the chastened crowd, the favored site for the great mass gatherings was not the square facing the parliament. In the war enthusiasm of 1914, Hungary relished the integrative powers of the crowd, celebrated itself, but this alternative to revolution brought catastrophe. Never did Hungarians feel farther from the sense of defeat, never was Hungary closer to it.

Official March 15 demonstration in front of the National Museum steps in Budapest, 1989. Photograph by Zoltan Fejér

11

Epilogue: 1989

The role of the chastened crowd in Hungarian history and the powerful potential of the myths of the defeated revolutions of 1848 and 1956 were again made evident in 1989. On March 15, 1987, and 1988, sizable crowds confronted a newly formed riot squad. In the dispersal of these crowds, there were some beatings and arrests. For over a decade March 15 was the day that the precocious counter-elite might taunt the Communist regime. "By now the March fifteenth nationalist demonstrations have become institutions! Nationalistic demonstrations!" complained János Kádár in a speech to the Central Committee in 1973. "We had one this year, too. There were about three to four thousand people. We had twenty-five hundred observers . . . a few hundred social and official observers, and five to six hundred nationalist demonstrators. Of these there were a few hundred well-meaning idiots out for a 'rumble' and the [showing] of the national colors—however, somebody had to organize it in the first place. And it is quite possible for three to four scoundrels to get together and, before you know it, it is in the world press that there is an annual nationalist demonstration in Hungary."[1] The regime tried numerous tactics to ghettoize the day as a student holiday. There were commemorations at school. Although a workday, students were released at midday. Sometimes they moved on to the streets, daring authorities. Reciting the same Sándor Petőfi poems that were part of the standard school curriculum on the public squares on March 15 could be viewed as incendiary and cause for arrest.

Every ritual system sows the seeds of its own collapse. In the *annus mirabilis* of 1989—an 1848 with an Americanized "happy ending"—the Communist regimes of Eastern Europe were toppled, in part, by their inability to handle the very crowds they had theoretically embraced. Despite their sponsorship of lavish crowd display, the Communists labored under the potent contradiction between the idealized crowd of the past, especially those of May Day, 1890–1914, and their fear of spontaneous crowd action. Communists had learned a valuable lesson from the success of the propaganda offices of World War I.

Exuberant crowds marked both the beginning and the end of World War I in Hungary.[2] In the shuffle for power in 1918, the Leninist convert György Lukács and his friends, including Béla Balázs and Karl Mannheim, joined a demonstration organized on behalf of the moderate "Wilsonian" revolutionary Mihály Károlyi, the liberal prime minister who attempted to bring Hungary into line with Woodrow Wilson's fourteen points. Lukács took over the crowd with shouts of "To Buda!" "To Buda!" Suddenly, Lukács was reenacting Sándor Petőfi's charismatic march across the Danube on March 15, 1848.[3] Since the revolution of 1905, Lukács and the Budapest literati were drawn to the revolutionism of the Russian intelligentsia. Ady's cult of Petőfi, Szabó's syndicalism, and Rosa Luxemburg's faith in the spontaneity of revolutionary mass action, became the linchpins of a Hungarian leftist crowd theory in the interwar period. As Lukács put it later, "Thanks to Ervin Szabó, my knowledge of Georges Sorel helped me to develop the combined Hegel-Ady-Dostoevsky experience into a sort of ideology that I then considered to be revolutionary."[4]

While the left succeeded only in parodying 1848, the Horthy regime proved masters of the art of crowd politics. In the politics of revanche, festivity multiplied. Perhaps, nothing holds together a crowd better than a sense of shared defeat; constructed historicism fed the illusion of greatness robbed. March 15, 1848 was a malleable icon—reinvoked by every subsequent Hungarian regime. It was a great nationalist anniversary during the Horthy regime, but in 1942 March 15 also served in its other capacity, as an opportunity for antifascist demonstrators to publicly protest the alliance with Nazism. (A rock opera in 1998 opens by smashing the icon of this antifascist March 15, 1942. In its place 1848 became a morality play that emphasized home, faith, and nation, and dispensed with much of 1848's radicalism, revolutionism, or individualism in the process.)[5]

Communism in Eastern Europe was imposed in a festive vacuum. In the postwar popular front regimes, March 15 briefly reasserted its prominence in Hungary. The newspapers celebrated the "Holiday of the Free Press," while the Provisional National Government announced its land reform program on March 15, 1945. In 1848 the serfs were freed; in 1945 the great estates were to be cut down to size. Festive holidays were particularly important in the immediate postwar rubble years. The novelty of paid holidays marked the dawn of a new day. The Marxist pageant masters produced organized mass events not only to head off future disorganized eruptions, but to convince the public of the camaraderie and efficacy of the new structures. Although the pretense of coalition government remained, the Communists demanded not only dominance in the police and security apparatus but a lion's share of public festivity. But what distinguished the Eastern European from the Soviet experience was the quarter century of nationalist, counterrevolutionary, and fascist festivity that had to be displaced or incorporated. March 15 would always present the communists with a dilemma. In 1947 the holiday was marginalized. But in 1948 the centennial celebration of the revolution came at an opportune moment to cloak the Communist seizure of power in the raiments of the nationalist revolution.[6]

The propaganda offices of Mátyás Rákosi's regime were developing a new calendar centered around May Day.[7] May Day legitimated the Communist regime, but St. Stephen's Day had to be revamped. Whereas the Horthy regime turned St. Stephen's Day into an anti-socialist holiday, the Communists initially insinuated into it an anti-German strain by emphasizing the eastern origins of the Magyars.[8] In 1948 they sought to revamp the holiday entirely. In order to defuse the religious character of the celebration, they proclaimed a folkloric "New Bread Day." János Kádár was the keynote speaker. The event sought to tap the traditional influx of peasants into Budapest on St. Stephen's Day and was meant to mark the end of the rural-urban dichotomy. Although a plethora of street entertainment was provided, New Bread Day was a flop, and the following year St. Stephen's Day became Constitution Day.[9]

The stultifying nature of Stalinist festivity manufactured crowds that were passive to a degree that would have been unimaginable to syndicalists like Szabó. The routinization of charisma led to tired May Day processionals and stage-managed folk dance extravaganzas.[10] Ritual specialists erected an edifice of rites and ceremonies to dampen the volatility of the revolutionary crowd. State festivity supplanted religious rites of marriage and to a lesser extent funerals, and in place of confirmation, so-called "cultural educators" concocted a new ceremony around the receipt of one's internal passport at sixteen.[11] The propaganda ministry continued to publish tracts justifying or laying out these new ritual traditions into the 1970s, but most fell into disuse long before that. A belief in the crowd as the antidote to totalitarianism lurked below the surface. Mikhail Bakhtin had juxtaposed the authentic crowd to the stultifying, choreographed festivity of the Stalinist Russia of his day. His study of Rabelais placed carnival and popular festivity within a liberating history of laughter. Popular merriment possessed potential as a weapon against totalitarian politics, for when the masses gathered in laughter, they mocked rulers and flaunted excess.[12]

The Hungarian Revolution of 1956 demonstrated the possibility of spontaneous revolt. On October 6, 1956, two weeks before the tearing down of the Stalin statue, two-hundred thousand Hungarians marched silently through the city in a reburial ceremony for László Rajk and three other victims of the 1949 Hungarian Communist Party purge. Rajk's widow had led the agitation for his rehabilitation. She wanted her murdered husband to be dug up from the pit of lime where he had been thrown, and reburied with fitting ceremony in the Kerepesi cemetery alongside Hungary's other great figures. The mass of demonstrators marched in complete silence, recalling the old feudal Hungarian tradition of the ordeal by the bier: each member of the community was required to pass in single file before the corpse of an unsolved murder on the supposition that when the murderer passed by, the dead victim's wound would reopen and begin to bleed.[13] It rained during the Rajk funeral, so laden with recrimination. Imre Nagy, the reform Communist leader in 1956, had attended. "When hundreds of thousands march past the coffins," one commentator wrote, "they are not only paying the last honors to the victims, but it is their passionate desire, their unshakable determination to bury a whole era."[14]

The Hungarian revolution began, according to Hannah Arendt, as "an unarmed and essentially harmless student demonstration" that mushroomed from a few thousand "suddenly and spontaneously" into a revolutionary crowd when it marched to the large festival plaza at the edge of the City Park and toppled the Stalin statue in the center.[15] By the next day, "no programs, points, or manifestos played any role," Arendt wrote. "What carried the revolution was the sheer momentum of acting-together of the whole people whose demands were so obvious that they hardly needed elaborate formulation."[16] The revolution lasted only days and perhaps never had any possibility for success. Yet Hannah Arendt, in her epilogue to the second edition of *The Origins of Totalitarianism*, acclaimed the Hungarian revolution as an example of a "pure" revolution. But if it were a real revolution, it was one not because it created a dramatic and lasting political convulsion, but rather because it was a gesture, a demonstration of a will to freedom, tinged with a recovered sense of nationalism. As such, it blurred the distinction between political revolution and political festivity.

For a third of a century the ghost of 1956 would haunt Hungarian politics. A tacit bargain of the reform "Goulash" Communism of the decades of détente was that 1956 not be a focus of discussion or commemoration, for János Kádár, Communist Party secretary, was directly implicated in the execution of Imre Nagy, the principal martyr of 1956, and about four hundred others. The charge levied against the regime in 1988–9 was that even in its more moderate form, the government represented a miscarriage of history. The system's legitimacy was attacked as a discontinuity in the national past. In the late 1980s, while American historians anguished over "the crisis of objectivity," or one might say Marxism, Hungarian historians were taking to the tribunes. In Eastern Europe the crisis in Marxism was not a crisis in history, rather it was a crisis of politics expressed through a reassessment of history. Historians were prominent in the democratic opposition as spokespersons for an anti-Marxist path, and they were also among the first beneficiaries of the Hungarian revolution of 1989. Assuming key positions in the immediate post-Communist Hungarian government were, for instance, József Antall, an intellectual historian of the mid-nineteenth century, who assumed the prime ministership, and leadership of the parliament was entrusted to a historian of 1848, György Szabad. Numerous historians were appointed to cabinet positions.

While the economy, politics, and the Warsaw Pact alliances were crumbling, the Hungarian revolution was unique in that a rather open discourse on historical revision propelled events forward. The Hungarian was, perhaps, the most historically minded of the series of related revolutions in 1989. In early 1988 five-hundred Hungarian historians, archivists, social scientists, and journalists met to urge repeal of the Archive Law, but they called their program: "Silence and Distortions, or On the Possibility of Examining Recent Hungarian History." Participants spoke boldly. The Communist Central Committee soon thereafter dislodged a central fiction by changing the designation of 1956 from "counter-revolution" to "popular insurrection." When a special Communist Party conference in May 1988 removed János Kádár and seven septuagenarians from the politburo, they also established a historical commission to reexamine 1956. Hungary's reform Communists hoped that this would be an act of reconciliation. Given that Imre Nagy, the martyred leader of 1956, was a reform Communist, the reformers believed they could lay claim to the Nagy inheritance. But the question had taken on a dynamic of its own. The "Committee for Historical Justice," demanded that the thirtieth anniversary of his execution be commemorated, that the graves of the victims of 1956 be honored and that

survivors and dependents of the victims gain the tangible rewards of rehabilitation, such as pensions. The "precondition for any ethical and political
renewal in Hungary" was "confronting the facts of 1956," the committee
proclaimed. All Communist Party members who "have never supported
the bloody terror" should face the past and thereby "free themselves of a
psychological burden."[17] Rehabilitation of previously purged individuals
had been the traditional method resorted to by the Soviet-style communist
regimes for announcing policy reversals, or proclaiming new political
agendas, and the Hungarian opposition now organized behind the demand
for a formal rehabilitation and ceremonial reburial.[18]

On the afternoon of June 16, 1988, the anniversary of Nagy's death, a
crowd officially estimated at four hundred (the protesters claimed one
thousand) gathered in Heroes Square. When they attempted to lay wreaths
and make speeches, the police ran identity checks and the crowd dispersed,
only to reassemble later at the Batthyány Memorial Flame where a police
cordon surrounded the memorial to the martyr of 1849. The crowd was
dispersed and fifteen were taken into custody. The new post-Kádár leadership decided it was best to conciliate. During his trip to America, Prime
Minister Károly Grosz promised to allow the reburial of Nagy. Still eva-
sions and delays continued. March 15, however, could not be postponed.
In 1989 the government gave in to the opposition's demand for the recognition of March 15 as a national holiday. They hoped that a collective commemoration of loyal and opposition forces would demonstrate a national
consensus for the new political reforms, and bring credit upon their regime, placing them within the tradition of the liberal reform demands of
1848. The political duality of 1989 was played out in a double demonstration. The communist reform leadership and spokespersons of the political
opposition publicly jockeyed for the moral high ground, using this political holiday to play out the rivalry over historical inheritance. The government sponsored a commemoration at the National Museum steps, where
the drama of 1848 had crystallized. But the Communist regime had held
too many events at the National Museum steps, robbing the location of its
subversive air. The official event was dwarfed by the counter demonstration that followed. A huge throng retraced the path taken on that epic day
in 1848. They visited the sites of March 15, as pilgrims at the Stations of
the Cross. At each site the history was retold. The history was to be felt
again, as if for the first time. A bitter indictment of the regime was that it
had robbed the public of its historical memory. "Generations have grown
up in darkness. Young Hungarians know their own country's history only

the way an abandoned child knows his parent's past."[19] The holiday had retained its edge.

Public politics was reinvigorated that day. The sociologist Tamás Hofer recounted the euphoria of the March 15, 1989, demonstration, the symbolic battlefield on which the Communist regime was beaten. The streets and squares of Budapest became "a substitution for a parliament" on which the "gentle crowd" mobilized against the party state. At first glance, this seems to confirm the powerful democratic nature of the iconoclastic crowd challenging order and defying authority. The opposition in 1989 depended upon the crowd, believing that such active public support, more than the compromised ballot box, would keep the "huge" bureaucratic "pyramid" from "crushing" the opposition.[20] But Hofer needed to label this demonstration as a "gentle" crowd to divorce it from the "tough" crowd of fascism.[21] Hungarian tradition has remembered the spontaneous actions of past crowds as "authentic," while parliamentary elections have been manipulated. But the dangerous precedents in Hungarian history of crowd-based populism are well-known: euphoric crowds buoyed hyper-nationalism, legitimated the war call in 1914, and cheered on the authoritarian/fascist state. So the emphasis at this demonstration was on "gentle," and the task since the change in power has been to construct an ethos of gentle crowds and parliamentary systems within the framework of mass politics. The demonstrators on March 15, 1989, were presenting an agenda for the future rather than directly confrontational. Hanging a banner proclaiming "Free Hungarian Television" on the studio facade sufficed. March 15 was as joyous a day as the anniversary it commemorated. Perhaps, the most dramatic statement made on that holiday was not in Hungary at all, but in the shopping districts of Vienna where an even larger Hungarian crowd had traveled to celebrate consumerism. Although the political were galvanized by history, the spontaneous, iconoclastic crowd replaced the hedonism of laughter with that of shopping.

The crowd was visible, while the "negotiated revolution" was still largely hidden from public view. Television cameras relayed the images, and foreign Communist publics were reacting to the surge of energy. Far more ink was spilt over the demonstrative opposition than the political reforms taking place behind the scenes. Scholars, on the other hand, have naturally ferreted out the hidden story of the "negotiated" or "the lawful revolution." The assumption is that history of "the transformation" was determined by the Communist reformers willing to relinquish power and the opposition eager to assume control. In these analyses demonstrations are primarily of symbolic importance. But for a moment the crowd, the opposition, and reform communists had been joined. Crowd demonstrations would not have had the character they did, and certainly not the result, were it not for a framework of toleration and a determination for systemic change. Nevertheless, the demonstrations were like electric shocks that shot through the system with stunning effect. It is the obvious story of 1989, but it should not, therefore, be obscured in the writing of the history, or perhaps, we should say the myth of 1989.

The crowd on March 15, 1989, had confronted a hypocrisy, but the funeral for Imre Nagy confronted a taboo. The press, armed with new freedom, took up the issue of Nagy's rehabilitation, and on June 16, 1989, a crowd of a quarter-million people gathered in Heroes Square; organizers had expected around ten thousand. Millions watched on television. The columns in the square were wrapped in black crepe. The opposition now sought to raise the posthumous Nagy against an ailing Kádár. Kádár's dilemma, like Franz Joseph's before him, was that however acceptable a milder regime may have become, he could not deny his rise to power came with the crushing of the revolution. The disparity between the official interpretation and the popular narrative of 1956 betrayed a legitimacy problem for the regime that became intolerable with liberalization. Three weeks after the funeral demonstration, the Hungarian Supreme Court announced Nagy's full rehabilitation, and on that day life-supports were removed and Kádár died. From 1848 to 1989 a tradition evolved around the lament over failed revolution. Nagy's reburial was less a revolution than a funeral of an era. Demonstrators aimed at a "transformation"; few desired full-scale, violent revolution. The wish was simply to continue or accelerate the process of change. What is unique about the Hungarian case is the mix of martyrology with a mythology of revolution in the hope of producing an enduring chastened crowd.

Notes

Chapter 1, The Chastened Crowd

1. Elias Canetti, *Crowds and Power*, trans. Carol Stewart (New York, 1973), 16, 59, 305–6, 315–6, 327, 329.

2. What Deák did, in fact, say was "We don't know whether we should be glad or sorry if our army is beaten. It is uncertain which will be to the country's advantage." Béla K. Király, *Ferenc Deák* (Boston, 1975), 177.

3. This dialectic is, perhaps, more commonplace than generally thought. The American labor movement, for instance, filled its Labor Day festivities with wholesome celebration meant to please its followers and calm its critics. See, for example, Michael Kazin and Steven J. Ross, "America's Labor Day: The Dilemma of a Workers' Celebration," *Journal of American History* 78 (March 1992): 1294–1323.

4. Eric Hobsbawm, *Nations and Nationalism since 1780. Programme, Myth, Reality* (Cambridge, Eng., 1992). The word crowd does not appear, although in his discussion of Miroslav Hroch, *Social Preconditions of National Revival in Europe: A Comparative Analysis of the Social Composition of Patriotic Groups among the Smaller European Nations* (Cambridge, Eng., 1985), an abstract concept of a mass is used, 11–12, 104.

5. Georges Lefebvre, *The Great Fear of 1789: Rural Panic in Revolutionary France* (New York, 1973); Albert Soboul, *The Parisian Sans-culottes and the French Revolution, 1793–4* (Oxford, Eng., 1964); George Rudé, *The Crowd in the French Revolution* (London, 1959); *The Crowd in History, 1730–1848* (New York, 1970). Other key articles are E. P. Thompson, "The Moral Economy of the English Crowd in the Eighteenth Century," *Past and Present* 50 (1971): 76–136; and Natalie Zemon Davis, "The Rites of Violence: Religious Riot in Sixteenth-century France," *Past and Present* 59 (1973): 51–91.

6. Benedict Anderson, *Imagined Communities: Reflections on the Origin and Spread of Nationalism* (London, 1983). See also Karl W. Deutsch, *Nationalism and Social Communication* (Cambridge, Mass., 1966).

7. Gustave Le Bon, *The Crowd: A Study of the Popular Mind* (New York, 1960).

8. Mark Harrison, *Crowds and History: Mass Phenomena in English Towns, 1790–1835* (Cambridge, Eng., 1988); Tim Harris, *London Crowds in the Reign of*

Charles II: Propaganda and Politics from the Restoration until the Exclusion Crisis (Cambridge, Eng., 1987); Tony Hayter, *The Army and the Crowd in Mid-Georgian England* (Totowa, N.J., 1978); Charles Tilly, *Popular Contention in Great Britain, 1758–1834* (Cambridge, Mass., 1995); Barry Faulk, "The Public Execution: Urban Rhetoric and Victorian Crowds," in William B. Thesing, ed., *Executions and the British Experience from the 17th to the 20th Century: A Collection of Essays* (Jefferson, N.C., 1990).

9. Lynn Hunt, Thomas R. Martin, Barbara H. Rosenwein, R. Po-chia Hsia, and Bonnie G. Smith, *The Challenge of the West: Peoples and Cultures from 1787 to the Global Age* (Lexington, Mass., 1995).

10. Manfred Häckel, "Der Befreiungskampf des ungarischen Volkes 1848/49 in der deutschen Literatur der Zeit," in Leopold Magon, Gerhard Steiner, Wolfgang Steinitz, Miklós Szabolcsi, and György Mihály Vajda, eds., *Studien zur Geschichte der Deutsch-Ungarischen Literarischen Beziehungen* (East Berlin, 1969), 305.

11. István Deák, *The Lawful Revolution: Kossuth and the Hungarians, 1848–1849* (New York, 1979), argued for the legality at the base of even the revolutionary impulse. He does not, however, suggest that it was not, nonetheless, a revolution.

12. See András A. Gergely, *Kisebbség, etnikum, regionalizmus* [Minorities, ethnicities, regionalism] (Budapest, 1997); Ernő Gáll, *A nacionalizmus színeváltozásal* [Nationalism's color change] (Nagyvárad [Oradea], 1994); Liah Greenfeld, *Nationalism: Five Roads to Modernity* (Cambridge, Mass., 1992); Theodor Schieder, *Nationalismus und Nationalstaat* (Göttingen, 1992); Jonathan Arac and Harriet Ritvo, eds., *Macropolitics of Nineteenth-Century Literature: Nationalism, Exoticism, Imperialism* (Philadelphia, 1991); Homi K. Bhabha, *Nation and Narration* (London, 1990); Anthony Smith, *The Ethnic Origin of Nations* (Oxford, Eng., 1986); Walker Connor, *Ethnonationalism, The Quest for Understanding* (Princeton, N.J., 1994); Ernst B. Haas, "What Is Nationalism and Why Should We Study It?" *International Organizaton* 40 (Summer 1986): 708–44; Ernest Gellner, *Nations and Nationalism* (Ithaca, 1983); John Breuilly, *Nationalism and the State* (New York, 1982); John A. Armstrong, *Nations before Nationalism* (Chapel Hill, N.C., 1982); *Nationalism in the Twentieth Century* (New York, 1979); Elie Kedourie, *Nationalism* (London, 1960); Hans Kohn, *Nationalism. Its Meaning and History* (New York, 1955).

13. Rudé, *The Crowd in the French Revolution*, 1.

14. George Rudé, *The Crowd in History, 1730–1848* (New York, 1970), 4.

15. José Ortega y Gasset, *The Revolt of the Masses* (New York, 1932).

16. Pierre Ayçoberry, *The Nazi Question: An Essay on the Interpretations of National Socialism (1922–1975)* (New York, 1981), 31.

17. George Mosse, *The Nationalization of the Masses* (New York, 1975).

18. Adam Gopnik, "Noël Contendere: A Political Impasse Gives Way to a Literary Scandale," *The New Yorker*, December 28, 1998, and January 4, 1999, 65–66.

19. Tom Furniss, "The Genesis of the Reflections: Resisting the irresistible voice of the multitude," *Edmund Burke's Aesthetic Ideology* (Cambridge, Eng., 1993), 115–37.

20. J. S. McClelland, *The Crowd and the Mob: From Plato to Canetti* (London, 1989), 115. On crowd festivity in the French Revolution, see Mona Ozouf, *Festivals and the French Revolution*, trans. Alan Sheridan (Cambridge, Mass., 1988); David Lloyd Dowd, *Pageant-Master of the Republic. Jacques-Louis David and the French Revolution* (Lincoln, Neb., 1948). See also, Lynn Hunt, *Politics, Culture, and Class in the French Revolution* (Berkeley, 1984).

21. In his preface to *Le Peuple* (1846), Michelet declared, "Frenchmen of every circumstance, of every class and of every party, remember one thing, you have on this earth only one true friend, and that friend is France. You will always be guilty, in the eyes of the eternal coalition of aristocracies, of one crime, of having, fifty years ago, sought to deliver the world. They have not forgiven it, they will not forgive it. You are always their peril. You may be distinguished among yourselves by different party names, but you are, as Frenchmen, condemned together. In the eyes of Europe, let it be known, France will always have but one inexpiable name, which is her true name in eternity: the Revolution." Cited in Roland Barthes, *Michelet* (New York, 1987), 77.

22. László Deme, *The Radical Left in the Hungarian Revolution of 1848* (Boulder, Colo., 1976), 10.

23. Deme, *Radical Left*, 10. See also, László Deme, "Echoes of the French Revolution in 1848 Hungary," *East European Quarterly* 25 (March 1991): 103–12.

24. Anton Ernstberger, "Charles Mackay und die Idee der Vereinigten Staaten von Europa," *Historische Zeitschrift* 146 (1932): 263–302.

25. Charles Mackay, *Extraordinary Popular Delusions and the Madness of Crowds* (New York, 1974. First revised ed., 1852.), xvii.

26. Mackay, *Extraordinary Popular Delusions*, xx.

27. Karl Marx, *The Communist Manifesto*, last page on utopian socialism. See also, François Melis, "Neue Forschungsergebnisse zu den Artikeln von Friedrich Engels in der 'Neuen Rheinischen Zeitung' über die ungarische Revolution" *Marx-Engels-Jahrbuch* 11 (1989): 242–57.

28. "Die Feste, die Presse und der Frankfurter Abgeordnetentag. Drei Symptome des öffentlichen Geistes," Rhenish speech delivered September 1863, in *Ferdinand Lassalle, Reden und Schriften*, ed. Friedrich Jeneczek (Munich, 1970), 354.

29. Jacob Burckhardt, *The Civilization of the Renaissance in Italy*, vol. 2 (New York, 1958), 401.

30. Emil Dürr, ed., *Jacob Burckhardt als Politischer Publizist* (Zurich, 1937), 43.

31. Dürr, 55.

32. *Origins of Contemporary France* (New York, 1876), 129.

33. Peter Bergmann, *Nietzsche, "the Last Antipolitical German"* (Bloomington, Ind., 1986).

34. Jaap van Ginneken, *Crowds, Psychology, and Politics 1871–1900* (Cambridge, Eng., 1992), 1.

35. Scipio Sighele, *La folla delinquente* (Torino, 1891); Gabriel de Tarde, *L'opinion et la foule* (Paris, 1901). For a contemporary Hungarian analysis of this literature, see Károly Pekár, "Az ember tömegek psychologiája," *Athenaeum* (1899): 103–10, 221–34.

36. On Le Bon, see Susanna Barrows, *Distorted Mirrors. Visions of the Crowd in Late Nineteenth-Century France* (New Haven, Conn., 1981). For other literature on the crowd, see Marc Traugott, ed., *Repertoires and Cycles of Collective Action* (Durham, N.C., 1995); Sidney Tarrow, *Power in Movement; Social Movements and Contentious Politics* (Cambridge, Eng., 1993); Clark McPhail, *The Myth of the Madding Crowd* (New York, 1991); Rob Sindall, *Street Violence in the Nineteenth Century: Media Panic or Real Danger?* (Leicester, Eng., 1990); George Gaskell and Robert Benewick, eds., *The Crowd in Contemporary Britain* (London, 1987); C. F. Graumann and S. Moscovici, eds., *Changing Perceptions of the Crowd Mind and Behavior* (New York, 1986); Nicolaus Mills, *The Crowd in American Literature* (Baton Rouge, La., 1986);

Roger Geiger, "Democracy and the Crowd: The Social History of an Idea in France and Italy, 1890–1914," *Societas* 7 (Winter 1977): 47–71.

37. *The Historical Novel* (New York, 1965), 23.

38. Georges Sorel, *Reflections of Violence* (New York, 1999, first published 1906).

39. Lajos Varga, *A Magyarországi Szociáldemokrata Párt ellenzéke és tevékenysége, 1906–1911* [The Hungarian Social-Democratic Party opposition and activity] (Budapest, 1973), 72–3.

40. György Litván and János Bak, eds., *Socialism and Social Science: Selected Writings of Ervin Szabó* (London, 1982), 170. See also György Király, "A 48-as forradalom legendája," *Nyugat* 15 (1922): 34–39.

41. Jászi Viktor. "A tömeg" [The crowd], selection from *A kollektív lélek* [The collective spirit], in *A szociológia első magyar műhelye: A Huszadik Század köre* [Sociology's first laboratory: The Twentieth Century Circle], ed. György Litván, vol. 1 (Budapest, 1973), 501–16.

42. Pál Angyal, *A tömeg bűntettei* [Crowd Punishments] (Budapest, 1905), 9–11.

43. J. M. Golby and A. W. Purdue, *The Civilisation of the Crowd: Popular Culture in England, 1750–1900* (New York, 1985); Harold Perkin, *The Structured Crowd: Essays in English Social History* (Sussex, Eng., 1981).

44. Carl Schorske, *Fin-de-Siècle Vienna: Politics and Culture* (New York, 1981).

45. Sigmund Freud, *Group Psychology and the Analysis of the Ego* (New York, 1922), 51; Wilfred Trotter, *Instincts of the Herd in Peace and War* (London, 1923). See also, Kristóf Nyíri, *A Monarchia szellemi életéről: Filozófiatörténeti tanulmányok* [On the monarchy's intellectual life: Studies in the history of philosophy] (Budapest, 1980), 137–43.

46. Gábor Gyáni, *Az utca és a szalon: A társadalmi térhasználat Budapesten, 1870–1940* [The street and the salon: Social use of public squares in Budapest] (Budapest, 1998).

47. See Pieter M. Judson, *Exclusive Revolutionaries. Liberal Politics, Social Experience, and National Identity in the Austrian Empire, 1848–1914* (Ann Arbor, Mich., 1996); Lothar Höbelt, *Kornblume und Kaiseradler: Die deutschfreiheitlichen Parteien Altösterreichs, 1882–1918* (Vienna, 1993); Leopold Kammerhofer, ed., *Studien zum Deutschliberalismus in Zisleithanien 1873–1879* (Vienna, 1992); John W. Boyer, *Political Radicalism in Late Imperial Vienna: Origins of the Christian Social Movement, 1848–1897* (Chicago, 1981). For the Hungarian view of the problem, see Éva Somogyi, *Vom Zentralismus zum Dualismus: Der Weg der deutschösterreichischen Liberalen zum Ausgleich von 1867* (Budapest, 1983).

48. David Blackbourn and Geoff Eley, *The Peculiarities of German History: Bourgeois Society and Politics in Nineteenth-Century Germany* (Oxford, Eng., 1984).

49. Mária Ormos, "The Early Interwar Years, 1921–1938" in *A History of Hungary*, ed. Peter F. Sugar (Bloomington, Ind., 1990), 314.

50. Homi Bhabha, *Nation and Narration* (London, 1990), 3.

51. Trotter, *Instincts of the Herd*.

52. Károly Kerényi was among the many who sought refuge in such festivity, which he thought brought a sense of reality to the religious or the supernatural. Out of the peak moments of the festival sprang, according to Kerényi, "something more than present." Károly Kerényi, "Vom Wesen des Festes," *Paideuma* 1, no. 2 (1938): 63.

53. Quoted in Steven Bela Vardy, *Modern Hungarian Historiography* (New York, 1976), 46–7 and 70. See also Irene Raab Epstein, *Gyula Szekfű: A Study in the Political Basis of Hungarian Historiography* (New York, 1987).

54. Iván T. Berend, *The European Periphery and Industrialization, 1780–1914* (Cambridge, Eng., 1982).

55. Andrew Janos, *The Politics of Backwardness in Hungary, 1825–1945* (Princeton, N.J., 1982), 92.

56. László Tarr, *A délibábok országa* [The country of mirages] (Budapest, 1976), and András Gerő, *The Hungarian Parliament, 1867–1918: A Mirage of Power* (New York, 1997).

57. On liberalism and the making of a civil society, see András Gerő, *Modern Hungarian Society in the Making, The Unfinished Experience* (Budapest, 1995). In the discussion concerning liberalism, Máté Szabó argued that the political crowd was one of liberalism's most salient features, an important vehicle for garnering a mass constituency. "Mi a liberalizmus?" [What is liberalism], in *Válság és reform* [Crisis and reform] (Budapest, 1987), 129–30. See also Miklós Szabó, "A liberalizmus utópiája és a 'létező' liberalizmus" [Liberal utopia and feasible liberalism], *Válság és reform*, 151–7.

58. *Szekfű Gyula: Három nemzedék és ami utána következik* [G. S.: Three Generations and what followed it] (Budapest, 1989), xxviii–xxix.

59. Gabor Vermes, *István Tisza: The Liberal Vision and Conservative Statecraft of a Magyar Nationalist* (New York, 1985), 39.

Chapter 2, The Crowd as Threshold of the Nation

1. Eric Hobsbawm, *Nations and Nationalism since 1780: Programme, Myth, Reality* (Cambridge, Eng., 1992), 31; Roman Rosdolsky, "Friedrich Engels und das Problem der 'geschichtslosen Völker,'" *Archiv für Sozialgeschichte* 4 (1964): 87–282.

2. Kölcsey's "Himnusz" was set to music in 1844 by Ferenc Erkel. The national militia battled to its somber message in 1848, and it has been the national anthem despite changes in regimes.

3. Lóránt Czigány, *The Oxford History of Hungarian Literature: From the Earliest Times to the Present* (Oxford, 1984), 128.

4. C. M. B. Brann, "National Language Policy and Planning: France 1789, Nigeria 1989," *History of European Ideas* 13 (1991): 98.

5. *Ungarische Wirren und Zerwürfnisse* (Leipzig, 1842), 58.

6. See Edith Császár Mályusz, *The Theater and National Awakening* (Atlanta, 1980).

7. See Heinz Kindermann, *Realismus*, Theatergeschichte Europas, vol. 7 (Salzburg, 1965), 404–11; Laurence Senelick, ed., *National Theatre in Northern and Eastern Europe, 1746–1900* (Cambridge, Eng., 1991).

8. Friedrich Gottas, "Die Deutschen in den Ländern der Ungarischen Krone (1790–1867)," in *Land an der Donau, Deutsche Geschichte im Osten Europas*, ed. Günter Schödl (Berlin, 1995), 220–21.

9. The author was Frentzel, a military officer; see Lajos Laurisin, *A Magyar Király Operaház* [The Hungarian Royal Theater] (Budapest, 1941), 18.

10. Laurisin, *Operaház*, 17–18.

11. A useful and detailed monograph on the German theater in Budapest is Wolfgang Binal, *Deutschsprachiges Theater in Budapest von den Anfängen bis zum Brand des Theaters in der Wollgasse (1889)* (Vienna, 1972).

12. See in particular the essays by György Mihály Vajda, "Zur Geschichte der ungarisch-deutschen Literaturbeziehungen," and Antal Mádl, "Karl Beck. Ein Vermit-

tler zwischen ungarischer, österreichischer und deutscher Literatur," in Leopold Magon, Gerhard Steiner, Wolfgang Steinitz, Miklós Szabolcsi, and György Mihály Vajda, eds., *Studien zur Geschichte der Deutsch-Ungarischen Literarischen Beziehungen* (East Berlin, 1969), 9–31 and 202–13. On Lenau see, Agnes Huszar Vardy, *A Study in Austrian Romanticism: Hungarian Influences in Lenau's Poetry* (Buffalo, 1973).

13. Susan Gal, *Language Shift: Social Determinants of Linguistic Change in Bilingual Austria* (New York, 1978).

14. Gottas, "Die Deutschen," 219–90; Béla Bellér, "Das ungarnländische Deutschtum im Reformzeitalter, während der bürgerlichen Revolution und Absolutismus," in Wendelin Hambuch, ed., *300 Jahre Zusammenleben-Aus der Geschichte der Ungarndeutschen. 300 éves együttélés-A magyarországi németek történetéből*, vol. 1 (Budapest, 1988), 53–61.

15. Karl v. Klempa, *Die kulturpolitischen Bestrebungen des Grafen Georg Festetics* (Győr, 1939).

16. Pál Gyulai, "Nemzeti szinház és drámai irodalmunk" [National theater and dramatic literature] *Budapesti Szemle* 1, no. 1 (1857): 120.

17. For a general overview of the development of national theater in Eastern Europe, see Emil Niederhauser, *A nemzeti megújulási mozgalmak Kelet-Európában* [Movements of national renewal in Eastern Europe] (Budapest, 1977), 204–11.

18. Gyulai, "Nemzeti szinház," 124.

19. Ibid., 127.

20. Binal, *Deutschsprachiges Theater*, 94–5, 98, 110–11, 101, 129.

21. Gyulai, "Nemzeti szinház," 120.

22. Richard Sennett, *The Fall of Public Man* (New York, 1977), 203.

23. On this theater question, see Laurisin, *Operaház*, 19; Mályusz, *Theater and National Awakening*, 282.

24. Sennett, *The Fall of Public Man*, 203.

25. József Madarász, *Emlékirataim, 1831–1881* [My memoirs] (Budapest, 1883), 8. See also Gernot Seide, *Regierungspolitik und öffentliche Meinung im Kaisertum Österreich anläßlich der polnischen Novemberrevolution, 1830–1831* (Wiesbaden, 1971), 107–43.

26. Ludwig von Wirkner, *Meine Erlebnisse: Blätter aus dem Tagebuche meines öffentliche Wirkens vom Jahre, 1825–1852* (Pressburg, 1880), 56–64. Wirkner was dispatched to conduct trials of peasants.

27. Zsigmond Kemény, *A rajongók* (Budapest, 1858–9).

28. Veit Valentin, *Das Hambacher Nationalfest* (Berlin, 1932), 31.

29. Franz Schnabel, "Die Denkmalskunst und der Geist des 19. Jahrhunderts," in *Abhandlungen und Vorträge, 1914–1965* (Basel, 1970), 150. See also Thomas Nipperdey, "Nationalidee und Nationaldenkmal im Deutschland in 19. Jahrhundert," *Historische Zeitschrift* 206, no. 3: 529–85.

30. Theo Gantner, *Der Festumzug: Ein volkskundlicher Beitrag zum Festwesen des 19. Jahrhunderts in der Schweiz* (Basel, 1970), 24–5.

31. Emil Dürr, ed., *Jacob Burckhardt als Politischer Publizist* (Zurich, 1937), 43.

32. Dürr, *Jacob Burckhardt*, 43.

33. Ibid., 43–6.

34. Ibid., 55.

35. *Der Ungar*, August 25, 1846. See László Molnár, "Das Pester Modeblatt (Pesti Divatlap) und das Ungarische Kunstgewerbe," *Annales Sectio Historia* 11 (1970):

256–68; László Molnár, *Iparművészeti törekvések a reformkori Magyarországon* [Industrial arts advances in Reform-era Hungary] (Budapest, 1976).

36. István Fenyő, György Kókay, Domokos Kosáry, Ilona T. Erdélyi, Aranka Ugrin, *A magyar sajtó története* [A History of the Hungarian Press], vol. 1, *1705–1808* (Budapest, 1979), 665–713.

37. See Götz Mavius, *Dénes von Pázmándy der Jüngere, 1816–1856: Ein Beitrag zur Geschichte des Parlamentarismus in Ungarn* (Munich, 1986).

38. For a general discussion of fairs see Günter D. Roth, *Messen und Märkte* (Munich, 1965); Helen Augur, *The Book of Fairs* (New York, 1939); Felix Milleker, *Geschichte der Banater Jahrmärkte* (Wrschatz, 1927), 10–11.

39. Julius Seidlitz, "Das erste Volksfest in Pesth," *Der Ungar,* June 24, 1845, and June 25, 1845.

40. *Pester Lloyd,* September 5, 1862; for the development of urban parks, see Zoltán Gombos, *Régi kertek Pesten és Budán* [Pest and Buda's old gardens] (Budapest, 1974), 175–96.

41. Moritz [Mór] Gelléri, *Der Ungarische Landes-Industrieverein, 1842–1912* (Budapest, 1912), 12. On the early history of Hungarian exhibitions see Gábor Nyárády, *Az első magyar iparműkiállítás* [The first Hungarian industrial arts exhibition] (Budapest, 1962), and Mór Gelléri, *A kiállítások története, fejlődése és rendszeresítése* [A history of exhibitions, their development and organization] (Budapest, 1885), 79–150; Béla Kenéz, *Ipari öntudatunk ébresztői és munkálói* [Awakeners and achievers in industry] (Budapest, 1943); G. L. Feldmann, "Die Pester Industrieausstellung im Jahre 1846," *Der Ungar*, August 25, September 2, 8, and 12, 1846. A new festive mood seemed to infuse Pest in 1845, see the *Der Ungar* articles: "Das erste Volksfest in Pesth," June 22 and 25, 1845; "Das St. Stephans-Fest in Ungarn," August 19, 1845, and the celebration of fifty-year jubilee of the Palatine, "Das Jubiläumsfeier," September 24, 1845.

42. Madarász, *Emlékirataim*, 101.

43. Zsigmond Kemény, *Naplója* [His diary] (Bucharest, 1966), 159, 185.

44. On Széchenyi's treatise *Hitel* [On credit], and his role as a reformer, see George Bárány, *Stephen Széchenyi and the Awakening of Hungarian Nationalism, 1791–1841* (Princeton, NJ, 1968). See also András Gergely, *Széchenyi eszmerendszerének kialakulása* [The formation of Széchenyi's thought] (Budapest, 1972).

45. Lajos Kossuth, *Írásai és beszédei 1848–1849-ből* [His writings and speeches from 1848–49] (Budapest, 1987), 19.

46. Jankotyckh v. Adlerstein, *Chronologisches Tagebuch der magyarischen Revolution,* vol. 1 (Vienna, 1851), 84; István Barta, ed., *Kossuth Lajos 1848/49-ben* (Budapest, 1951), vol. 1 in *Kossuth Lajos összes munkai* [L. K.'s collected works], 11 vols. (Budapest, 1951–7), 216.

47. On the statue raising plans of the mid-nineteenth century see, László Pusztai, "A korszak szobrászata," *Művészet Magyarországon, 1830–70* [Art in Hungary], vol. 1 (Budapest, 1981).

48. Adlerstein, *Chronologisches Tagebuch*, 75.

49. Dávid Angyal, *Az ifjú Ferenc József* [The young F. J.] (Budapest, 1942), 26–7.

50. Ferenc Toldy, *Irodalmi beszédei* [His literary speeches], vol. 1 (Pest, 1872), 226.

51. Adolph Kohut, *Kaiser Franz Josef I. als König von Ungarn* (Berlin, 1916), 25.

52. Franz Schnürer, *Briefe Kaiser Franz Josephs I. an seine Mutter, 1838–1872* (Munich, 1930), 84.

53. Adlerstein, *Chronologisches Tagebuch*, 83.

54. Tivadar Ács, ed., *A száműzöttek. Fiala János 1848–49-i honvédalezredes emlékiratai az emigrációból* [The exiles: Lt. Col. J. F.'s memoirs from emigration] (Budapest, 1943), 45. The conscripts would be punished by transfer to restricted quarters in Arad.

55. Adlerstein, *Chronologisches Tagebuch*, 83–84; Barta, *Kossuth Lajos*, vol. 1: 216.

56. Barta, *Kossuth 1848–49-ben*, I: 216.

57. Adlerstein, *Chronologisches Tagebuch*, 84.

58. Ibid., 88.

59. Kossuth, *Írásai és beszédei*, 19; ed. István Barta, *Kossuth Lajos 1848–49-ben*, vol. 1, *Kossuth Lajos az utolsó rendi országgyűlésen*, [L. K. at the last diet of the estates], Kossuth Lajos összes munkái [L. K.'s collected works] (Budapest, 1951), xi, 772.

60. Elias Canetti, "Open and Closed Crowd," *Crowds and Power* (New York, 1978), 16–17.

Chapter 3, Crowds Shaking Nations

1. Sándor Lestyán, *1848 március 15, a Pilvax forradalma* [March 15, 1848, the Pilvax Revolution] (Budapest, 1948); Lajos Hatvany, *Így élt Petőfi* [Thus lived Petőfi] (Budapest, 1967), 2 vols.; László Deme, *The Radical Left in the Hungarian Revolution of 1848* (New York, 1976), 14–23; György Spira, *A magyar forradalom, 1848–49-ben* [The Hungarian Revolution] (Budapest, 1959), 71–90; György Spira, *Petőfi napja* [Petőfi's day] (Budapest, 1975); "Polgári forradalom (1848–1849)" [The bourgeois revolution] in *Magyarország története, 1848–1890* [History of Hungary], ed. Endre Kovács (Budapest, 1979), vol. 1: 76–80; and the contemporary accounts of Alajos Degré, *Visszaemlékezéseim* [My recollections] (Budapest, 1983), 177–95; Ákos Egressy, *Emlékeim, az 1848–49-dik évi szabadságharcz idejéből* [My memories, from the time of the 1848–49 War of Independence] (Budapest, 1909), 1–7.

2. Wolfram Siemann, *Die deutsche Revolution von 1848/49* (Frankfurt am Main, 1985), 177; R. John Rath, *The Viennese Revolution of 1848* (New York, 1969); Carl Göllner, *Die Siebenbürger Sachsen in den Revolutionsjahren 1848–1849* (Bucharest, 1967); Irmgard Martius, *Großösterreich und die Siebenbürger Sachsen 1848–1859* (Munich, 1957).

3. Éva Haraszti, *Az angol külpolitika a magyar szabadságharc ellen* [English foreign policy against the Hungarian revolution] (Budapest, 1951), 109–10.

4. Edsel Walter Stroup, *Hungary in Early 1848: The Constitutional Struggle against Absolutism in Contemporary Eyes* (Buffalo, 1977), 87; István Major, *Honvédélményeim 1848–49-ből* [My experiences as a Honvéd] (Budapest, 1973), 15–16. See also, George Barany, "Two Revolutions in 1848: Vienna and Pest," in *Hungarian History—World History*, Indiana University Studies on Hungary (Budapest, 1984), vol. 1: 62.

5. Zoltán Vas, *Kossuth Lajos élete* [Lajos Kossuth's life] (Budapest, 2nd ed. 1965), vol. 1: 231–56.

6. Participants and historians have cited a range of numbers from 6 or 7 to 10 through 15. Including those who overslept but joined up with the band later, a higher figure is probably correct.

7. György Spira, *A Hungarian Count in the Revolution of 1848* (Budapest, 1974), 50.

8. Spira, in "Polgári forradalom," 72.

9. The text of the Twelve Points was:

WHAT DOES THE HUNGARIAN NATION WISH? THAT THERE SHOULD BE PEACE, FREEDOM AND CONCORD

1. We wish the freedom of the press and the abolition of censorship
2. Responsible government in Budapest
3. Annual meetings of the parliament in Pest
4. Equality before the law in civil and religious matters
5. A national guard
6. Equality of taxation
7. Abolition of feudal burdens
8. Jury system on the basis of representation and equality
9. A national bank
10. The armed forces should swear allegiance to the constitution; our Hungarian soldiers should not be sent abroad; foreign soldiers should be removed from our soil
11. Political prisoners of state should be freed
12. Union with Transylvania
    Equality, Liberty, Fraternity!

Trans. in Deme, *Radical Left*, 16–17.

10. György Spira, *Négy magyar sors* (Budapest, 1983), 100.

11. Mór Jókai, *Életemből* [From my life] (Budapest, 1898), vol. 1: 190.

12. Adolf Ágai [Csicseri Bors], *Budapesti Hirlap*, supplement, October 11 and October 15, 1882; Hatvany, *Így élt Petőfi*, vol. 2: 285.

13. Degré, *Visszaemlékezéseim,* 178.

14. From *Életképek*, March 19, 1848, cited in Hatvany, *Így élt Petőfi*, vol. 2: 268–9. Dániel Hamary, *Hazánk* (June 1886), 553–54, and János Vajda, *Összes művei* [Collected works] (Budapest, [1944]), 1838, 1943.

15. Elek Magyar, *Pesti históriák* [Pest Stories] (Budapest, 1920), 27–31; Hatvany, *Így élt Petőfi*, vol. 2: 273.

16. Péter Hatala, *Petőfi-Album* (Budapest, 1898), 160–2; in Hatvany, *Így élt Petőfi*, vol. 2: 270.

17. Izidor Kálnoki, *Az Ujság* [The newspaper], March 15, 1906; Lestyán, *1848 március 15*, 36; Alajos Degré, *Budapest,* February, 1883, p. 5–6, cited in Hatvany, *Így élt Petőfi*, vol. 2: 273.

18. Domokos G. Kosáry, *The Press during the Hungarian Revolution of 1848–1849* (Highland Lakes, N.J., 1986), 28.

19. Jókai, *Életemből,* vol. 1: 190–1.

20. Klára Lövei [Leövey], *Történelmi Lapok* 6 (March 15, 1894): 53–4; Hatvany, *Így élt Petőfi*, vol. 2: 284.

21. Many gave speeches. Most notably: József Irinyi, Pál Vasvári, Gyula Bulyovszky, Gábor Egressy, Dániel Irányi, Mór Jókai, and a few in German also. From *Életképek*, March 19, 1848, in Ferenc Bay, ed., *1848 napi-sajtója* [1848 daily press] (Budapest, 1948), 16. Hatvany, *Így élt Petőfi*, vol. 2: 282–3; Károly Firtinger, *Ötven esztendő a magyarországi könyvnyomtatás közelmúltjából* [Fifty years of Hungarian book printing from the recent past] (Budapest, 1900), 134; Mrs. Sándor Vachott, "Első és utolsó találkozás Petőfivel," *Petőfiana. Évkönyv* (Budapest, 1888), 2: 64–6, in Hatvány, *Így élt Petőfi*, vol. 2: 227.

22. Degré, *Visszaemlékezéseim,* 189.

23. Adolf Ágai, *Budapesti Hirlap*, (October 15, 1882); Degré, *Visszaemlékezéseim,* 180; Hatvany, *Így élt Petőfi*, vol. 2: 283.

24. Siemann, *Die deutsche Revolution*, 108; Ágai, *Budapesti Hirlap* (October 15, 1882).

25. Imre Deák, ed., *1848, a szabadságharc története levelekben ahogyan a kortársak látták* [1848: The history of the War of Independence in letters as contemporaries saw it] (Budapest, 1942), 27.

26. Spira, *Petőfi napja,* 67.

27. Hamary, *Hazánk*, June 1886; Hatvany, *Így élt Petőfi*, vol. 2: 269, 285.

28. Stroup, *Hungary in Early 1848*, 111.

29. Dénes Lengyel, *Irodalmi kirándulások* [Literary meanderings] (Budapest, 2nd ed., 1977), 16.

30. Gusztáv Zerffi, *Mártius 15dike 1848 Pesten* [March 15th 1848 in Pest] in Sándor Lestyán, *Az ismeretlen Táncsics* (Budapest, 1945), 15.

31. *Életképek*, March 19, 1848, in Mór Jókai, *Cikkek a forradalom évéből* [Articles from the revolutionary year] *Jókai Mór munkái: Gyűjteményes díszkiadás* [Works of M. J.: Collected anniversary edition], 38 (Budapest, 1994), 10.

32. *Életképek*, March 19, 1848, in Jókai, *Cikkek*, 5.

33. János Arany, *Népies politikai cikkek* (1848) [Folkish political articles], October 1, 1848 (Budapest, 1982), 3.

34. *Életképek*, March 19, 1848, in Jókai, *Cikkek*, 9.

35. Egressy, *Emlékeim*, 5. Petőfi's "National Song" was hurriedly put to music by Béni Egressy and József Szerdahelyi, with Ferenc Erkel assisting in the arrangement. Dezső Legány, *Erkel Ferenc, művei és korabeli történetük* [Ferenc Erkel, His works and their contemporary influence] (Budapest, 1975), 61.

36. Kosáry, *Press*, 30–31.

37. Jókai, *Életemből*, vol. 1: 193, in Deme, *Radical Left*, 25.

38. *Pesti Hirlap*, March 18, 1848, in Bay, *1848 napisajtója*, 23.

39. *Életképek*, March 19, 1848, in Jókai, *Cikkek*, 11.

40. Egressy, *Emlékeim*, 2.

41. Imre Deák, *1848 levelekben*, 29. Báró Samu Jósika to Gróf József Teleki.

42. Major, *Honvédélményeim*, 15–6.

43. István Kováts, *Egy szegény pórfiú önéletrajza* [The autobiography of a serf lad] (Budapest, 1981), 262.

44. Egressy, *Emlékeim*, 2; Jókai, *Életemből*, vol. 1: 193.

45. *Budapesti Híradó*, March 22, 1848, in Bay, *1848 napisajtója*, 27.

46. Imre Deák, Palatine Stephen's telegram to Court Chancellor László Szőgyény, no. 22, 33, trans. Deme, *Radical Left, 27.*

47. György Spira, in "Polgári forradalom," 85. See also Josef Polisensky, *Aristocrats and the Crowd in the Revolutionary Year 1848. A Contribution to the History of Revolution and Counter-Revolution in Austria* (Albany, N.Y., 1980), 124; Stanley Z. Pech, *The Czech Revolution of 1848* (Chapel Hill, N.C., 1969). One week later there was a major panic in Baden spread by rumors; see Ralph C. Carevali, "The 'False French Alarm': Revolutionary Panic in Baden, 1848," *Central European History* 18 (1985): 119–42.

48. Cited in Deme, *Radical Left, 27.* Frigyes Podmaniczky expressed the same fear, *Naplótöredékek* [Parts of a diary] (Budapest, 1887), vol. 2: 230. Imre Deák, 33, letter to Court Chancellor László Szőgyény. See Spira, "Polgári forradalom," 73.

49. Iván T. Berend and György Ránki, *Economic Development in East-Central Europe in the 19th and 20th Centuries* (New York, 1974), 33; János Varga, "A forradalom és a parasztság," in *A negyvennyolcas forradalom kérdései*, György Spira and Jenő Szücs, eds. (Budapest, 1976), 82.

50. István Deák, *The Lawful Revolution: Louis Kossuth and the Hungarians, 1848–1849* (New York, 1979), 85; *Kossuth Lajos 1848–49-ben*, vol. 1, *Kossuth Lajos az utolsó rendi országgyűlésen* [L. K. at the last diet of the estates], *Kossuth Lajos összes munkái* [L. K.'s collected works], ed. István Barta (Budapest, 1951), 675; László Deme, "Echoes of the French Revolution in 1848 Hungary," *East European Quarterly* 25 (March 1991): 105.

51. *Márczius Tizenötödike*, March 21, 1848, pp. 11–2, cited in Deme, "Echoes of the French Revolution," 106.

52. Lajos Kovács, March 20, 1848, in Spira, *Hungarian Count*, 54–5.

53. Miklós Wesselényi to Kossuth, Zsibó, Transylvania, March 23, 1848, in Imre Deák, *1848 levelekben*, 41.

54. In Stroup, *Hungary in Early 1848*, 154.

55. Kosáry, *Press*, 34.

56. Ibid., 34. Spira, *Magyarország története*, vol. 1, 94.

57. Cited in Kosáry, *Press*, 36.

58. Deák, *Lawful Revolution*, 95.

59. Stroup, *Hungary in Early 1848*, 161.

60. Ibid., 171.

61. Spira, *Hungarian Count*, 86.

62. Deák, *Lawful Revolution*, 95; Stroup, *Hungary in Early 1848*, 172

63. Deák, *Lawful Revolution*, 95

64. Stroup, *Hungary in Early 1848*, 173.

65. Deák, *Lawful Revolution*, 95.

66. Ibid.

67. Speech by Beöthy Ödön, cited in Tibor Vágvölgyi, *A magyar jakobinusok köztársasági mozgalma* [The Hungarian jacobin republican movement] (Budapest, 1968), 180.

68. István Deák, "The Revolution and the War of Independence, 1848–1849," in Peter Sugar, ed., *A History of Hungary* (Bloomington, Ind., 1994), 211.

69. Translation is my own. For a different recent translation, see George Szirtes, "The Whole Sea has Revolted . . . ," in *The Lost Rider: A bilingual anthology*, Péter Dávidházi, Győző Ferencz, László Kúnos, Szabolcs Várady, and George Szirtes, eds. (Budapest, 1997), 132–3. The anthology also includes a Szirtes translation of Petőfi's "National Song."

70. Deák, *Lawful Revolution*, 96.

71. József M. Értavy-Baráth, *Petőfi* (Buffalo, 1973), 261.

72. Értavy-Baráth, *Petőfi*, 267.

73. For a numerical population table see, György Spira, *The Nationality Issue in the Hungary of 1848–49*, trans. Zsuzsa Béres (Budapest, 1992), 13.

74. Ferenc Deák to József Oszterhuber, Pozsony, March 28, 1848, in Imre Deák, *1848 levelekben*, 52.

75. Wolfgang Häusler, *Von der Massenarmut zur Arbeiterbewegung. Demokratie und soziale Frage in der Wiener Revolution von 1848* (Vienna, 1979), 153–6.

76. Joseph Berg, *Geschichte der Ungarischen Juden* (Leipzig, 1879), 99.

77. Spira, *Hungarian Count*, 55–6. On the pogroms in Sopron see Max Pollak, *Die Geschichte der Juden in Oedenburg* (Vienna, 1929), 95.

78. "Mit nem beszél a német" [What the Germans do not say]. See also, Értavy-Baráth, *Petőfi*, 258–9.

79. Kosáry, *Press*, 263–4.

80. Deák, *Lawful Revolution*, 86.

81. Ibid., 113.

82. *Pesti Divatlap*, April 29, 1848; Blanka Teleki in *Életképek Népszava*, May 8, 1848. See Károly P. Szathmáry, *Gróf Teleki Blanka életrajza* [The biography of Countess Blanka Teleki] (Budapest, 1886); Antonina De Gerando, *Gróf Teleki Blanka élete: A Teleki Blanka kör számára* [The life of B. T.: For the B. T. circle] (Budapest, 1892); *Karacs Teréz, Teleki Blanka, Lővei Klára: Teleki Blanka és köre* [B. T. and her circle] (Budapest, 1963).

83. Ernest Bauer, *Joseph Graf Jellachich: Banus von Kroatien* (Vienna, 1975), 84.

84. Ibid., 81.

85. Ibid., 85–91.

86. Spira, *Nationality Issue*, 44.

87. Ibid., 38.

88. For early disturbances in southern Hungary, see Hermann Meynert, *Geschichte der Ereignisse in der österreichischen Monarchie während der Jahre 1848 und 1849* (Vienna, 1853), 448–64. See also, Zoltán Szász, *Erdély története, III, 1830-tól napjainkig* [History of Transylvania, 1830–present] (Budapest, 1987), 1356–78; J. Subbotic, *Authentische Darstellung der Ursachen der Entstehung, Entwicklung und Führungsart des Krieges zwischen Serben und Magyaren im Jahre 1848* (Zagreb, 1849).

89. *Márczius Tizenötödike*, April 20, 1848, 133, in Deme, *Radical Left,* 48.

90. *Okmánytár Magyarország függetlenségi harczának történetéhez* [Collection of documents for the history of Hungary's War of Independence], ed. Dénes Pap (Pest, 1868–9), vol. 1: 57–9, in Deme, *Radical Left,* 48.

91. Deme, *Radical Left,* 48.

92. Meynert, *Geschichte der Ereignisse in der österreichischen Monarchie,* 221.

93. Ibid., 443–4.

94. Ibid.

95. Deák, *Lawful Revolution*, 113–14.

96. Spira, *Nationality Issue*, 26.

97. Imre Deák, *1848 levelekben*, 75.

98. *Budapesti Híradó*, May 17, 1848, in Hatvany, *Így élt Petőfi*, vol. 2: 379.

99. Spira, *Hungarian Count*, 197.

100. Deák, *Lawful Revolution*, 137.

101. Spira, *Nationality Issue*, 28.

102. Polisensky, *Aristocrats and the Crowd*, 157–64.

103. Egressy, *Emlékeim,* 11–12.

104. Kováts, *Egy szegény pórfiú*, 265–7.

105. Károly Francsics, *Kis kamorámban gyertyát gyújték* [I light a candle in my small chamber] (Budapest, 1973), 245.

106. In Bachó László Dezséri, *Gyöngyös város, 1848/49-ben* [The city of Gyöngyös] (Gyöngyös, 1939), 41–2.

107. Spira, *Magyar forradalom*, 245.

108. József Madarász, *Emlékirataim, 1831–1881* (My memoir) (Budapest, 1883), 154.

109. Kornél Ábrányi, sr., *Életemből és emlékeimből* [Of my life and memories] (Budapest, 1897), 85.

110. Endre Nizsalovszky and Sándor Lukácsy, *Eötvös József levelei Szalay Lász-lóhoz* [József Eötvös's letters to László Szalay] (Budapest, 1967), 168–9; Johann Weber, *Eötvös und die ungarische Nationalitätenfrage* (Munich, 1966), 88.

111. Ábrányi, *Életemből*, 83.

112. P. C. Headley, *The Life of Louis Kossuth, Governor of Hungary. Including No-tices of the Men and Scenes of the Hungarian Revolution. Appendix: His Principal Speeches* (Auburn, N.Y., 1852), 115.

113. *Székely vértanúk, 1854* [The Székely martyrs], ed. Dénes Károlyi (Bucharest, 1975). See also Erzsébet Kertész, *Kossuth Zsuzsanna* (Budapest, 1983).

114. István Deák, *Lawful Revolution*, 170.

115. Ibid., 170.

116. "Nép" [Volk], *Életképek*, May 21, 1848, in Jókai, *Cikkek*, 79.

117. Kossuth's announcement of September 24, 1848, to the parliament at the be-ginning of his recruitment tour, Lajos Kossuth, *Írások és beszédek 1848–1849-ből* [Writings and speeches] (Budapest, 1987), 168.

118. To Dénes Pázmándy, October 1, 1848, in Kossuth, *Írások*, 176.

119. István Barta, *Kossuth alföldi toborzó körútja 1848 őszén* [Kossuth's alföld re-cruitment tour in autumn 1848] (Budapest, 1952), 6. See also I. Lukinich, "Adalék Kossuth toborzó körútjának történetéhez," *Hadtört. Közlemények* (1937), 263.

120. The most famous was the September 24, 1848 speech at Cegléd, memorialzed in Gyula Tury's painting, see *Cegléd története* [History of Cegléd], ed. Nándor Irkvai (Szentendre, 1982), 189–208.

121. Barta, *Kossuth alföldi körútja*, 6.

122. Ibid., 9.

123. Ibid., 7.

124. Csaba Csorba, *Esztergom hadi krónikája* [The military chronicle of Eszter-gom] (Budapest, 1978), 218. On the buoying effect of the crowd on Kossuth, see Vas, *Kossuth L. élete*, vol. 1: 325–7.

125. Cited in Deák, *Lawful Revolution*, 163–4. Kempen would make similar complaints.

126. Anonymous, *Kossuth unter dem Sezirmesser eines Schwarzgelben* (Leipzig, 1849), 28–9; Spira, *Nationality Issue,* 116.

127. John Keegan, *A History of Warfare* (London, 1993), 16.

128. Spira, *Nationality Issue,* 136.

129. *Pesti Hirlap*, November 28, 1848, in Bay, *1848 napisajtója*, 113.

130. Lajos Kossuth, *Hirlap*, December 14, 1848, in Bay, *1848 napisajtója*, 114.

131. "Kossuth felhívása az általános népfelkelésre," Budapest, December 22, 1848, in Kossuth, *Írások*, 249.

132. Petőfi Sándor, *Dicsértessék a nép neve . . .* [Praise the people's name], ed. Sán-dor Lukácsy (Budapest, n.d), 126–7.

133. Baroness Wilhelmine von Beck, *Personal Adventures during the Late War of Independence in Hungary* (London, 1851), 74–5.

134. György Spira in *Budapest története, a márciusi forradalomtól az őszirózsás forradalomig* [The history of Budapest, from the March Revolution to the Chrysanthe-mum Revolution] (Budapest, 1978), vol. 4: 72.

135. For a description of the occupation, see Károly Madách's letter of January 6, 1849, and January 5, 1849, Pest declaration of surrender and expression of loyalty to Emperor Francis in *Források Buda, Pest és Óbuda történetéhez, 1686–1873* [Sources

in the History of Buda, Pest, and Óbuda], vol. 1, ed. Vera Bácskai; *Források Budapest múltjából* [Sources from Budapest's past], no. 98–100 (Budapest, 1971), 182–4.

136. Károly Madách to Imre Madách, January 6, 1849, in Bácskai, vol.1, *Források*, no. 100: 186.

137. Ibid., see also, Zoltán Ferenczi, *Deák élete* (Budapest, 1904), vol. 2: 218.

138. Gusztáv Beksics, *Kemény Zsigmond: A forradalom s a kiegyezés* (Budapest, 1883), 104.

139. Francsics, *Kis kamorámban*, 228.

140. Beck, *Personal Adventures*, 119.

141. József Nagy, *Eger története* (Budapest, 1978), 283.

142. György Gracza, *Az 1848–49-iki magyar szabadságharcz története* [History of the 1848–49 Magyar War of Independence] (Budapest, n.d.), vol. 4: 197–200; F. A., "Márczius 15-ike az abszolutizmusban," *Magyar Hirlap*, March 15, 1906.

143. Gracza, *1848–49-iki magyar szabadságharcz*, 201–2.

144. Ibid., 202–3.

145. Francsics, *Kis kamorámban*, 212.

146. Ibid.

147. *Közlöny*, March 14, 1849.

148. Francsics, *Kis kamorámban*, 222.

149. Josef Némedy, *Die Belagerungen der Festung Ofen in den Jahren 1686 und 1849* (Pest 1852), 70–71.

150. Ibid., 139.

151. On the military miscalculations involved in the drawn out campaign, see Deák, *Lawful Revolution*, 270–4.

152. Charles Loring Brace, *Hungary in 1851; with an Experience of the Austrian Police* (New York, 1852), 39–40.

153. Anonymous, *Die magyarische Revolution im Jahre 1848 und 1849* (Pest, 1852), vol. 2: 41–42.

154. Ibid., vol. 2: 42.

155. Beck, *Personal Adventures*, 202.

156. Ibid., 254.

157. Értavy-Baráth, *Petőfi*, 367. See also, Madarász, *Emlékirataim*, 261 and 294.

158. Francsics, *Kis kamorámban*, 232.

159. Ibid., 230.

160. Ibid., 232–3.

161. Ibid., 234.

162. Ibid., 232.

163. In "Fekete-piros dal" [Black-red song], he wrote *Petőfi Sándor: Összes művei.* [S. P.: Complete works], ed. Béla Varjas (Budapest, 1951), vol. 3: 65.

Chapter 4, The Martyrology of Revolutionary Defeat

1. Károly Vörös, ed., "Pest-Budától Budapestig 1849–1873" [From Pest-Buda to Budapest], in *Budapest története, a márciusi forradalomtól az őszirózsás forradalomig* [From the March Revolution to the Chrysanthemum Revolution], Károly Vörös, ed. (Budapest, 1978), vol. 4: 121.

2. Vörös, "Pest-Budától Budapestig," vol. 4: 121. The most recent treatment of this period is, György Spira, *A pestiek Petőfi és Haynau között* [Pest citizens between Petőfi and Haynau] (Budapest, 1998).

3. Cited in Barry Faulk, "The Public Execution: Urban Rhetoric and Victorian Crowds," in William B. Thesing, *Executions and the British Experience from the 17th to the 20th Century: A Collection of Essays* (Jefferson, N.C., 1990), 57.

4. Vörös, "Pest-Budától Budapestig," vol. 4: 122.

5. Lajos Steier, *Haynau és Paskievics* (Budapest, n.d.), vol. 2: 175.

6. Linda Dégh, *A szabadságharc népköltészete* [Folk poetry of the War of Independence] (Budapest, 1952), 100.

7. József Madarász, *Emlékirataim, 1831–1881* [My memoirs] (Budapest, 1883), 265.

8. Sándor Szilágyi, *Rajzok a forradalom utáni időkből* [Sketches of the post-revolutionary time] (Budapest, 1876), 7.

9. Ladislaus Újházy, *A Brief Explanatory Report, as to the Termination of the Hungarian Struggle; the Capitulation of the Fortress of Comorn; and the Objects, Probable Extent, and other Circumstances of the Hungarian Emigration* (New York, 1850), 12.

10. István Sándor, *Világos és Arad a magyar néphagyományban* [Világos and Arad in Magyar folk tradition] (Budapest, 1953), 113.

11. István Kováts, *Egy szegény pórfiú önéletrajza* [The autobiography of a poor serf-lad] (Budapest, 1981), 291–2.

12. See Friedrich Walter, "Von Windischgrätz über Welden zu Haynau, Wiener Regierung und Armee-Oberkommando in Ungarn 1849/50," in Friedrich Walter and Harold Steinacker, *Die Nationalitätenfrage im alten Ungarn und die Südostpolitik Wiens* (Munich, 1959), 68–161; Karl Freiherr von Schönals, *Biografie des k. k. Feldzeugmeister Julius Freiherrn von Haynau* (Graz, 1853), 106–8.

13. Paul Müller, *Feldmarschall Fürst Windischgrätz, Revolution und Gegenrevolution in Österreich* (Graz, 1934), 170–239; Walter Rogge, *Österreich von Világos bis zur Gegenwart* (Leipzig, 1872), 1: 105ff.

14. Steier, *Haynau és Paskievics*, vol. 2: 420; see Éva H. Haraszti, *Az angol külpolitika a magyar szabadságharc ellen* [English foreign policy against the Hungarian War of Independence] (Budapest, 1951), 244.

15. Steier, *Haynau és Paskievics*, vol. 2: 357.

16. Ibid., 359.

17. Ibid., 420.

18. Ibid., 421.

19. Dávid Angyal, *Az ifjú Ferenc József* [The Young Franz Joseph] (Budapest, 1942), 110.

20. Steier, *Haynau és Paskievics*, vol. 2: 256.

21. July 19, 1849, edict in *Források Buda, Pest és Óbuda történetéhez, 1686–1873* [Sources in the history of Buda, Pest, and Óbuda, 1686–1873], Vera Bácskai, ed., vol. 1, *Források Budapest múltjából* [Sources from Budapest's past], no. 110 (Budapest, 1971), 193–4.

22. For the prison correspondence of the thirteen generals, see Tamás Katona, ed., *Az aradi vértanúk* [The Arad martyrs] (Budapest, 1983), vol. 1: 89–318.

23. János Földy, *Világostól Josephstadtig, 1849–1856* [From Világos to Josephstadt] (Budapest, 1939), 35.

24. See Földy, 125. The biographies of women political prisoners still await their historian.

25. Aladár Urbán, "Batthyány Lajosné visszaemlékezései férje fogságára és halálára" [Mrs. Lajos Batthyány's recollections of her husband's imprisonment and death], in *Századok* 115, no. 3 (1981): 598. When Batthyány was imprisoned, Deák provided Mrs. Batthyány with legal advice and urged patience, reassuring her also that his wealth would not be sequestered. Zoltán Ferenczi, *Deák élete* [Deák's life] (Budapest, 1904), vol. 2: 218.

26. István Deák, *The Lawful Revolution: Louis Kossuth and the Hungarians, 1848–1849* (New York, 1979), 334.

27. Erzsébet Andics, *A nagybirtokos arisztokrácia ellenforradalmi szerepe 1848–49-ben* [The counter-revolutionary role of the great estate owner aristocracy in 1848–9] (Budapest, 1981), vol. 1: 445. For official correspondence and trial proceedings, see also Katona, *Az aradi vértanúk*, vol. 2. S. Horváth, *Graf Ludwig Batthyány, ein politischer Märtyrer aus Ungarns Revolutionsgeschichte und der 6. Oktober 1849 in Ungarn* (Hamburg, 1850), estimates the crowd at the funeral to have been some 3,000, a figure that was low since throughout that day there had been rumors of his death by suicide.

28. The priest seems not to have been reprimanded. Katona, *A aradi vértanuk*, vol. 1: 66. See also, Albert Bartha, *Az aradi 13 vértanú pörének és kivégzésének hiteles története* [The entreaties of the 13 Arad martyrs and the official history of their executions] (Budapest, 1930).

29. Vörös, "Pest-Budától Budapestig," 122.

30. Mrs. János Lónyay, diary excerpt in *A föld megőszült: Emlékiratok, naplók az abszolutizmus (Bach) korából* [The world turned grey. Memoirs and diaries from the Absolutist (Bach) era], Gyula Tóth, ed. (Budapest, 1985), 161.

31. Ákos Egressy, *Emlékeim, az 1848–49-dik évi szabadságharcz idejéből* [My memories, from the time of the 1848–49 War of Independence (Budapest, 1909), 167.

32. Ludwig Franz Deinhardstein, *Gesammelte dramatische Werke* (Leipzig, 1857), vol. 6; Tivadar Rédey, *A Nemzeti Színház története: Az első félszázad* [A history of the National Theater: The first half-century] (Budapest, 1937), 241.

33. Vörös, "Pest-Budától Budapestig," vol. 4:124; Spira, *A pestiek*, 659.

34. For an analysis of the Hungarian theater see Pál Gyulai, "Nemzeti színház és drámai irodalmunk" [National theater and dramatic literature] *Budapesti Szemle,* 1, no. 1 (Pest, 1857), 120–39. For a general overview of the development of national theater in Eastern Europe see, Emil Niederhauser, *A nemzeti megújulási mozgalmak Kelet-Európában* [Movements of national renewal in Eastern Europe] (Budapest, 1977), 204–11.

35. The military districts were Sopron, Pozsony, Kassa, Buda-Pest, Nagyvárad.

36. Károly Francsics, *Kis kamorámban gyertyát gyújték* [I light a candle in my small chamber] (Budapest, 1973), 257–8; see also Judit Brody, "The Széchenyi Chain Bridge at Budapest," *Technology and Culture* 29, no. 1 (1988): 104–17; Spira, *A pestiek,* 696–7.

37. David F. Good, *The Economic Rise of the Habsburg Empire, 1750–1914* (Berkeley, 1984), 100.

38. George Bárány, "Ungarns Verwaltung: 1848–1919," in Adam Wandruszka and Peter Urbanitsch, *Die Habsburgermonarchie, 1848–1918,* vol. 2, *Verwaltung und Rechtswesen* (Vienna, 1975), 347.

39. Josef Karl Mayr, ed., *Das Tagebuch des Polizeiministers Kempen von 1848 bis 1859* (Vienna, 1931), 253.

40. Pál Somssich, *Magyarországnak és királyának törvényes joga [Das legitime Recht Ungarns und seines Königs]* (Vienna, 1850), Hungarian edition, 14, 18.

41. Ibid., 14.

42. Somssich, *Das legitime Recht Ungarns und seines Königs,* 112.

43. Somssich, *Magyarországnak és királyának törvényes joga,* 15–7.

44. Somssich, *Das legitime Recht Ungarns und seines Königs,* 113.

45. János Asbóth, *Jellemrajzok és tanulmányok korunk történetéhez* [Portraits and Studies in the History of our Epoch] (Budapest, 1892), 122–3.

46. OL, D36, k. k. A C für Ungarn und Sieben. Polizei Section. Titkos iratok, no. 439, (May 26, 1850), 72.

47. Anonymous, *Biografie des k. k. Feldzeugmeisters Juilius Freiherrn von Haynau* (Graz, 1853), 114. The British government issued a white paper, "Correspondence respecting the Assault committed upon Marshal Haynau" (1851); see Yulug Tekin Kurat, *The European Powers and the Question of the Hungarian Refugees of 1849* (Ph.D. diss., University of London), 1958.

48. Charles Loring Brace, *Hungary in 1851, with an Experience of the Austrian Police* (New York, 1852), 199–200.

49. Péter Búsbach, *Egy viharos emberöltő: Korrajz* [A turbulent generation: Portrait of an epoch] (Budapest, 1898), vol. 1: 285.

50. Rogge, *Österreich,* vol. 1: 227.

51. Ibid., 223, 227.

52. Lónyay, diary, 162.

53. Berzeviczy, *Régi emlékek, 1853–1870* (Budapest, 1907), 63.

54. Johann Heinrich Schwicker, *Geschichte der Ungarischen Literatur* (Leipzig, 1889), 729.

55. For example, see Mrs. János Bánffy (née Wesselényi Józefa), *Emlékirata, 1848–49-i élményeiről* [Memoir of her experiences in 1848–49] (Kolozsvár, 1931).

56. See George C. Rable, *Civil Wars. Women and the Crisis of Southern Nationalism* (Urbana, Ill., 1989); Charles Reagan Wilson, *Baptized in Blood: The Religion of the Lost Cause, 1865–1920* (Athens, Ga., 1980).

57. Lónyay, diary, 164.

58. See Berzeviczy, *Régi emlékek,* 73–4.

59. György Szabad, *Hungarian Political Trends between the Revolution and the Compromise (1849–1867)* (Budapest, 1977), 63.

60. Lónyay, diary, 162–3.

61. József Nagy, *Eger története* [History of Eger] (Budapest, 1978), 285.

62. F. A. "Márczius 15-ike az abszolutizmusban," *Magyar Hirlap,* March 15, 1906.

63. Nándor Borostyáni, "A feketesárga évekből," *Pesti Hirlap,* October 23, 1885.

64. Kováts, *Egy szegény pórfiú önéletrajza,* 337.

65. Rédey,. *A Nemzeti Szinház története,* 241.

66. Ibid., 243. Lajos Lukács, *Magyar függetlenségi és alkotmányos mozgalmak, 1849–1867* [Hungarian independence and constitutional movements] (Budapest, 1955).

67. Bácskai, *Források,* no. 117, p. 200.

68. Hadtörténelmi Intézet Levéltára (hereafter HIL), Militär-Districts-Commando, Pesth (1850), 4.b-485, 519 res., cited in Lukács, *Magyar függetlenségi és alkotmányos mozgalmak,* 35.

69. Ibid., 35.

70. In Selmecbánya, Kassa, and Lőcse. Országos Levéltár, (National Archive, hereafter OL), Geringer-iratok, Pr. 1852–1901, 1954, cited in Lukács, *Magyar függetlenségi és alkotmányos mozgalmak,* 35.

71. Lóránt Czigány, *Oxford History of Hungarian Literature, From the Earliest Times to the Present* (Oxford, Eng., 1984), 138; Mihály Vörösmarty, *Összes munkái* [Collected works], vol. 1; *Lírai és vegyes költemények, 1821–1855* [Lyrics and other poetry, 1821–1855] (Budapest, 1884–5).

72. Czigány, *History of Hungarian Literature,* 137.

73. András Cserbák, *Kalendárium-típusok a Néprajzi Múzeum gyűjteményében* [Types of calendars in the Ethnographic Museum collection] (Budapest, n.d.), 15. Alajos Bucsánszky's publishing house boasted a circulation of 100,000 for their three calendars. See also Gábor I. Kovács, *Kis magyar kalendáriumtörténet 1880-ig: A magyar kalendáriumok történeti és művelődésszociológiai vizsgálata* [The history of small Hungarian calendars until 1880] (Budapest, 1989), 113–39.

74. Szilágyi, *Rajzok,* 8.

75. Pál Gyulai (1826–1909), a Transylvanian Calvinist, co-authored a volume of revolutionary political verse, *National Colors,* with Károly Szász and Ferenc Mentovich. His significant career as a literary critic would begin in the early 1850s with articles in the *Pesti röpívek.*

76. Szilágyi, *Rajzok,* 20.

77. *Magyar Hirlap,* April 25, 1850; see also, Elek Benedek, *Nagy magyarok élete* [The lives of great Magyars] (Budapest, 1979), 254. Newpaper coverage was very slight. Aside from the brief description of the funeral, there is an article on April 26, 1850, reporting the results of the autopsy: pneumonia.

78. *Magyar Hirlap,* April 26, 1850, report from Temesi Banat.

79. Szilágyi, *Rajzok,* 41.

80. Egressy, *Magyar Hirlap,* "Pályám emlékeiből," Dec. 25, 1904, 54.

81. Búsbach, *Korrajz,* vol. 1: 281.

82. Szilágyi, *Rajzok,* 8.

83. Ibid., 21.

84. Búsbach, *Korrajz,* vol. 1: 290.

85. OL, D51b, spy report, no. 580.

86. Gellért Váry, "A Bach-korszak csongrádon," in *A föld megőszült,* ed. Toth, 24.

87. Ibid., 25.

88. Bartholomew [Bertalan] de Szemere, *Hungary from 1848 to 1860,* 36–7. On the Kossuth emigration and the peasantry, see Tibor Csabai, *Kossuth Lajos és az irodalom* [Lajos Kossuth and the literature] (Budapest, 1961), 220–225.

89. Szemere, *Hungary from 1848–60,* 46.

90. Berzeviczy, *Régi emlékek,* 68.

91. Kornél Ábrányi, Sr., *Életemből és emlékeimből* [From my life and memories] (Budapest, 1897), 125.

92. Váry, "A Bach-korszak csongrádon," 22.

93. *Magyar Hirlap,* April 25, 1850.

94. See E. J. Hobsbawm, *Primitive Rebels: Studies in Archaic Forms of Social Movement in the 19th and 20th Centuries* (New York, 1959), 13–29.

95. His name was Pista Cseho. Váry, "A Bach-korszak csongrádon," 23.

96. Sándor Rózsa (Szeged, July 16, 1813–Szamosújvár, November 22, 1878) was a shepherd, imprisoned for the first time in 1836. In 1845 his appeal for clemency was refused, but in 1848 he collected his men and joined the Honvéd army, fighting on the

southern front. His unsupervised fighting troop of *betyárs* probably continued to steal, and the unit was disbanded by the Magyar military command. In 1857 he was captured and tried, but after a clamor of public opinion he was freed in the amnesty that followed the coronation. He returned to the *puszta*, and the same crime pattern resumed in the Szeged area. He was recaptured and died in prison. For Sándor Rózsa's place in the Hungarian imagination see Sándor Szücs, *Betyárok, pandúrok, és hírességek* [Betyárs, gendarmes, and other famous people] (Budapest, 1969); Agnes and Steven Várdy, "Robin Hoods of the Puszta, Hungarian Betyárs: Rebels against Hapsburg Absolutism," *The World and I* (September and October, 1991). See also the novels of Gyula Krúdy, *Rózsa Sándor: A betyárok csillaga* [S. R.: The star of the bandits] (1923) and Móricz Zsigmond, *Rózsa Sándor,* 2 vols. (1949).

97. Dégh, *Szabadságharc népköltészete,* 150.

98. Lukács, *Magyar függetlenségi és alkotmányos mozgalmak,* 396.

99. Dégh, *Szabadságharc népköltészete,* 150, 148; See the tale "Lajos Kossuth and Sándor Rózsa" in Linda Dégh, ed., *Folktales of Hungary* (London, 1965), 223–34.

100. Dégh, *Szabadságharc népköltészete,* 108.

101. Francsics, *Kis kamorámban,* entry of April, 14, 1851, 291–2.

102. "Siralomház" (1869); "Elítélt" [The Condemned] (1872). Pál Karták, *Munkácsy Mihály: Eletrajzi vázlat* [M. M.: A skeleton biography] (Pozsony and Budapest, 1929, 15. Béla Lázár, *Munkácsy Mihály (1844–1944), emlékek és emlékezések* [Memories and remembrances] (Budapest, [1944]), 33.

103. Dezső Dercsényi and Anna Zádor, *A magyarországi művészet története* [The history of Hungarian art] (Budapest, 4th ed., 1970), 1: 426.

104. Dercsényi and Zádor, *Művészet története,* 2: 330.

105. Dercsényi and Zádor, *Művészet története,* 1: 426.

106. Headley, *Kossuth,* 382–3.

107. Görgey as "The Scapegoat of Defeat," see László Pusztaszeri, "General Görgey's Military and Political Role: Civil-Military Relations during the Hungarian Revolution," in *East Central European Society and War in the Era of Revolutions, 1775–1856* (New York, 1984), 473–518.

108. Dégh, *Szabadságharc népköltészete,* 98–9, 101, and 121.

109. The Kossuth and Rákóczi statues were placed in the same square in Pest. Dénes Lengyel, *Irodalmi kirándulások* [Literary meanderings] (Budapest, 2nd ed., 1977), 34–6.

110. Imre Ferenczi, "History, Folk Legend, and Oral Tradition," in *Studies in East European Folk Narrative,* Indiana University Folklore Monograph Series, 25 (Bloomington, Ind., 1978), 96–128.

111. Gyula Ortutay, "The Kossuth Song," in *Folklore Today,* ed. Linda Dégh and H. Glassie (Bloomington, Ind., 1976), 399–401. Gyula Ortutay, "Kossuth," *Ethnographia,* vol. 58 (1952), 263–307.

112. Brace, *Hungary in 1851,* 43.

113. Búsbach, *Korrajz,* vol. 1: 283, 291–3.

114. Lukács, *Magyar függetlenségi és alkotmányos mozgalmak,* 35.

115. Andor Klay, *Daring Diplomacy: The Case of the First American Ultimatum* (Minneapolis, 1957); Yulug Tekin Kurat, *The European Powers and the Question of the Hungarian Refugees of 1849* (Ph.D. diss., University of London), 1958.

116. Headley, *Kossuth,* 323.

117. "Two years after the bloody day of Arad, I first landed on the shores of England, a homeless wanderer, powerless and poor; and I saw my landing become the signal for a universal outburst of sympathy with my country's wrongs, such as no people

ever experienced from a foreign nation. Hungary, a couple of years before, scarcely known by name, I found a household word in every British heart . . ." "My Country and English Sympathy," *The Atlas*, October 13, 1855, in Éva H. Haraszti, ed., *Kossuth as an English Journalist* (Budapest, 1990), 292.

118. Thomas Kabdebo, "Reception of Kossuth in England and the Magazine *Punch* in 1851," in *Hungarian Studies*, vol. 1, no. 2 (1985): 225–34. See also John Komlos, *Louis Kossuth in America, 1851–1852* (Buffalo, N.Y., 1973); Herbert Alan Johnson, "Magyar-mania in New York City. Louis Kossuth and American Politics," *The New-York Historical Society Quarterly* (July 1964) 237–49; Sándor Szilassy, "America and the Hungarian Revolution of 1848–9," *Slavonic and East European Review* 102 (January 1966): 179–96. For the French, Hungarian émigrés juxtaposed Hungarian and Polish independence to the specter of Pan-Slavism, J. Boldényi, *Das Magyarenthum oder der Krieg der Nationalitäten* (Leipzig 1851) [trans. from the French], 110.

119. Headley, *Kossuth*, 241.

120. Ibid., 234.

121. Ibid., 387.

122. Ibid., 247. See also József Ferenczy, *Kossuth Lajos* (Pozsony and Budapest, 1885), 61–4.

123. François Melis, "Neue Forschungsergebnisse zu den Artikeln von Friedrich Engels in der 'Neuen Rheinischen Zeitung' über die ungarische Revolution," *Marx-Engels-Jahrbuch* 11 (1989): 242–57. See also Manfred Häckel, "Der Befreiungskampf des ungarischen Volkes 1848/49 in der deutschen Literatur der Zeit," and Gerhard Steiner, "Die Anfänge der Rezeption des ungarischen Volksliedes in Deutschland" in Leopold Magon, Gerhard Steiner, Wolfgang Steinitz, Miklós Szabolcsi and György Mihály Vajda, eds., *Studien zur Geschichte der Deutsch-Ungarischen Literarischen Beziehungen* (Berlin, 1969), 298– 319 and 247–74. In the post-revolutionary Germany one could at least lament Hungarian revolutionary defeat, if not one's own. For example, Ferdinand Gregorovius, *Polen- und Magyarenlieder* (Königsberg, 1849); Adolf Bucheim and Osjar Falke, *Nationalgesänge der Magyaren* (Kassel, 1850–1); Wolfgang Menzel, *Die Gesänge der Völker: Lyrische Mustersammlung in nationalen Parallelen* (Leipzig, 1851); Karl Maria Kertbeny, *Ausgewählte ungarische Volkslieder* (Darmstadt, 1851); Karl Beck's poem "Honvéds" in *Aus der Heimat, Gesänge* (Dresden, 1852); and Karl Obermann, *Die Ungarische Revolution von 1848/49 und die Demokratische Bewegung in Deutschland* (Budapest, 1971).

124. Headley, *Kossuth*, 215.

125. Ibid., 266.

126. Ibid., 255; György Szabad, "Kossuth on the Political System of the United States of America," *Études Historiques Hongroises 1975* (Budapest, 1975) 1: 501–30; Anna Katona, "American Influences on Hungarian Political Thinking from the American Revolution to the Centennial," *Canadian-American Review of Hungarian Studies*, 5 (Spring, 1978): 13–28.

127. Headley, *Kossuth*, 460.

128. Ibid., 380.

129. Ibid., 280.

130. Ibid., 344.

131. Ibid., 249.

132. Ibid., 247.

133. *Early Christian Writings*, trans. Maxwell Staniforth (Middlesex, 1968), 162. See also Elaine Pagels, *The Gnostic Gospels* (New York, 1979), 70–101.

134. Headley, *Kossuth,* 261.

135. Dégh, *Folktales of Hungary,* 224–5.

136. For the history of the Hungarian emigration see, Lajos Lukács, *Magyar politikai emigráció, 1849–1867* [The Magyar political emigration] (Budapest, 1984); Tibor Frank, *Marx és Kossuth* [Marx and Kossuth] (Budapest, 1985); Thomas Kabdebo, *Diplomat in Exile, Francis Pulszky's Political Activities in England, 1849–1860* (New York, 1979); Tibor Tóth Somlyói, *Diplomácia és emigráció "Kossuthiana"* [Diplomacy and emigration "Kossuthiana"] (Budapest, 1985). For a contemporary account, see Dániel Kászonyi, *Magyarhon négy korszaka* [*Ungarns Vier Zeitalter* (1st ed. Leipzig, 1868)] (Budapest, 1977), 397–512.

137. See also Loránt Hegedűs, *Kossuth Lajos, legendák hőse* [Lajos Kossuth, The hero of legends] (Budapest, 1934); József Ádámfy, *A világ Kossuth-szobrai* [Kossuth statues of the world] (Budapest, [1982]).

138. Headley, *Kossuth,* 323.

139. Ibid., 215.

Chapter 5, The Unquiet Wait

1. Vincze Jankovich, *Korrajzok és eszmetöredékek, 1850–1867 évszakból.* Based on Vincze Jankovich's diary (Budapest, 1871), 23, 26.

2. Christoph Stölzl, *Die Ära Bach in Böhmen: Sozialgeschichtliche Studien zum Neoabsolutismus 1849–1859* (Munich and Vienna, 1971), 261.

3. On the Bach system see László Révész, "Die Bedeutung des Neoabsolutismus für Ungarn," vol. 14, no. 3, *Der Donauraum* (1969): 142–159.

4. Heinrich Friedjung, "Alexander Bachs Jugend und Bildungsjahre," *Historische Aufsätze* (Stuttgart, 1919), 24.

5. Gábor Adriányi, *Die Stellung der ungarischen Kirche zum österreichischen Konkordat von 1855* (Rome, 1963), 30.

6. Friedrich Engel-Jánosi, *Österreich und der Vatikan 1846–1918* (Graz, 1958), 1: 68.

7. Eduard Winter, *Revolution, Neoabsolutismus und Liberalismus in der Donaumonarchie* (Vienna, 1969), 78.

8. Országos Levéltár (National Archive, hereafter OL), kk A C für Ungarn und Sieben. Polizei Section, Titkos iratok, D36 folder 439, no. 306, January 16, 1850.

9. Károly Francsics, *Kis kamorámban gyertyát gyújték* [I light a candle in my small chamber] (Budapest, 1973), 270–1. See also, Walter Rogge, *Österreich von Világos bis zur Gegenwart* (Leipzig, 1872), 1: 223.

10. *Pester Zeitung,* July 9, 1851.

11. Anton Heinrich Springer, *Oestreich nach der Revolution* (Leipzig 1850), 47.

12. *Briefe von Johann Philipp Freiherrn von Wessenberg aus den Jahren 1848–1858 an Isordink-Kostnitz* (Leipzig 1877), l: 181.

13. OL, kk A C für Ministerial Commisarrats Amt des Kaschauer, D 51b–333, Nov 1850.

14. OL, kk A C für Ungarn und Sieben, Polizei Section, Titkos iratok, D36, 301–600, P. J., internal memorandum of September 18, 1850, no. 392.

15. Bartholomew de [Bertalan] Szemere, *Hungary from 1848 to 1860* (London, 1860), 35.

16. Ibid., 33–4.

17. Ibid., 34–35.

18. Ibid., 36.

19. Karl Megner, *Beamte. Wirtschafts- und sozialgeschichtliche Aspekte des k. k. Beamtentums* (Vienna, 1985), 258–62.

20. Szemere, *Hungary*, 36.

21. Gellért Váry, "A Bach-korszak Csongrádon" [The Bach era in Csongrád], in *A föld megőszült, emlékiratok, naplók az abszolutizmus (Bach) korából* [The world turned gray, memoirs and diaries from the Absolutist (Bach) era], ed. Gyula Tóth (Budapest, 1985), 1: 24.

22. István Széchenyi, *Ein Blick auf den anonymen "Rückblick" welcher für einen vertrauten Kreis, in verhältnissmässig wenigen Exemplaren im Monate October 1857, in Wien, erschien* (London, 1859); Albert Berzeviczy, *Régi emlékek, 1853–1870* [Old memories] (Budapest, 1907), 69.

23. Augsburger *Allgemeine Zeitung*, as cited in Rogge, *Österreich*, 1: 228.

24. The historiograph of this mood was Albert Berzeviczy, *Az abszolutizmus kora Magyarországon* [The Era of Absolutism in Hungary] (Budapest, 1922–37), 4 vols., and Berzeviczy, *Régi emlékek*.

25. Emmanuel Le Roy Ladurie, *Carnival in Romans* (New York, 1979), 316–7; Mikhail Bakhtin, *Rabelais and His World* (Bloomington, Ind., 1984). On the politics of festivity, see also Michael Müller, "Karneval als Politikum: Zum Verhältnis zwischen Preussen und dem Rheinland im 19. Jahrhundert," in Kurt Duewell and Wolfgang Koellmann, eds., *Von der Entstehung der Provinzen bis zur Reichsgründung* (Wuppertal, 1987), vol.1, *Rheinland-Westfalen im Industriezeitalter*, 207–23. See also Gail Kligman, *Calus, Symbolic Transformation in Romanian Ritual* (Chicago, 1981).

26. Francsics, *Kis kamorámban*, February, 1851, 289–90.

27. Váry, "A Bach-korszak Csongrádon," in Tóth, ed., *A föld megőszült*, 1: 22. In Vienna also "the carnival of 1851 was celebrated as the most sumptuous and light-hearted that Vienna had ever known." Rogge, *Österreich*, 1: 473.

28. Francsics, *Kis kamorámban*, Ash Wednesday, 1851, 290.

29. OL, D129, kk Statthalterei Abtheilung Kaschau Elnöki titkos iratok. Bericht Polizei Direktion, Kaschau, March 16, 1857, no. 71 pras, p. 697.

30. Francsics, *Kis kamorámban*, February 1851, 290.

31. OL, D129, kk Staathatleriei Abtheilung Kaschau, Polizei, March 3, 1858, 95. A fascinating memoir of one anonymous Bohemian official in the Slovak hinterlands is Einem k.k. Stuhlrichter, *Acht Jahre Amtsleben in Ungarn* (Leipzig 1861).

32. Brigitte Hamann, "Erzherzog Albrecht—die graue Eminenz," in I. Ackerl, W. Humelberger and H. Mommsen, eds., *Politik und Gesellschaft im Alten und Neuen Österreich. Festschrift für Rudolf Neck zum 60. Geburtstag* (Vienna, 1981), 62–77.

33. In the battles over the citadel of Buda the southern wing and center of the castle were almost burned to rubble. What survived the flames was scarred by the siege, when Habsburg soldiers fled into the palace, were pursued by Honvéds and fighting ensued inside the castle. Miklós Horler, *Budapest műemlékei* [Budapest monuments] (Budapest, 1955), 1: 296. The new facade of 1851 was remodeled again at the turn-of-the-century in order to expand the space. A single grand ballroom was inadequate for the second capital of the monarchy. Horler, *Budapest műemlékei*, 308.

34. Joseph Redlich, *Emperor Francis Joseph of Austria* (New York, 1929), 194.

35. For discussion of Franz Joseph's political persona see Redlich, *Emperor Francis Joseph of Austria*; Steven Beller, *Francis Joseph* (London and New York, 1996); Jean-Paul Bled, *Franz Joseph*, trans. Teresa Bridgeman (Oxford, Eng. and Cambridge, Mass.,

1992); Éva Somogyi, *Ferenc József* (Budapest, 1989); András Gerő, *Ferenc József, a magyarok királya* [Franz Joseph, King of the Hungarians] (Budapest, 1988); Ottokar Janetschek, *Kaiser Franz Joseph* (Vienna, 1949); Adolph Kohut, *Kaiser Franz Josef I. als König von Ungarn* (Berlin, 1916); Karl Tschuppik, *Francis Joseph I, The Downfall of an Empire* (New York, 1930). For useful details of Franz Joseph's public life, see the monarchist brochures *Unser Kaiser im Glanze festlicher Ereignisse* (Vienna, n.d. [1881]) and *Unser Kaiser auf Reisen und als Gastfreund* (Vienna, n.d. [1881]).

36. Rogge, *Österreich*, 1: 252.

37. Váry, "A Bach-korszak Csongrádon," in Tóth, ed., *A föld megőszült*, 1: 20.

38. OL, Stimmungsbericht, Protmann, Protmann des kk Polizei Direktion von Ofen-Pest, D44, II, May 28, 1852.

39. OL, Stimmungsbericht, Protmann, D44, no. 1128, April 30, 1852.

40. Johann Janstyck von Adlerstein, *Die Rundreise Sr. k. k. apost. Majestät Franz Joseph des Ersten durch Ungarn und Siebenbürgen im Jahre 1852* (Vienna, 1852), 3.

41. Josef Karl Mayr, ed., *Das Tagebuch des Polizeiministers Kempen von 1848 bis 1859* (Vienna, 1931), 256.

42. See Richard Wortman, "Rule by Sentiment: Alexander II's Journeys through the Russian Empire, *American Historical Review*, vol. 95, no. 3 (June 1990): 745–71; Richard Wortman, *Scenarios of Power. Myth and Ceremony in Russian Monarchy*, vol. 1 (Princeton, 1995).

43. Adlerstein, *Die Rundreise Franz Joseph im Jahre 1852*, 9.

44. Ibid., 32.

45. Ibid., 39–40.

46. Adolf Kohut, *Bismarck és Magyarország* (Budapest, 1915), 15; Redlich, 116. Bismarck was so impressed by the peasant response to Franz Joseph, that in the 1870s he still thought, "If Franz Joseph went in Hussar uniform through Hungary, he would be received with unparalleled cheers everywhere." At another time he conjectured, that "If constitutional life ends there [in Austria] one day, then after the end of dualism, it would remain strong in Hungary, because in the country, especially amongst the peasants, they have an unbounded attachment to the Habsburg dynasty." Kohut, *Bismarck*, 28.

47. *Pester Lloyd*, November 17, 1859.

48. Adlerstein, *Die Rundreise Franz Joseph im Jahre 1852*, 69

49. Kohut, *Bismarck*, 78; Heinrich Friedjung, *Österreich von 1848 bis 1860* (Stuttgart, 1912 [2nd ed.]), 1: 431–3.

50. Gyula Kabdebo, *A szobrászat története* (Budapest, 1909), 165.

51. László Pusztai, "A korszak szobrászata," ["The era's statuary"] in *Művészet Magyarországon, 1830–70* [Art in Hungary] (Budapest, 1981), 1: 33.

52. See József Ádámfy, *A világ Kossuth-szobrai* [Kossuth statues of the world] (Budapest, [1982]).

53. Götz Mavius, "Ungarische Denkmalskunst zwischen Tafelrichterstil und Millennium," *Ungarn-Jahrbuch*, 11 (1980–81): 155.

54. Horler, *Budapest műemlékei*, 1: 586.

55. Endre Liber, *Budapest szobrai és emléktáblái* [Budapest's statues and memorial plaques] (Budapest, 1934), 64; Horler, *Budapest műemlékei*, 1: 586.

56. Liber, *Budapest szobrai*, 64.

57. Rogge, *Österreich*, 1: 274. Robert Kann, "The Dynasty and the Imperial Idea," *Austrian History Yearbook*, 3 (1967): 11–31.

58. OL, correspondence to Agusz Antal, D–41, no. 223/852.

59. Rogge, *Österreich*, 1: 274.

60. Berzeviczy, *Régi emlékek*, 67.

61. Rogge, *Österreich*, 1: 275.

62. Adlerstein, *Die Rundreise Franz Joseph im Jahre 1852*, 174.

63. Rogge, *Österreich*, 1: 301–2.

64. Adolf Frankenburg, "Bécsi élményeim," [My experiences in Vienna], 1–2, (1880), in Tóth, ed., *A föld megőszült*, 1: 121.

65. Carl E. Schorske, *Fin-de-siècle Vienna: Politics and Culture* (New York, 1981), 30.

66. Francsics, *Kis kamorámban*, February 22, 1853, 310.

67. See also, Oszkár Sashegyi, *Ungarns politische Verwaltung in der Ära Bach 1849–1860* (Graz, 1979), 84.

68. György Szabad, *Hungarian Political Trends Between the Revolution and the Compromise (1849–1867)* (Budapest, 1977), 64–65.

69. Rogge, *Österreich*, 1: 285–6.

70. Of 806 lawyers, 176 lost the right to practice. Rogge, *Österreich*, 1: 290; see also József Nagy Szárazberky, "Kiszabadulásom. Szerepem a Bach-korszak alatt" [My liberation. My role during the Bach period] in Tóth, ed., *A föld megőszült*, 1: 143–56.

71. Francsics, *Kis kamorámban*, April 13, 1853, 318; March 15, 1853, 313.

72. By chance, in Trafalgar Square an Austrian spy extracted the information from a disgruntled Hungarian forty-eighter who had witnessed the burial of the crown. Kálmán Benda and Erik Fügedi, *A magyar korona regénye* [The story of the Hungarian Crown] (Budapest, 1979), 201. Tibor Frank, "The War Without Arms: The Secret Service of the Habsburg Monarchy, 1849–65," in Béla K. Király, ed., *The Crucial Decade: East Central European Society and National Defense, 1859–1870* (New York, 1984), 429–43. For Ferenc Házmán's account, see "A korona elásása" ["Burial of the crown"] in *A korona kilenc évszázada, történelmi források a magyar koronáról* [The crown's 900 years, historical documents concerning the Magyar crown], ed. Tamás Katona (Budapest, 1979), 278–80.

73. Benda and Fügedi, *A magyar korona regénye*, 207–8.

74. Ferenc Bonitz, *Gróf Zichy Nándor, élet- és jellemrajz* [Count Nándor Zichy, life and character study] (Budapest, 1912), 37; Benda and Fügedi, 208–9; Rogge, *Österreich*, 1: 290.

75. Lajos Lukács, ed., *The Vatican and Hungary 1846–1878. Reports and Correspondence on Hungary of the Apostolic Nuncios in Vienna* (Budapest, 1982).

76. James Schedel, "Emperor, Church and People: Religion and Dynastic Loyalty During the Golden Jubilee of Franz Joseph," *The Catholic Historical Review*, 76 (1990): 71–92.

77. Rogge, *Österreich*, 1: 223.

78. OL, KK Ministerium des Cultus und Unterrichts, D4, packet 2: 2, no. 3754, 8, Sept 15, 1852.

79. OL, KK Ministerium des Cultus und Unterrichts, D4, packet 2: 2; no. 1348, Ministry of the Interior, January 21, 1858; no. 9078, Ministry of the Interior, May 30,1858; no. 9078, Ministry of the Interior, May 30, 1858.

80. Jenő F. Bangó's vivid account of the pilgrimage, in *Die Wahlfahrt in Ungarn* (Vienna, 1978), while drawn from contemporary sources, nevertheless captures the pilgrimage culture as it developed amongst the post-serf peasantry. See further, Gábor Tüskés, "Religiöse Volkskunde in Ungarn," *Jahrbuch für Volkskunde*, 4 (1981); A.

Vajkai, "A csatkai búcsú," *Ethnographia* (1940), 50–73; Imre Takács, "Vallomás a búcsúról," *Jelenkor* (1969), 786–792; Ernő Kunt, "A magyar népi temetők szemiotikai elemzése," *A miskolci Hermann Ottó Múzeum*, 13/14 (1974). For articles on nineteenth-century Hungarian religious customs, see *Népi kultúra-népi társadolom* [Folk culture, folk society] (Budapest, 1971); on Hungarian-Jewish folklore, see Sándor Schreiber, *Folklór és tárgytörténet* (Budapest, 1975).

81. Berzeviczy, *Régi emlékek*, 104–5.

82. Ibid.

83. Bangó, *Die Wahlfahrt in Ungarn*, 37.

84. Rogge, *Österreich*, 1: 311.

85. Bangó, *Die Wahlfahrt in Ungarn*, 134.

86. The Hungarian pilgrimage movement continued the eighteenth century effort to restore shrines destroyed in the years of Turkish rule. Tekla Dömötör, *Hungarian Folk Belief* (Bloomington, Ind., 1981), 246–7. See also Zsolt K. Lengyel, "Katholische Glaube und ungarische Muttersprache. Zur Wahlfahrt in Csíksomlyó," *Ungarn-Jahrbuch*, 15 (1987): 210–18.

87. Garay died November 5, 1853 and was buried in the Kerepesi cemetery. In 1908 his remains were placed in a more decorative grave. József Ferenczy, *Garay János életrajza* [Biography of J. G.] (Budapest, 1883); János Jeney, *Garay János* (Budapest, 1932); and István Bodnár, *Garay-Album. Garay János emlékszobránek leleplezése ünnepére* [J. G. Album. On the occasion of the unveiling of his memorial statue] (Budapest, 1898).

88. *Hölgyfutár*, February 6, 1850.

89. James Steven Curl, *The Victorian Celebration of Death* (London, 1972), 20.

90. "Mihály Vörösmarty," *Báró Kemény Zsigmond munkáiból* [From Z. K.'s work], ed. Pál Gyulai (Budapest, 1905; February, 1864), 265.

91. László Tarr, *A régi Váci utca regényes krónikája* [Literary Chronicle of Old Váci Street] (Budapest, 1984), 74.

92. Józscf Eötvös, "Vörösmarty emlékezete," [In remembrance of Vörösmarty] *Budapesti Szemle*, vol. 4, no. 14 (1858): 492–501.

93. Mihály Vörösmarty, *Zalán futása*; Loránt Czigány, *The Oxford History of Hungarian Literature, From the Earliest Times to the Present* (Oxford, 1984), 139; See also László Deme, "The Romantic Image of Military Conquest and National Defense: The Poetry of Mihály Vörösmarty," in *East Central European Society and War in the Era of Revolutions, 1775–1856* (New York, 1984), 356–65.

94. For the importance of Vörösmarty to the "cultural program" of nationalism, see Emil Niederhauser, *A nemzeti megújulási mozgalmak kelet-európában* [Movements of national renewal in Eastern Europe] (Budapest, 1977), 150.

95. Tarr, *Váci utca*, 113.

96. Géza Lengyel, "Vörösmarty szobra" [The Vörösmarty statue], *Nyugat*, 1 (1908), 625–6.

97. Lengyel, "Vörösmarty szobra," *Nyugat*, 1 (1908), 625.

98. Mrs. József Rudnay, as cited in Tarr, *Váci utca*, 74.

99. Tarr, *Váci utca*, 74; Tivadar Rédey, *A Nemzeti Szinház története, Az első félszázad* [History of the National Theater: The first half century] (Budapest, 1937), 264.

100. Szabad, *Hungarian Political Trends*, 65.

101. Gábor Preisich, *Budapest városépítésének története* [History of Budapest City Planning] (Budapest, 1960), 1: 75. In 1857 the Pest beautification and town planning commissions were reconstituted, 1: 73.

102. Richard Radó, _Pest-budai emlékek a xix. századból_ [Nineteenth-century Pest-Buda monuments] (Budapest, 1941), 82–3.

103. Francsics, _Kis kamorámban_, October 13, 1857, 385; May 8, 1859, 400; June 30, 1860, 400. Impressions of Pest in entry of February 9, 1860, 405.

104. _Budapesti Hírlap_, June 8, 1853, as cited in Tarr, Váci utca, 76.

105. Tarr, _Váci utca_, 14.

106. Ludmila Kybalová, Olga Herbenová, Milena Lamarová, _The Pictorial Encyclopedia of Fashion_ (London, 1968), 271–2.

107. Honoré Daumier, "Le Charivari," 1857.

108. _Hölgyfutár_, 1857, as cited in Tarr, 65.

109. Tarr, _Váci utca_, 40.

110. See Czigány, _Hungarian Literature_, 198–216.

111. Gusztáv Beksics, _Kemény Zsigmond, A forradalom s a kiegyezés_ [Z. K., The revolution and compromise] (Budapest, 1883), 104.

112. Ibid., 114–6.

113. Zsigmond Kemény, _Forradalom után_ [After the revolution] (Pest, 1850), 1; See also Kristóf Nyíri, _A Monarchia szellemi életéről, Filozófiatörténeti tanulmányok_ [On the intellectual life of the monarchy: Studies in the history of philosophy] (Budapest, 1980), 35–65; Tibor Csabai, _Kossuth Lajos és az irodalom_ [Lajos Kossuth and Literature] (Budapest, 1961), 242–6.

114. Kemény, _Forradalom után_, 2.

115. Ibid., 1.

116. Ibid., 3.

117. Ibid., 2.

118. Pál Gyulai's _Petőfi Sándor és lírai költészetünk_ [S. P. and lyrical poetry], written in the mid-fifties, served as a position statement for Magyar literary realism. Other leaders of the Deák party were Antal Csengery and János Arany. See _Levelezése 1843–tól 1867-ig_ [Correspondence from 1843 to 1867], ed. Sándor Somogyi (Budapest, 1961). For a contemporary assessment of the change in poetic sensibilities and the theater, see János Erdélyi, "A legujabb magyar lyra" [The newest Magyar lyric poems], _Budapesti Szemle_, 5 (1859), 16–17: 211–32; Pál Gyulai, "Nemzeti szinház és drámai irodalmunk" [The National Theater and our dramatic literature] _Budapesti Szemle_ 1 (1857), 1: 120–39. On Hungarian fine arts, see Károly Lyka, _Nemzeti Romantika, Magyar Művészet, 1850–1867_ [National romantics, Hungarian Art] (Budapest, 1942). He contends the fine arts took root in Hungary in this period.

119. Sándor Szilágyi, _Rajzok a forradalom utáni időkből_ [Sketches of the post-revolutionary time] (Budapest, 1876), 101.

120. Kemény, _Forradalom után_, 3.

121. Gyulai, "Nemzeti szinház," 126.

122. Ibid., 131.

123. Ibid., 127.

124. "Gazdag nő" [The Rich Woman], _Hőlgyfutár_, December 21, 1849.

125. _PZ_, June 21, 1851; Binal, _Deutschsprachiges Theater_, 227.

126. In contrast, the Viennese only performed two Hungarian plays in a hundred years, one play by Therese Artner (1772–1829) in 1821 and another by Mór Jókai in 1885. Otto Rub, _Das Burgtheater: Statischer Rückblick_ (Vienna, 1913), 304.

127. Wolfgang Binal, _Deutschsprachiges Theater in Budapest_ (Vienna, 1972), 226.

128. Rogge, _Österreich_, September, 1856, 1: 455.

129. Friedrich Engel-Janosi, *Österreich und der Vatikan 1846–1918* (Graz, 1958), 1: 80–1.

130. Stölzl, *Die Ära Bach in Böhmen*, 115–8.

131. Cited in Wilma Abeles Iggers, *Women of Prague, Ethnic Diversity and Social Change from the Eighteenth Century to the Present* (Providence, R.I., 1995), letters of January 22, 1851, June 22, 1851, May 17, 1853, and May 9, 1853: 58–9, 62.

132. *PL*, January 28, 1857.

133. Ibid.

134. János Arany, "A Walesi bárdok;" N. Mastermann, "The Massacre of the Bards," *Welsh Review*, 1948. Arany sustained his animosity toward Franz Joseph, repeating the same theme of mass suicide in "Inauguration of the Margaret Bridge" (1877). See also, F. Reidl, *Arany János* (Budapest, 1957; 1887).

135. Berzeviczy, *Régi emlékek*, 71; on preparations see, *PL*, March 8, 1857; *PL*, April 2, 1857.

136. Cited in Rogge, *Österreich*, 1: 480–1.

137. *PL*, May 5, 1857; Rogge, *Österreich*, 1: 481–8.

138. *PL*, May 5, 1857.

139. *PL*, May 10, 1857.

140. Adlerstein, 16. *Temesvaren Zeitung. Die Rundreise Allerhöchsten kais. königl. Majestäten in Ungarn in der Zeit vom 4. bis 30, Mai 1857* (Temesvár, 1857); *Temesvaren Zeitung, Die Rundreise Allerhöchsten kais. königl. Majestäten in Ungarn in der Zeit vom 8. August bis 5, September1857* (Temesvár, 1857).

141. Binal, *Deutschsprachiges Theater*, 243.

142. Rogge, *Österreich*, 1: 482–3.

143. *PL*, May 8, 1857.

144. On the nationalist role of the National Agricultural Association, see Arpád Balás von Sipek, *Kurzer Abriss der Geschichte der Ungarischen Landwirtschaft* (Budapest, 1897).

145. Christopher Hobhouse, *1851 and the Crystal Palace* (New York, 1937).

146. Martin J. Wiener, *English Culture and the Decline of the Industrial Spirit, 1850–1980* (Cambridge, 1981).

147. On Hcvcs county exhibition of November 20–22, 1858, *PN*, Dec. 3, 1858.

148. *PL*, May 9 and 16, 1857.

149. *PL*, May 13 and 24, 1857.

150. In the absence of the sovereign, the Kóztelek exhibition was convened by Archduke Albrecht. *PL*, May 31, 1857; *PL*, June 4, 7, 8, and 11, 1857. *PL*, June 24, 1857 complains of the weak attendance at the Kassau exhibition.

151. *PL*, May 26, 1857.

152. *PL*, June 3, 1857.

153. *PL*, May 31, 1857.

154. *PL*, August 11, 1857. Alexander Bertók, *Andenken an die Allerhöchste Anwesenheit Sr. k. k. Apost. Majestät Franz Josef I. Kaiser von Oesterreich, König von Ungarn etc am 8., 9., 10, und 11. August 1857 in Oedenburg* (Oedenburg, 1857).

155. *PL*, September 9, 1857.

156. *PL*, September 6 and 11, 1857; Szabad, 65.

157. Rogge, *Österreich*, 1: 360.

158. The Dessewffy family played a leading role in fashioning Hungarian conservatism. The father Joseph (1771–1843), a friend of Széchenyi, had believed that only

the Austrian connection prevented Hungary from experiencing the fate of Poland. His three sons, Aurel (1808–1842), Marzel (1812–1886), and Emil (1813–1866), each played an important role in fashioning a reformist Hungarian conservatism. See Béla Menczer, "Ungarischer Konservatismus," in Gerd-Klaus Kaltenbrunner, ed., *Rekonstruktion des Konservatismus* (Freiburg, 1972), 219–40.

159. *PN*, December 22, 1858; also articles of December 21, 23, and 25, 1858.

160. Ágnes R. Varkonyi, "Polgári és nemesi, racionális és romantikus tudománypolitikai elvek ütközőjén" [The conflict between bourgeois and gentry, rationalism and romanticism in intellectual politics], in Sándor Kónya, Domokos Kosáry, László Makkai, Ervin Pamlényi, Lóránt Tilkovszky, Ágnes R. Várkonyi, László Vekerdi, Antal Vörös, *A Magyar Tudományos Akadémia másfél évszázada, 1825–1975* [A century and a half of the Magyar Academy of Science, 1825–1975] (Budapest, 1975), 90–96. See also István Sőtér: *A sas és a serleg. Akadémiai arcképek* [The eagle and the chalice, Portraits of the Academy] (Budapest, 1975).

161. OL, Staathatleriei Abtheilung (SA) Kaschau, 1859, D129, packet 4, no. 132, 112 (May 7, 1859); D129, SA Kaschau, 1859, packet 3, no. 39, 195–7; D129, 1859, packet 4, no. 11.

162. OL, D129, SA Kaschau, 1859, packet 4, no. 124, 60 (Feb. 23, 1859).

163. OL, D129, SA Kaschau, 1859, packet 4, no. 158, 449 (Nov. 24, 1859).

164. OL, D129, SA Kaschau, 1859, packet 4, no. 132, 112 (May 7, 1859).

165. OL, D129, SA Kaschau, 1859, packet 4, no. 132, 143 (May 31, 1859).

166. Péter Búsbach, *Egy viharos emberöltő; korrajz* [A turbulent generation; Portrait of an epoch] (Budapest, 1899), 2: 26.

167. For a synopsis of Jókai's journalistic career, see József Ferenczy, *Irodalmi dolgozatok* [Literary papers] (Budapest, 1899), 1–22.

168. Liber, *Budapest szobrai*, 67.

169. Rédey, *A Nemzeti Szinház története*, 268.

170. Liber, *Budapest szobrai*, 67.

171. Sculpted by László Dunaiszky. Liber, *Budapest szobrai*, 68; Mavius, "Ungarische Denkmalskunst," 158–61.

172. Liber, *Budapest szobrai*, 68, and drawing of the statue, 73.

Chapter 6, The Emergence of the Chastened Crowd

1. János Reizner, *Szeged története* [History of Szeged] (Szeged, 1899), vol. 2: 229.

2. On the development of a Hungarian newspaper culture, see Béla Dezsényi and György Nemes, *A magyar sajtó 250 éve,* [250 Years of the Hungarian Press], vol.1 (Budapest, 1954); György Kókay, ed., *A magyar sajtó története* [History of the Hungarian Press], 2 vols. (Budapest, 1979). Domokos Kosáry and Béla Németh, eds., *A magyar sajtó története* [History of the Hungarian Press], vol. 2/1 and 2/2, 1848–67 (Budapest, 1985). *Magyar folyóiratok programcikkeinek válogatott gyűjteménye* [A Selected collection of manifestos from Hungarian journals], György Kókay, Ambrus Oltványi, and Kálmán Vargha, eds. (Budapest, 1978), 186–95.

3. According to Albert Berzeviczy in *Régi emlékek, 1853–1870* [Old memories] (Budapest, 1907), 32–3, in lyric poetry and general usage contemporaries called the revolution "the revolution," until Mihály Horvát referred to it as "the war of Hungarian independence" in *Magyarország függetlenségi harcának története 1848 és 1849-*

ben [History of Hungary's War of Independence in 1848 and 1849], 3 vols. (Pest, 1871–2).

4. Louis Kossuth, *Memoirs of My Exile* (New York, 1880), 402.

5. Ernst Birke, *Frankreich und Ostmitteleuropa im 19. Jahrhundert* (Cologne, 1960), 211–19. See Lajos Lukács, "Military Organizations of the Hungarian Exiles, 1859–67"; Thomas Kabdebo, "The Hungarian National Directorate and the 1859 War"; and Paolo Santarcangeli, "Hungarian Armed Units in Italy, 1848–67," in Béla K. Király, ed., *The Crucial Decade: East Central European Society and National Defense, 1859–1870* (New York, 1984), 457–68; 469–82; 483–95. The appeal of Generals Klapka and Perczel on May 20, 1859, 629–30.

6. OL, D129, 1859, packet 3, no. 73, p. 290.

7. Kossuth, *Memoirs of My Exile*, 405.

8. Reizner, *Szeged története*, vol. 2: 228.

9. Országos Levéltár (National Archive, hereafter OL), kk Staathalterei Abtheilung Kaschau, D129, 1859, packet 3, no. 40, Buda, May 28, 1859.

10. OL, D129, 1859, packet 3, no. 42, p. 216, June 9,1859.

11. OL, D129, 1859, packet 3, no. 61, p. 245, Vienna Ministry of Interior to Poche.

12. OL, D129, 1859, packet 3, no. 80, p. 341 and 343.

13. OL, D129, 1859, packet 3, no. 80, p. 345.

14. József Nagy, *Eger története* [History of Eger] (Budapest, 1978), 286–7.

15. See István Deák, "Defeat at Solferino: The Nationality Question and the Habsburg Army in the War of 1859," in Béla K. Király, ed., *The Crucial Decade. East Central European Society and National Defense, 1859–1870* (New York 1984), 496–516.

16. Oskar Sashegyi, *Ungarns politische Verwaltung in der Ära Bach 1849–1860* (Graz, 1979). General Crenneville, who succeeded General Grünne, wrote his wife, "Bach's resignation resembles a victory." Klaus Koch, *Generaladjutant Franz Crenneville. Politik und Militär zwischen Krimkrieg und Königgrätz* (Vienna, 1984), 108.

17. On the patent see Friedrich Gottas, *Die Frage der Protestanten in Ungarn in der Ära des Neoabsolutismus. Das ungarische Protestantenpatent vom I. September 1859* (Munich, 1965).

18. Walter Rogge, *Österreich von Világos bis zur Gegenwart* (Leipzig, 1872), vol. 2: 19; see also Gottas *Die Frage der Protestanten*, 90.

19. Gottas, *Die Frage der Protestanten*, 88.

20. *Österreichisches Zeitung* article publicized the sharp criticism, cited in Gottas, *Die Frage der Protestanten*, 85.

21. Imre Visi, *Tisza Kálmán: Politikai jellemrajz, a tízéves miniszterelnöki jubilaeum alkalmából* [Kálmán Tisza: Political portrait, on the occasion of his tenth year as minister president] (Pozsony, 1885), 17. Lajos Lukács, *Magyar függetlenségi és alkotmányos mozgalmak, 1849–1867* [Hungarian independence and constitutionalist movements, 1849–1867] (Budapest, 1955).

22. Béla Király, *Hungary in the Late Eighteenth Century: The Decline of Enlightened Despotism* (New York, 1969), 270; See also Ernst Wangermann, *From Joseph II to the Jacobin Trials: Government Policy and Public Opinion in the Habsburg Dominions in the Period of the French Revolution*, 2d ed. (Westport, Conn., 1969).

23. *Pesti Napló* (hereafter *PN*), October 31, 1859.

24. László Négyesy, *Kazinczy pályálya* [Kazinczy's Career] (Budapest, 1931), 167.

25. Négyesy, *Kazinczy pályálya*, 167; Sándor Fekete, *Számadás az ünnepről. Régi viták—mai megközelítésben* [An Account of the holiday] (Budapest, 1975), 148.

26. *PN,* October 9, 1859.

27. On "the philological-lexiographic revolution," see Benedict Anderson, *Imagined Communities, Reflections on the Origin and Spread of Nationalism* (London, 1983), 80.

28. Lajos Kéky, *A százéves Kisfaludy Társaság, 1836–1936* [The Centennial of the Kisfaludy Society] (Budapest, 1936), 104–5. Ultimately, though, nationalism was built on a martyrology that was essentially emotional and poetic. The Kisfaludy Society was reconstituted in 1860 and a Kazinczy Society was never organized.

29. For an analysis of the Schiller rhetoric of these years see, Alex Gehring, *Genie und Verehrergemeinde* (Bonn, 1968), 75. See also pp. 72–87, 96–114. On the émigrés' press campaign for Kazinczy celebration, see Harald Stein, *Die Stellungnahmen der grossen Pariser Presse zum Österreichischen Verfassungs- und Reichsproblem in den Jahren 1859 bis 1861 unter besonderer Berücksichtigung des Österreichisch-Ungarischen Verfassungskonfliktes* (Cologne, 1970).

30. *Pester Lloyd* (hereafter *PL*), October 28, 1859.

31. "We will not bow so low as to respond," wrote the *PN*, but then proceeded to quote other derogatory statements made by Austrians, such as that "Hungarians are wild and lazy." *PN,* October 30, 1859 and *PL*, October 29, 1859.

32. *PL*, October 25, 1859.

33. *PL*, October 28, 1859.

34. *PL*, November 19, 1859 report from the *Szerbszski Dnevnik.*

35. *PL*, October 28, 1859.

36. Ibid.

37. The poem was written by Károly Szász. József Eötvös, "Kazinczy Ferencz," in *Beszédek* [Speeches] (Budapest, n.d.), vol. 1: 74–94. Paul Bödy, *Joseph Eötvös and the Modernization of Hungary, 1840–1870* (New York, 2d ed., 1985), 75–9. See also Steven Várdy, *Baron Joseph Eötvös, 1813–1871: A literary biography* (New York, 1987). Toldy related Kazinczy's career and rushed to press with the first Kazinczy biography: Ferenc Toldy, *Kazinczy Ferenc és kora* [Ferencz Kazinczy and his times] (Pest, 1859). Editing of Kazinczy's correspondence followed promptly.

38. *PN,* October 29, 1859; *PL,* October 28, 1859; see also Péter Hanák, *The First Attempt at the Austro-Hungarian Compromise, 1859–1860* (Budapest, 1975), 14. On Deák see, Béla Király, *Ferenc Deák* (Boston, 1975).

39. *PL*, November 25, 1859.

40. *PL*, November 6, 1859.

41. *PL*, November 1, 1859.

42. *PN*, November 4, 1859.

43. Tibor Csabai, *Kossuth Lajos és az irodalom* [Lajos Kossuth and the literature] (Budapest, 1961), 227.

44. *PN*, November 5, 1859.

45. Négyesy, *Kazinczy pályálya*, 168.

46. *PL*, December 30, 1859; January 1, 1860.

47. János Erdélyi, *Úti levelek, naplók* [Travel letters, diaries] (Budapest, 1985), 113.

48. Ibid., 111.

49. Ibid., 113.

50. Ibid., 115.

51. *PN*, November 4, 1859.

52. Sándor Halmágyi, "We are living in serious and instructive times!" *PN*, November 6, 1859.

53. Keith Hitchins, *Orthodoxy and Nationality: Andreiu Şaguna and the Rumanians of Transylvania, 1846–1873* (Cambridge, Mass., 1977), 255. Permission was denied until November 1861.

54. Hitchins, *Orthodoxy and Nationality*, 100.

55. Irmgard Martius, *Großösterreich und die Siebenbürger Sachsen 1848–1859* (Munich, 1957).

56. Hitchins, *Orthodoxy and Nationality*, 115.

57. *PL*, November 23, 1859.

58. József Eötvös, *Összes művei* [Collected Works], vol. 8: 1, *Beszédek* [Speeches], (Budapest, 1902), 235–8.

59. László Katus, "József Eötvös and Ferenc Deák: Laws on Nationalities," in *Geopolitics in the Danube Region, Hungarian Reconciliation Efforts, 1848–1998*, ed. Ignác Romsics and Béla K. Király (Budapest, 1999), 139.

60. Eduard von Wertheimer, *Graf Julius Andrássy: Sein Leben und seine Zeit* (Stuttgart, 1910), vol. 1: 118. Two banquets were hosted by the primate for the occasion. One was laid for 500, while the most elite were invited to a banquet for 125. The confrontation took place at this elite gathering. See also Dávid Angyal, *Gróf Andrássy Gyula (1823–1890)* [Count G. Andrássy] (Budapest, 1941).

61. Wertheimer, 1: 118.

62. November 21, Pest. János Szeberényi, *A császár-király és a reformata vallás, vagyis: Boldogházy István R . . . falusi jegyző és fia közti levelezés az 1859-ki sept. 1-én kelt cs. kir nyiltparancsra vonatkozólag* [The Emperor-King and the protestant religion, or: Stephen Boldogházy village R. notary and son's correspondence concerning the September 1, 1859 patent decree] (Pest, 1860), 14.

63. Gottas, *Die Frage der Protestanten*, 145.

64. Among the publicists of the Hungarian Protestant cause were Mór Ballagi, *Die Protestantenfrage in Ungarn und die Politik Österreichs* (Hamburg, 1860), 2 vols.; Sándor Imre, "Emlékbeszéd Ballagi Mór Magyar Tudományos Akadémiai rendes tagról" [Memorial speech in honor of Mór Ballagi, regular member of the Hungarian Academy of Sciences], *Magyar Tudományos Akadémiai emlékbeszédek* [Commemorative addresses of the Hungarian Academy of Sciences], vol. 7, no. 7, 175.

65. Gottas, *Die Frage der Protestanten*, 85–9.

66. Jenő Rados, *Magyar építészet történet* [Architectural history of Hungary] (Budapest, 3d ed., 1975), 292. In smaller and larger ways signs of the oppressive years were disappearing. For instance, "Haynau Square" in Pozsony was to be called "Charity Square" again. *PL*, January 15, 1860. The bank made their contribution public on January 27, 1860. The government contribution was 5,000 forints.

67. Péter Búsbach, *Egy viharos emberöltő: Korrajz* [A turbulent generation; Portrait of an epoch] (Budapest, 1899), vol. 2: 22.

68. Albert Berzeviczy, *Régi emlékek, 1853–1870* [Old Memories] (Budapest, 1907), 122.

69. Berzeviczy, *Régi emlékek*, 124–5.

70. Ibid., 125.

71. Károly Francsics, *Kis kamorámban gyertyát gyújték* [I light a candle in my small chamber] (Budapest, 1973), April 8, 1860, 413–4.

72. Szabolcs Seléndy, ed., *Temetőkert. Magyar és külföldi temetők története és művészete fejfák, sírkövek, kolumbáriumok, a temetőkert díszítése és ápolása, a tervezés feladatai—jogok és kötelességek, sírgondozási, szolgáltatások, növényválasztási tanácsok* [Cemetery Gardens: The history of Hungarian and foreign cemeteries . . .]

(Budapest, 1972), 38; See also, Judit Lakner, *Halál a századfordulón* [Death at the turn of the century] (Budapest, 1993).

73. Búsbach, *Egy viharos emberöltő*, vol. 2: 23.

74. *PL,* April 3, 1857, article called for a series of monuments throughout the land, including a Széchenyi statue in Suspension Bridge Square in Pest. It also visualized some great monument at Mohács which every Hungarian would feel obliged to visit once in his lifetime. See also George L. Mosse, "National Cemeteries and National Revival: The Cult of the Fallen Soldiers in Germany," *Journal of Contemporary History* 14 (1979): 1–20.

75. *PL*, November 23, 1859.

76. Ferenc Toldy, *Új Magyar Múzeum* (1860).

77. *PL*, November 1, 1859.

78. *PL*, March 16, 1860. For helping to draft the student proclamation of 1860, Árpád Hindy and his brother were arrested on charges of treason a few days before March 15. See also, Lukács, *Magyar függetlenségi és alkotmányos mozgalmak.* Táncsics was also arrested again.

79. *PL*, March 25, 1860.

80. *VÚ*, April 8, 1860; *PL*, April 5, 1860; László Tarr, *A régi Váci utca regényes krónikája* [Literary chronicle of old Váci Street] (Budapest, 1984), 21.

81. András Gerő, "15 March," in Irén Pilaszanovich, *Nemzeti szabadságünnepünk kalandos története: Fényképkiállítás* [The changing face of our Independence Day through history: Exhibition of photographs] (Budapest, 1992), 14.

82. Berzeviczy, *Régi emlékek*, 128.

83. Von einem Ungarn [Stephen Széchenyi], *Ein Blick auf den anonymen 'Rückblick' welcher für einen vertrauten Kreis, in verhältnismässig wenigen exemplaren im Monate October 1857, in Wien, erschien* (London, 1859).

84. Aurél Kecskeméthy, *Széchenyi István utolsó évei és halála (1849–1860).* It appeared in German as *Graf Stephan Széchenyi's staatsmännische Laufbahn, seine letzten Lebensjahre in der Döblinger Irrenanstalt und sein Tod* (Pest, 1866).

85. *PN*, April 16, 1860; Lakner, *Halál a századfordulón*, 25.

86. See also Wertheimer, *Andrássy*, vol. 1: 120.

87. The day after Széchenyi's burial the Pest university church was again filled for a requiem for Forinyák. *PL*, April 13, 1860.

88. *PN*, April 22, 1860. By mid-May there were also advertisements for Széchenyi figurines. *PN*, May 16, 1860.

89. *PL*, June 23, 1860.

90. For example, see the Széchenyi funeral service in Karcag, a Kuman village, that drew 10,000 people from the outlying area. *PN*, April 10, 1860; see also *PN*, May 5 and 9 for continuing regional reports. Zoltán Varga, *A Széchenyi-ábrázolás fő irányai a magyar történetírásban (1851–1918)* [The main thrusts of the Széchenyi debate in historical writing] (Budapest, 1963).

91. *PL*, June 15, 1860.

92. *PN*, May 1, 1860.

93. Ibid.

94. Búsbach, *Egy viharos emberöltő*, vol. 2: 26.

95. Reizner, *Szeged története*, vol. 2: 232.

96. *Allgemeine Zeitung,* April 9, 1860.

97. Oskar Regele, *Feldzeugmeister Benedek, Der Weg nach Königgrätz* (Vienna, 1960), 186–91.

98. *PL*, May 4, 1860; *PL*, May 21, 1860.

99. *PL*, May 25, 1860.

100. Gottas, *Die Frage der Protestanten*, 145–46. The Szózat would be sung at the Dohány Street synagogue for the first time for a Jewish-Magyar friendship holiday on December 20, 1860. József Katona, *A 90 éves Dohány-utcai templom* (Budapest, 1949), 9.

101. *PL*, July 13, 1860; *PN*, July 13, 1860.

102. *PL*, July 13, 1860.

103. *PL*, July 13, 1860; *PN*, July 12 and 14, 1860.

104. *PN*, July 13, 1860.

105. See also Endre Liber, *Budapest szobrai és emléktáblái* [Budapest's statues and memorial plaques] (Budapest, 1934). "The vivid color, Berzsenyi's passionate patriotic songs could not be fashioned in these times," wrote János Erdélyi, in a 1859 review article on the state of lyric poetry in Hungary. "A legújabb magyar lyra" [The newest Magyar lyric poems] *Budapesti Szemle,* vol. 5 (1859), 16–17: 215.

106. *PL*, May 22, 1860. A Kölcsey statue was also unveiled in Szatmár, September 25, 1860, *PN*.

107. *PN*, June 20, 1860; *PL*, June 27, 1860.

108. *PN*, June 20, 1860.

109. *PN*, June 12, 13, and 20, 1860; *PL*, June 14 and 20 1860.

110. *PN*, June 14, 1860.

111. Reizner, *Szeged története*, vol. 2: 229.

112. *PL*, July 19, 1860.

113. Búsbach, *Egy viharos emberöltő*, chapter entitled, "The mute country," vol. 2: 12.

114. For a portrait of the theater life in an ethnically mixed area see Alojz Ujes, "Das Publikum der wandernden Schauspieltruppen in der Vojvodina im 19. Jahrhundert," in *Das Theater und sein Publikum*, Öst. Akad. der Wissenschaften, Philosophisch-Historische Klasse no. 327, 206–217.

115. *PL*, May 23 and 26, 1860; Búsbach, *Egy viharos emberöltő*, 27.

116. Reizner, *Szeged története*, vol. 2: 229. In 1860 Heinz Kindermann estimates there were around four hundred Hungarian actors traveling around the country. *Theatergeschichte Europas*, vol. 7 (Salzburg, 1965), 411.

117. Búsbach, *Egy viharos emberöltő*, 18.

118. *PL*, July 21, 1860.

119. *PL*, July 24 and July 28, 1860.

120. *PL*, August 16, 1860. Certain types of walking sticks also were declared "banned weapons." *PL*, September 16, 1860.

121. Búsbach, *Egy viharos emberöltő*, 3–12.

122. Nagy, *Eger története*, 287.

123. György Szabad, *Hungarian Political Trends Between the Revolution and the Compromise (1849–1867)* (Budapest, 1977), 82–3.

124. Ibid., 83.

125. Ibid., 82; See Heinrich Friedjung, ed., *Benedeks nachgelassene Papiere* (Dresden, 1904).

126. Reizner, *Szeged története*, vol. 2: 232; *PL,* August 17, 22, 23, 26, 31.

127. *PL*, August 22 and August 23, 1860.

128. *PN,* August 22, 1860. *PL*, August 16 lists the sixteen different contingents of the procession, including guilds, schools, infantry, top officials, monks and other clergy, and aristocrats.

129. *PL*, August 23, 1860. The Primate was greeted by a large crowd when he arrived in Pest and was treated as a hero during the St. Stephen's day ceremonial. *PL*, August 19, 22, and 23, 1860.

130. *PN*, August 22, 1860.

131. *PN*, August 22 & 24, 1860.

132. Police report of August 21, 1860, cited in Vera Bácskai, ed., *Források Buda, Pest és Óbuda történetéhez, 1686–1873* [Sources in the History of Buda, Pest, and Óbuda, 1686–1873], vol. 1, in *Források Budapest múltjából* [Sources in Budapest's Past], ed. Ágnes Ságvári, no. 130: 231–2.

133. Szabad, *Hungarian Political Trends*, 83–4.

134. Regele, *Feldzeugmeister Benedek*, 187–191.

135. *PL,* September 13, 1860.

136. *PL*, September 12, 1860.

137. Károly Kisfaludy, *Mohács* (1824), 522.

138. *VÚ*, June 24, 1860; *PL*, June 26, 1860.

139. Arthur Patterson, *The Magyars: Their Country and Institutions* (London, 1869), 21.

140. Dániel Kászonyi, *Magyarhon négy korszaka* [*Ungarns vier Zeitalter*] (Budapest, 1977; Leipzig, 1868), 409.

141. Kászonyi, *Magyarhon,* 409.

Chapter 7, The Celebration of Compromise

1. *Kann Franz Joseph in Ungarn gekrönt werden? Eine Antwort auf ungarisch-französische Theorien* (Leipzig, 1861), 10–11.

2. See Heinz Schomann, *Kaiserkrönung, Wahl und Krönung in Frankfurt nach den Bildern der Festbücher* (Harenberg, 1982).

3. Iván Bertényi, *A magyar korona története* [History of the Hungarian crown] (Budapest, 2d rev. ed., 1980), 112.

4. Heinrich Friedjung, "Das österreichische Kaiserkrone," in *Historische Aufsätze* (Stuttgart 1919), 9–23.

5. Max Falk and Adolf Dux, *Krönungs-Album. 8. Juni 1867* (Pest, [1867]), 11.

6. *Krönungs-Kalender. Führer durch Pest-Ofen während der Krönungsfestlichkeiten* (Pest, 1867), 5. See also Max Falk, "Die Krönung des Königs von Ungarn," and Adolf Dux, "Die Krönung im Jahre 1867," both in Falk, *Krönungs-Album.*

7. See Emma Bartoniek, *A magyar királykoronázások története* [The history of the coronation of Magyar kings] (Budapest, 1939); Ferenc Eckhart, *A szentkorona-eszme története* [History of the idea of the Holy Crown] (Budapest, 1941); István Csekey, *A magyar trónöröklési jog. Jogtörténelmi és közjogi tanulmány oklevélmellékletekkel* [The law of inheritance of the Hungarian throne. Legal history with appendix of common law documents] (Budapest, 1917). Anton Radvánszky, "Das Amt des Kronhüters im Staatsrecht und in der Geschichte Ungarns," *Ungarn-Jahrbuch*, vol. 11 (1980–81), 1–62.

8. Iván Bertényi, *A magyar korona története*, 97 and 102.

9. Ibid., 108.

10. Oskar Regele, *Feldzeugmeister Benedek, Der Weg nach Königgrätz* (Vienna, 1960), 190; Antonio Schmidt-Brentano, *Die Armee in Österreich. Militär, Staat und Gesellschaft 1848–1867* (Boppard am Rhein, 1975), 382.

11. Károly Francsics, *Kis kamorámban gyertyát gyújték* [I light a candle in my small chamber] (Budapest, 1973), diary entry of October 22, 417–18.

12. *Pester Lloyd* (hereafter *PL*), October 26, 1860.

13. *PL*, December 7, 1860.

14. Anonymous, *Drei Jahre Verfassungsstreit. Beiträge zur jüngsten Geschichte Oesterreichs von einem Ungar* (Leipzig, 1864), 66.

15. Antonio Schmidt-Brentano, *Die Armee in Österreich. Militär: Staat und Gesellschaft 1848–1867* (Boppard am Rhein, 1975), 382.

16. Regele, *Feldzeugmeister Benedek*, 190.

17. László Tarr, *A régi Váci utca regényes krónikája* [Novelistic annals of old Váci Street] (Budapest, 1984), 114.

18. *PL*, October 27, 1860.

19. *Pest-Ofener Zeitung*, cited in *PL*, December 4, 1860.

20. *PL*, Dec. 3, 1860. A similar event took place in Nyíregyháza where intoxicated men, armed with axes, smashed windows and doors. Troops stepped in. Most of those arrested were servants, day laborers, or cart drivers. A curfew was announced, and a warning was issued to employers that they would be held responsible for their servants. *PL*, Dec. 3, 1860.

21. *PL*, December 6, 1860.

22. Országos Levéltár (hereafter OL), D185, kanc. Elnöki iratok, 1861, no. 489, May 17, 1861.

23. For example, Count Nándor Zichy began his political career in these elections. Ferenc Bonitz, *Gróf Zichy Nándor: Élet- és jellemrajz* [Life and character study] (Budapest 1912), 42; József Madarász, *Emlékirataim, 1831–1881* [My memoirs] (Budapest, 1883), 332–8.

24. OL, D185, kanc. Elnöki iratok, 1861, no. 90, Jan. 24, 1861, and no. 164, Vienna, Feb. 5, 1861 to Vay; OL, D185, kanc. Elnöki iratok, 1861, no. 179.

25. As an example of the publicistic literature, see Lajos Ambrózy, *Béküljünk ki! Okt. 1861* [Let's make up!] (Temesvár, 1861); Anonymous, *Die Pacificirung Ungarns* (Pest 1861); Anonymous, *Restauratió vagy revolutio? Oszinte szó a magyar nemzethez* [Restoration or revolution? An honest word to the Hungarian nation] (Leipzig, 1861).

26. *Vasarnapi Újság* (hereafter *VÚ*), March 31, 1861.

27. In the 343-seat lower house of the Reichsrat, where Hungary was allocated only eighty-five seats, with another twenty-six for Transylvania, and nine for Croatia. Bohemia would be represented by eighty-two seats in a "full parliament" and be Austria's partner in the "narrower parliament" from which Hungary was excluded.

28. *Magyar Ország*, no. 47, cited in OL, D185, kanc. Elnöki iratok, 1861, no. 312, Vienna, March 11, 1861, Polizeiministerium to Hofkanzlei.

29. OL, D185, kanc, Elnöki iratok, 1861, no. 375, March 25, 1861.

30. *VÚ*, March 31, 1861. For a description of the development of parties in the 1860s see Adalbert Toth, *Parteien und Reichstagswahlen in Ungarn, 1848–1892* (Munich, 1973), 23–30.

31. See also Péter Hanák, *A dualizmus korának történeti problémái* [The historical problems of the dualist period] (Budapest, 1971), 25–26.

32. Cited in András Gerő, *The Hungarian Parliament (1867–1918): A Mirage of Power*, trans. James Patterson and Enikő Koncz (New York, 1997), 70–1.

33. *Pesti Napló* (hereafter *PN*), March 31, 1861; on the commemoration ceremonies see *PN*, April 9, 1861.

34. *VÚ*, May 12, 1861, 217.

35. Mór Jókai, "Teleki László meghalt" [László Teleki died], *VÚ*, May 12, 1861, 217; *PN*, May 14, 1861; see György Szabad, *Miért halt meg Teleki László?* [Why did Teleki die?] (Budapest, 1985).

36. OL, D185 kanc. Elnöki iratok, 1861, no. 1. For Pest Police Captain Elek Thaisz's report see Vera Bácskai, ed., *Források Buda, Pest és Óbuda történetéhez, 1686–1873* [Sources in the History of Buda, Pest, and Óbuda, 1686–1873], vol. 1, in *Források Budapest múltjából* [Sources in Budapest's Past], ed. Ágnes Ságvári, no. 135: 237–9.

37. *VÚ*, May 12, 1861, p. 216.

38. OL, kanc. D185, Elnöki iratok, 1861, no. 56, Vienna, Jan. 14, 1861 to Váy.

39. *VÚ*, May 12, 1861, p. 216. György Szabad, *Forradalom és kiegyezés válaszútján, 1860–61* [On the crossroads between revolution and compromise] (Budapest, 1967), 211.

40. OL, D185, kanc. Elnöki iratok, 1861, no. 754, Sept. 18, 1861, Buda, László Károlyi to Antal Forgách, Vienna.

41. *VÚ*, May 19, 1861, p. 236.

42. May 12 service in K.-Apáthi, *VÚ*, May 19, 1861, p. 236.

43. OL, D185, kanc. Elnöki iratok, 1861, no. 489. May 17, 1861

44. OL, D185, kanc. Elnöki iratok, 1861, no. 754, September 18, 1861, László Károlyi in Buda to Antal Forgách in Vienna.

45. OL, D185, kanc. Elnöki iratok, 1861, no. 416, May 16, 1861, Polizeiminister to Hofkanzlers von Szőgényi.

46. OL, D185, Kanc. Elnöki iratok, 1861, no. 630, Aug. 22, 1861.

47. OL, D185, Kanc. Elnöki iratok, no. 126, Jan. 31, 1861.

48. Ibid.

49. *VÚ*, February 17, 1861.

50. OL, D185, Kanc. Elnöki iratok, 1861, no. 478, May 12, 1861.

51. OL, D185, Kanc. Elnöki iratok, 1861, no. 579, July 10, 1861, and no. 891, Pest, July 12, 1861. Police to Praes.

52. Stefan Malfer, "Az adómegtagadás és adóvégrehajtás Magyarországon 1860 és 1862 között" [Tax evasion and tax collection in Hungary between 1860 and 1862], vol. 25, no. 4, *Történelmi Szemle* (1982), 662–72.

Percentage of Taxes Owed, by Fiscal Quarter

	I	II	III	IV
1858–9	60%	43%	33–8%	19%
1860	61	44	39	26
1861	88	89	76	39
1862	43	32	28	16
1863	56	40	37	26

In comparison, by the end of the second quarter over half had been collected in Austria.

53. Bertalan Szemere, *Levelek, 1849–1862* [Letters] (Pest, 1870), 130–31. Szemere to György Majláth, July 6, 1861.

54. *PN*, July 14, 1861.

55. Dávid Angyal, *Gróf Andrássy Gyula (1823–1890)* [Count G. Andrássy] (Budapest, 1941), 23–4.

56. *PL*, April 6, 1862; *VÚ*, February 17, 1861, reports Dessewffy had issued a statement that "The nation's Széchenyi statue question was no longer just an idea."

57. *PL*, August 17, 1862.

58. *PL*, November 28, 1862. On the change in artistic style preferences, see "Gróf Széchenyi István emléke milyen legyen?" *Koszorú*, 1863.

59. *PN* and *PL*, October 5, 1864.

60. OL, Kanc. Elnöki iratok, D185, no. 230, February 19, 1864. Banquet of February 1, 1864.

61. *PL*, February 7 and February 8, 1862.

62. For example, *PN*, on April 1 and April 7, 1864, published a long list of contributors and the amount of their donation.

63. OL, Kanc. Elnöki iratok, D185, no. 561 April 20, 1864, Vienna Polizeiministerium, no. 84, Jan. 28, 1865.

64. Sándor Asbóth, *Adalékok a kényuralom-ellenes mozgalmak történetéhez. Az Asbóth-család irataiból* [Additions to the history of the movements against despotism] (Budapest, 1888), 174.

65. OL, Kanc. Elnöki iratok, D185, no. 377, Abschrift eines von der Pesther kk Polizedirektion unter 14 März 1864 an Staatshalterei-Präsidium Ofen.

66. *Der Ungar*, June 24, 1845; *PL*, September 10, and September 13, 1859; *PL*, September 10, 1862.

67. *PL*, August 31, September 6 and 7, 1862.

68. *PL*, June 24 and June 25, 1862.

69. One benefit of the improved Austro-Hungarian relations was the possibility of such travel. Pest was also easier to reach and easy to tour. In 1862 steamboat service between Pest, Buda, and Óbuda expanded to hourly. *PN*, April 9, 1862.

70. *PL*, September 5 and 10, 1862. For the development of urban parks see Zoltán Gombos, *Régi kertek Pesten és Budán* [Pest and Buda's old gardens] (Budapest, 1974), 175–96.

71. *PL*, September 11, 1862.

72. Lajos Cenner, *A szent jobb, vagyis: az I. apostoli király dicsőséges szent jobb kezének története* [The history of the apostolic king's blessed right hand] (Budapest, 1900), 14.

73. *PL*, August 22, 1862.

74. See Éva Somogyi, *Vom Zentralismus zum Dualismus. Der Weg der deutschösterreichischen Liberalen zum Ausgleich von 1867* (Budapest, 1983).

75. OL, Kanc. Elnöki iratok, D185, no. 590–91, May 28, 1863; no. 162, Feb. 12, 1863, no. 836, July 10, 1863; no. 836, July 4, 1863; no. 110, Dec. 3, 1863, no. 1471; no. 256 March 11, 1863, p. 10; no. 364 April 4, 1863; no. 99 Jan. 26, 1863; no. 162 Feb. 12, 1863, no. 256, March 15, 1963, p.1., no. 245, March 26, 1863, no. 358, April 2, 1863, no. 316, April 4, 1863; no. 556, May 15, 1863, p. 2. For instance, Kálmán Csáky's father in law claims he was tied up and forced to incriminate his son-in-law.

76. OL, Kanc. Elnöki iratok, D185, no. 110, February 7, 1865, no. 188, February 17, 1865.

77. Franz Joseph made a "sudden reckless decision" to go to Budapest in June 1865. Edward Crankshaw, *The Fall of the House of Habsburg* (New York, 1963), 201.

78. To Mihály Horváth Letter June 4, Sándor Márki, *Horváth Mihály, 1809–1878* (Budapest, 1917), 295.

79. His first gesture was to visit the race track at Pozsony on April 30, 1865. He was greeted with exuberant éljen cries. Eduard von Wertheimer, *Graf Julius Andrássy. Sein Leben und seine Zeit* (Stuttgart, 1910), vol. 1: 171.

80. *PN*, March 17, 1864 on the "tremendous efforts being made to improve material well-being." Article emphasized railroad building, state support of agricultural investment and agricultural mechanization.

81. *PN*, March 22, 1864, on tenth anniversary meeting of Magyar Gazdasági Egyesület.

82. *PL*, June 6, 1865.

83. *PL*, June 4, 1865.

84. *PL*, June 6, 1865.

85. Ibid.

86. *VÚ*, June 11, 1865.

87. Joan Haslip, *The Lonely Empress: A Biography of Elizabeth of Austria* (Cleveland, 1965), 184–5.

88. *PL*, June 4, 1865.

89. *PL,* June 7, 1865; On Festetics, see Anonymous, *Fotografien aus dem Ungarischen Reichstage* (Pest, 1869), 62–6.

90. *PL,* June 7, 1865.

91. *VÚ*, July 16, 1865, p. 359.

92. Head of the Pest police telegraphed Vienna on June 6, 1865, "Gross war der Jubel," Wertheimer, *Julius Andrássy*, vol. 1:174.

93. While Toldy waxed poetic in his correspondence about "the new times," Batthyány's widow was angry at the display of public enthusiasm. Márki, *Horváth Mihály*, 37.

94. Imre Lukinich, ed., *Báró Eötvös József Naplójegyzetek-Gondolatok, 1864–1868* [B. József Eötvös diary notes and thoughts, 1864–1868] (Budapest, 1941), June 13, 1865, 114–5.

95. Austrian military circles were still convinced that neither the conciliatory manner of the Emperor nor the appearance of the Empress in Pest would settle the outstanding issues. Only cannons could do that, Count Coudenhove told the Prussian military attache in Vienna. Wertheimer, *Julius Andrássy*, vol. 1: 191.

96. Hitchins, *Orthodoxy and Nationality, Andreiu Şaguna and the Rumanians of Transylvania, 1846–1873* (Cambridge, Mass., 1977), 148.

97. *PL*, August 19, 1865.

98. *PL*, morning edition, August 17, 1865; "Pest ünnepélyei" [Pest holidays] *PN,* August 28, 1865. In 1866 much was made of the sovereign's name day, as well. *PN*, March 28, 1866.

99. *PN,* August 20, 1865.

100. *PL*, August 13, 1865, August 17, 1865, August 19, 1865. A singer's festival was also held in Arad in March 1866. *PN*, March 28, 1866.

101. *PN*, August 22, 1865; Tamás Nádor, *Liszt Ferenc életének krónikája* [A chronology of Franz Liszt's life] (Budapest, 1977), 250.

102. Imre Keszi, *Pest-Buda* (Budapest, 1973), on Liszt, 35–8; Tibor Frank, "Liszt, Brahms, Mahler: Music in Late Nineteenth Century Budapest," in *Hungary and European Civilization*, ed. György Ránki (Budapest, 1989), 343–59; on Liszt's subsequent career see Dezső Legány, *Liszt Ferenc Magyarországon, 1869–1873* [Franz Liszt in Hungary, 1869–1873] (Budapest, 1976).

103. Haslip, *The Lonely Empress*, 178–9.

104. Serious study of Hungarian began in February 1863; Rödhammer, 322.

105. Brigitte Hamann, *Elisabeth: Kaiserin wider Willen* (Vienna, 1982), 227.

106. Judit Garamvölgyi, ed., *Quellen zur Genesis des Ungarischen Ausgleichsgesetzes von 1867* (Munich, 1979), 53–6; *PN,* December 13–15, 1865; *PL,* December 12–15, 1865; "Egy képviselő napló-jegyzetei az 1865. deczember 10-kén megnyilt országgyülés alatt" [A representative's diary notations during the parliamentary session opened Dec. 10, 1865], Bácskai, *Források,* no. 138: 243.

107. Haslip, *The Lonely Empress,* 186.

108. László Tarr, *A délibábok országa* [The country of mirages] (Budapest, 1976), 12.

109. See Hamann, *Elisabeth*; Gyöngyvér Czére, *A koronás szépasszony (Erzsébet magyar királyné)* [The crowning beauty (Elizabeth, the Magyar queen)] (Budapest, 1989); Emil Niederhauser, *Merénylet Erzsébet királyné ellen* [The Assassination of Queen Elizabeth] (Budapest, 1985). See for example the last chapter of Captain Walter Wyatt, *Hungarian Celebrities* (London, 1871).

110. Lajos Bátorfi, *Tíz év emléke Zalában, 1867–1876* [Memories of a decade in Zala] (Nagy-kanizsa, 1878), 141.

111. Hans Rödhammer, ed., *Elisabeth: Kaiserin von Österreich und Königin von Ungarn, 1837–1898* (Linz, 1983), 131.

112. Haslip, *The Lonely Empress,* 188–9.

113. Sándor Pethő, ed., "Első lépések a politikában" [First Steps in Politics], in *Emlékkönyv Zichy Nándor gróf születésének századik évfordulójára, 1829–1929* [Commemorative volume on Count N. Zichy's 100th birthday], ed. Anonymous (Budapest, 1929), February 26, 1866, 49. Bonitz, *Zichy Nándor,* 96–109.

114. Pethő, "Első lépések a politikában," March 2, 1866, 49.

115. Pethő, "Első lépések a politikában," March 4, 1866, 5.

116. Haslip, *The Lonely Empress,* 189.

117. Their rivalry persisted into the 1890's when ostentatious mourning for both again became an affirmation or rejection of the Ausgleich. See Anonymous, *The Martyrdom of an Empress* (New York, 1900).

118. A. Kienast, *Die Legion Klapka* (Vienna, 1900), 100. See also, Michael Károlyi, *Memoirs of Michael Karolyi. Faith Without Illusion* (New York, 1957), 19.

119. Zoltán Vas, *Kossuth Lajos élete* [L. Kossuth's life] (Budapest, 2d ed. 1965), vol. 2, 384–459. See also György Szabad, *Kossuth politikai pályája* [Kossuth's political career] (Budapest, 1977), 191–9.

120. Friedrich Cornelius, *Der Friede von Nikolsburg und die öffentliche Meinung in Österreich: Eine Studie zur Völkerpsychologie* (Munich, 1927); Adam Wandruszka, *Schicksalsjahr 1866* (Graz, 1966); the reaction in the army is discussed in Walter Wagner, *Geschichte des k. k. Kriegs-Ministerium 1866–1888* (Vienna, 1971).

121. Haslip, *The Lonely Empress,* 195.

122. Ibid., 194.

123. *PN* viewed Bismarck as a Bonapartist. "The driving force behind the anti-Bismarck feeling of European liberalism was the universal liberal solidarity." István Dioszegi, *Hungarians in the Ballhausplatz: Studies on the Austro-Hungarian Common Foreign Policy* (Budapest, 1983), 98–9.

124. Haslip, *The Lonely Empress,* 196.

125. Mrs. Bánffy, born Ágnes Esterházy, Duchess Stefánia Almásy-Wenckheim, Duchess Katalin Andrássy-Kendeffy, Duchess Gabriella Andrássy-Pálffy, Duchess Franciska Bombelles-Hunyady. OL, Miniszterelnökség, 1867 K26 ME Segédkönyv.

126. Kornél Ábrányi, Jr., "A kiegyezés" [The Compromise], in *Nemzeti ideál,* ed. János Hock (Budapest, 1901).

127. See Friedrich Ferdinand Beust, *Memoirs of Friedrich Ferdinand Count von Beust*, vol. 2 (St. Clair Shores, Mich., 1972). On the Ausgleich see, Gunter E. Rothenberg, "The Military Compromise of 1868 and Hungary," 519–32, in *The Crucial Decade. East Central European Society and National Defense, 1859–1870*, ed. Béla K. Király (New York, 1984); Gunter E. Rothenberg, *The Army of Francis Joseph* (West Lafayette, Ind., 1976).

128. *Vasárnapi Újság*, March 3, 1867. Demonstration was February 18, 1867.

129. Vas, *Kossuth Lajos élete*, ch. 4, "A Cassandra-levél," 460–554.

130. Tarr, *A délibábok országa*, 7.

131. Ralph E. Giesey, "Inaugural Aspects of French Royal Ceremonials" in *Coronations: Medieval and Early Modern Monarchic Ritual,* ed. János M. Bak (Berkeley, 1990), 35.

132. Madarász, *Emlékirataim*, 361.

133. OL, K26 ME, 1867, packets 116, 199, 212, 216, 246, 249.

134. OL, K26 ME Segédkönyv, 1867, 210.

135. These were often delicate, tangled decisions, as for example, drawing up the membership list for the highest honor of the Golden Fleece. OL, K26 ME Segédkönyv, 1867, packets 246, 249.

136. Teréz Forray, *A magyar királyok koronázási szertartásai* [Ceremonies of the Hungarian royal coronation] (Szeged, 1929), 40.

137. *PL*, May 9, 1867.

138. *PL*, May 7, 1867.

139. Forray, *A magyar királyok koronázási szertartásai*, 40.

140. See also Lawrence M. Bryant, *The King and the City in the Parisian Royal Entry Ceremony* (Geneva, 1986).

141. Péter Búsbach, *Egy viharos emberöltő, korrajz* [A turbulent generation; portrait of an epoch] (Budapest, 1899), 209–210. The eight-year-old Rudolf would describe the coronation in his German essay book, "Die ungarische Königskrönung," which captured both the excitement and the tedium of the event ("much Latin was read") in Hamann, *Elisabeth,* 387–8.

142. Counties attempted to collect their soil from their historic sites, such as Aba Sámuel's grave in Heves County, the Alpár cliffs in Pest, and Ferenc Deák's birthplace in Zala. Mihály Latkóczy, *Korona és koronázás. Ünnepi emlék 1892, Junius 8-ára* [Crown and Coronation. In holiday memory of June 8, 1892] (Budapest, 1892), 1–39.

143. The people of Pest-Buda welcoming the king was all Hungary welcoming him. Giesey, "Inaugural Aspects of French Royal Ceremonials" in Bak, *Coronations*, 40.

144. Lukinich, *Eötvös József Naplójegyzetek*, June 7, 1867, 233.

145. Gusztáv Gratz, *A dualizmus kora, Magyarország története, 1867–1918* [The dualist era; History of Hungary] (Budapest, 1934), 1:81.

146. Arthur J. May, *The Hapsburg Monarchy, 1867–1914* (Cambridge, Mass., 1951), 62.

147. For one example of sarcasm toward the 'defiant' Croats and Bohemians see *Spatzenkalender zum Krönungsfest* by Robert Boldini, editor of the *Fackel* and *Spatzenversammlung* (Pest, 1869). The Czechs were characterized as "all Russians" who own a third of Vienna.

148. Kálmán Benda and Erik Fügedi, *A magyar korona regénye* [The story of the Hungarian crown] (Budapest, 1979), 211.

149. Latkóczy, *Korona és koronázás,* 33ff.

150. For Pest city council's description of the procession, see Bácskai, *Források,* 243–5.

151. "Coronation of the King of Hungary," *The Illustrated London News* (hereafter ILN), 50: 1433 (June 29, 1867), 644.

152. Latkóczy, *Korona és koronázás,* 1892.

153. Anton Radvánszky, "Das Amt des Kronhüters im Staatsrecht und in der Geschichte Ungarns," *Ungarn-Jahrbuch* 11 (1980–81): 1–62.

154. "Coronation of the King of Hungary," *ILN,* 50: 1433 (June 29, 1867), 644–5.

155. Bartoniek, *A magyar királykoronázások,* 26. The traditional three questions were omitted.

156. Bátorfi, *Tiz év emléke Zalában,* 142.

157. Gyula Szekfü, "Az öreg Kossuth, 1867–1894" [The old Kossuth, 1867–1894], in *Emlékkönyv Kossuth Lajos születésének 150. évfordulójára* [Commemorative volume for Lajos Kossuth's 150th Birthday], ed. Zoltán I. Tóth (Budapest, 1952), vol. 2: 341–433.

158. Firm measures would be taken to stifle open dissent by Kossuthites in the first years of the new order. Sándor Sebestény, "Regierungsfeindliches Auftreten der Oppositionskräfte des Komitates Heves nach dem Ausgleich vom Jahre 1867," *Annales Sectio Historia,* vol. 15 (1974): 195–219.

159. Miklós Lukácsy, "Az október hatodiki gyászünnepélyek" [The October sixth memorial celebrations], in Ottó Varga, ed., *Aradi vértanúk albuma* [Album of the Arad martyrs] (Budapest, n.d.), 217.

160. *PL,* March 15, 1868.

161. Wertheimer, *Julius Andrássy,* 1: 333.

162. *PL,* March 15, 1868.

163. *Neue Politische Journal* (hereafter *NPJ*), December 2, 1873.

164. *NPJ,* January 20, February 5, December 2, 1873.

165. Lukácsy, "Az október hatodiki gyászünnepélyek," 221. On the critical army issue at this moment see Rothenberg, "The Military Compromise of 1868 and Hungary;" Zoltán Szász, "The Founding of the *Honvédség* and the Hungarian Ministry of Defense, 1867–1870"; and János Décsy, "Gyula Andrássy and the Founding of the *Honvédség*" in Király, *Crucial Decade,* 519–32, 533–9, 540–50.

166. Cited in Tarr, *A délibábok országa,* 19.

Chapter 8, The Exhibition of Liberalism

1. András Gergely and Zoltán Szász, *Kiegyezés után* [After the compromise] (Budapest, 1978); Gusztáv Gratz, *A dualizmus kora* [The dualist era], 2 vols. (Budapest, 1934); Friedrich Gottas, *Ungarn im Zeitalter des Hochliberalismus: Studien zur Tisza-Ära 1875–1890* (Vienna, 1976). István Nemeskürty, *A kőszívű ember unokái: A kiegyezés utáni első nemzedék, 1867–1896* [The stone-"hearted" man's nephews: The first generation after the compromise] (Budapest, 1987).

2. *Mikszáth Kálmán összes művei* [Complete works of K. M.], vol. 53, *Cikkek és karcolatok* [Articles and sketches], III, 1877, p. 42, #160. July 11.

3. Kornél Ábrányi, Jr. [pseud. Kakas Aranyos II], *Tisza Kálmán* (Budapest, 1878), 6. Unfortunately we lack a modern biography of Kálmán Tisza. See also Imre Visi, *Tisza Kálmán politikai jellemrajz, a tizéves jubilaeum alkalmából* [Political portrait of

K. T., on the occasion of his ten-year jubilee] (Pozsony, 1885); Kálmán Mikszáth, *Az én kortársaim* [My contemporaries] (Budapest, 1904); and Tamás Vécsey, *Tisza Kálmán. Politikai és publicisztikai tanulmány* [K. T.: A political and publicistic study] (Celldömölk, 1931).

4. Kornél Ábrányi, Jr., "A kiegyezés" [The Compromise], in János Hock, ed., *Nemzeti dicsőségünk: fényes korszakok a magyar nemzet történelméből* [Our national glory: The great eras in Hungarian national history] (Budapest, 1906), 281. For a description of the funeral, see Judit Lakner, *Halál a századfordulón* [Death at the turn of the century] (Budapest, 1993), 27.

5. *Neue Politische Journal* (hereafter *NPJ*), February 12, 1876.

6. *NPJ*, February 17, 1876.

7. *NPJ*, February 29, 1876.

8. *NPJ*, March 15, 1876.

9. See *The Hungarian Parliament (1867–1918): A Mirage of Power* (New York, 1997).

10. Robert W. Rydell, *All the World's a Fair: Visions of Empire at American International Expositions, 1876–1916* (Chicago, 1984), 2; Paul Greenhalgh, *Ephemeral Vistas: The Expositions Universelles, Great Exhibitions and World's Fairs, 1851–1939* (Manchester, 1988); Burton Benedict et al., *The Anthropology of World's Fairs* (Berkeley, 1983); John Allwood, *The Great Exhibitions* (London, 1977); Richard D. Mandell, *Paris 1900: The Great World's Fair* (Toronto, 1967). Attendance at the millennium exhibition was probably significantly higher, with 2,978,027 paid visitors.

11. *Pester Lloyd* (hereafter *PL*), January 21, 1862, February 23, 1862. No wonder that hardly anyone bothered to visit the Pest exhibit of 386 objects displayed in London. The sixteen-day exhibition drew 832 visitors, amounting to "about two people per object," the *Pesti Napló* (hereafter *PN*) complained (March 25, 1862).

12. *PN,* April 9, 1862.

13. On Hungarian planning for their part in the 1862 London World Exhibition see, *PN*, July 14, July 25, and November 29, 1861; on handling objects and response, *PN,* January 18 and March 9, 1862. *PL,* January 21, 1862, February 23, 1862. Delegation listed, March 16, 1862, June 26, 1862, July 2, 1862, July 10, 1862, July 13, 1862, May 1, May 2, May 3, 1862, July, 16, 17, 18, 1862.

14. *Bürgerfreund,* August 8, 1869. Open letter from Count József Zichy, Jr., president of the provisional exhibition committee.

15. Jutta Pemsel, *Die Wiener Weltausstellung von 1873* (Vienna, 1989).

16. *PN*, September 2, 1872.

17. *PN,* September 3, 1872. Of the 575 exhibitors, 30 percent were from Kecskemét and its environs; 40 percent came from Budapest. The fair broke even. *Az 1885-évi budapesti országos általános kiállitás közleményei* [The 1885 Budapest National Universal Exhibition communiques], no. 1 (April 5, 1883), 4–5.

18. See Tamás Hofer, "Peasant Culture and Urban Culture in the Period of Modernization: Delineation of a Problem Area Based on Data from Hungary," in *The Peasant and the City in Eastern Europe: Interpenetrating Structures*, ed. Irene Portis Winner and Thomas G. Winner (Cambridge, Mass., 1984). Péter Hidas, "The Peasants of Hungary Between Revolution and Compromise," *East European Quarterly* 19 (June 1985): 191–200.

19. Felix Milleker, *Geschichte der Banater Jahrmärkte* (Wrschatz, 1927), 10–11; Felix Milleker, *Die Banater Eisenbahnen: Ihre Entstehung und Entwicklung, 1847–1917* (Crkva, 1927).

20. *PN,* September 2 and 3, 1872.

21. Pemsel, *Die Wiener Weltausstellung,* 77.

22. Ibid., 17, 47.

23. Ibid., 77

24. *NPJ,* July 19, 1876.

25. *NPJ,* August 20, 1876, and August 26, 1876.

26. *NPJ,* August 20, 1876. See John Komlos, *The Habsburg Monarchy as a Customs Union: Economic Development in Austria-Hungary in the Nineteenth Century* (Princeton, N.J., 1983).

27. *NPJ,* May 19, 1879.

28. *NPJ,* August 21, 1876; *Magyar Napló* (hereafter *MN*), August 22, 1876; *Hon,* August 22, 1876.

29. *NPJ,* May 16, 1879. On Zichy see, Sándor Hartman, *Zichy Jenő gróf és a magyar világ-kiállítás* [Count J. Z. and the Hungarian world exhibition] (Budapest 1891).

30. *NPJ,* May 18, 1879.

31. See David F. Good, *The Economic Rise of the Habsburg Empire, 1750–1914* (Berkeley, 1984), 86–95.

32. Scott M. Eddie, "The Changing Pattern of Land Ownership in Hungary, 1867–1914," *The Economic History Review* 20 (1967): 304, 309; Scott M. Eddie, "Agriculture as a Source of Supply: Conjectures from the History of Hungary, 1870–1913," in *Economic Development in the Habsburg Monarchy in the Nineteenth Century,* ed. John Komlos (Boulder, Colo., 1983), 101–4. See also Hans Rosenberg, *Grosse Depression und Bismarckzeit* (Berlin, 1967).

33. *NPJ,* May 20, 1879. Jenő Zichy was a colorful magnate, who continued to serve as an exhibition pageant master, and in his philanthropic role, bequeathed his substantial art collection to the nation before he died in a pistol duel in March of 1906.

34. *NPJ,* May 25, 1879. Only 8 percent of the 3,271 exhibitors were from Székesfehérvár, but this exhibition had a decidedly provincial flavor, with 72 percent of the remaining exhibitors coming from the provinces. The fair ran a deficit of 26,704 ft. *Az 1885-évi budapesti országos általános kiállitás közleményei,* 5.

35. Urban growth: Percentage increase of population from 1801 to 1891

Budapest	90.7%	Paris	38.1%
Berlin	88.2	London	37.7
Glasgow	70.7	Hamburg	37.1
Manchester	65.5	St. Petersburg	37.0
Liverpool	63.6	Moscow	16.8
Vienna	53.9	Naples	4.0

Source: Gusztáv Thirring, *Budapest székes főváros statisztikai évkönyve* [Budapest capital and residential statistical yearbook] (Budapest, 1895–6), vol. 2: 50.

36. Thirring, *Budapest statisztikai évkönyve,* 1895–6, 2: 50.

37. *The Growth of the Cities in the Nineteenth Century* (New York, 1899), 1.

38. *Neue Freie Presse* (hereafter *NFP*) (Vienna), May 1, 1885.

39. László Siklóssy, *Hogyan épült Budapest? (1870–1930)* [How was Budapest built?] (Budapest, 1931), 135–6.

40. Gábor Preisich, *Budapest városépítésének története: A kiegyezéstől a tanácsköztársaságig* [Budapest urban planning history: From the Compromise to the Socialist Republic] (Budapest, 1964), vol. 2: 23; see also, Károly Vörös, *Egy világváros születése* [The birth of a world city] (Budapest, 1973).

41. István Pintér, *Rendnek muszáj lenni* [There must be order] (Budapest, 1973).

42. László Tarr, *A délibábok országa* [The country of mirages] (Budapest, 1976), 66.

43. *PN*, Oct. 8, 1872.

44. Pinter, *Rendnek muszáj lenni*, 6.

45. *NPJ*, October 27, 1876.

46. S. Vincze Edit, *A hűtlenségi per, 1871–1872* [The treason trial] (Budapest, 1971), 40.

47. Beatrix W. Bouvier, *Französische Revolution und deutsche Arbeiterbewegung* (Bonn, 1982).

48. *NPJ*, October 26, 1876.

49. *NPJ*, October 26, 1876.

50. *NPJ*, October 27, 1876.

51. *Magyarisierung in Ungarn. (Nach den Debatten des ungarischen Reichstages über den obligaten Unterricht der magyarischen Sprache in sämmtlichen Volksschulen.)* (Munich, 1879), viii.

52. Gusztáv Gratz, *A dualizmus kora: magyarország története, 1867–1918* [The dualist era: The history of Hungary] (Budapest, 1934).

53. Gale Stokes, *Legitimacy Through Liberalism: Vladimir Jovanvić and the Transformation of Serbian Politics* (Seattle, 1975), 111.

54. *NPJ*, March 13, 1879.

55. Lajos Kossuth to Ferdinand Bakay, March 22, 1879. Printed in *NPJ*, March 31, 1879.

56. *NPJ*, March 17, 1879.

57. *Neues Politisches Volksblatt* (hereafter *NPV*), August 23, 1880. See also Gergely and Szász, *Kiegyezés után*, 115–20. On the contradictions in the internal administration of the compromise, see Éva Somogyi, *Kormányzati rendszer a dualista Habsburg Monarchiában (A közös minisztertanács), 1867–1906* [The administrative system in the dualist Habsburg Monarchy (The joint ministerial council)] (Budapest, 1996).

58. *Siebenburgen Tagesblatt*, August 21, 1875; Friedrich Gottas, "Die Deutschen in den Ländern der Ungarischen Krone (1790–1867)," in *Land an der Donau*, ed. Günter Schödl (Berlin, 1995), 363.

59. *NPV*, August 21, 1880.

60. *Hon*, December 28, 1871, 1.

61. Ibid.; Götz Mavius, "Ungarische Denkmäler—Made in Austria," *Hungarian Studies* 3 (1987): 157–70, notes that most statues, even the most nationalistic, were cast in Vienna.

62. *NPV*, October 18, 1880.

63. *NPV*, October 16, 1882. On the subsequent proliferation of Petőfi statues see, Károly Varjas, *Petőfi szobrok hazánkban és határainkon túl /1850–1988/* (Budapest, 1989). On the art history of Hungarian statuary see, Károly Lyka, *Közönség és művészet a századvégen, 1867–1896* [The public and the arts at the turn of the century] (Budapest, 1947); Károly Lyka, *Szobrászatunk a századfordulón, Magyar müvészet, 1896–1914* [Our statuary at the turn of the century: The art of Hungary] (Budapest, 2d ed., 1983); Lajos Németh, *A százéves Budapest szobraiból* [Of a century of Budapest statuary] (Budapest, 1972); Endre Liber, *Budapest szobrai és emléktáblái* [The statues and memorial plaques of Budapest] (Budapest, 1934); László Siklóssy, *Hogyan épült Budapest? (1870–1930)* [How was Budapest built?] (Budapest, 1931). See also Mihály T. Révész, *A sajtó szabadság érvényesülése Magyarországon, 1867–1875* [Achievement of freedom of the press in Hungary] (Budapest, 1986).

64. On the politics of nationality in the dualist period, see Gergely and Szász, *Kiegyezés után*, 198–206, and in today's political context, see András A. Gergely, *Kisebbség, etnikum, regionalizmus* [Minorities, ethnicities, and regionalism] (Budapest, 1997).

65. Cited in *NPV*, September 11, 1880.

66. Gottas, "Die Deutschen in den Ländern der Ungarischen Krone," 363.

67. Ferenc Glatz, "Das Deutschtum in Ungarn im Zeitalter der industriellen Entwicklung," in *300 Jahre Zusammenleben—Aus der Geschichte der Ungarndeutschen. 300 éves együttélés—A magyarországi németek történetéből*, ed. Wendelin Hambuch (Budapest, 1988), 1: 74.

68. *NPV*, September 16, 1880.

69. *NPV*, September 21, 1880.

70. *Hon*, October 24, 1880; *NPV*, October 24, 1880.

71. *NPV*, December 10 and 11, 1880.

72. *NPV,* May 1, 1882.

73. Adolf Silberstein (also known as Ötvös), "Jubiläum des ungarischen Nationaltheaters (1837–1887)," *Im Strome der Zeit*, vol. 3 (Budapest, 1895), 3–4.

74. Silberstein, "Jubiläum des ungarischen Nationaltheaters," 1–27. See also A. Ötvös, "Die ungarische Schauspielkunst," in *Das moderne Ungarn*, ed. Ambrus Neményi (Berlin, 1883), 178–93.

75. Silberstein, "Jubiläum des ungarischen Nationaltheaters," 2. By 1900 parliament would be bemoaning the declining public interest in the Hungarian National Theater, most especially its loss of pedagogic purpose. *PL*, February 24, 1900.

76. Wolfgang Binal, *Deutschsprachiges Theater in Budapest von den Anfängen bis zum Brand des Theaters in der Wollgasse (1889)* (Vienna, 1972), 422. The de-Germanization of the Pest stage fanned Pan-German resentment. A pamphlet of 1895, *Greater Germany and Mitteleuropa in the Year 1950*, projected one state including all Germans and millions of Germanized Slovaks, Slovenes, and Hungarians. Wolfgang Mommsen, "Österreich-Ungarn aus der Sicht des deutschen Kaiserreichs," in *Der autoritäre Nationalstaat. Verfassung: Gesellschaft und Kultur im deutschen Kaiserreich* (Frankfurt am Main, 1990), 225.

77. Pinter, *Rendnek muszáj lenni*, 27.

78. Andrew Handler, *Blood Libel at Tiszaeszlár* (New York, 1980); Judit Kubinsky, *Politikai antiszemitizmus Magyarországon (1875–1890)* [Political antisemitism in Hungary] (Budapest, 1976); Iván Sándor, *A vizsgálat iratai* [The investigation records] (Budapest, 1976); William O. McCagg, *Jewish Notables and Geniuses in Modern Hungary* (New York 1972); Sándor Hegedüs, *A tiszaeszlári vér vád* [Blood ritual trial of Tiszaeszlár] (Budapest, 1966); Gyula Krúdy, *A tiszaeszlári Solymosi Eszter* [E. S. of Tiszaeszlár] (Budapest, 1975).

79. Handler, *Blood Libel*, 176.

80. *NPV*, August 9, 10, 11, 12, 13, 1883.

81. *NPV*, August 27, 28, 29, 30, 31, September 1, 1883.

82. *NPV*, August 10, 1883.

83. *NPV*, August 12, 1883.

84. Cited in Tibor Frank, "Hungary and the dual monarchy, 1867–1890," Peter F. Sugar, Péter Hanák, and Tibor Frank, *A History of Hungary* (Bloomington, Ind., 1994), 264.

85. *NPV*, March 16, 1884.

86. Frank, "Hungary and the dual monarchy," 264.

87. István Pintér, *Rendnek muszáj lenni* [There must be order] (Budapest, 1973), 30.

88. Ibid., 36.

89. *Az 1885-évi budapesti országos általános kiállitás közleményei* [The 1885 Budapest National Universal Exhibition proceedings], vol. 2 (April 19, 1883), 25.

90. Mór Gelléri, *Budapest a kiállitás alatt: Fővárosi kalauz és tájékoztató mindenki számára* [Budapest during the exhibition: Everyone's guide to Budapest during the time of the exhibition] (Budapest, 1885), 96. Ferenc Heltai, "A budapesti országos általános kiállitás," in *Az "Athanaeum" nagy képes naptára az 1885-dik évre* [The Athanaeum's large picture calendar of 1885], ed. Károly Concha (Budapest, 1885), 60.

91. *NPV,* September 27–30, 1883.

92. Mór Gelléri, *Matlekovits Sándor: Élete és működése* [S. M.: His life and work] (Budapest, 1908); Ferenc Heltai, "Dr. Matlekovits Sándor," in *Az "Athanaeum" nagy képes naptára*, 63–6; Károly Ráth, *Országos iparos-gyülések, 1872–1899* [National industrial meetings] (Budapest, 1899); Béla Kenéz, *Ipari öntudatunk ébresztői és munkálói* [The awakeners and achievers in industry] (Budapest, 1943), 174–80; Mór Gelléri, *A kiállitások története: Fejlődedés és rendszeresitése* [A history of exhibitions: Their development and organization] (Budapest, 1885). On exhibitions and the development of consumerism, see Thomas Richards, *The Commodity Culture of Victorian England: Advertising and Spectacle, 1851–1914* (Stanford, Calif., 1990).

93. Heltai, "Dr. Matlekovits Sándor," 63.

94. Judit Kubinsky, *Politikai antiszemitizmus magyarországon (1875–1890)* [Political antisemitism in Hungary, 1875–1890] (Budapest, 1976); Handler, *Blood Libel*; William O. McCagg, *Jewish Notables and Geniuses in Modern Hungary* (New York, 1972).

95. *Budapesti Hirlap*, February 6, 1885. Avoiding deficits "is the fundamental thing," instructed Crown Prince Rudolf.

96. Károly Gerlóczy, *Zárjelentése* [Closing statement] (Budapest, 1896), 25. Final cost overruns for neither the capital's exhibit nor the National Exhibition were substantial.

97. *NPV* February 15, 1885.

98. *NPJ*, May 13, 1873; Tarr, *A délibábok országa,* 247. See Lászlo Siklóssy, "King Edward VII in Hungary," *Hungarian Quarterly* 5 (1939): 61–77.

99. *Magyar Korona* (hereafter MK), May 3, 1885.

100. Good, *The Economic Rise of the Habsburg Empire*, 139.

101. *Der Bauunternehmer: Ausstellung Zeitung*, February 15, 1885.

102. *NPV,* February 23, 1885.

103. *Der Bauunternehmer*, April 12, 1885.

104. *The Times* of London, September 29, 1885.

105. Ibid.

106. "A kiforditott főváros" [The capital turned inside out], *PN*, August 20, 1885.

107. Gelléri, *Budapest a kiállitás alatt*, 49.

108. Edmund Steinacker, *Budapest, Together with an Appendix on the National Hungarian Exhibition of 1885 at Budapest with a Ground Plan of the Exhibition* (London, 1885). *MK,* February 16, 1885; Hugó Ilosvai, *Magyarország és az ezredéves ünnepély* [Hungary and the thousand-year celebration] (Budapest, 1896).

109. Catherine Albrecht, "Pride in Production: The Jubilee Exhibition of 1891 and Economic Competition between Czechs and Germans in Bohemia," *Austrian History Yearbook* 24 (1993): 105.

110. *MK*, May 2, 1885.

111. *NFP*, May 2, 1885.

112. *NPV*, February 23, 1885.
113. *Ország-Világ*, September 19, 1885.
114. *NFP*, May 1, 1885.

Chapter 9, Memorializing

1. *Neues Politisches Volksblatt* (hereafter *NPV*), Jan 1, 1888.
2. *NPV*, March 17, 1888.
3. *NPV*, March 16, 1888.
4. Tisza's parliamentary speech of May 26, 1888. *NPV*, May 27, 1888–May 29, 1888.
5. On the military culture of East Central Europe, see Béla K. Király and Walter Scott Dillard, eds., *The East Central European Officer Corps 1740–1920s: Social Origins, Selection, Education, and Training* (Boulder, Colo., 1988).
6. Kornél Ábrányi, Jr., *A király: Magyarország közélete az ezredik évforduló korszakában* [The king: Hungarian public life in the era of the thousand-year anniversary], vol. 1 (Budapest, 1896), 132.
7. Adolph Kohut, *Kaiser Franz Josef I. als König von Ungarn* (Berlin, 1916), 344.
8. *NPV*, February 12, 1889.
9. Empress Elisabeth, *Das poetische Tagebuch*, ed. Brigitte Hamann (Vienna, 1984), 341.
10. *NPV*, February 14, 1889.
11. Ferenc Pölöskei, *István Tisza. Ein ungarischer Staatsmann in Krisenzeiten* (Budapest, 1994), 30.
12. *NPV*, February 8 and 20, 1889.
13. *NPV*, February 8, 1889.
14. *NPV*, February 21, 1889.
15. György Gracza, *Kossuth Lajos: Élete, működése és halála* [L. K.: Life, activities, and death] (3d ed., Budapest, [1893]), 232–3.
16. *NPV*, April 14, 1890.
17. *NPV*, May 1, 1892.
18. *NPV*, April 19, 1890.
19. *NPV*, October 7, 1890.
20. *NPV*, October 5, 1890.
21. *NPV*, May 1, 1892, p. 3.
22. *Budapest*, May 2, 1892; *NPV*, May 2, 1890.
23. Vilmos Borross, *Koronázási emlékkönyv Ő felsége Ferencz József Magyarország királya és érzsébet királyné Ő felsége megkoronáztatásának huszonötödik évfordulójára* [Commemorative volume on the twenty-fifth anniversary of the coronation as Hungarian king of his Apostolic Majesty Franz Joseph and her Apostolic Queen Elizabeth] (Budapest, 1892), 5.
24. Moritz Csáky, *Der Kulturkampf in Ungarn* (Graz, 1967).
25. *Budapest főváros levéltára, közgyülési jegyzököny* [Archives of the Budapest Capital City Council (henceforth BFL)] April 20, 1892, in *Források Budapest történetéhez, 1873–1919* [Documents of Budapest's History], ed. Mária H. Kohut, vol. 2, *Források Budapest multjából* [Documents from Budapest's Past] (Budapest, 1971), no. 123, 268.
26. *Vasárnapi Ujság* (henceforth *VU*), June 5, 1892, 386, 400, 404–5.

27. Országos Levéltár [National Archive (henceforth OL)], K26, 1892, no. 445 (1311) in *Források Budapest multjából*, no. 14, p. 45.

28. *VU*, June 5, 1892, 409.

29. *Neue Freie Presse* (henceforth *NFP*), June 7, 1892; Augsburger *Allgemeine Zeitung* (henceforth *AZ*), June 29, 1892.

30. *NFP*, June 7, 1892.

31. *NFP*, June 7, 1892, and *AZ*, June 9, 1892. For a parallel see, E. Hammerton and D. Cannadine, "Conflict and Consensus on a Ceremonial Occasion: The Diamond Jubilee in Cambridge in 1897," *Historical Journal* 24 (1981): 111–46.

32. *NFP*, June 8, 1892.

33. *NFP*, June 7, 1892.

34. Franz Joseph, it was widely noted, was not accompanied by members of the Austrian court. *NFP*, June 9, 1892.

35. Dániel Szabó, "Mária kútja Szentpéteren," in *Hid a századok felett: Tanulmányok Katus László 70. Szuletesnapjara* [Bridge to the century: Studies in honor of L. K.'s 70th birthday], ed. Mariann Nagy (Pécs, 1997), 281–94.

36. *Emlékkönyv Zichy Nándor Gróf születésének századik évfordulójára, 1829–1929* [Commemorative volume on Count N. Zichy's hundredth birthday] (Budapest, 1929), June 1894, 71–2; *Katholikus Szemle*, 8: 449.

37. *NPV*, March 5, 1894.

38. Lakner, Judit, *Halál a századfordulón* (Budapest, 1993), 28–9; for the funeral and memorialization of Kossuth, see Gracza, *Kossuth Lajos*, 238–302.

39. Budapest főváros levéltára, *Közgyülési iratok*, [Archives of the Capital City Budapest, Parliamentary documents], 184–9, excerpt entry 87, pp. 187–8.

40. Alajos Bucsánsky, *Nagy képes naptára az 1896 évre* [Large Picture Calendar for 1896] (Budapest, 1896), 2. See also András Gerő, *Heroes' Square Budapest. Hungary's History in Stone and Bronze* (Budapest, 1990).

41. "The founding of a nation is celebrated best if the country has been able to advance its culture, economy, and constitutional situation." The government allocated over fl. 3,000,000 for construction of the industrial arts museum, planned an industrial arts school in Budapest, and funded four hundred new primary schools. OL, K26, ME (Ministerelnökség), Milleneumi ünnepségekkel kapcsolatos ügyek (Millenneum-related issues), packet 332, no. 524, 1895. Decree of Ministry of Religion and Public Education and March 17, 1896 legislative proposal by Prime Minister Dezső Bánffy. The ethnographic museum and a new fine arts museum were also direct legacies of the millennium exhibition, and the Vajdahunyad Castle would become the National Museum of Agriculture.

42. *NPV*, June 11, 1890.

43. OL, K26, ME, 1895, packet 332, no. 524.

44. See John Lukacs, *Budapest 1900: A Historical Portrait of a City and Its Culture* (New York, 1988).

45. *NPV*, May 18, 1890.

46. *NPV*, May 24, 1890.

47. *NPV*, November 14, 1890.

48. Zoltán Bálint, *Die Architektur der Millenniums-Ausstellung* (Vienna, 1896), 14.

49. John E. Findling, *Chicago's Great World's Fair* (Manchester, England, 1994); Robert Muccigrosso, *Celebrating the New World: Chicago's Columbian Exposition of 1893* (Chicago, 1993); David F. Burg, *Chicago's White City of 1893* (Lexington, Kentucky, 1976).

50. Bálint, *Die Architektur der Millenniums-Ausstellung,* 12.

51. George Eisen, "The 'Budapest Option': The Hungarian Alternative to the First Modern Olympic Games," *International Journal of the History of Sport* 8 (1991): 124–32; David Young, *The Modern Olympics: A Struggle for Revival* (Baltimore, 1996); Pierre de Coubertin, *Une Campagne de 21 Ans* (Paris, 1908), 111.

52. Bálint, *Die Architektur der Millenniums-Ausstellung*, 12.

53. On the initial plans see, *Az 1896-iki ezredéves országos kiállitás közleményei* [The 1896 1000-year exhibition proceedings], vol. 1 (1892), 62.

54. Bálint, *Die Architektur der Millenniums-Ausstellung*, 12.

55. The exhibition commission requested 100 percent more space than in 1885. *1896-iki kiállitás közleményei* 3 (March 9, 1893): 228

56. István Hermann, *Die Gedankenwelt von Georg Lukács* (Budapest, 1978), 24.

57. David E. Nye, "Electrifying Expositions, 1880–1939," in *Fair Representations: World's Fairs and the Modern World*, ed. Robert Rydell and Nancy E. Gwinn (Amsterdam, 1994), 140–56.

58. *1896-iki kiállitás közleményei* 3 (March 9, 1893): 382, 812–3, 1123.

59. Bálint, *Die Architektur der Millenniums-Ausstellung*, 13, 25.

60. For a description of the architectural conception and building process, see Ignác Alpár, *Az 1000-éves országos kiállítás* [The thousand-year National Exhibition] (Budapest, 1896).

61. *NFP*, May 2, 1896, and *PL*, May 2, 1896.

62. The Romanesque structure on the historic island housed the Habsburg exhibit and included a balcony for viewing. *1896-iki kiállitás közleményei* 3 (March 9, 1893): 311–2, 721.

63. F. Hopkinson Smith, "The Hungarian Millennium," *Harper's New Monthly Magazine* (June 1897–November 1897): 401. The restaurant was Gerbaud.

64. "A Penultimate Exhibition," *Saturday Review* (London), May 16, 1896, 470.

65. Smith, "The Hungarian Millennium," 401.

66. *1896-iki kiállitás közleményei* (January 1896), 1123. The exhibition received 10 percent of amusement park entrance fees.

67. Ibid., 814, 1101.

68. Ibid., 1120, 1104.

69. Smith, "The Hungarian Millennium," 401.

70. *1896-iki kiállitás közleményei* 3 (March 9, 1893): 356, 575.

71. "A Penultimate Exhibition," 497.

72. Paul Greenhalgh, *Ephemeral Vistas: The Expositions Universelles, Great Exhibitions, and World's Fairs, 1851–1939* (Manchester, 1988), 20. Hungarians participated at the Paris fair in 1900. Zsolnay ceramics won some acclaim, but their most striking contribution was a replica of the Vajdahunyad Castle on the Avenue des Puissances Étrangères. Györgyi Kálmán, "Az iparművészet a párizsi kiállításon" [Hungarian industrial arts at the Paris exhibition], *Magyar Iparművéset*, September 1900, 209–45.

73. *Vasárnapi Ujság* (hereafter *VU*), January 19, 1996, 45. OL, K26, ME, packet 332, parliamentary debate of February 4, 1894.

74. *VU*, January 19, 1896, 45; OL, K26, ME, packet 332 (March 17, 1896).

75. *NPV,* May 7, 1896.

76. "The Impudent Sparrow and the Patient Elephant," *NPV*, May 9, 1896. For parliamentary debate on the flag-burning, see *NPV,* May 7, 1896.

77. *NPV,* May 8, 1896.

78. *Stenographische Protokolle, über die Sitzungen des Hauses der Abgeordneten des österreichischen Reichsrathes im Jahre 1896.* Eleventh Session, 20 (Vienna, 1896),

490–510. The magnate Zsigmond Csáky-Pallavicini, derisively referred to as the drunken count (*palinkás gróf*), sought to mobilize a similar demagogic, antisemitic political movement, but with limited success. *Egyenlőség*, March 29, 1895. Hungarian Jews, in turn, connected themselves with the thousand-year tradition. Rabbi Sámuel Kohn argued that "of all religions in our nation, ours is the oldest. . . . Our religion had existed in this land before it became the country of the Magyars, and also accompanied them [the Magyars] when they arrived here and conquered the land with their blood. We, to whose joy this nation has acknowledged the legality of our religion, not only feel but *know* that we are Magyars. For us the word Israelite . . . is the adjective of the word Magyar. . . . It signifies a Jewish Magyar"; "Elnöki megnyitó" [Presidential opening address], in *Évkönyv* [Yearbook], ed. Vilmos Bacher and József Bánóczi (Budapest, 1897), 7–8.

79. The banderium marched from the castle to Mátyás Church where the crown and regalia had been on public display from June 5–8. OL, K26 ME, 1896, packet 361, March 9, 1896, and May 3, 1896.

80. *NPV*, June 9, 1896.

81. István Hermann, *Die Gedankenwelt von Georg Lukács* (Budapest, 1978), 24.

82. Smith, "The Hungarian Millennium," 402. See also, Richard Harding Davis, "The Millennial Celebration at Budapest," in *A Year from a Reporter's Note-book* (New York, 1903), 66–99.

83. Smith, "The Hungarian Millennium," 399–400.

Chapter 10, The Loss of the Streets

1. Mór Szatmári, ed., *Kossuth Ferencz harmincz parlamenti beszéde, életrajzi adatokkal* [Thirty parliamentary addresses by F. Kossuth, with biographical information] (Budapest, 1906), includes paintings by F. Kossuth of his wife, Teréz, and a portrait and bust of his father, 30, 39, 43 and 59.

2. *Népszava* [hereafter *Nsz*], March 15, September 18, October 7, in Ervin Szabó, *Szabó Ervin történeti írásai*, ed. György Litván (Budapest, 1979).

3. György Litván, and János Bak, *Socialism and Social Science: Selected Writings of Ervin Szabó* (London 1982), 158. On the aesthetic criticism of this sudden profusion of statuary in Budapest, see Károly Lyka, *Szobrászatunk a századfordulón: Magyar művészet, 1896–1914* [Our statuary at the turn-of-the-century: Art of Hungary] (Budapest, 2d ed., 1983).

4. Litván and Bak, *Selected Writings of Ervin Szabó,* 158.

5. *Volksstimme*, November 24, 1897.

6. Keith Hitchins, *Rumania, 1866–1947* (Oxford, Eng., 1994), 207.

7. *Neues Politisches Volksblatt* (hereafter, *NPV*), March 12, 1898.

8. In addition to the *Népszava* edition, also seized were ten thousand copies of a socialist tract in mid-March, 1898. *NPV*, March 6, 1898.

9. *NPV*, March 16, 1898. On popular theater see, Nagy Ildikó, "Polgárosuló színház a polgári Budapesten" [Developing bourgeois theater in bourgeois Budapest], *A tudománytól a tömegkultúráig; Művelődéstörténeti tanulmányok, 1890–1945* [From scholarly to popular culture] (Budapest, 1994), 191–216.

10. *NPV,* March 18, 1898.

11. *NPV*, April 20, 1898.

12. *NPV*, May 3, 1898.

13. *Az 1848–49-iki magyar szabadságharcz története* [History of the 1848–49 Hungarian War of Independence], 5 vols. (Budapest, 1894–8).

14. OL, K26 ME, packet 446. See Emil Niederhauser, *Merénylet Erzsébet királyné ellen* [The Assassination of Queen Elizabeth] (Budapest, 1985).

15. *PL,* March 16, 1900.

16. *NPV*, March 15, 1902. Perhaps indicative of Kálmán Tisza's continued obscurity is that a recent anthology of Hungarian prime ministers misdated Tisza's death to March 28 (*Magyarország miniszterelnökei, 1848–1990* [Budapest, 1993], 42), and in two chronologies of Hungarian history, one does not include Kálmán Tisza's death and the other misdated it as March 3 rather than March 23. *Magyar történelmi kronológia. Az őstörténettől 1970-ig* [Chronology of Hungarian history] (Budapest, 1981); *Magyarország törgéneti kronológiája, III, 1848–1944* [Historical chronology of Hungary] (Budapest, 1983), 801.

17. *NPV*, March 25, 1902.

18. *NPV*, March 16, 1902.

19. In 1900 strikes included the Ganz factory (May 28–June 8) and streetcar employees (June 24–5). Unemployed demonstrated in Budapest on February 15, 1900 and January 4, 1901. Twelve thousand demonstrated on February 15 and ten thousand on December 21. *Nsz*. See also, Albert Lichtblau, "Boycott-Krawall-Gewalt-Demonstration: Die Budapester Mieterbewegung 1906 bis 1912 und exkursive Vergleiche zu ähnlichen Vorgängen in Wien," *Archiv 1992. Jahrbuchs des Vereins für Geschichte der Arbeiterbewegung* (Vienna, 1992): 65–82; Michael John, " 'Strassenkrawalle und Excesse': Formen des sozialen Protests der Unterschichten in Wien 1880 bis 1918," in *Wien-Prag-Budapest: Blütezeit der Habsburgermetropolen; Urbanisierung, Kommunalpolitik, gesellschaftliche Konflikte (1867–1918)*, ed. Gerhard Melinz and Susan Zimmermann (Vienna, 1996), 230–44.

20. *NPV*, August 12, 1903.

21. Kálmán Thaly, *Rákóczi-emlékek törökországban, és II. Rákóczi Ferencz fejedelem hamvainak föltalálása* [Rákóczi memorials in Turkey, and the discovery of Prince F. Rákóczi II's remains] (Budapest, 1893).

22. *NPV*, October 7, 1903.

23. *Budapester Tagblatt*, September 8, 1904. On István Tisza, see Gabor Vermes, *István Tisza: The Liberal Vision and Conservative Statecraft of a Magyar Nationalist* (New York, 1985); Ferenc Pölöskei, *Tisza István* (Budapest, 1985); also appeared as *István Tisza. Ein ungarischer Staatsmann in Krisenzeiten* (Budapest, 1994), 79; István Dolmányos, *A koalíció az 1905–1906. évi kormányzati válság idején idején* [The coalition during the 1905–6 government crisis period] (Budapest, 1976).

24. *BT*, November 21, 1904.

25. Ibid.

26. Ibid., January 28, 1905.

27. *Nsz*, March 16, 1905.

28. Éva Somogyi, ed., *Die Protokolle des gemeinsamen Ministerrates der österreichisch-ungarischen Monarchie. 1896–1907* (Budapest, 1991), 457–8.

29. Ludwig Mangold, *Zur Geschichte des Kabinetts Fejérváry* (Leipzig, n.d. [1909]), 31. See Peter F. Sugar, "An Underrated Event: The Hungarian Constitutional Crisis of 1905–6," *East European Quarterly* 15, no. 3 (September 1981): 281–306.

30. *BT,* October 1, 1905.

31. William Alexander Jenks, *The Austrian Electoral Reform of 1907* (New York, 1974).

32. *NPV*, March 21, 1903.

33. Rudolf Sieghart, *Die letzten Jahrzehnte einer Grossmacht* (Berlin, 1932), 81–118.

34. *NPV*, February 20 and 22, 1906.

35. Mangold, *Zur Geschichte des Kabinetts Fejérváry*, 57.

36. *NPV*, March 16, 1906.

37. Éva Gyulai, "Borsod vármegye Rákóczi hamvainak hazahozatalánál, adalékok az ünnepek viselettörténetéhez," in *A Herman Ottó Múzeum évkönyve*, vols. 25–6 (1986–7): 393–6. Another example of the popular historical writings generated by the reburial was János Hock's *Rákóczi Ferencné: történeti elbeszélés* [Mrs. F. Rákóczi: Historical essay] (Budapest, 1907).

38. Géza Kassai, *Magyar történelmi sorsfordulók és a nemzetiségi kérdés* [Hungarian history's turns of fate and the nationality question] (Budapest, 1959), 86.

39. *Libertatea* (1906), no. 20, quoted in Sándor Biró, *The Nationalities Program in Transylvania, 1867–1940: A Social History of the Romanian Minority Under Hungarian Rule, 1867–1918 and of the Hungarian Minority under Romanian Rule, 1918–1940* (New York, 1992), 333.

40. Biró, *Nationalities Program in Transylvania*, 333.

41. Robert William Seton-Watson, *Racial Problems in Hungary* (New York, 1972; 1908). See also, Robert William Seton-Watson, *Corruption and Reform in Hungary; A Study of Electoral Practice* (London, 1911).

42. Lajos Varga, *A Magyarországi Szociáldemokrata Párt ellenzéke és tevékenysége, 1906–1911* [The Hungarian Social-Democratic Party opposition and activities] (Budapest, 1973), 58–9, 69–70.

43. *A nemzeti államok kialakulása és a nemzetiségi kérdés* [The Evolution of National States and the Nationality Question] (Budapest, 1912). See also, "Oszkár Jászi's Danube Federation Theories," *Geopolitics in the Danube Region, Hungarian Reconciliation Efforts, 1848–1998*, ed. Ignác Romsics and Béla K. Király (Budapest, 1999), 227–8.

44. Robert Musil, *Man Without Qualities* (New York, 1965), 33.

45. T. M. Islamow, "Die ungarländische Arbeiterbewegung zur Zeit der Koalitionsregierung (1907–1909)," *Acta Historica* 16 (1970): 105–50. Three months later the dedication of a statue to Elizabeth in Szeged became a melancholy occasion to recall her visit in 1857, with its folk festival and fish soup cooked in a huge silver pot. *Pesti Hirlap* (hereafter *PH*), September 29, 1907.

46. Islamow, "Die ungarländische Arbeiterbewegung," 116.

47. András Sipos, " 'Stammeshäuptlinge' und Reformer. Kräfteverhältnisse und Strukturen in der Budapester Kommunalpolitik 1873 bis 1914," in *Wien-Prag-Budapest: Blütezeit der Habsburgermetropolen; Urbanisierung, Kommunalpolitik, gesellschaftliche Konflikte (1867–1918)*, ed. Gerhard Melinz and Susan Zimmermann (Vienna, 1996), 121. See also Vilmos Vázsonyi, *Vázsonyi Vilmos beszédei és írásai* [Speeches and writings of V. V.], 2 vols. (Budapest, 1927).

48. Thomas Lindenberger, *Strassenpolitik. Zur Sozialgeschichte der öffentliche Ordnung in Berlin 1900 bis 1914* (Bonn, 1995), 366–7.

49. *Nsz*, January 31, 1912; *Vasárnapi Újság*, February 25, 1906, 117.

50. Robert A. Kann, "Die Statuen vor dem Wiener Rathaus," *Mitteilungen des Österreichischen Staatsarchivs* 33 (1980): 277ff. On the role of statues in Hungarian political culture see, Dénes Lengyel, *Irodalmi kirándulások* [Literary Meanderings] (2d

ed., Budapest, 1977); József Ádámfy, *A világ Kossuth-szobrai* [Kossuth Statues of the World] (Budapest, 1982); *Monumentumok az elsö háborúból* [Monuments of the First World War], ed. Gábor Feuer and Ákos Kovács (Budapest, 1985).

51. László Remete, *Barikádok Budapest utcáin/1912* (Budapest, 1972).
52. *Nsz*, March 5, 1912.
53. *NPV*, March 1, 1913.
54. *NPV*, March 4 and 5, 1913.
55. *NPV*, March 6, 1913.
56. *NPV*, March 21, 1912; *NPV*, March 21, 1914.
57. *NPV*, May 27, 1914.
58. *NPV*, May 29, 1914; *VU*, June 7, 1914; *PH*, May 29, 1914, 33. See also, Gyula Krúdy, *Kossuth fia* [Kossuth's son] (Budapest, 1976).
59. *NPV*, June 5, 1914.
60. *PH*, June 9 and June 12, 1914, 2; *Nsz*, June 10, 1914, p. 8.
61. *NPV*, June 24, 1914.
62. *NPV*, June 27, 1914.
63. *Szabadság*, June 29, 1914, 1
64. *PH*, July 1, 1914, 8.
65. *NPV*, July 9, 1914.
66. *NPV*, July 11, 1914.
67. *NPV*, July 2, 1914.
68. *PH*, August 1, 1914, 5.
69. Ibid.
70. *PH*, August 2, 1914, 12.
71. *PH*, August 1, 1914, 5.
72. Ibid.
73. *NPV*, August 3, 1914.
74. *PH*, August 3, 1914, 6–8.

Chapter 11, Epilogue: 1989

1. Rudolf L. Tőkés, *Hungary's Negotiated Revolution: Economic Reform, Social Change and Political Succession* (Cambridge, Eng., 1996), 172.
2. Julius Hay, *Born 1900, Memoirs*, trans. J. A. Underwood (La Salle, Ill., 1975), 50–5.
3. Arpad Kadarkay, *Georg Lukács: Life, Thought, and Politics* (Cambridge, Mass., 1991), 307.
4. Judith Marcus and Zoltán Tar, eds., *Georg Lukács: Theory, Culture, and Politics* (New Brunswick, N.J., 1989), 156.
5. *Zúgjatok harangok! 1848, Forradalmi rockfantázia* [Let the church bells ring! 1848, Revolutionary rock opera], dir. Gábor Koltay, Budapest, July 24–5, 1998.
6. See András Gerő, *Az államosított forradalom, 1848 centenáriuma* [The nationalized revolution, the 1848 centenary] (Budapest, 1998).
7. "The holiday of the free press," *Magyar Nemzet* (hereafter *MN*), March 15, 1947.
8. *MN*, August 20, 1947, and August 20, 1948.
9. *MN*, August 22, 1948. The retelling of the history of St. Stephen was one of the markers of the political transformation. See György Györffy, *King Saint Stephen of Hungary* (New York, 1994).

10. See Róbert Vértes, *Nemzeti és mozgalmi ünnepeink* [Holidays of the nation and the movement] (Budapest, 1966).

11. See Pál Földi, *A szocialista családi és társadalmi ünnepek rendezése kézikönyv* [Handbook for the organization of socialist family and social holidays] (Eger, 1962).

12. Mikhail Bakhtin, *Rabelais and His World* (Bloomington, Ind., 1984). Similarly Johan Huizinga, writing under German occupation, extolled man's capacity for play, *Homo Ludens, A Study of the Play Element in Culture* (Boston, 1950).

13. Tamas Aczel and Tibor Meray, *The Revolt of the Mind* (New York, 1959), 420, and Melvin J. Lasky, ed., *The Hungarian Revolution* (New York, 1957).

14. Aczel and Meray, *The Revolt of the Mind,* 439.

15. Hannah Arendt, *The Origins of Totalitarianism* (New York, 1958), 496.

16. Arendt, *The Origins of Totalitarianism,* 496.

17. *Die Welt,* June 10, 1988.

18. Hungarians were quick to pick up Gorbachev's rehabilitation of Bukharin, and the first biography of Bukharin, by Miklos Kun, published in a Communist country appeared in Hungary in 1988.

19. Zoltán Panek, in *Magyar Forum,* as cited in Ferenc Kulin, "Pártok és elvek, a dinamikus ellentétek egységét akarjuk," *Világosság* 4 (1991): 249–56. See also, interview with Géza Jeszensky by Charles Hebbert, "Hungary, Winners and Losers," in *East European Reporter* (Spring/Summer 1990).

20. Tamás Hofer, "The Demonstration of March 15, 1989, in Budapest: A Struggle for Public Memory," Program on Central and Eastern Europe, Working Paper Series 16 (Cambridge, Mass., 1991), 2.

21. Hofer, "The Demonstration of March 15, 1989," 2.

Index

abolition of serfdom, 53, 73; later conditions, 109; noble-peasant cooperation, 100; nobles, 53; pilgrimages, 140

Academy of Music, 207

actors, 27, 32, 147–48, 182–83, 349n116

Address Party, 196, 199

aestheticism, 147

agora, marketplace, 39

agricultural exhibitions: Bach system, 152–53; background to, 230; Franz Joseph visit, 204; National Universal Exhibition, 249–54; Slovakia, 182

agricultural machines, 204

Agyagfalva (Lutița), 79

air travel, 298

Albrecht, Archduke: appointment, 127; assassination attempt on emperor, 137; nationalism offending, 173; replaced, 180; royal tour of 1857, 151; St. Stephen's crown, 138; underground organizations, 211

All Saints Day, 262

Almássy, Móricz, 49

Almásy conspiracy, 202

Alnoch, Alois (Col.), 133

Alsó-Fehér, 80

amnesty: Haynau, 94, 99; royal tour, 130; Russians, 93; Teleki, 197

Anarchists, 11

Andrássy, Gyula: Beust, 212; coronation, 215, 217, 218–19; death, 260; Elizabeth, 208, 211; Honvéd question, 221–22; Kazinczy centennial, 166, 171; marginalizing Kossuth, 221; "mirage" of liberal era, 22–23; moderate nationalist, 199

Andrássy, Gyula, Jr., 290, 291, 292, 296

Angyal, Pál, 14–15

Antall, Jószef, 313

antisemitic crowds, 248

371

1298/222   £ 32.00.
4709-2107/028.
⑦.3873438.
    15.11.04.